Wilkie Collins

Wilkie Collins
Interdisciplinary Essays

Edited by

Andrew Mangham

CAMBRIDGE SCHOLARS PUBLISHING

Wilkie Collins: Interdisciplinary Essays, edited by Andrew Mangham

This book first published 2007 by

Cambridge Scholars Publishing

15 Angerton Gardens, Newcastle, NE5 2JA, UK

British Library Cataloguing in Publication Data
A catalogue record for this book is available from the British Library

In loving memory of Alex and Jade

TABLE OF CONTENTS

LIST OF ILLUSTRATIONS

ACKNOWLEDGEMENTS

This book is a result of the "Wilkie Collins Conference" held at the University of Sheffield in 2005. I would like to thank the delegates at that event (many of whom are contributors to this collection) for their enthusiasm and patience. I would like to thank the Department of English Literature at Sheffield for hosting the conference and for offering administrative and financial support. I am particularly indebted to Heather Lonsdale and Josephine Liptrott for helping with the paperwork and finding me a space in which to complete this book. Various people have given valuable suggestions at different stages of the project. These include Jenny Bourne Taylor, Angela Wright, and Goran Stanivukovic. I would like to thank them for listening to my thoughts and sharing the benefits of their expertise and experience. I would like to give special thanks to Janice M. Allan for reading through the whole manuscript and spotting a number of typos. I am grateful also for Greta Depledge's offer to stand in last minute with her contribution and for chasing a couple of references. Graham Law kindly helped me locate and access a number of Collins sources and Amanda Millar at Cambridge Scholars Publishing spent a great deal of time and effort on the proofs for this volume. My work on this project has benefited a great deal from the guidance of Sally Shuttleworth. Although busy with her own work, she kindly set aside time to offer advice at all stages of this venture and read my own contribution. Any faults with my work, however, are completely my own responsibility.

A. M.
Reading, 2006.

INTRODUCTION

Wilkie Collins was, as this collection aims to show, an author who was not afraid to experiment with different styles, genres, and ideas. Throughout his prolific and profitable career he wrote novels, plays, journalism, social commentary, histories, guidebooks, and much more besides. It is hardly surprising, therefore, that some scholars have identified him as an author who is difficult to categorise. In a recent collection of essays, for instance, Maria Bachman and Don Richard Cox have commented that, because Collins's work defies attempts to bracket or label it, the time has now arrived for students of Victorian literature to begin appreciating the author as more than just a sensation novelist (Bachman and Cox 2003, xxiv). Literary criticism since the 1980s, however, has frequently concluded that there is more to Collins than sensational tales of feverish suspense. What our book aims to do is suggest that Collins's varied writings are best understood by approaches that take account of their interdisciplinarity and intertextuality.

More specifically, Collins's work frequently refers to ideas that one would ordinarily expect to be exclusive to other fields of expertise. Legal, artistic, scientific, and theatrical technicalities, for instance, appear in books with which Collins intended to electrify readers with a range of sensational effects. As Jenny Bourne Taylor's seminal book on Collins makes clear, the author is thus ideally suited as the focus of interdisciplinary study. Such research has had a surge of interest in recent years. Although this collection enters into that energetic and active field of research, it does not ignore–as is often the case with such studies–the complex reasons for why ideas from widely varying disciplines appear in the work of this Victorian popular writer. This is not a book satisfied with recording where specialised ideas appear in Collins's work; rather, it is concerned with how and why they traveled across disciplinary boundaries and what this tells us about Victorian media and literature more generally.

This collection opens, therefore, with two essays that discuss Collins's experimentations with genre and his place within the periodical press. In exploring these areas we aim to offer some account of why Collins's work was experimental and interdisciplinary. Focusing specifically on Collins's 1879 novel *The Fallen Leaves*, Anne-Marie Beller begins this volume with an appraisal of the "generic indeterminacy" of Collins's work. She aims to explain the "failure" of *The Fallen Leaves* (as understood by Victorian and modern critics) as a result of the author's "experimental approach to genre". The text, Beller claims, offers a "challenging example of [...] how nineteenth-century popular fiction [...] provided a shared space in which classes came together".

As recent research has shown, the Victorian family magazine, a vehicle for most of Collins's fiction, was a complex forum in which a broad range of ideas, fictional and non-fictional, came together.[1] Deborah Wynne has noted that editors of periodicals would attempt to "draw out the themes and ideas of the serial novels" in ways that would relate to the "factual" material they were printed alongside. This, Wynne suggests, aimed to "enhance reading pleasure and generate debate" (Wynne 2001, 3). Holly Furneaux's essay, the second in this collection, analyses Collins's journalism within the context of Dickens's *Household Words*. She demonstrates how crucial the journalistic context is to understanding the serialised novel and reassesses contemporary critical thoughts on how Collins and Dickens influenced each other's work. Far from the notion that the latter censored the writing of the former, Furneaux suggests that Collins's non-fictional celebrations of bachelorhood were selected and emphasised by Dickens to support his characterisations of bachelors. This "suggests a mutual sexual radicalism" between the two authors and hints at the intricate intellectual relationships that existed between contributors to Victorian magazines.

The serialisation of nineteenth-century fiction also allowed novelists like Collins to respond to important contemporary events. Real crimes, in particular, were a frequent source of inspiration for popular novelists. If "a crime of extraordinary horror figures among our *causes célèbres*", wrote the Reverend Mansel in 1863, "the sensationist is immediately at hand to weave the incident into a thrilling tale, with names and circumstances slightly disguised" (Mansel 1863, 449). In 1860 the *Lancet* associated the growth of popular newspaper reports with the "literature of a certain class". Although it does not mention sensation fiction (or Wilkie Collins) directly, it is clear that such works were the article's intended critical target. Newspapers and popular fiction, it complained, were responsible for acquainting the general public with the knowledge of how to murder:

> We almost shudder at the widespread knowledge which must exist among those least to be trusted with it of how best to destroy life with the least chance of being discovered. In these days of cheapening everything for the "million", the means of murdering have become popularised. The well-reported history of one case of poisoning forms but the rehearsal for the second; nay, the very processes employed for unraveling the mysteries of one tragedy are registered for the purposes of another. (Anon. 1860, 217)

What is interesting here is how "mass" journalism and popular fiction are viewed as united in their ability to corrupt readers with a single unhealthy narrative. In the eyes of this writer, journalism and fiction are not distinct disciplines but rather two styles of writing that cooperated in a way that rendered them virtually indistinguishable. Indeed, the boundaries between the fictional and non-fictional, in the intellectual climate of the mid-nineteenth century were not altogether distinct.

Thus, many of the essays featured in this book were written with the view that, in order to fully understand a Wilkie Collins text, one needs to engage with the complex network of ideas that each one operated within. In Tatiana Kontou's essay, for instance, it is shown how mid-Victorian reports of spiritualist practice, and the real cases of alleged mediums, form a crucial backdrop to one of Collins's best-known characterisations and themes. She argues that Magdalen Vanstone in *No Name* (1862) has much in common with female mediums of the mid-nineteenth century. "The sensation heroine (as an actress)", she writes, "and the medium (as a sensation heroine) […] demonstrate the extent to which these different cultural registers influenced and broadened each other".

As Kontou suggests, séances, whether they were believed in or not, involved a thorough engagement with the visual. Each spiritualist "subject" was an image to be viewed and judged. This may, therefore, have spoken to Collins's long-standing interests in both the perfomative and visual arts. Art was important to Collins for a number of reasons. His novels frequently appeared alongside illustrations of their key episodes. As biographies and collections of Collins's letters make clear, the author also had strong links with a number of artists. Most notably, his father was a Royal Academedian who knew many of his own contemporaries. These included Sir David Wilkie (after whom his son was named) and William Blake, a man whose art often blurred the boundaries between the written and the visual. Collins's aunt, Margaret Carpenter, was also a famous painter of picturesque still life and his brother Charles Allston was an artist who worked on the fringes of the Pre-Raphaelite Brotherhood. Wilkie Collins knew key members of the brotherhood intimately. It seems, therefore, that he swam against the tide by becoming a novelist instead of a painter. Indeed, he felt from an early age that he was destined to follow in his father's footsteps.

Clare Douglass's essay, "Text and Image Together", considers why art, in the form of periodical illustrations, became a crucial part of the reading experience with regards to Collins's work. She argues that acknowledging the illustrations Collins's novels often appeared with is an important factor in reading and criticising Victorian popular novels. Douglass writes: "The power and significance, creatively and historically, of this experience calls for he recovery of not only Collins's other illustrated work but that of the many other Victorian writers whose illustrated fiction has long been forgotten".

As Aoife Leahy demonstrates in the sixth essay, Collins's artistic heritage is something he never entirely abandoned. Despite the fact that he was often criticised for concentrating more on plot than on character, his stories are packed with meticulous descriptions of people and landscapes. Leahy concentrates on images of evil. She demonstrates how Collins's depictions of handsome, masculine villains entered into contemporaneous discussions of Raphaelesque beauty. More specifically, she contests that, like Noel Paton's *The Adversary* (1879), Collins's beautiful villains concur with Pre-Raphaelite thinking by linking idealised appearances with evil. Thus, concludes Leahy, "*The Adversary* helps us to see the fiend that is lurking at the heart of many a Collins villain, despite the diabolical charm of such characters as Godfrey Ablewhite, through a Ruskinian suspicion of ideal beauty".

Considering less-canonical texts like *The Guilty River* (1886) and *Hide and Seek* (1854), Leahy shows how this is a volume that aims to appreciate the wealth of Collins material that is still relatively unknown to modern research. Although Wilkie Collins criticism is now what Lyn Pykett calls "as voluminous and as contradictory as the novels on which it comments" (Pykett 2005, 226), literary critics still appear preoccupied with the small sample of work Collins produced in the 1860s: namely *The Woman in White, No Name, Armadale* (1866), and *The Moonstone* (1868). Although this book suggests that much is still to be gained by offering new approaches to these better-known texts, it also aims to reveal that a great deal remains to be learned by considering the writings produced before and after Collins's most successful decade.

Hence, I aim to demonstrate the importance of Collins's second, and unjustly neglected, novel *Antonina, or the Fall of Rome* (1850). This novel, it is argued, offers a unique commentary on the turbulent politics of the 1840s through a historical retelling of the decline of the Roman Empire. In particular, my essay suggests that the similarities between images of political crisis and psychological breakdown supply Collins with a means of expressing his own ambivalence towards the European revolutions and Chartist movements of the early Victorian period. This is the first of five contributions to consider Collins's use of medical imagery. In her essay on physiognomy and the depiction of heroines, Jessica Cox focuses on how the author's female characters reproduce the physiognomic ideas introduced by John Caspar Lavater at the end of the eighteenth century. Cox's essay takes a broad sweep of the Collins canon and argues that nineteenth-century physiognomical ideas are crucial to the understanding of Wilkie Collins's women. In accordance with the sensation genre, Cox maintains, Collins employs such "ideas as a means of both creating and confusing the reader's impressions of character". Although discredited by modern science, Cox demonstrates how "physiognomical ideas remain an important key for reading character in nineteenth-century fiction".

In 1982 Barbara Foss Leavy offered an account of the social and intellectual connections between Wilkie Collins and key nineteenth-century psychiatrists.[2] In "Questioning Moral Inheritance in *The Legacy of Cain*", Amanda Mordavsky Caleb takes advantage of such links to offer a detailed analysis of the ways in which the author explores and reworks the predominantly-scientific images of degeneration and biological determinism. Concentrating on the author's penultimate novel, *The Legacy of Cain* (1889), Caleb argues that Collins aimed to reveal the "complexities of the 'nature-versus-nurture' debate" and "the potential dangers involved in accepting inheritance theories". *The Legacy of Cain* is, according to Caleb, a novel that provides a "case study", through the characters of Eunice and Helena Gracedeui, which explores the Victorian notions of heredity and degeneration. Caleb's is an essay that views the aging Wilkie Collins's work as an anticipation of the *fin-de-siècle* and the cultural anxieties that that era brought. William Hughes similarly demonstrates how Collins's best-known novel, *The Woman in White*, explored a range of ideas that were central to Bram Stoker's *Dracula* (1897). Hughes argues that both *The Woman in White* and *Dracula* share a concern with the nineteenth-century belief in "an identifiable medical discourse–a systematic, physiologically orientated psychology" championed by the influential psychologist William Carpenter. This notion of "unconscious cerebration", Hughes suggests, is something that drives representations of asylums and alienists in each author's most canonical text. While in *The Woman in White* the asylum comes to represent "the wrongful incarceration of the innocent and the apparently sane", *Dracula* presents the same as an arena where patient "abuse is knowingly and deliberately undertaken by the presiding physician".

Of the scores of books and essays written about Collins and sensation fiction, many concentrate on the author's representation of femininity. He was, as many have argued, particularly sensitive to the legal plights of women. In the eleventh essay in this collection, Greta Depledge suggests that such concerns with the rights of women extend to an interest in their *medical* treatment as well. Expanding the theme of medical malpractice, as raised by William Hughes, Depledge suggests that *Heart and Science* (1883) "provides a challenging literary representation of the complexities that surround medicine for women in the nineteenth century". Depledge observes that the text's representation of Dr Benjulia has as much to say on the medical (mis)treatment of women as it does the vivisection debates. Collins's text, she maintains, operates as part of the period's concerns over what lengths men will go to in the name of science.

As hinted above, the legal statuses of women is a recurrent focus in Collins's fiction. Collins initially trained as a barrister, though he never practiced as one. This no doubt cemented a long-standing interest in legal issues. In her essay, "The Scottish Verdict and Irregular Marriages", Anne

Longmuir considers how the intricate and often frustrating workings of nineteenth-century Scottish law provide Collins with the tools to present British identity as beset with "uncertainty" and "irrationality". Longmuir reveals how Scots law, in the nineteenth-century, was itself a paradigm of "epistemological uncertainty". With its loose definitions of marriage and "Not Proven" verdict, law in Scotland became emblematic of all that was "primitive", misleading, and uncertain. In *The Law and the Lady* (1875) and *Man and Wife* (1870), Longmuir reveals, these ideas are a powerful method of generating sensational plots and commenting on the essentially unstable nature of British selfhood. Such connections, she continues, offer innovative alternatives to "the pre-Freudian Victorian ideal of the whole and essential self".

Taking advantage of recent research into Collins's letters, Graham Law's essay on Collins and international copyright provides an exploration of the author's interests in the perceived faults in the Anglo-American legal system. Through two journalistic pieces of Collins's, "A National Wrong" (1870) and "Consideration on the Copyright Question" (1880), Law provides a useful account of the legal, economic, and political technicalities surrounding the publication of Collins's novels. These two pieces of journalism, in particular, "provide […] a context for a reading […] Collins's [ideas …] on the issue of international copyright". Although Collins offered no "theoretical basis" for his interest in the copyright issue, Law maintains that the author took his lead from Dickens in feeling a great sense of injustice in regards to the lack of legal provisions for protecting the "intellectual property" of the novelist.

From copyright law we move on to a consideration of family law in Lynn Parker's "The Dangerous Brother: Family Transgression in *The Haunted Hotel*". With reference to Collins's 1879 novella, Parker suggests that "Collins employs this spectral narrative to explore flaws in the nature of sibling bonds, 'bonds', moreover, that were considered central to the affectionate Victorian family". Although Parker discusses the impact of "The Deceased Wife's Sister's Bill" (1835) on nineteenth-century familial relationships, her focus is mainly on the ideological laws of sisterly self-sacrifice as propounded by domestic manuals like Sarah Stickney Ellis's *The Woman of England* (1843). In *The Haunted Hotel,* Parker claims, Collins portrays a "darker possibility" lurking beneath the veneer of familial ideology and ultimately reveals "the inability of those bonds to function successfully in the Victorian social realm".

As Collins's biographers have discussed, the author was not only an avid follower of stage performances but an active participant in them. He initially met his close friend and advisor, Charles Dickens, through their participation in Sir Edward Bulwer-Lytton's 1851 play *Not So Bad as We Seem.* He also wrote above fifteen plays including a melodramatic collaboration with Dickens, *No Thoroughfare* (1867), and *Black and White,* a love story first performed at the Adelphi theatre in 1869. Many of Collins's novels are indebted to the author's fascination with the stage. *No Name,* for instance, tells the story of an actress through chapters defined as "scenes"; *The New Magdalen* (1873) was originally conceived as a drama and went on to be successfully reproduced for the stage.

As Richard Pearson and Janice Norwood show in this book, however, Collins's most sustained engagements with the theatre came through his adaptations of *The Woman in White* and *The Moonstone.* Since then, as Stefani Brusberg-Kiermeier highlights in the last essay, these stories have gone on to be filmed for cinema and television with differing results. Pearson analyses dramatic adaptations of Collins's *The Moonstone* in "'Twin Sisters and Theatrical Thieves'". He aims to redress a prevailing critical assumption that "Collins either dashed off his [theatre] adaptations to secure dramatic copyright against pirated stage versions, or that he produced mistakes, full of 'drastic changes', that scarcely reward investigation". In comparing Collins's 1877 adaptation of *The Moonstone* with the original novel, Pearson shows that, rather than being a pale imitation, the play ought to stand alone as an impressive contribution to nineteenth-century drama.

Janice Norwood discusses the various adaptations of the *The Woman in White* from Collins's own rewriting in 1871 to Andrew Lloyd-Webber's recent transformation of the text into a stage musical. She questions whether Collins's adaptation can be considered a "sensation drama"–a type of theatre that emerged alongside the sensation novels of the 1860s. Comparing the 1871 adaptation with other sensation plays and the original novel, Norwood not only highlights the challenges Collins faced in transferring his best-known work to the stage, but also underscores how its production was more sophisticated than the average sensation drama. "It should", claims Norwood, "be recognised as a valid drama in its own right" and an anticipation of the "new psychological dramas of the late-nineteenth century".

In the final study for this book, Stefani Brusberg-Kiermeier speculates on the relevance Collins has for modern television and film audiences. Brusberg-Kiermeier analyses the specific pressures faced by film and television makers in adapting Collins's writings for the screen. The current trend for producing Collins-inspired films, she suggests, testifies to the "topical or even timeless appeal of Collins's plots" and has important modern signification. "The subversiveness of Collins's characters", it is poignantly concluded, "might indeed enhance a political consciousness for social inequality" in our own time.

This book focuses on the life and works of Wilkie Collins in order to bring together a range of voices, each with its own idea of what constitutes interdisciplinarity, to show the importance of situating popular Victorian fiction within a wide and varied cultural framework. This collection intends to widen our current understanding of Collins's work by reasserting its function as part of a complex and contradictory culture. Yet we also hope to introduce new ways of thinking about literature more generally. How, for instance, can an interdisciplinary framework bring little-known texts like *Antonina* and *The Fallen Leaves* to the forefront? How might such an approach benefit research into more canonical works like *The Woman in White* and *No Name*? Collins's body of work encompasses both neglected and widely known texts. In offering essays on both, we aim to go some way to answering the above questions and, with the aid of Janice M. Allan's concluding remarks, speculate about the theoretical future of Collins research.

Notes

[1] See, for example, Cantor and Shuttleworth 2004, Cantor, et al. 2004, and Wynne 2001.
[2] See Leavy 1982.

Works Cited

Anon. 1860. The Science of Murder. *Lancet*. II: 217-8.
Bachman Maria K. and Don Richard Cox. 2003. *Reality's Dark Light: The Sensational Wilkie Collins*. Knoxville: University of Tennessee Press.
Baker, William. 2002. *Wilkie Collins's Library: A Reconstruction*. London: Greenwood Press.
Cantor, Geoffrey. and Sally Shuttleworth, eds. 2004. *Science Serialized: Representations of the Sciences in Nineteenth-Century Periodicals*. Cambridge, MA: The Massachusetts Institute of Technology Press.
Cantor, Geoffrey, Gowan Dawson, Graeme Gooday, Richard Noakes, Sally Shuttleworth, and Jonathan Topham. 2004. *Science in the Nineteenth-Century Periodical*. Cambridge: Cambridge University Press.
Leavy, Barbara Foss. 1982. Wilkie Collins's Cinderella: The History of Psychology and *The Woman in White*. *Dickens Studies Annual* 10: 91-141.
Mansel, Henry. 1863. Sensation Novels. *Quarterly Review* 117: 481-514.
Pykett, Lyn. 2005. *Authors in Context: Wilkie Collins*. Oxford: Oxford University Press.
Taylor, Jenny Bourne. 1988. *In the Secret Theatre of Home: Wilkie Collins, Sensation Narrative and Nineteenth-Century Psychology*. London: Routledge.
Wynne, Deborah. 2001. *The Sensation Novel and the Victorian Family Magazine*. Hampshire: Palgrave.

PART I:
COLLINS IN CONTEXT

"TOO ABSURDLY REPULSIVE": GENERIC INDETERMINACY AND THE FAILURE OF *THE FALLEN LEAVES*

ANNE-MARIE BELLER

The Fallen Leaves (1879) is viewed by the majority of Collins scholars as aesthetically inferior to his other works, and is considered expressively to summarise the deterioration of the later novels. A. C. Swinburne summed up its contemporary lack of success, in both critical and commercial terms, when he described it as "ludicrously loathsome" (Page 1974, 27) and "too absurdly repulsive for comment or endurance" (Winnifrith 1996, 140), and in the *Critical Heritage* (1974) Norman Page appears to endorse this opinion, claiming that "by general consent then and now" *The Fallen Leaves* is "a dismal failure" (Page 1974, 2).

The aim of this essay is to examine the reasons for the almost universal disparagement and neglect of Collins's 1879 novel, and to consider the implications of Swinburne's choice of the epithets "ludicrous" and "absurd". I want to suggest that these terms are prompted by the structural and formal elements of *The Fallen Leaves*, rather than simply its thematic content, and to focus particularly on Collins's flouting of accepted notions of generic classifications. Jenny Bourne Taylor has argued of Collins's later work that it

> continually shifts between genres though on the whole the novels are clearly recognizable within definite categories, as purpose novels, high melodrama, domestic realism. They adapt a shared stock of conventions from the earlier sensation fiction, yet it is impossible to draw precise generic boundaries around them. (Taylor 1988, 211)

While agreeing broadly with this statement, I would argue that *The Fallen Leaves* constitutes an exception, in that it is not clearly recognisable within one definite category, and that its extreme generic indeterminacy is a key factor in the difficulty that readers and critics alike have experienced in approaching this novel. Before considering the specific problems raised by *The Fallen Leaves*, I want to offer a brief context for my discussion by highlighting some of the contradictions inherent in Victorian (and later) negotiations of genre.

In some senses, the Victorians' relationship to genre was characterised by contradiction and paradox. On the one hand, the entire concept of genre was at a critical juncture: traditional Aristotelian and neo-classicist ideas about genre had been challenged and undermined by the Romantics, so that, in the nineteenth century the stability and hierarchical nature of the established literary categories became questionable for the first time. In addition, the novel's appearance as a distinct literary type in the eighteenth century posed other problems. Not only did the novel resist traditional categories by refusing to conform to their criterion, but the nature of its form undermined the very concept of "literariness" upon which theories of genre were based.

On the other hand, however, Victorian culture was characterised by a zeal for taxonomy, by a drive toward classification in all areas of the social and natural world. If species, races, classes, and the disciplines of science, anthropology, and the law were subject to this movement toward codification, then so too was the area of literature. Thus, the Victorians were arguably faced with a conflict between their innate desire for classification and the specific problems attaching to questions of genre.

The often arbitrary distinction between "sensational" and "realistic", which held sway in the nineteenth century, has remained largely unquestioned until relatively recent times. Similarly, Victorian sub-categories of fiction have influenced modern scholars in their perception of various "minor" writers and the genres in which they worked. In 1870, *Temple Bar* ran a series of articles on contemporary fiction in which the critic and future Poet Laureate, Alfred Austin, discussed the major trends in novel writing. He separated contemporary fiction into three categories or schools: "fast", "sensational", and "simple". Austin's definition of the last category, which he saw as deriving from Samuel Richardson, accords with that of the "sentimental novel" and is represented by writers such as Charlotte Yonge and Florence Marryat. Collins, Braddon, and Wood head the "sensation" school and, for Austin at least, the "fast" school is typified by the novels of female writers like Ouida (Austin 1870).[1]

Given that these three categories purport to contain the sum of contemporary fiction, the question arises as to where Austin accommodates the novels of such writers as Thackeray, Trollope, or Gaskell. The implicit suggestion is that writers working within the framework of social realism or the "novel of character" somehow transcend genre. By omitting "realism" as a category Austin invests it with a "natural" status, a given, against which other forms must define themselves in negative opposition. This naturalisation of genre, and the notion that genuine artists are above generic conventions, remains current as demonstrated by the modern label "genre fiction", typically applied to popular or "lower" forms, often mass-produced and formulaic, and which implies that superior authors work outside genre. A recent critic, neatly illustrating these assumptions, has made the comment that: "[Dickens] is of far too great a stature to be bounded by genres" (Punter 1996, 188).

Austin's articles also highlight the subjective and fluid nature of genre, in that many of the authors detailed above are perceived to belong in different categories by various critics. Rhoda Broughton, for example, is often associated with sensation fiction and was also identified by Margaret Oliphant, on the basis of her candid depictions of female passion, as decidedly "fast". Sally Mitchell's article "Sentiment and Suffering" (1977), however, locates Broughton as a writer of the sentimental novel.[2] In the same way, Ouida is alternately seen as "fast", "sensational", and "sentimental", just as all three categories can be, and are, applied to Florence Marryat. All this would suggest not only a confusion on the part of mid-Victorian reviewers as to the agreed criteria for genre allocation, but also a continued sense among modern critics of the inadequacy of traditional concepts of genre.

To return to Collins, it is reasonable to say that he showed a marked disregard for the authoritarian aspects of genre throughout his career, repeatedly playing with and deliberately subverting the conventions of different genres (such as stage melodrama, gothic, penny fiction, and contemporary newspaper journalism) in novels from *Antonina, or The Fall of Rome* (1850) onwards. It might also be argued that Collins's critical reception has suffered because of this disrespectful attitude towards generic rules, and through early critics' inability to comprehend Collins's unorthodox approach to genre. Philip O'Neill has employed the useful term "critical straitjacketing", arguing that the determination to view *The Moonstone* (1868) as the prototypical detective novel "misses much of the substance of the novel as a whole" (O'Neill 1988, 3).

Without doubt this tendency toward generic indeterminacy increased in the latter stages of Collins's career, which arguably relates to the negative critical opinion of the later work. Robert Ashley, for example, noted in his 1952 biography that "[d]uring [the 1870s and 80s] Collins seems to have been unable to make up his mind just what kind of novelist he wanted to be, sensationalist, or social critic, romanticist or realist, with the result that his fiction follows no consistent line of development" (Ashley 1952, 113). Ashley sees this "indecisiveness" as occurring mainly from book to book, yet in many of the later novels the movement between different genres that he identifies is present in the same work. In *The Fallen Leaves* Collins's hybridisation of genre is at its most extreme, and results in an apparent disunity, which I believe accounts, to a considerable degree for the extensive judgments of aesthetic failure.

Recent critics have drawn attention to the fact that, from the beginning of his career, Collins was interested in a wide range of different literary types. Lillian Nayder, for example, discusses his "early experimentation with various genres" and points out that "Collins produced melodramas, short stories, travel narratives, and journalism", as well as a novella and a memoir (Nayder 1997, 13, 15). Though he decided to focus on novel writing, this initial experimentation with a variety of literary forms continued to inform Collins's fiction, and he repeatedly subverted the conventions of a host of genres within his novels, producing new directions and innovations, with the result that his oeuvre as a whole defies easy classification in traditional generic terms. Nayder has also suggested that a tension existed between Collins's desire to be seen as a serious author and his conflicting desire to explore subjects and themes that were associated with "lower" forms, such as the penny dreadfuls, female melodrama, and the gothic. This conflict, she argues, was evident early in Collins's career and affected his working relationship with Dickens:

> Hoping to succeed as a middle-class professional yet troubled by his perception of working-class injuries, gender inequities, and imperial wrongdoing, Collins not only complies with but works against Dickens from nearly the start of their collaborations. (Nayder 2002, 8)

Tamar Heller is another scholar who has examined Collins's ambiguous position in the Victorian literary marketplace. Heller's study of the influence of Radcliffean gothic in Collins's work illustrates the way in which his interest in the themes of female subordination, victimisation, and rebellion led to his appropriation of genres perceived as feminine, and consequently his marginalisation in a literary arena that was witnessing the professionalisation, and therefore masculinisation, of novel writing. As Heller also notes, this marginalisation continued into the twentieth century, "a period of aggressive canonisation" (Heller 1992, 5), largely because "Collins'[s] association with 'subliterary' genres caused him to be considered a minor writer not worthy of serious critical study" (ibid., 5). Both Nayder and Heller question the ideological basis of aesthetic judgments, pointing out the "shifting beliefs in what constitutes literary value" (ibid., 6), and suggesting the "need to reexamine our ideas of literary value and to broaden our conceptions of a novel's worth" (Nayder 1997, 139). Nevertheless, the principal focus of both studies remains on the celebrated novels of the 1860s, with neither critic engaging with Collins's later neglected fiction in any real depth, and Heller unconsciously replicates earlier judgments when she refers to "the aesthetic awkwardness of a novel like *The Fallen Leaves*" (Heller 1992, 166).

In one of the rare modern discussions of the work, Jenny Bourne Taylor has pointed out that *The Fallen Leaves* is "Collins's most politically explicit novel" (Taylor 1988, 232), and it may be argued that this overt political content is connected to the spectacular lack of success in popular and critical terms, though not in any straightforward way. It is not merely the obtrusive polemical style of portions of the novel which is responsible for its failure but, more subtly, the fact that Collins's political views had direct implications on his ideas about literature and the content of his fiction. The enthusiastic democracy that floods the pages of *The Fallen Leaves*, signalled most clearly by the hero's Christian Socialist beliefs, was also evident in Collins's deliberate embracing of the widening reading public, a stance that was not widely shared by the literary elite in the mid to late Victorian period. Indeed, as Peter McDonald has recently shown, many influential figures of the late nineteenth-century literary scene viewed the enlarged reading public–produced by both the electoral reforms and the post 1870 Education acts–as a pernicious threat to literary standards (McDonald 1997, 6-7). Writing of the attitudes of a growing literary and critical elite, McDonald claims that "far from being intrinsic [...] the value of literary forms was [...] dependent on the limited size and specific gender of their readership" (ibid., 6). Collins, as a writer whose greatest successes were inextricably connected with the popular and female-associated genre of sensation fiction, represented the antithesis of such views. His belief in the desirability of a democratised and ever-widening readership, first articulated in the 1858 essay "The Unknown Public" (Collins 1858), continued to inform his ideology, leading increasingly to a stance, by the end of his career, which was decidedly at odds with that of the literary elite. Inevitably, this endorsement of the popular impacted on the writer's critical reception. Collins's optimistic statement that *The Fallen Leaves* would achieve its due recognition from "the great audience of the English people" (Collins 1887, iii) is echoed in a letter dated the 22 June 1880. He writes:

> The Second Series [of *The Fallen Leaves*] will be written [...] when our English system of publication sanctions the issue of the first cheap Edition which really appeals to the people. I know "the General reader", by experience, as my best friend and ally when I have certain cliques and classes in this country arrayed against me. (Baker and Clarke 1999, 429)

Yet Collins's reliance on the popular vote as a reliable indication of his novel's worth was a view that was becoming distinctly outmoded, with many commentators believing the obverse to be in fact true. As one reviewer phrased it: "books and poems are not to be esteemed, like loaves of bread or pots of ale, by the number of their purchasers; [...] popularity [...] is the most fallible of tests; [...] literature exists of itself and for itself" (Anon. 1892, 265).

Collins believed that the failure of *The Fallen Leaves* to secure widespread popularity upon first issue was largely explained by the prudish, middle-class distaste for his choice of subject matter. In the preface to his following novel, *Jezebel's Daughter* (1880), Collins complained with reference to *The Fallen Leaves* that there are certain important social topics which are held to be forbidden to the English novelist (no matter how seriously and how delicately he may treat them), by a narrow minded minority of readers, and by the critics who flatter their prejudices. (Collins 1887, iii)

He goes on to acknowledge the similar complaints levelled against *Basil* (1852), *Armadale* (1866) and *The New Magdalen* (1873). Yet, what Collins fails to consider is that, despite objections about the perceived immorality of these works, all of them achieved some measure of critical approval and significant popularity in terms of sales. Dickens greatly admired *Basil*, while, as S. M. Ellis claims, *The New Magdalen* "was a favourite tale of Matthew Arnold's, though he as a rule was not addicted to the reading of sensational fiction" (Ellis 1951, 47). Thus, while Collins is undoubtedly correct in citing distaste for the content of *The Fallen Leaves* as one element in its celebrated lack of success, it cannot wholly account for the continued neglect and critical disdain.

Comparisons with *The New Magdalen* are illuminating because, thematically, *The Fallen Leaves* closely resembles Collins's earlier novel about a reformed prostitute, with both works positing the fallen woman as victim and attacking social hypocrisy through the framework of Christian Socialism. Yet despite the common concern with identity, perceptions of innocence and purity, and the paradox underlying social respectability, and Collins's notion of true morality, the two novels are in fact very different. A significant departure in *The Fallen Leaves* is the shift in focus from female identity to male. In common with most of Collins's earlier novels, and indeed sensation fiction more generally, the central character of *The New Magdalen* is its heroine, Mercy Merrick. Jenny Bourne Taylor justifiably states that "the moral centre of the story is the Christian Socialist priest, Julian Gray" (Taylor 1988, 218), but it is Mercy's story, her quest for identity and acceptance with which Collins is primarily concerned. By contrast, in *The Fallen Leaves* it is the hero, Amelius Goldenheart, whose emotional and moral journey provides the trajectory of the novel. Several separate narratives converge and are resolved through the figure of Goldenheart who operates, as his name indicates, on an almost mythical level throughout.

Temporarily exiled from the Eden, which the novel casts in general terms as America, and specifically as the Christian Socialist Community at Tadmoor, Amelius emerges as a Christ-like figure, drawing to himself a collection of troubled people, the "fallen leaves" of the title. The Christ motif is emphasised throughout the novel, notably in Amelius's evangelical preaching at the "fatal lecture" and in his redemption of the Mary Magdalen figure, Simple Sally. Collins sets up an opposition between the prostitute Sally and the cold Madonna, Regina. Yet, perhaps the most interesting woman with whom Amelius becomes involved is Mrs Farnaby, in whom the roles of suffering

Madonna and fallen Magdalen are combined. The different stories that each of these women represent are tenuously held together by Amelius until the end, when all three women are found to be related to one another. The mythical quality embodied by the idealistic figure of Amelius is extended to Collins's treatment of Simple Sally. Here again is evidence of the difference between *The New Magdalen* and *The Fallen Leaves*, for although the ideological perspective in both novels casts the prostitute firmly in the role of victim, Sally lacks the independence, resourcefulness, and intelligence of her predecessor Mercy. On first meeting Sally, Amelius is struck by the girl's fragility and innocence:

> His heart ached as he looked at her, she was so poor and so young. The lost creature had [...] barely passed the boundary between childhood and girlhood. [...] Her eyes of the purest and loveliest blue rested on Amelius with a vacantly patient look, like the eyes of a suffering child. (Collins 1879, 185)

What are most apparent in the scenes describing Sally and the sordid environs she inhabits are the apparently unconscious contradictions of Collins's approach. The writing is characterised by both a brutal realism and an implausible sentimentality, which sit oddly together and are, in some ways, reminiscent of early Dickens novels such as *Oliver Twist* (1837-9). Collins vividly describes a London that would have been shocking and alien to the majority of his readers, and he does so with a persuasive knowledge and compassion that is compelling. The effect is intensified by being filtered through the youthful idealism of Amelius, to whom such unfamiliar scenes are tantamount to a vision of hell:

> On the floor of a kitchen, men, women, and children lay all huddled together in closely packed rows. Ghastly faces rose terrified out of the seething obscurity when the light of the lantern fell on them. The stench drove Amelius back, sickened and shuddering. (Collins 1879, 190)

The realism evinced here and in comparable scenes is, however, undermined by a persistent sentimentality in the characterisation of Sally and the other prostitutes, of whom Collins writes: "All that is most unselfish, all that is most divinely compassionate and self-sacrificing in a woman's nature, was as beautiful and as undefiled as ever in these women" (ibid., 187). The insistent idealisation of the street women, whom Collins presents as wholly untouched by the corruption and misery surrounding them, creates a romantic note which, paradoxically, weakens his argument against the injustice suffered by this underclass. Sally's relatively untroubled transformation from half-starved, abused street urchin to ideal Victorian lady is similarly unconvincing, jarring with the implicit premise of the novel regarding the inexorable and inescapable plight of the London poor.

Such contradictions stem largely from Collins's apparent inability (or unwillingness) to locate *The Fallen Leaves* within a specific genre of fiction. The narrative moves between realism and romanticism, between social critique and high melodrama, in a way that often appears disjointed. It is interesting to view the various women who hold claim to Amelius's attention as symbolic of the different genres with which the novel flirts. Just as Collins the author cannot decide ultimately upon one generic mode for *The Fallen Leaves*, so too does his main character oscillate indecisively between the various women in his life and what they represent.

The genre of sensation fiction, and to a lesser extent the gothic, are personified by Mrs Farnaby, who draws Amelius into her tragic story and persuades him to search for her lost daughter. In Emma Farnaby, Collins revisits many of the typical sensation tropes from his fiction of the sixties, including seduction, illegitimacy, the "stolen" child, and a melodramatic death from strychnine poisoning. The other central modes in the novel are the conventional love story, represented by Regina, and the propaganda or social reform novel embodied by the prostitute Simple Sally.[3] Chiefly divided between these different literary genres, Amelius is also drawn briefly into other forms by minor characters, such as the servant, Phoebe, from whose overly-dramatic and excessive style Amelius anxiously retreats. "'She shall rue the day', cried Phoebe, relapsing into melodrama again [...] 'Come! Come!' said Amelius, sharply, 'You mustn't speak in that way'" (ibid., 144). Her constant declamations in the style of a Mrs Siddons, her victimisation and deception by the would-be-villainous Jervy, and her lower-class status all serve to align Phoebe with Victorian stage melodrama.

As Amelius becomes more involved with Regina he rejects both "sensation" and "melodrama", to the disapproval of Mrs Farnaby, who tells him that "keeping company with Regina has made you a milksop already" (ibid., 146). Constant references are made to Regina's placidity and, above all, her conventionality. These are linked overtly, by the narrator, to her lack of depth and inability to feel passion. When Amelius suggests that they should defy convention and marry out of hand, Regina is appalled: "Without my uncle to give me away! [...] Without my Aunt! With no bridesmaids, and no friends, and no wedding breakfast! Oh Amelius, what can you be thinking of?" (ibid., 133). At a later point, Amelius beseeches Regina: "Oh, my dear girl, do have some *feeling* for me! Do for once have a will of your own" (ibid., 216, italics added).

Ultimately, Amelius resists the conventional love story that Regina embodies, and concurs with the narrator in condemning both her coldness and conventional restraint. In effect, Regina is criticised for not being a sensation heroine. She loses Amelius because she is unable to feel deeply or expressively enough, in contrast to the 1860s sensation heroine who was continually castigated for feeling too much and too vividly (see, for example, Oliphant 1867). Regina, in fact, has more in common with the heroine of domestic fiction: "You are so nice, dear [...] when you are not violent and unreasonable. It is such a pity you were brought up in America. Won't you stay to lunch?" (Collins 1879, 217). Regina represents the antithesis of characters such as Lydia Gwilt and Magdalen Vanstone, and her lack of "sensation" causes her finally to lose the prize.

Metaphorically, Amelius's futile attempts to resist being drawn into the stories of Mrs Farnaby and Simple Sally echo Collins's own failure to shun the lures of sensationalism and the Propaganda novel. Mrs Farnaby's confidence that Amelius will not fail to help her, despite his misgivings, might be viewed as Collins's acknowledgement of his own inability as a writer to resist the tendency toward dramatic incident and sensational device. "Do you think I don't know you better than you know yourself", Mrs Farnaby tells Amelius (ibid., 147).

Appropriately, the different generic choices symbolised by the various women in the novel are dominantly genres associated with the female. Because the Victorian ideological construction of genre was both classed and gendered, Collins could be seen to be disrupting not only aesthetic categories, but also, by moving between male genres (realism, bildungsroman, the thesis novel) and female genres (sensation, melodrama, gothic, sentimentalism) to be potentially destabilising gender boundaries in an unsettling way. Such ambivalence inevitably affected the critical perception of Collins's writing, especially during the later years of his career when the boundaries between "high" and "low" were being aggressively asserted. As Heller points out:

> Collins'[s] position in this changing Victorian literary marketplace was in many ways a double one, both feminine and masculine. Collins was associated with the "low" and heavily feminine genres of the Gothic and sensation fiction, yet he was an active participant in the process of professionalisation. (Heller 1992, 7)

In *The Fallen Leaves*, Collins's dilemma is metaphorically played out by Amelius who must choose between respectability, through an alliance with Regina, and the approval of figures representing compliance with social orthodoxy, such as Farnaby, or a career in the margins of society through an alliance with Sally and Mrs Farnaby, who represent feminine excess and emotionality.

Amelius's ultimate marriage with Sally would suggest Collins's final choice of genre as the novel of social reform; the rejection of Regina is symbolic of his dissatisfaction with the conventional romance and the restrictions imposed by it. However, Collins's desire to produce something more than a simple love story, and his consequent experimentation with one generic form after another finally leads to a lack of coherence and unity that, in terms of dominant theories of fiction, seriously flaws the novel.

Modern genre theory has moved away from the more prescriptive and static formulations of genre, recognizing the evolutionary and morphological aspects of generic development. Some theorists have rejected the notion of genre entirely, seeing generic classification as counter-productive to artistic creation, and misrepresentative of the way in which true works of art tend to violate such rules.[4] Jacques Derrida takes this anti-generic stance, interpreting the "law" of genre as a demarcation and thus, the imposition of a limit. Genres are implicitly separate from one another, since the definition of a generic mode depends on its difference from other modes. Therefore, the "law" dictates that a genre possesses its own unity and should not be mixed with other genres. However, as Derrida suggests, that which defines a genre is actually outside of, and thus absent from, the genre, and yet at the same time present, because properties within the genre are "marked" by it (Derrida 1992, 230). The "law of genre" is therefore one of impurity and "genre always potentially exceeds the boundaries that bring it into being" (ibid., 221).

Derrida claims that it is impossible *not* to mix genres since, by their very nature, genres inevitably cross boundaries: "Every text *participates* in one or several genres, there is no genreless text, there is always a genre and genres, yet such participation never amounts to belonging" (ibid., 230, italics in original). Victorian critics, of course, were uncomfortable with this wilful confusion of categories and, indeed, many modern scholars would subscribe to the view that there must be a limit, an extent to which genres may be mixed within the same work before they lose coherency. Thus, in aesthetic terms, *The Fallen Leaves* might be viewed by many as generic hybridity taken to an absurd extreme, which consequently fails to emerge as a unified whole.

However, developments in twentieth-century literary theory, such as deconstruction and post-structuralism, have inevitably meant that traditional "organicist" theories of fiction have been challenged. Terry Eagleton has argued that the dogmatic presumption of critics "that literary works form organic wholes" is an "arbitrary prejudice". He writes:

> It is true that this prejudice runs so deep in modern critics that it is difficult to see it as just that–a doctrinal predilection, which is no less arguable and contentious than any other. There is absolutely no need to suppose that works of literature either do or should constitute harmonious wholes, and many suggestive frictions and collisions of meaning must be blandly "processed" by literary criticism to induce them to do so. (Eagleton 2001, 70)

Thus, it may be possible to view the incoherency of *The Fallen Leaves*, not as a failure of organic unity, but rather as a challenging example of form successfully dramatising the contradictions and ambiguities that Collins's novel seeks to articulate.

An important section of the novel is "the fatal lecture", where Amelius gives a public talk about his unusual life and his ideology, much to the anger of Mr Farnaby and his sense of respectability. Taylor identifies this episode as the chief vehicle for the expounding of Amelius's/Collins's socio-political views, but she also notes that a vital function of the lecture lies in its provision of a setting where the various classes can be brought together and, at the level of plot, enable Mr Farnaby to be recognised. As Taylor suggests: "It loosens the fixed separatedness of the different classes of London" (Taylor 1988, 235). It is possible to extend this observation and suggest a parallel between the way in which the "fatal lecture" operates and the function of Collins's novel itself. For, just like the lecture, nineteenth-century popular fiction also provided a shared space in which different classes came together, often provoking a response of hostility or resistance. Amelius's "fatal lecture" might be seen as the central metaphor of the novel, echoing not only the controversial breaking down of class boundaries that popular novels were accused of fostering, but also Collins's blending of disparate styles and literary methods which culminates, like the "fatal lecture", in a disastrous critical reception. The ridicule that Amelius endures as a result is shared by Collins through such judgments as Swinburne's "absurd" and "ludicrous". In the same way that Amelius is unable to unite people with his idealistic Christian Socialism, so too does his author, in the opinion of the Victorian literary establishment, fail to derive coherence or structure from his experimental approach to genre.

Notes

[1] Austin does not name authors explicitly in his essays, but his descriptions of the novels he cites point to the identifications I have made. Eileen Bigland notes that Ouida and Austin met at Lord Lytton's country house, and that they argued tremendously. See Bigland 1951, 190.

[2] Mitchell also identifies Ouida, Caroline Norton, and Ellen Wood as writers of the sentimental novel, all of whom have also been considered sensation authors.

[3] The bildungsroman is another literary type on which *The Fallen Leaves* draws, chiefly apparent in the development of Amelius, his journey towards maturity, and in the relationship with Rufus, his older mentor.

[4] See, for example, Croce 2000, 25-8.

Works Cited

Anon. 1892. The Cheapening of Poetry. *National Observer* 5:625.
Ashley, Robert. 1952. *Wilkie Collins*. London: Arthur Barker.

Attridge, Derek (ed.). 1992. *Acts of Literature*. London: Routledge.

Austin, Alfred. Our Novels: The Fast School; The Sensational School; The Simple School. *Temple Bar* 29:177-94; 410-24; 488-503.

Baker, William. and William M. Clarke, eds. 1999. *The Letters of Wilkie Collins.* 2 vols. Basingstoke: Macmillan.

Bigland, Eileen. 1951. *Ouida: The Passionate Victorian*. London: Jarrolds.

Collins, Wilkie. 1858. The Unknown Public. *Household Words* 21:217-20.

—. 1887. *Jezebel's Daughter*. London: Chatto and Windus.

—. 1879. *The Fallen Leaves*. London: Chatto and Windus, 1890.

Croce, Benedetto. 2000. Criticism of the Theory of Artistic and Literary Kinds, in Duff 2000. 25-8.

Derrida, Jacques. 1992. The Law of Genre, in Attridge 1992. 221-52.

Duff, David, ed. 2000. *Modern Genre Theory*. London: Longman.

Eagleton, Terry. 2001. *Literary Theory*. Oxford: Blackwell.

Ellis, S. M. 1951. *Wilkie Collins, Le Fanu and Others*. London: Constable.

Heller, Tamar. 1992. *Dead Secrets: Wilkie Collins and the Female Gothic*. New Haven: Yale University Press.

McDonald, Peter. 1997. *British Literary Culture and Publishing Practice 1880-1914*. Cambridge: Cambridge University Press.

Mitchell, Sally. 1977. Sentiment and Suffering: Women's Recreational Reading in the 1860s. *Victorian Studies* 21:29-45.

Nayder, Lillian. 1997. *Wilkie Collins*. New York: Twayne.

—. 2002. *Unequal Partners: Charles Dickens, Wilkie Collins and Victorian Authorship*. London: Cornell University Press.

Oliphant, Margaret. 1867. Novels. *Blackwood's Edinburgh Magazine* 102:257-80.

O'Neill, Philip. 1988. *Wilkie Collins: Women, Property and Propriety*. London: Macmillan.

Page, Norman. 1974. *Wilkie Collins: The Critical Heritage*. London: Routledge and Kegan Paul.

Punter, David. 1996. *The Literature of Terror*. 2 vols. Essex: Longman.

Taylor, Jenny Bourne. 1988. *In the Secret Theatre of Home: Wilkie Collins, Sensation Narrative and Nineteenth-Century Psychology*. London: Routledge.

Winnifrith, Tom. 1996. *Fallen Women in the Nineteenth Century*. Hampshire: Macmillan.

A DISTASTE FOR MATRIMONIAL SAUCE: THE CELEBRATION OF BACHELORHOOD IN THE JOURNALISM AND FICTION OF COLLINS AND DICKENS

HOLLY FURNEAUX

In a mischievous 1859 article for Dickens's *All the Year Round*, Collins critiques the "monotonous flavour of matrimonial sauce" that pervaded contemporary representations of bachelorhood (Collins 1859, 355). In both his fiction and his journalism Collins devotes a great deal of attention and energy to lifestyles that preclude matrimony. This essay focuses on his celebratory bachelor pieces for Dickens's journals, *Household Words* and, later, *All the Year Round*, and examines Dickens's tactical interspersion of Collins's valorisation of the unmarried man with his serialised, fictional ruminations on the same theme. Far from repressing such material, Dickens as editor prominently positioned Collins's often controversial paeans to the joys of unmarried life, strategically deploying Collins's pieces to support and recommend the treatment of bachelorhood in his own part-published novels.

Through scrutiny of the complex relationship between Collins and Dickens's journalistic and fictional output, this article resists the now pervasive belief that Dickens consistently repressed potentially "offensive" material in his friend's work. In the past two decades critics have started to look at Dickens as an impediment on Collins's writing, figuring the older and more established author as a prudish and unhelpful restraint on socially subversive aspects of Collins's fiction. This now typical interpretation is based on the powerful mantra that "Dickens was conscious of the susceptibilities of his readers and protected them assiduously, whether on sex, marriage, religion, or class" (Clarke 1988, 66).[1] The critical revision of the friends' working relationship offers an important corrective to the long-held view that, while Collins's career was enormously benefited by Dickens's interventions, Collins had nothing but a damaging influence on Dickens's work. It is important to see their relationship as mutually beneficial (and perhaps occasionally reciprocally detrimental).[2] The recent backlash, however, against Dickens's alleged conservatism fails to account for their shared interest in exploring those who failed, or refused, to become accommodated within a rigid family model.

Various advocates of the idea of Dickens as Collins's censor quote Dickens's letter to Wills, with whom he edited *Household Words*:

> I particularly wish you to look well to Wilkie's article about the Wigan schoolmaster, and not to leave anything in it that may be sweeping and unnecessarily offensive to the middle-class. He always has a tendency to overdo that–and such a subject gives him a fresh temptation. Don't be afraid of the Truth, in the least, but don't be unjust. (Tillotson, et al. 1965-2002, vol. 6, 664)

In the article referred to, Collins attacks the prejudice and ignorance of middle-class parents in selecting schools. Dickens, at times, was clearly anxious about alienating his journal's predominantly middle-class, family audiences. Contrary, however, to the received view of Dickens as foremost champion of an intensely heterosexual hearth and home, I argue that, on issues of sexuality, Dickens's fiction supported, promoted, and even went beyond Collins's exploration of alternative desires and lifestyles.

Collins vehemently repudiated the idea, still propounded today, that Dickens's fiction entirely avoids discussion of adult sexuality. He responded angrily in the margins of his copy of Forster's biography of Dickens to the author's statement that there is scarcely a page of Dickens's work that "might not be put into the hand of a child":

> If it is true, which it is not, it would imply the condemnation of Dickens's books as works of art, it would declare him to be guilty of deliberately presenting to his readers a false reflection of human life. If this wretched English claptrap means anything it means the novelist is forbidden to touch on the sexual relations which literally swarm about him, and influence the lives of millions of his fellow creatures[, restricting fiction to] those relations licensed by [...] the ceremony called marriage. (Quoted in Lonoff 1980, 156-7)

Dickens's radical stance on sexual issues can be indicated through his response to Collins's 1852 novel *Basil*. While most reviewers concentrated on what they called the "unfortunate selection" of "absolutely disgusting", sexually explicit content, Dickens wrote to Collins in praise for the work (Nayder 1997, 36). Dickens makes no reference to the scandal raised by the novel, writing instead in terms of moral approbation: "I have made Basil's acquaintance with great gratification, and entertain a high respect for him. And I hope that I shall become intimate with many worthy descendants of his" (Tillotson, et al. 1965-2002, vol. 6, 824).

As their literary and personal relationship deepened, Dickens consistently supported Collins's interest in those whose "aberrant" desires excluded them from the respectable family and developed these themes in his own novels. It is surely no accident that only months after being deeply moved by Collins's portrayal of Anne Rodway, Dickens should write his most explicit exploration of the extremes of female friendship in *Little Dorrit* (1857). "The Diary of Anne Rodway" (1856), published in two short instalments in *Household Words*, depicts a seamstress driven to turn amateur detective by the murder of her intimate female friend. Dickens responded to Collins's story with almost hyperbolic enthusiasm, recommending it to his closest friends and writing to Collins of the tale's emotional affect on him: "My behaviour [...] was weak in the extreme, for I cried as much as you could possibly desire" (Tillotson, et al. 1965-2002, vol. 8, 165). Anne Rodway's frank detailing of her intense, but indefinable attachment to Mary anticipates the same-sex passions explored in "The History of a Self Tormentor" that Dickens pens as Miss Wade. Both Anne Rodway and Miss Wade can convincingly be read as proto-lesbian.[3] Anne says of the friend she has "take[n] a fancy to":

> My heart warmed to her when we first met in the same lodging-house, two years ago; and although I am not one of the over-affectionate sort myself, I feel as if I could go to the world's end to serve that girl. Yet, strange to say, if I was asked why I was so fond of her, I don't think I should know how to answer the question. (Collins 1856a, 2)

The diary is punctuated with Anne's physical appreciations of her friend; she says "Mary is a very pretty girl", "she looked so pretty and so delicate as she fell asleep that it quite made my heart ache to see her" (ibid., 1, 2). Although Anne finally marries the fiancé who has hovered on the peripheries of the story, it is clear that her relationship with him is subordinate to her feelings for her lost friend. Throughout the diary Anne chastises herself for failing to think about her husband to be, and the final entry firmly places the emphasis on the inter-female bond: "I am not ungrateful for my blessings; but oh, how I miss that sweet face, on this morning of all others!". On her wedding day Anne carries a bouquet of flowers picked from Mary's grave in her bosom. And the diary closes with the words: "I can't forget Mary even on my wedding day" (ibid., 38). This displacement of marriage through same-sex attachments operates as a direct precursor to Dickens's description of the fiercely independent Miss Wade and her relationships with Charlotte and Tattycoram. Miss Wade famously entices Tattycoram away from the conventional family, rejecting marriage in favour of female cohabitation. For both Dickens and Collins these depictions of passionate, independent female cohabitation are not isolated anomalies. Both authors continue to explore these themes throughout their work.[4] Indeed these gender-nuanced depictions of female marital aversion reflect just one element of their shared attention to a wide variety of non-marital lifestyles and desires.[5]

While Dickens's approval of "The Diary of Anne Rodway" led him to suggest a future collaboration with Collins once he had finished *Little Dorrit*, their contributions to Dickens's *Household Words* can already be seen to collaborate in mapping out radical erotic and emotional alternatives to the family ideal.[6] At variance with his sexually conservative reputation, Dickens printed and endorsed Collins's fictional and journalistic pieces, such as the 1856 short piece "Bold Words by a Bachelor" in which Collins argued "that the general idea of the scope and purpose of the institution of Marriage is a miserably narrow one" (Collins 1856b, 507). The piece insists "that there are other affections in this world, which are noble and honourable, besides those of conjugal and parental origin". These "bold words" on the limitations of the familial model are delivered by the provocative figure of "an incurably-settled old bachelor" (ibid., 351). In an 1858 piece, "An Awful Warning to Bachelors", Collins adopts a similar persona. This incurable bachelor declares: "I have the strongest possible antipathy to being settled in life; and that, if I thought either of my eyes were capable of fixing itself on a young woman, I would shut that eye up, by an effort of will, henceforth and forever" (Collins 1858, 337). Collins, albeit in a comic mode, expends a great deal of journalistic energy in defence of the wilfully single male. Both these pieces hold the prestigious opening article position in *Household Words*, suggesting Dickens's editorial support of their content. This support is further evinced by Dickens's vindication of bachelorhood in his own fiction.

The marital resistance exercised by the single male was experienced as particularly provoking during the nineteenth century. Many of the closest members of Dickens's literary and social circles, including Collins and George Cruikshank, entered often anxious debates about the nature and social impact of bachelorhood. Cruikshank's sketch series of 1844, *The Bachelor's Own Book, or, The Progress of Mr Lambkin (gent.), in the Pursuit of Pleasure and Amusement: and also in Search of Health and Happiness* distils a familiar "progress" trajectory into twenty-four plates, the substance of which is almost entirely revealed in the title, where "happiness" inevitably translates as marriage. Cruikshank stereotypically depicts a lonely illness attended by a hired nurse as the result of Lambkin's indulgence in the exclusively male "pleasure[s] and amusement[s]" of betting and heavy social drinking. Recovering his health, Mr Lambkin determines upon a more staid single lifestyle, "but feels buried alive in the Grand Mausoleum Club; and contemplating an old bachelor member who sits poring over the newspapers all day, he feels horror-struck at the possibility of such a fate becoming his own and determines to seek a reconciliation with the Lady of his affections" (Cruikshank 1844, plate 22). The perceived negative social consequences of the bachelor's departure from normative familial domesticity are emphasised by Cruikshank's inclusion of newspapers bearing the captions "Refuge for the Destitute", "Home for the Housewife", and "[...] on Solitude" in his depiction of the un(re)productive Mausoleum Club.[7] Through an abrupt reconciliation with familial domesticity, Cruikshank spares Mr Lambkin from the growing stigma surrounding wilful bachelorhood. The final plate of the series, portraying Lambkin's inevitable wedding breakfast, is accompanied by an inscription that concludes with Lambkin's marriage speech: "May the single be married and [...] married happily" (ibid., plate 24).

These common narratives of "bachelor development" were faithful to the etymological origins of the term. In its earliest uses, a bachelor was a noviciate, a junior in training, either for fully-fledged knighthood, craftsmanship, or a university degree. The most common sense of bachelor as "an unmarried man (of marriageable age)", has, from its origins, carried an implication of incompleteness.[8] Integral to this common use is a sense of transgression against the imperative of marriage. As Howard Chudacoff puts it, "in modern Western society, any choice of lifestyle that diverts or prevents a presumably marriageable person from the social obligation to settle down and start a family has been considered inappropriate" (Chudacoff 1999, 8).

Eve Sedgwick reads the nineteenth-century fictional bachelor as a visible emblem of the "refus[al] of sexual choice, in a society where sexual choice for men is both compulsory and always self contradictory" (Sedgwick 1986, 160). Bachelors circumvented the imperatives to marriage and heterosexuality as well as apparently rejecting the role of domestic provider, central to what Herbert Sussman has described as "normative bourgeois manliness":

> Bourgeois masculinity is also defined in relation to the domestic sphere within criteria that value the role of bread-winner for a domestic establishment and that situate affectionate as well as sexual life within marriage. In short, normative bourgeois masculinity enforces compulsory heterosexuality and compulsory matrimony. (Sussman 1995, 4-5)

Such normative expectations informed stereotypes of the "selfish" bachelor whose spending on himself rather than a family was perceived as deviant. These assumptions also contributed to deeply anxious responses, such as T. S. Arthur's paranoid 1845 description of bachelorhood as "strange, unnatural, criminal" (quoted in Boone 1987, 279).[9] The prevalence of anxieties surrounding the single male in the mid-nineteenth century is also clearly expressed through the repetition of a particular plot structure in popular bachelor narratives. The typical story of bachelor "development" refused to acknowledge the bachelor's rejection of otherwise compulsory heterosexuality, depicting his marital resistance only to resolve it through final nuptials.

Collins firmly rejects the repetitive, predictable plotting of bachelorhood-resolved in "The Bachelor Bedroom":

> The bachelor has been profusely served up on all sorts of literary tables; but the presentation of him has hitherto been remarkable for a singularly monotonous flavour of matrimonial sauce. We have heard of his loneliness, and its remedy; of his solitary position in illness, and its remedy; of the miserable neglect of his linen, and its remedy. (Collins 1859, 355)

In this article, Collins refuses to bemoan bachelor life, offering a rare celebration of the diversity of a "succession of remarkable bachelors" whose true characters–closely concealed in everyday society–unfold at night to a select, exclusively male group "in the loose atmosphere of the Bachelor Bedroom" (ibid., 355, 358). Collins parodies the social constraints on gendered behaviour, demonstrating that the daytime construction of ideal masculinity is utterly artificial. His bachelors are entirely transformed in the all-male space of the "Bedroom"; Mr Smart, for example, undergoes a complete change in demeanour, even shifting from a "highly-bred English" accent to a rich Irish brogue: "At the first round of the tumblers, the false Mr Smart began to disappear, and the true Mr Smart approached, as it were, from a visionary distance, and took his place among us" (ibid., 358). Mr Bigg undergoes a similar metamorphosis "in the select society of the bachelor bedroom, inspired by the surreptitious tray and the midnight secrecy, wrapped in clouds of tobacco smoke, and freed from the restraint of his own magnificent garments, the truth flies out of Mr Bigg" (ibid., 356). This carefully hidden truth is an eccentric literary obsession, which marks him out–through a popular contemporary code word for same-sex desire–as "an enthusiast".

The piece operates as the culmination of Collins's articles on bachelorhood for both of Dickens's journals. Importantly, Collins's enthusiastic portrayal of the variety of bachelor experience in "The Bachelor Bedroom" is both spatially and conceptually positioned amongst Dickens's comparable novelistic ruminations on the same theme. The 6 August issue of *All the Year Round* begins with the fifteenth and exactly central instalment of *A Tale of Two Cities* (1859, issued in thirty-one weekly parts) and closes with Collins's article, chased by an advertisement for the third monthly part of *A Tale of Two Cities*, which Dickens published in both weekly and monthly formats. The collective bound edition of the journal emphasises the continuity between these two texts; the sixteenth instalment of *A Tale of Two Cities,* which begins the following weekly number of 13 August, is positioned on the opposite page to Collins's "Bachelor Bedroom". In his novel Dickens offers the precise collation of bachelorhood minus the "matrimonial sauce" that Collins's piece promotes.

Fig. 1. Phiz, "Under the Plane Tree".

The immediate proximity between Collins's article and the closing advertisment for *A Tale of Two Cities* further suggests an overlap in purpose. Mark Turner has argued similarly for Anthony Trollope's use of positive bachelor discourse in contemporary periodicals to support his, albeit muted, novelistic affirmation of bachelorhood: "A sense of propriety would have prevented Trollope from being any more explicit about the pleasures a man gives up by marrying, but such open proclamations were unnecessary as the discourse of the bachelor circulated in magazines and pamphlets around the time of the serialisation of *The Belton Estate*" (Turner 2000, 117).

There is a close link between the positive treatment of bachelors in Collins's article and Dickens's representation of Mr Jarvis Lorry as bachelor hero. A "confidential bachelor clerk" whose fastidious attention to business is balanced by courage, loyalty, and emotional integrity, Mr Lorry presents a very rare example of bachelorhood positively represented, and even celebrated. Previous critics have noted that, in the fiction of Dickens's time, the bachelor is most often portrayed as a selfish, bitchy, hypochondriac (Sedgwick 1986, 155). These negative characteristics reflect a cultural anxiety about the figure of the wilfully unmarried male, whose refusal of matrimony was viewed with increasing concern throughout the nineteenth century. Through careful editorial positioning, Dickens employs Collins's critique to recommend the treatment of bachelorhood in his own serial, and to prime readers for a more favourable reception of the provocative figure of the volitionally single male.

The sixteenth instalment of *A Tale of Two Cities* returns to the unconventional, extended Manette "family", which accommodates elderly bachelor banker Mr Lorry, and former-nursemaid turned general carer and cook Miss Pross, as well as the more conventional father, daughter, suitor triad. Mr Lorry experiences the Manette household as "the sunny part of his life" (Dickens 1859, 96). A celebratory image of Lorry's non-conventional relationship to this family is incorporated within Sydney Carton's final vision of the Manettes: "I see the good old man, so long their friend, in ten years' time enriching them with all he has, and passing tranquilly to his reward" (Ibid., 389-90). Lorry's central role in this family of his own choosing is also expressed in Phiz's illustration, "Under the Plane Tree" (fig.1), which was prominently placed as frontispiece to the first bound edition. In contrast to the peripheral Sydney, Mr Lorry appears in the centre of the family grouping. Lorry is described as "thanking his bachelor stars for having lighted him in his declining years to a Home" (ibid., 103). The traditional domestic model evoked here by the reverent capitalisation of "Home" is immediately undercut. Mr Lorry's pleasure in this household is strictly one of "his declining years", which have released him from the imperative to marriage, allowing him to enter domestic life without becoming a spouse.

As an elderly "gentleman of sixty" (ibid., 20), who ages eighteen years throughout the novel's action, Mr Lorry comes under a category that was, as Snyder argues, treated with particular suspicion:

> The polymorphic variety of negative bachelor stereotypes reveals no single trajectory of aberrance, but any number of ways in which bachelors, especially those "old bachelors" who seemed to have run permanently off the rails of the marriage track, were seen as veering away from an acceptable performance of manhood. (Snyder 1999, 28)

In Donald Grant Mitchell's immensely popular *Reveries of a Bachelor: Or a Book of the Heart* (1850) the young single protagonist, despite his ambivalence towards marriage, marks elderly unreformed bachelorhood as aberrant: "I will never [...] live a bachelor till sixty; never so surely as there is hope in man, or charity in woman, or faith in both" (Marvel 1850, 65).[10]

In the sixteenth instalment (the number directly after Collins's article) Dickens elaborates on the perfect appropriateness of Mr Lorry's permanent bachelordom. In an exchange between Mr Lorry and Miss Pross, Dickens provides an emphatic statement of his divergence from the cultural expectation of the bachelor's "rehabilitation" through marriage:

> "Dear, dear, dear! To think that there might have been a Mrs Lorry, any time these fifty years almost!"
> "Not at all!" from Miss Pross.
> "You think there might never have been a Mrs Lorry?" asked the gentleman of that name.
> "Pooh!" rejoined Miss Pross; "you were a bachelor in your cradle".
> "Well!" observed Mr Lorry, beamingly adjusting his little wig, "that seems probable, too".
> "And you were cut out for a bachelor", pursued Miss Pross, "before you were put in your cradle".
> "Then, I think", said Mr Lorry, "that I was very unhandsomely dealt with, and that I ought to have had a voice in the selection of my pattern". (Dickens 1859, 200)

Although Mr Lorry pays lip service to dominant contemporary perceptions of bachelorhood as an "unhandsome" state, this is at variance with his cheerful and immediate acceptance of Miss Pross's suggestions. His "beaming" agreement with her conception of him as a bachelor from inception suggests a pleasure in her observations, as well as a desire to justify what was increasingly perceived as a deviant or perverse lifestyle.

Dickens employs a model of born and fated bachelorhood, predestined by "bachelor stars", to further naturalise Lorry's unmarried status. In his insistence on Mr Lorry's experience of bachelorhood as natural and unavoidable, Dickens resists contemporary perceptions of unmarried men as either failed or wilfully aberrant. In this, he anticipates (albeit in a novelistic rather than a clinical register), the strategies employed by Havelock Ellis, and other sexologists at the end of the century, to de-stigmatise homosexuality by arguing for its non-volitional, congenital basis.[11]

The challenge to the normative family presented by the bachelor's marital resistance has been elided within Dickens criticism through a pervasive de-sexing of Dickens's single men (Sedgwick 1986, 154). Readings of Dickens's bachelors as asexual work to contain and conceal the willing abstainer's repudiation of a public sexuality that must always be heterosexual. Although Sedgwick has described the bachelor's potential to "startlingly desexualise [...] the question of male sexual choice" (ibid., 154), a more enabling approach has been recommended by Karma Lochrie at a paper delivered at the "Queer Matters" seminar, King's College London, May 2004, in which the refusal of sexual activity does not indicate asexuality, but rather constitutes a sexuality based on what one *will not* do. In her account of the "stone butch lesbian", who "does not let her partner touch her sexually", Judith Halberstam explores the ways in which a refusal of sexual acts can be just as meaningful as a performance of them: "Nonperformance, in this formulation, signifies as heavily as performance and reveals the ways in which performativity itself is as much a record of what a body will not do as what it might do" (Halberstam 1998, 126).

Given the absolute bias in current critical and popular thought towards defining sexuality through the type of person or acts selected, Lochrie and Halberstam's oppositional call for attention to the significance of the type of person or acts rejected offers a bold (although still gestural) attempt to rethink sexual categories. Halberstam asserts that "the stone butch has the dubious distinction of being possibly the only sexual identity defined almost solely in terms of what practices she does *not* engage in. Is there any other sexual identity, we might ask, defined by what a person will not do? Furthermore, could we even imagine designating male sexual identities in terms of non-performance?" (ibid., 123). Vincent Bertolini suggests that bachelorhood may offer just such an identity, as it is "defined negatively by its total lack of explicit sexual content, since all practices single, or reciprocal, are proscribed (hence the double meaning, which persists as a Latin trace in modern romance languages, of *celibate* as 'unmarried male' and 'sexually abstinent')" (Bertolini 1996, 709, italics in original).

This article's exploration of the anxieties surrounding the single male during the period of Collins's and Dickens's career suggests that perceptions of bachelorhood as sexual in its non-performance of marital heterosexuality contributed to the problematisation of the wilfully unmarried male. Sussman convincingly demonstrates that, in this period, uses of the term "bachelor" reflected "a construction of masculinity developed in the nineteenth century to code the rejection of heterosexuality". As he argues, such a rejection incited both "suspicion" of the bachelor and "social pressure compel[ling] him toward a marriage that is necessary to his self-fashioning as bourgeois man" (Sussman 1995, 66). Mr Lorry's refusal of the only publicly available form of sexuality propels him into an apparently paradoxical asexual experience of bachelorhood, a sexual category defined by what he will not do. His repudiation of heterosexuality contributes importantly to the plethora of non-heterosexual and non-reproductive choices insistently celebrated in Dickens's fiction.[12] The naturalisation and valorisation of bachelorhood in the works of both Collins and Dickens clearly demonstrate their mutual appreciation of the insufficiency of marriage as the exclusive mechanism for domestic fulfilment. In Mr Lorry's selection of the Manettes as his family of choice, he achieves a domestic idyll that is singularly untied to the demands of reproductive sexuality.

Collins's resistance to the rigid ideals of family, gender, and sexuality has long been recognised.[13] Far from repressing potentially "offensive" material in Collins's work, Dickens supported and printed these pieces in a dialogue with his own overlapping fiction. Reading Dickens's novels within the original periodical context that he, as editor, constructed for his work, enables recognition of Dickens's effort to provide a coherent exploration of the alternatives to marriage in both the fictional and non-fictional content of his serials. Attention to Dickens's strategic use of Collins's journalistic critiques of marriage presents a challenge to under-scrutinised critical imaginings of Dickens as foremost champion of a vehemently heterosexual hearth and home. The consensus between Dickens and Collins on exploring alternative lifestyles and desires, which cannot be accommodated within a conventional model of family, suggests a mutual sexual radicalism.

Notes

I would like to give my thanks to participants of Birkbeck College's 2004 "Dickens Day" and University of Sheffield's "Wilkie Collins Conference" for comments on early versions of this piece. I am particularly grateful to Andrew Mangham for the exuberance he injects into Collins and Dickens studies.
[1] On the persistent perception of Dickens as Collins's censor see Lonoff 1982, 51, Heller 1992, 92-3, and Nayder 1997, 38.
[2] Important new work is beginning to explore the mutual fruitfulness of Collins's collaborations for Dickens. See Trodd 1999-2000.
[3] For homoerotic readings of Miss Wade see Jagose 1998, Wilson 1998, and Armstrong 1995.

[4] The unusual (albeit temporarily) successful and independent cohabitation of Miss Wade and Tattycoram anticipates the liberating partnership that Limping Lucy envisions for herself and Rosanna Spearman in Collins's much later novel, *The Moonstone*–serialised in *All the Year Round* from January to August 1868. Limping Lucy expresses an explicit aversion to the opposite sex: "What do you care? What does any man care? Oh! If she had only thought of the men as I think, she might have been living now" (Collins 1868, 206). As a distinct alternative to what Collins depicts in this novel as the extremely dubious "pleasures" of heterosexual romance, Limping Lucy hopes to provide her beloved friend with a self-sufficient, female domestic alternative to her unrequited love for Franklin Blake: "I loved her. [...] She was an angel. She might have been happy with me. I had a plan for our going to London together like sisters and living by our needles. That man came here, and spoilt it all. He bewitched her. [...] I meant to take her away from the mortification she was suffering here. We should have had a little lodging in London, and lived together like sisters [...] We might have got our living together nicely" (ibid., 206).

[5] Collins and Dickens are faithful to the disparity in contemporary attitudes towards unmarried men and women, at a time when spinsterhood was regarded even more pejoratively than bachelorhood. These very different, gender-nuanced examples are included in order to demonstrate the diversity of domestic alternatives endorsed in Collins's and Dickens's work.

[6] See his letter to W. H. Wills, 10 July 1856: "You had best give Collins £20 in a handsome note, stating that I had told you that I saw such pains in his story ["Anne Rodway"] and so much merit, that I wished to remove it from ordinary calculations. I have a floating idea in my mind that after *Little Dorrit* is finished [...] he and I might do something in *Household Words* together" (Tillotson et al. 1965-2002, vol. 8, 159).

[7] Cruikshank's headlines convey common contemporary concerns that bachelorhood contributed to increased numbers of so-called "redundant" women, and could result in more applications for charitable relief from those without families to financially support them. Demographic shifts throughout the nineteenth century resulted in a dramatic increase in the population of unmarried women (famously addressed in W. R. Greg's 1862 article "Why are Women Redundant?") and a corresponding escalation of anxieties surrounding the volitional bachelor.

[8] The *Oxford English Dictionary* records 1386 as the first use of the term in this sense.

[9] For a comprehensive treatment of negative bachelor stereotyping see Snyder 1999, 28-31; and for continuing concerns about volitional bachelorhood later in the century see Tosh 1999, 173 and Tosh 1991, 67.

[10] Snyder documents the popular success of this text, which went through over fifty unauthorised editions (Snyder 1999, 48).

[11] For a summary of the sexological "congenital homosexuality" intervention see Doan and Waters 1998, 42. These early sexologists did not necessarily believe in the theory of innate homosexuality, but used the congenital argument strategically to encourage tolerance by countering claims of deliberate depravity. Chris White, for example has questioned the veracity of sexologists' congenital thesis, suggesting the tactical value of such a position: "It is impossible to know to what extent these theorists genuinely believed in the theory of innate homosexuality, or to what extent it was a vital strategic device in arguing for toleration and acceptance" (White 1999, 3).

[12] For an exploration of Dickens's career-long commitment to homoerotic articulation see Furneaux 2005.
[13] Powerful examples of homoerotic, male marital resistance permeate Collins's fiction. See, for example, the passionate friendships of Zack Thorpe and Mat Grice in *Hide and Seek* (1854) and Allan Armadale and Ozias Midwinter in *Armadale* (1866).

Works Cited

Armstrong, Mary. 1995. "What Can You Two Be Together?": Charles Dickens, Female Homoerotic Desire and the Work of Heterosexual Recovery. Unpublished doctoral thesis. Duke University.

Bertolini, Vincent, 1996. Fireside Chastity: The Erotics of Sentimental Bachelorhood in the 1850s. *American Literature* 68: 707-37.

Bland, Lucy. and Laura Doan. 1998. *Sexology Uncensored: The Documents of Sexual Science*. Cambridge: Polity Press.

Boone, Joseph. 1987. *Tradition Counter Tradition: Love and the Form of Fiction*. Chicago and London: University of Chicago Press.

Bowen, John. 2000. *Other Dickens: Pickwick to Chuzzlewit*. Oxford: Oxford University Press.

Chase, Karen. and Michael Levenson. 2000. *The Spectacle of Intimacy: A Public Life for the Victorian Family*. Princeton, NJ: Princeton University Press.

Chudacoff, Howard. 1999. *The Age of the Bachelor: Creating an American Subculture*. Princeton, NJ: Princeton University Press.

Clarke, William. 1988. *The Secret Life of Wilkie Collins*. London: Allison and Busby.

Collins, Wilkie. 1858. An Awful Warning to Bachelors. *Household Words*, 17:337-40.

—. 1859. The Bachelor Bedroom. *All the Year Round* 15:355-60.

—. 1856a. The Diary of Anne Rodway. *Household Words* 14:1-7 and 30-8.

—. 1856b. Bold Words by a Bachelor. *Household Words* 14:505-7.

—. 1868. *The Moonstone*. Oxford: Oxford University Press, 1982.

Cruikshank, George. 1844. *The Bachelor's Own Book*. Glasgow: David Bryce, 1888.

Dickens, Charles. 1859. *A Tale of Two Cities*. London: Penguin, 2003.

Doan, Laura. and Chris Waters. 1998. Homosexualities, in Bland and Doan 1998, 42.

Furneaux, Holly. 2005. "It is Impossible to be Gentler": The Homoerotics of Male Nursing in Dickens's Fiction. *Critical Survey* 17:34-47.

Halberstam, Judith. 1998. *Female Masculinity*. Durham and London: Duke University Press.

Hall, Donald. 1996. *Fixing Patriarchy: Feminism and Mid-Victorian Male Novelists*. Basingstoke: Macmillan.

Heller, Tamar. 1992. *Dead Secrets: Wilkie Collins and the Female Gothic*. New Haven: Yale University Press.

Jagose, Annamarie. 1998. Remembering Miss Wade: *Little Dorrit* and the Historicizing of Female Perversity". *GLQ* 4:423-51.

Lonoff, Sue. 1980. Charles Dickens and Wilkie Collins. *Nineteenth-Century Fiction* 35:150-70.

—. 1982. *Wilkie Collins and his Victorian Readers: A Study in the Rhetoric of Authorship*. New York: AMA Press.

Marvel, I. K. 1850. *Reveries of a Bachelor*. London: David Bogue, 1852.

Nayder, Lillian. 1997. *Wilkie Collins*. New York: Twayne.

Roper, Michael. and John Tosh (eds). 1991. *Manful Assertions: Masculinities in Britain since 1800*. London: Routledge.

Sedgwick, Eve Kosofsky. 1986. The Beast in the Closet: James and the Writing of Homosexual Panic, in Yeazell 1986, 148-86.

Snyder, Katherine. 1999. *Bachelors, Manhood and the Novel 1850-1925*. Cambridge: Cambridge University Press.

Sussman, Herbert. 1995. *Victorian Masculinities: Manhood and Masculine Poetics in Early Victorian Literature and Art*. Cambridge: Cambridge University Press.

Tillotson, K., G. Storey, et al. (eds). 1965-2002. *The Letters of Charles Dickens*. 12 vols. Oxford: Clarendon.

Tosh, John. 1991. Domesticity and Manliness in the Victorian Middle Class: The Family of Edward Benson White, in Roper and Tosh 1991, 44-73.

—. 1999. *A Man's Place: Masculinity and the Middle-Class Home in Victorian England*. New Haven and London: Yale University Press.

Trodd, Anthea. 1999-2000. Collaborating in Open Boats: Dickens, Collins, Franklin and Bligh. *Victorian Studies* 42:201-25

Turner, Mark. 2000. *Trollope and the Magazines: Gendered Issues in Mid-Victorian Britain*. Basingstoke: Macmillan.

White, Chris (ed.). 1999. *Nineteenth-Century Writings on Homosexuality: A Sourcebook*. London: Routledge.

Wilson, Anna, 1998. On History, Case History, and Deviance: Miss Wade's Symptoms and Their Interpretation. *Dickens Studies Annual* 26:187-201.

Yeazell, Ruth Bernard. 1986. *Sex, Politics and Science in the Nineteenth-Century Novel*. Baltimore and London: Johns Hopkins University Press.

AWFUL APPARITION!

Mrs. T. (to T., who has been reading the popular novel). "PRAY, MR. TOMKINS, ARE YOU NEVER COMING UP-STAIRS? HOW MUCH LONGER ARE YOU GOING TO SIT UP WITH THAT 'WOMAN IN WHITE?'"

Fig. 2. "Awful Apparition", *Punch* (1861).

THE AWFUL APPARITION

THAT APPEARED TO MR. BRIGGS, ON GETTING HOME AFTER THE SPIRITUAL SEANCE (AND LITTLE SUPPER), AND WHICH HAD SUCH AN EFFECT ON HIS NERVES THAT HE COULD NOT GO TO BUSINESS THE NEXT DAY.

Fig. 3. "The Awful Apparition", *Punch* (1864).

PARALLEL WORLDS: COLLINS'S SENSATIONALISM AND SPIRITUALIST PRACTICE

TATIANA KONTOU

The two engravings on the facing page (figs 2 and 3), which appeared in *Punch* in 1861 and 1864 respectively, satirise the soaring popularity of two major cultural phenomena—sensation fiction and spiritualism. The gentleman who has been reading Collins's *The Woman in White* is startled by the "apparition" of his rather stern housekeeper, while the figure in the second illustration (who has returned home from a séance) is dumbstruck by a ghostly image formed by two hats and an oil lamp. The two pieces are clearly poking fun at these fragile men—playfully demonstrating that becoming immersed in the vicarious drama of sensation novels or interacting with spirits can have a detrimental effect on the nervous system. Nevertheless, in spite of their almost identical titles (they are separated only by a point of grammar, "Awful Apparition" and "*The* Awful Apparition"), these caricatures do not appear to share any other common factors. Sensation fiction and spiritualism, though embedded in the same historical moment, have been recorded as entirely separate strands of Victorian life and culture. Indeed, we might argue that, while the sensation genre diverged from its gothic predecessors by locating its narratives in contemporary households and eliminating aspects of supernatural interference, spiritualism domesticated supernatural encounters in a very different way by introducing a systematic communication between the living and the dead.[1]

However, although séances do not figure in the sensation novels of the 1860s and mediums claimed that spirit manifestations were genuine supernatural encounters rather than "sensational plots" to dupe patrons out of their fortunes, a closer analysis of certain aspects of both the genre and the spiritualist practices of the time reveals the numerous points at which the novel and the séance intersect.

This essay will therefore locate Wilkie Collins's sensation fiction and spiritualism in their proper historical context and attempt to draw parallels between the two discourses. As I have already mentioned, a "comparative" analysis of these two phenomena might seem unyielding on the surface but it is my aim here to trace and examine the various ways in which text and the séance meet through their acute emphasis on the politics of sex and gender and their use of theatrical or melodramatic narrative tropes. The incorporation of spiritualist elements into sensation fiction and the deployment of sensational motifs during séances will constitute the main focus of the essay, where I will argue that the two forms exploited each other's narrative potential and dramatic imagery. This argument will pivot around the close textual analysis of selected episodes in Wilkie Collins's *No Name* (1862) which will be read alongside séance reports and descriptions of spirit encounters. The lines which separate the sensation heroine and the medium, as I will show throughout, are not as rigid as they first appear.

The protagonist of *No Name*, Magdalen Vanstone, blurs the boundaries between stage and drawing-room, between "real" and assumed identities, by taking part in amateur dramatics or, by deploying her professional acting skills off the stage. These different levels of performance are depicted through a variety of mediumistic tropes which connect the figure of the sensation heroine to that of the spirit medium more concretely. I will therefore argue that mediums were blurring similar boundaries by oscillating between the world of the living and the dead, all the while creating an ambiguity as to the extent to which their manifestations were authentic, fraudulent, or an amalgam of both. Thus, the figure of the domestic actress in both *No Name* and the séance is the crucial point of convergence here.

The duplicitous qualities of sensation fiction were the source of much anxiety to high-minded critics of the era and the genre was condemned as the product of "morbid imagination" (Oliphant 1867, 258) or dismissed as "mere trash" (Mansel 1863, 488). Sensation novels were considered morally unfit for the reading public. However, the representation of "high-strung women, full of passion, purpose and movement", in stark contrast to the "passive", "angelic", and "insipid" (Dallas 1862, 8) heroines of old, did not just provoke the disapproval of critics. In fact, it was one of the key factors behind the genre's phenomenal popularity (sensation novels were especially enjoyed by women but also, it should be noted, by significant numbers of men). The insights of E. S. Dallas, a more sympathetic critic of sensation fiction, are particularly useful here in terms of foregrounding the complexities and contradictions of the genre. Somewhat perversely, Dallas linked the "feminine influence" (Dallas 1866, 295) that these narratives displayed and exerted (from the production of sensation fiction by women to the representation of heroines) to the systematic blurring of consistent gender behaviour.[2] According to this logic, the "natural" passivity of women made them unfit to lead the action in a novel and, as a result, novelists reverted to creating unrealistic or "masculinised" heroines. As Dallas explains:

> When women are […] put forward to lead the action of a plot, they must be
> urged into a false position. To get vigorous action they are described as rushing
> into crime, and doing masculine deeds. […] If the novelist depends for his
> sensation upon the action of a woman, the chances are that he will attain his end
> by unnatural means. (Dallas 1866, 297)

These "unnatural means" stem from an ambivalence about the divisions
between masculine and feminine behaviour. If these heroines were successfully
imitating their male counterparts, what was this saying about a culture that was
apparently so preoccupied with maintaining the boundaries of sex and gender?
What exactly *was* "unnatural" about these emulations? And, most pressingly,
what does the reading of sensation fiction and the spell it cast over the female
public tell us about our current understanding of gender, sexuality, and identity
in the nineteenth century?

Before such questions can be tackled, concepts such as "feminine
influence" and "unnatural means", even though they remain hazily defined and
historically bound to the specific controversy caused by sensation fiction,
become relevant in the discussion of spiritualism. From its origins in 1848 to its
heyday in the 1870s,[3] the "language" of the séance—passivity, possession,
trance, and materialisation—imbued the spiritualist experience with a deeply
gendered vocabulary. Or, put another way, Victorian femininity was both
articulated through, and influenced by, the practice of mediumship. Moreover,
the debates and criticisms put forward by skeptics in response to the behaviour
of mediums are consistently concerned with the "unnatural" (as opposed to the
*super*natural) elements of the phenomena. The history of spiritualism, from its
beginnings to its peak, appears to be haunted by this issue.

Thus, Margaret and Kate Fox, the teenage sisters who famously
claimed to have established communication with the spirit of a murdered pedlar
in Hydesville, New York on 31 March 1848, could well be conceived as models
for sensation heroines. Their spectacular rise and fall (eventually descending
into poverty and alcoholism) displays all the necessary ingredients of a thrilling
story.[4] Margaret and Kate's contact with the spirits was comprised of a series of
questions and answers which were expressed in the form of rappings—a process
that Arthur Conan Doyle described as a "'telegraphic' communication from the
other side" (Doyle 1926, 57). Surely enough, like any scandalous tale, the Fox
sisters' reputation reached gargantuan proportions—polarising America into
advocates and skeptics but uniting all in curiosity.

In 1852, the American medium Mrs Hayden, respectable wife of a New
England journalist, crossed the Atlantic to hold séances for an enthusiastic and
inquisitive public. Frank Podmore describes the instant popularity of
spiritualism as "an epidemic of table-turning" (Podmore 1902, vol. 2, 7) in order
to fully convey the "contagious" appeal of spiritualism in all levels of society.[5]

Victorian England had its share of phrenologists, physiognomists, and mesmerists and was now eager to experiment with the other world.[6] These spirit communications were similar in form to those demonstrated by the Fox sisters. By pointing at the letters of a printed alphabet until a rap indicated the correct choice, eventually forming words and sentences, the spirit communicated with those asking the questions (ibid., 4).

As the spiritualist "epidemic" spread across the country, the form of spirit manifestations began to vary—tilting tables, moving furniture, invisible hands playing music instruments, written messages and, eventually, fully-formed apparitions became part of the repertoire developed by indigenous mediums. In some ways mirroring the criticism of sensation fiction, the press viewed the spiritualist movement with hostility. At best, it was condemned as a short-lived and ridiculous fad. At worst, it was a pathological problem or the product of mental illness.[7] An article in *Chambers Journal* defined spiritualism as "a singular retrogression into effete superstitions" (Anon. 1853, 321), while a piece in *All the Year Round*, described mediumship as "an abnormal condition of the brain and nervous system" (Anon. 1860, 370), comparing mediums to persons "afflicted with hysteria, epilepsy, catalepsy, and other congenital diseases" (ibid.). These responses to spiritualism clearly run parallel to the anxieties produced by sensation fiction as both phenomena are defined in terms of "weak" or vulnerable femininity. Moreover, the mental diseases mentioned here often actually figured in the plots of sensation novels as justifications for irrational behaviour.[8] In a spiritualist context though, trance, possession, and unconventional behaviour were acceptable, even desirable, forms of expression—proofs of spirit intervention, of real contact with the other side.

So far, I have sketched the typical characteristics of the sensation genre and the development of spiritualism in Victorian England. With this backdrop in place, it is now time to address the question of gender (or, more specifically, the question of femininity) in more rigorous detail. With the exception of Daniel Dunglas Home, the most powerful and popular mediums were women.[9] Women's "natural" passivity was the key element, or so it appears, in the successful development of mediumship as it prepared the medium for a process in which she would "empty out" her own self in order to host a spirit. W. H. Harrison, the editor of *The Spiritualist*, one of the most eminent newspapers dedicated to the subject of spiritualism, explained this transition within the familiar terms of mesmerism, a practice which was heavily saturated with gendered power relations in the nineteenth-century imagination[10]—"the spirit out of the body mesmerises the medium, and by the exercise of will-power causes the sensitive to speak or see what the controlling power wishes" (Harrison 1876, 4). Irrespective of the spirit's gender, the disembodied entity occupies the masculine position of power and influence while the "sensitive", a term conventionally associated with femininity and feminine weakness, is used here to represent the medium.

In another description of materialisation séances, the medium is portrayed as submissive to both the will of the spirit and to the desires of the séance sitters:

> A physical medium is entirely passive, and, in truth, performs no work at all. He or she places him or herself into the hands of the circle or investigators, sits on whatever position he or she is assigned, undergoes any tests or fastenings which may be adjudged necessary to render it certain that the phenomena observed are not due to the tricks of said medium. (Adshead 1879, v)

The passivity of the medium, so crucial to achieving successful contact with the dead, is therefore ambiguous or multi-faceted—it is a decisive factor in confirming that the manifestations are not fraudulent but it also functions as evidence that they are not influenced by the medium's own decision (conscious or not) to construct a spiritual "Other". Returning to Dallas's comments regarding the "unnatural" energetic drive of sensation heroines, we can therefore argue that the categories of activity and passivity are both encompassed and overturned within a spiritualist context. The extreme passivity of the medium, the process of becoming an empty vessel, senseless and inert, is at the same time responsible for the vibrant display of (after)life that constitutes the spirit manifestation. Thus, there is an intricate pattern of subversion beginning to emerge here. Both sensation heroines and mediums assume a false passivity, a docile or domestic exterior, in order to create spectral doubles and mysterious afterlives—alternative selves through which socially unacceptable forms of behaviour can be enacted. In doing so, both heroines and mediums challenge the concept of "unnatural" behaviour. Indeed, they transgress the preconceived notion of a single, concrete identity by portraying a diverse range of vivid personae.

Alex Owen comments that "spiritualist mediumship was both expressive of an inner struggle with the problem of femininity and instrumental in reconciling that tension" (Owen 1989, 209). Perhaps the reconciliation could therefore be found during the séance, where (somewhat paradoxically) the medium protected her social identity by dissolving it: "[the medium] passes into the unconscious trance, and loses his or her individuality, as when in deep sleep, till the conclusion of the séance, and in this state the medium is supposed to be subject to the control of his or her own particular guides" (Adshead 1879, vi). This "loss" of the social and psychical self was especially important to the manifestation of spirits who differed from the medium in terms of gender and personality. In sensation fiction, the enactment of multiple personalities and identities does not provide such a clear-cut resolution of "inner struggle" because it is not situated in the realm of the other world but within the cultural and legal systems of society (albeit a fictional one). Thus, the heroine's psychical duplicity is often expressed through bigamy or class transgression and many sensation plots, with *No Name* being an illuminating example, revolve around the exposure of female dishonesty and impersonation.

As Ann Cvetkovich points out, it is the amalgamation of beauty and evil which produces the strong effects of sensationalism: "The apparent naturalness of these connections between the visible, the real, and the affectively powerful can be called into question at moments when the meaning of a visible event is not as natural or self-evident as the emotions it produces seem to be" (Cvetkovich 1992, 24). The appearances of sensation heroines conceal hidden, dangerous selves—helping these protagonists commit their crimes and (however temporarily) to escape detection or punishment. Appearances are also crucial to any understanding of spiritualist experience. The distinction between what *appears* and what actually *is* is inextricably bound to the question of mediumship and to the proceedings of the séance, where fantasy and reality intermingle in similar ways.

Of course, when mediums were exposed as frauds, caught in the act of imitating the spirits, this play between appearance and reality was swiftly terminated. The mediumship of Mary Rosina Showers provides an excellent example of how spirit manifestations force us to question the ways in which we "read" identity according to criteria such as social standing and exterior beauty. The daughter of a former army officer in Bombay, Rosina developed her skills at the age of sixteen and gave private séances to select circles where the embodied spirits of men and women appeared and conversed with the sitters. During these interactions she would confine herself to a make-shift cabinet situated in the séance room and fall into a deep trance.[11] To the sitters, her elevated social status and her beauty guaranteed that the young medium was genuine. The revelation of her pretense came as a huge surprise to her admirers. Showers, alongside another youthful materialisation medium named Florence Cook, had given joint séances where spirits walked hand in hand. The failure of spiritualist investigators to expose Showers as a fraud early on in her career can only be explained by the innocence, good nature, and passivity such mediums were seen to represent. As Frank Podmore remarked:

> That an imposture so naïve and so flagrant should have escaped detection for so long in itself requires explanation, that explanation is, no doubt, to be found in the peculiar conditions of the exhibition. The two principal performers were, as we have seen, young girls little more than children in years, and one of them at least possessed of considerable personal attractions. (Podmore 1902, vol. 2, 102)

What must be acknowledged here, however, is that Podmore reads these spirit impersonations within a "childish" context rather than in terms of dangerous femininity. He is protecting and reinforcing the idea that young girls are not capable of serious or malicious imposture. Indeed, Mary Rosina's appearance creates a veil for her behaviour and Podmore implies that it is the beauty of the young woman which fools the sitters rather than her cunning intelligence. Crucially, were he to focus on the girls' ingenious minds or acting talents, he would also have to question the extent to which other young mediums were simulating manifestations and the extent to which gender norms were also "performed" and exaggerated during séances. These questions could then be transferred to a wider, non-spiritualist, non-fictional framework which would not only press for the re-definition of mediumship but also the re-definition of femininity. In fact, the entire edifice of Victorian identity, implausible though it may seem, is threatened by the ghostly projections of such girls.

However, it is my aim here to demonstrate how the question of performance and theatricality brings three discourses (novel, séance, and stage) into a ghostly interchange. To make this relationship clearer, it should be noted that the fictional heroines of sensation novels were often closely associated with the figure of the actress, either directly (when these heroines are actresses themselves or perform in amateur theatricals) or indirectly (when they mask their real feelings and motives by playing a series of different "roles"). Similarly, mediums were also defined in terms of performativity—most obviously when they were caught in the act of "embodying" the spirit but perhaps more interestingly, when they evoked elements of the theatre in their séances.[12] I will therefore examine the presence of theatrical motifs in *No Name* and compare them to the theatrics of the séance. I will map out the ways in which the "actress" and, more broadly, the absorption of theatrical techniques (melodrama, spectacle, the somatic representation of emotion, and so on) become suited to a critical discussion of the polymorphism of the Victorian psyche.

What is significant about all three of these discourses is that the act of metamorphosis is ambiguous or untraceable—it is realised away from the public gaze. The transition from self to other-self is, fundamentally, a veiled or invisible process. It is interesting to note that questions of concealment and doubling are also very prominent in Victorian discussions of the relationship between the conscious and unconscious mind. This brings the performances of sensation heroines and materialisation mediums into a wider network of discourses about the constituents of the self. Consider, for example, the term "hidden soul" as it is used by E. S. Dallas to describe our subconscious being (Dallas 1866, 199). Dallas perceives the human soul as a "double [...] or at least as leading a double life" (ibid., 200), immediately recalling the psychical duality embodied by heroines and mediums alike. Indeed, stage, séance, and text can all be interpreted through this register of visibility, concealment, and duplicity (showing how the analysis of these ghostly theatrics goes far beyond questions of surface appearance). This point will inform the remainder of this essay (and I will return to it later using specific examples). For now, however, I will focus attention on the development of the theatrical séance.

In 1872, an English medium named Mrs Guppy withdrew into a cabinet. After falling into a trance, Guppy produced a series of pale spirit faces which appeared at the opening of the cabinet and resembled, according to Podmore, "a Punch and Judy show" (Podmore 1902, vol. 2, 96).[13] It was a defining moment in the history of spiritualism. However, it was not Guppy but Florence Cook, who almost single-handedly developed and defined the materialisation séances of the 1870s.[14] From the confines of a cabinet, the entranced Florence would produce the spirit of Katie King, a beautiful young woman with flowing hair, a white dress and a turban who would socialise with the astonished séance sitters (Michelson 1922, 7). Similar mediumship developed among other young girls, including Mary Rosina Showers, Catherine Wood, and (much later) Elizabeth d'Espérance. Each one of these girls would follow a similar procedure to Cook, gaining fame and notoriety in the process. Each one gave up their minds and bodies to become a living portal for their spectral "others".

My focus is on how materialisation séances contributed to the domestication of the theatre and the extent to which Victorian identity was defined through performative registers. The figure of the "domestic actress"—confined yet mercurial—was especially key to the links between *No Name* and the séance.

The narrative of Collins's *No Name* pivots around Magdalen Vanstone's uncanny ability to transform into a variety of characters, each of which is in some way representative of domesticity and Victorian femininity (she portrays a governess, a young maiden, and a servant). After the death of her parents, it is revealed that both Magdalen and her older sister Norah are illegitimate. They must forsake their elevated social status and comfortable lifestyle as their fortune is bequeathed to Michael, the next of kin and legal heir. Although Norah surrenders to her fate and assumes the respectable role of a governess, Magdalen decides to become an actress to support herself financially. Acting, however, is more than just a profession to Magdalen—it shapes her desires and sense of justice, fixing and dividing her identity at the same time. She skillfully employs her talents off the stage in order to regain her lost fortune and the family's good name.

Magdalen's initial transgression can therefore be located in her choice of profession. Acting was associated with impropriety and loose morals, a public life that was not suitable for Victorian ladies.[15] We can argue, however, that Magdalen's deeper, more significant transgression lies in her carefully constructed simulations of the characters she encounters in her life (such as her old governess Miss Garth and her young maid Louisa). These impersonations blur the boundaries between selves and question the extent to which gendered personality is individual and unique or culturally "programmed". What is more, Collins frames Magdalen's various transformations using a series of mediumistic tropes and spirit vocabularies, turning the heroine into both a medium and an embodied spirit.

Consider, for example, Magdalen's dramatic declaration that she and her sister are "Nobody's Children" after losing their social standing (Collins 1862, 125). Magdalen's face, "always remarkable for its want of colour" becomes "startling to contemplate, in its blank bloodless pallor" (ibid., 121), after the heroine is informed of her social demise. In a sense then, Collins turns his heroine into a kind of apparition—pallid, nameless, and without a fixed position within society. Her pale face becomes a somatic representation of Magdalen's "spectralisation" and indeterminable status, directly evoking the portrayal of spirits during séances. In a séance performed by Mary Rosina Showers, for example, the materialised spirit Florence Maple is described by one sitter in very similar terms to those used by Collins—"we all noticed the extreme pallor of her features, the open, starring, never-winking eyes".[16] In both novel and séance, "pallor" becomes a powerful signifier of ghostliness, of an ethereal plane between visibility and invisibility, functioning on a "proper" and "improper" level. In addition, Collins makes a subtle connection between spectrality and acting by likening Magdalen's pale face to a *tabula rasa*—a blank, pliable space which facilitates the heroine's chameleonic changes.

The fact that Magdalen's physical appearance bears no resemblance to her parents further erodes her ties with her past life. However, as Jenny Bourne Taylor remarks, it "implies what turns out to be true, though in an unexpected way; that she is a bastard" (Taylor 1988, 143-4). This non-resemblance not only allows Magdalen to assume a series of roles "outside" of herself but also to re-enact elements of her past that have been taken from her and de-legitimised. She successfully assumes the character of her childhood governess and mimics the mannerisms of her beloved sister Norah. These deeply personal enactments appear to compensate for her lack of a visible, physical connection with the family line.

The shift from fixity to namelessness, from a stable position to social ambiguity, spectralises Magdalen but it also provides her with the power to go against social convention. With this point in mind, it is worth noting here that Magdalen's definition of herself as "Nobody's Child" and the novel's title, *No Name*, both recall the Cyclops episode in Homer's *Odyssey* (c. 760 B. C.). Just as Odysseus outwits his opponent by calling himself "Nobody", Magdalen uses namelessness in her struggle against a myopic society and legal system. With theatrical cunning, she morphs into a series of different characters, an "odyssey" that eventually leads her back to her original identity—Magdalen Vanstone, heir to the family fortune.[17] This circular movement, losing herself in order to find herself, is therefore closely associated with the way we can understand Victorian mediumship and the materialisation séance (where the boundaries of the self are stretched to include both the "real" and the "phantasmal" parts).

According to Alex Owen, the experience of the séance (in which everyday reality was suspended) was based around an interactive play of fantasises and desires between the sitters and the medium (Owen 1989, 221). Unidentified spirits could be recognised and claimed by the sitters as the very images of the dead they had been yearning to see:

> Spirits and sitters were involved in a complex exchange which can be understood as devolving, "as in the original fantasies, on positions of desire: active or passive, feminine or masculine, mother or son, father or daughter". As in daydreams and fantasies, these positions were interchangeable and could involve endless computations on a particular theme or scene. (ibid., 222)

Just as these dramatic moments are registered by both parties as embodiments of a psychical reality, Magdalen's transformations can be read through the same template. As I have already explained, her namelessness is both manifested and concealed in her performances. They take her "outside" of herself but they also create links with her past identity—embodiments, like materialised spirits, of desire. However, we can also understand Magdalen's theatrics in terms of *failed* séances where the desires of the sitters and the spirit are differentiated. There are two episodes in the novel where this framework can be applied.

I will examine two scenes from *No Name* in which Magdalen assumes the role of Miss Garth, her childhood governess, using the unsuccessful séance as a kind of critical metaphor. In the role of Miss Garth, Magdalen intends to visit the house of Noel Vanstone, in whose hands the sisters' fortune now resides, in order to regain the loss. Prior to this meeting, Magdalen decides to test the strength of her metamorphosis by first presenting herself to her sister Norah. I will use both of these encounters (with Norah and with Noel) to construct my analysis here.

In this respect, it is significant that Magdalen's greatest challenge in performing the role of the governess is in accurately replicating Miss Garth's physical appearance as opposed to her personality and mannerisms. As Collins writes, there is a "vast difference between a disguise worn by gaslight, for the amusement of an audience, and a disguise assumed by daylight to deceive the searching eyes of two strangers" (Collins 1862, 217). Thus, the transition from the "artificiality" of night-time theatrical performances to everyday experience is problematised. Whereas the marks that Magdalen paints on her face to appear older have an "artificial nature" (ibid.), Miss Garth's *persona*—"the harsh voice, the blunt manner, the Northumbrian *burr*" (ibid., 218)— is so faithfully reproduced as to be "perfect" (ibid.). Although Miss Garth's "copy" would be deemed an artistic success on the stage, away from the theatre the transformation is "hideous" (ibid.). Nevertheless, the transgressive or unsettling element of Magdalen's performance is *not* located in her external appearance as the portrayal of old, menopausal women falls comfortably into the theatrical conventions of the time.[18] Rather, it can be found in her ability to psychologically morph into the identity of another woman.

Let us then examine the meeting between Magdalen and Norah in more detail—the first instance in which a private, domestic transformation (where bedroom becomes dressing-room) is put to the test in public. The encounter is permeated with intense emotion—Magdalen's "heart beat fast" and "a burning heat glowed in her as she thought of her false hair, her false colour, her false dress, and saw the dear familiar face coming nearer and nearer" (ibid., 221). In this dramatic moment, we can observe an emotional split between Magdalen's assumed character and her "true" identity. Rather than losing her cool and revealing her secret, Magdalen's consciousness of her artificial exterior becomes more and more acute—a play of surface and depth. Collins thus heightens the tension in this encounter, not with a moment of identification between the sisters, but with Norah's disinterested gaze: "[her] eyes looked up […] and looked away from [Magdalen's face] again, as from the face of a stranger" (ibid.). Family instinct and blood ties are called into question by the effectiveness of Magdalen's disguise. She has become invisible to her sister; her identity is entirely cocooned within Miss Garth. It is perhaps significant that Norah wears a veil during this scene—a clear signifier of mourning and loss. In a sense then, we might argue that Norah, who is clothed in formal mourning dress in memory of her parents, is grieving for her "lost" sister also. She is unable to see beyond the disguise and reclaim Magdalen from the theatrical, spectral realm; she commits the memory of Magdalen to an unrecoverable past.

Just as séances can be conceived as dramatic performances, in which desires are played out through spirits and sitters enacting roles for each other, the episode between Magdalen and Norah can be interpreted in a similar way. Like the proceedings of many séances, the drama here is both successfully and unsuccessfully enacted by the heroines. Magdalen's "manifestation" of Miss Garth is wholly successful in the sense that her own sister cannot recognise her. On the other hand, Magdalen's inner desire, a deep yearning to break out from her "shameful" disguise (ibid.), is unrealised. The dramatic potential of the scene, in which the sisters would be reunited like sitter and departed spirit, is not fulfilled.

A séance attended by the novelist Florence Marryat[19] is underscored by similar questions of family ties, identification, and "illegitimacy".[20] In her spiritualist memoir *There is No Death* (1891), Marryat describes her first encounter with spiritualism in February 1873, an event which proved crucial in the subsequent development of her beliefs. It may come as something of a surprise then that this formative experience with the American medium Mrs Holmes is actually a tale of misrecognition and misfired instincts. The face of a little girl materialises in the aperture of the spirit cabinet but Marryat is unable to identify any kind of familial or emotional connection with the ghostly image. The spirit child, covered in muslin, is prompted by the medium to move on as she has made a mistake:

> [She] did move on, but very slowly and reluctantly. I could read the disappointment in her eyes, and after she had disappeared, she peeped round the corner again and looked at me, longingly. This was "Florence", my dear *lost* child (as I then called her), whom had left me as a little infant of ten days old, and whom I could not at first recognise as a young girl of ten years. (Marryat 1891, 21, italics in original)

On the one hand then, we can read this unrecognised spirit as an optical illusion or dramatic effect intended to convince Marryat of the authenticity of the séance (a reading which turns the episode into a kind of failed theatrical scene). On the other, if we accept that the spirit child (at least symbolically) is indeed Marryat's dead daughter, we can argue that the girl becomes "nobody's child". Just like Magdalen, she is cast back into the netherworld, ostensibly unloved and unremembered. Moreover, it is also worth noting here that Victorian womanhood was very much defined in terms of childbearing and parental responsibility. As a result, the appearance of the child and the mother's delayed reaction pose more troubling and uncomfortable questions than any debate over the veracity of the manifestation. If Magdalen's "illegitimacy" is inscribed and enacted through the different identities she assumes, the unrecognised spirit girl is illegitimate because of the excluded position she occupies in Marryat's heart, memory, and family network. At this moment, she is twice dead.

Marryat remained uncertain of the child's identity for some time until a trance séance conducted by Mrs Cook convinced her otherwise.[21] Florence converses with her daughter in a dialogue that is clearly tinged with melodramatic hyperbole and emotional turmoil:

> "Mother! I am Florence. I must be very quiet. I want to feel I have a mother still. I am so lonely. Why should I be so? I cannot speak well. I want to be like one of

you. I want to feel I have a mother and sisters, I am so far away from you all now".

("But I always think of you my dear dead baby".)

"That's just it—your *baby*. But I'm not a baby now. I shall get nearer [...]. I know you think of me, but you think of me as a baby. You don't know me as I *am*". (ibid., 77, italics in original)

If we return to Owen's argument that séances were dramatic enactments of desire in which spirit and sitters could occupy multiple positions, then we can understand Florence's acceptance of her spirit daughter in precisely this way. Moreover, there is an additional fantasy being enacted here that goes beyond the various dramatic "positions" of the séance itself—the notion that the dead baby has grown up in the other world. There are uncanny parallel voices running through this scene, as Florence is the name shared by both mother and daughter. We must therefore take into account that the medium is not only acting as the mouthpiece for the spirit daughter but is also actively positioning herself into the dramatic equation. The medium plays out the role of the daughter that Marryat wishes to identify as her own and, at the same time, she questions the parameters of mediumistic consciousness by using the phrase "become like one of you" when in the guise of the spirit girl. Who is being ventriloquised, and who is actually speaking, is unclear during the séance—voices echo and distort through different levels of consciousness and performance. Reality and fantasy blend into each other, as do the public and the private. Thus, the extent to which these enactments are conscious theatrical renditions or "materialisations" of deeper, more intense psychical dramas is fundamentally, perhaps necessarily, ambiguous.

I will now return to *No Name* and the second episode that I outlined earlier (in which Magdalen, disguised as Miss Garth, visits Noel Vanstone and his housekeeper Mrs Lecount). Utterly convinced by the disguise, Vanstone proceeds to make a series of hurtful and insulting remarks about Magdalen and her sister (under the impression, of course, that he is speaking to Miss Garth). Shaken by his callousness, Magdalen momentarily forgets her assumed persona and speaks with her own voice. The effect of this is stranger than we might think. In a curious way, she ventriloquises *herself*—releasing long suppressed desires and frustrations through the external *façade* of Miss Garth, a "foreign" or spectral voice which briefly possesses its host vessel. Put another way, because her "real" voice is spoken through the lips of her assumed character, it is as if Miss Garth becomes the medium for Magdalen's spirit. Nevertheless, Magdalen is quick to compose herself and her long-practiced acting skills allow her to fall back into character:

Nothing but the habit of public performance saved her from making the serious error that she had committed more palpable still, by attempting to set it right.

Here, her past practice in the Entertainment came to her rescue, and urged her to
go on instantly, in Miss Garth's voice, as if nothing had happened. (Collins
1862, 235)

There are, however, further layers of deception in play. Later in the scene, the
housekeeper, Mrs Lecount, pretends to leave the room but is in fact hiding
behind Magdalen's chair. She succeeds in cutting away a piece from the inner
flounce of her gown—a detail which is later used to expose Magdalen's
performance (ibid., 237). The inner flounces of the costume therefore assume a
double (perhaps multiple) function here. On the one hand, they represent
Magdalen's "real" identity, the hidden layers beneath her disguise (it is
appropriate, in this sense, that the fragment of fabric is used to reveal the truth).
On the other hand, because the "brown alpaca dress" (ibid.) is a *costume*, a
surface adornment, the fabric demonstrates how Magdalen's false identity is
only skin deep—she steps out of character as if out of a dress. More broadly, it
could also be argued that (in light of the powerful connection between
conceptions of womanhood and decorative dressing) it is Magdalen's *femininity*
which betrays her. When Mrs Lecount declares that *"I hold you in the hollow of
my hand"* (ibid., 239, italics in original) while clutching the fragment, the point
is compounded—the dress, at least metaphorically, *is* Magdalen. She is defined
and controlled by these fabrics and flounces.

It is interesting to note that the exposure of Magdalen's performance is
closely reminiscent of failed séances in which sitters would grab the spirits and
accuse the medium of fraud. An illustration published in *The Graphic*, depicts
one of Florence Cook's spirit-grabbing episodes.[22] The incident is "narrated", as
it were, through a series of small pictures which perhaps resemble a cinematic
story-board to the twenty-first century viewer. The pictorial sequence therefore
transforms spirit-grabbing into a sensational narrative (which of course placed
great emphasis on the revelation of various kinds of fraud). What is more,
corset, stockings, and boots appear at the centre of the illustration, the "spiritual
garments", not only depicting the exposure of the medium but making the same
link between femininity and theatrical deception seen in *No Name* (as well as
eroticising this relationship). These feminine undergarments both exhibit and
conceal the medium's assumed identity; they bind this play of desire, secrecy,
and performance together. If the "exposure" of women is articulated in terms of
costume, then the question of gender itself, in both séance and novel, is also
closely associated with masquerade and performance.

In both sensation novels and spiritualist practice, the question of
theatrical performance is so profoundly ambiguous that it ultimately transcends
any debate over its "natural" or "artificial" status. In fact, these spectral
theatricals situate themselves at the very epicenter of the Victorian psyche.
"Acting", whether we locate it in the domestic sphere, the séance, or on the

stage, becomes essential to our own (constantly developing) understanding of how to read and define Victorian personalities. The sensation heroine (as an actress) and the medium (as a sensation heroine) also demonstrate the extent to which these different cultural registers influenced and broadened each other. With this in mind, what I have tried to show in this essay is how gendered identity was explored and defined through a series of complex and interdisciplinary links between sensation fiction and the séance.

Notes

[1] One of the sensation genre's most significant innovations was situating its tales of evil, murder, and destruction at the heart of the contemporary middle-class home. This was a source of much anxiety and concern amongst critics of the era, who perceived these scenarios not only as improbable but as morally threatening. For contemporary responses to the domestic settings of sensation fiction see Austin 1870, 421 and James 1865, 594.

[2] Lyn Pykett highlights the paradoxes inherent in the gendering of the sensation novel, as it was interpreted as a "feminine", "un-feminine", and "anti-feminine". See Pykett 1992, 31-5.

[3] For full length studies of spiritualism see Doyle 1926 and Podmore 1902. Oppenheim 1985 is also an invaluable resource.

[4] The Fox sisters were accused of simulating the spirit rapping by clicking their knee joints. In December 1850, three professors of medicine at the University of Buffalo named Flint, Lee, and Coventry wrote a joint public letter to the *Commercial Advertiser* explaining how these sounds could be produced by the clicking of toe or knee joints. See Podmore 1902, vol. 1, 184. As I have already intimated, both Kate and Margaret succumbed to alcoholism and died destitute in 1892 and 1893 respectively. See Owen 1989, 65.

[5] For analysis of the appeal spiritualism had in literary circles see Porter 1958. On the growing interest in spiritualism amongst the working-classes see Barrow 1986.

[6] In contrast, Podmore traced the emergence of spiritualism to magical and religious beliefs (Podmore 1902, vol. 1). Similarly, Oppenheim argues that the movement "drew much strength from indigenous cultural and anthropological traditions, in which religious faith and magic rituals were closely intertwined. In the second half of the nineteenth-century, nourished on rich deposits of spiritual lore from previous ages, spiritualism in Britain flourished in the specific conditions created by the troubled relations of science and religion" (Oppenheim 1985, 27).

[7] For an account of the medical response to spiritualism (which had a substantial influence on the mainstream press) see Shortt 1984, 339-45.

[8] For a discussion of the ways in which transgressive behaviour was depicted as mental malady and how the sensation genre was also considered to be threatening to one's health see Gilbert 1997 and Mangham 2003.

[9] Although there were a few notable male mediums, the spiritualist arena was dominated by women and, as a result, I am dealing exclusively with female mediums in this piece. A study of masculinity and mediumship has yet to be produced. For a discussion of

Daniel Dunglas Home's mediumship see Oppenheim 1985, Podmore 1902, vol. 2, Doyle 1926, vol. 2, and Home's own autobiography of 1878.

[10] For a discussion of the power relations and sexual chemistry that existed between the male mesmerist and his female patient see Winter 1998.

[11] See Owen 1989, Podmore 1902, vol. 2, and Marryat 1892.

[12] Emma Hardinge Britten, a successful trance lecturer on both sides of the Atlantic, had begun a career as an actress before she became a medium. See Oppenheim 1985, 7.

[13] Podmore also quotes from Robert Dale Owen's account of a séance with Kate Fox in October 1860 at which a "veiled and luminous female figure presented itself and walked about the room" (Podmore 1902, vol. 2, 96). Apart from this incident, materialisation séances seem to have developed concurrently in Britain and the States in early 1872.

[14] See Doyle 1926, vol. 2, Podmore 1902, vol. 2, Owen 1989, Oppenheim 1985, and Marryat 1892.

[15] For a discussion of the association between actresses and prostitutes see Davies 1991, 78-85.

[16] Letter by Dr Richardson to the *Medium and Daybreak*, reproduced in Podmore 1902, vol. 2, 101.

[17] Kate Flint remarks that however transgressive and undesirable the subject matter of sensation fiction, the resolution of the plot would always revert to the prevalent ideology and moral values of the epoch (Flint 1993, 281). In *No Name*, Magdalen reassumes her family name and inherited wealth through Norah's marriage to George Bartram (who takes on the Vanstone fortune later in the novel).

[18] For the portrayal of old women on the stage, a role also popular with cross-dressing actors, see Davies 1991, 113.

[19] Florence Marryat was a woman of many talents. She was a popular novelist, mostly of sensation fiction, an actress, opera singer, playwright, editor of *London Society* (1872-76) and an avid spiritualist whose experiences recorded in *There is No Death* and *The Spirit World* provide a vibrant account of Victorian spiritualism. For biographical information on Marryat see Black 1893 and Sutherland 1988.

[20] I am using "illegitimacy" here not in its legal context but metaphorically; for example, as a way of understanding mediums who would often materialise spirits claiming to be a lost daughter or friend. Illegitimacy can therefore be interpreted in terms of theatricality but also in terms of the "authenticity" of the séance itself—closer inspection of the physical appearance of spirits or more private questions would reveal that the materialised being was not who he or she was claiming to be.

[21] Mrs Cook, a private trance medium, is not to be confused with Florence Cook (the materialisation star of the 1870s).

[21] For a reproduction of this illustration see Oppenheim 1985.

Works Cited

Adshead, W. P. 1879. *Miss Wood in Derbyshire: Experiments Demonstrating the Fact that Spirits Can Appear in the Physical Form*. London: J Burns.

Anon. 1853. The Spirits Come to Town. *Chambers Edinburgh Journal* 19:321-4.

Anon. 1860. Modern Magic. *All the Year Round* 3:370-6.

Austin, Alfred. 1870. Our Novels: The Sensation School. *Temple Bar* 29:410-24.

Barrow, Logie. 1986. *Independent Spirits: Spiritualism and the English Plebeians 1850-1910.* London and New York: Routledge and Kegan Paul.

Black, Helen C. 1893. *Notable Women Authors of the Day, Biographical Sketches.* Glasgow: David Bryce and Son.

Collins, Wilkie. 1862. *No Name.* London: Penguin Books, 1994.

Cvetkovich, Ann. 1992. *Mixed Feelings: Feminism, Mass Culture and Victorian Sensationalism.* New Jersey: Rutgers University Press.

Davies, Tracy C. 1991. *Actresses as Working Women, their Social Identity in Victorian Culture.* London and New York: Routledge.

Doyle, Arthur Conan. 1926. *The History of Spiritualism.* 2 vols. London: Cassell and Company.

Flint, Kate. 1993. *The Woman Reader 1837-1914.* Oxford: Oxford University Press.

Gilbert, Pamela K. 1997. *Disease, Desire and the Body in Victorian Women's Popular Novels.* Cambridge: Cambridge University Press.

Harrison, W. H. 1876. *Mediumship: Its Nature and Varieties.* London: William H. Harrison.

Home, Daniel Dunglas. 1878. *Lights and Shadows of Spiritualism.* London: Virtue and Company.

James, Henry. 1865. Miss Braddon. *The Nation* 9:593-4.

Mangham, Andrew. 2003. Hysterical Fictions: Mid-Nineteenth-Century Constructions of Hysteria and the Fiction of Mary Elizabeth Braddon. *Wilkie Collins Society Journal* 6:35-52.

Marryat, Florence. 1891. *There is No Death.* London: Griffith Farran and Company.

Michelson, Herman. 1922. Who Was Katie King?. *New York Magazine* 16 July 1922. 7.

Oliphant, Margaret. 1867. Novels. *Blackwood's Edinburgh Magazine* 102:257-80.

Oppenheim, Janet. 1985. *The Other World: Spiritualism and Psychical Research in England, 1850-1914.* Cambridge: Cambridge University Press.

Owen, Alex. 1989. *The Darkened Room: Women, Power, and Spiritualism in Late Nineteenth Century England,* London: Virago Press.

Podmore, Frank. 1902. *Modern Spiritualism, A History and a Criticism in Two Volumes.* 2 vols. London: Methuen and Company.

Porter, Katherine H. 1958. *Through a Glass Darkly: Spiritualism in the Browning Circle.* Lawrence: University of Kansas Press.

Pykett, Lyn. 1992. *The Improper Feminine: The Woman's Sensation Novel and the New Woman Writing.* London: Routledge.

Shortt, S. E. D. 1984. Physicians and Psychics: The Anglo-American Medical Response to Spiritualism, 1870-1890. *Journal of the History of Medicine and Allied Sciences* 39:339-55.

Sutherland, John (ed.). 1988. *The Longman Companion to Victorian Fiction.* Essex: Longman Group.

Taylor, Jenny Bourne. 1988. *In the Secret Theatre of Home: Wilkie Collins, Sensation Narrative and Nineteenth-Century Psychology.* London and New York: Routledge.

Winter, Alison. 1998. *Mesmerized: Powers of Mind in Victorian Britain.* Chicago and London: The University of Chicago Press.

PART II:
COLLINS AND ART

TEXT AND IMAGE TOGETHER: THE INFLUENCE OF ILLUSTRATION AND THE VICTORIAN MARKET IN THE NOVELS OF WILKIE COLLINS

CLARE DOUGLASS

Illustration served both a practical and an aesthetic function in much of the popular fiction of the nineteenth-century. For Wilkie Collins the importance of visual art and illustration was so great that he underscored its significance by including art *within* the narratives of his fiction as well as in conjunction with them. Such is evident in one of his most famous novels, *The Woman in White* (1860). Walter Hartwright, one of several character narrators in the text, describes his brief career in illustration as a means of secretly supporting Laura Fairlie and her half-sister, Marian Halcombe: "I get my bread by drawing and engraving on wood for the cheap periodicals" (Collins 1860, 433). Although *The Woman in White* did not initially appear with illustrations in *All the Year Round* from 26 November 1859 to 25 August 1860, the fact that such a central character works as an illustrator of periodicals should not be overlooked. In fact, Walter's illustrating makes his and Marian's plan to regain Laura's name and rightful inheritance possible. Without this means of support, Laura would not have a home in which to recover from the ordeal of having been kidnapped and secreted in an asylum and these three characters could not discover what really happened to Anne and restore Laura to her family and society. So why then does Collins select this particular profession for the novel's hero? His knowledge of the publishing process makes it a practical choice–one that would give Walter, as he worked on a job-by-job basis, the time and privacy he needed to conduct his investigation and realise his plans for Laura. Though Walter refers to his career only in passing and sees it primarily as a means to an end rather than a life calling, Collins's interest in visual art and illustration makes his association of the novel's hero with this aesthetic pursuit an unsurprising one. We see in *The Woman in White* Collins's appreciation not only for the visual but for the artist who creates it and, perhaps even more significantly, for the type of artist with whom he worked time and time again. In this essay I will continue to situate Collins in this historical and creative context, highlighting the role of illustration within his texts and their relation to the Victorian market; I will focus on the social and experiential significance of these mixed-media works and the importance of reclaiming the image as a central part of the reading experience.

Illustration represents the cross-section of word and imagination in a space where the artist visually realises a moment of written narrative. Joachim Möller, in his introduction to a collection of essays titled *Imagination on a Long Rein: English Literature Illustrated* (1988), explores the creative and emotional side of this venture:

> She seeks to underpin the imagination, not to crush it, to point the way, not to tether. She is an unavowed love, and yet would wish to be more, for her place is often in the shade. All we usually know is that she exists. And yet she can be enchanting. Her name is illustration. This alone is certain; the rest is open. (Möller 1988, 7)

Though rather sentimental, Möller's description of illustration conveys its complex nature, which strikes its viewer on both an emotional and an intellectual level. Yet despite its capacity to impact all who view it, illustration resists universal interpretation. As Möller goes on to state, "illustrations […] elude the trite approach, being primarily the result of a personal response to the text, a no-man's-land for scholarly method, private property" (ibid.). However, we can, and do, still strive to place illustrations in the historical trajectory of marketing and publication as well as interpret their significance and impact in what Julie Stone Peters describes as the "theatre of the book" in a work bearing that title. Though a definitive explanation of the emotive power of an image may be beyond our reach, this does not mean that a sense of the cooperation, or contention, between image and text cannot be determined. In fact, careful scrutiny of the structure of an image and its relation to a specific moment in the text can reveal a great deal about the impact of illustrated works on their readers. Such comparisons compel us to appreciate the significance these mixed-media artifacts have for their audience and recognise Collins's role in navigating their market value.

Collins and Illustration: A Personal and Historical Context

Linda K. Hughes and Michael Lund, in their innovative work *The Victorian Serial* (1999), suggest that the format of the serial itself is inherently Victorian, reflecting both the changes and daily life of the period. Defining the serial as "a continuing story over an extended time with enforced interruptions", Hughes and Lund point out that the serial became so "pervasive" during this period that Thomas Arnold came to "consider it a new phenomenon in the 1830s, suggest[ing] that something in the culture of the time made it especially receptive to the serial". The increase in literacy and affordability of the serial made it more popular at this time. Its very form of alternating between periods of waiting and satisfaction reflected the middle-class work ethic (Hughes and Lund 1999, 1-4). Serialised fiction, with its installments often including an illustrated cover and two or more plates, served as both a reprieve from daily life and a mirror of it. Richard Altick suggests these illustrations served as a democratizing tool, citing Charles Knight's "emphasis upon pictures as a means of bringing printed matter to the attention of a public unaccustomed to reading" (Altick 1998, 332-5). Clearly, then, illustration is of great socio-historical *and* literary significance. According to Philip V. Allingham, each image also functioned as an "handy aide-mémoire" intended to remind readers of the events of previous installments (Allingham 2003, 113). But how do these images relate to the work of Wilkie Collins and how and where do we place him in the context of such mixed-media marketing and production? The answer may be found in his personal history and how this might have determined his interest in the visual.

Collins's complex personal history in a family working with visual art indicates his extensive familiarity with the medium. Between coming from a family in which several members were painters and his own meager training in art as a boy, (though he was in his own words "of the inferior, or embryo order of artists" (Collins 1851, 496)), it is not surprising that his work was shaped by the visual image. Collins's aunt on his mother's side, Margaret Carpenter, nèe Geddes, found success as a portrait painter. It was through her painting that she helped support her parents and sisters before moving to London to pursue her training and career. A year after the exhibition of her work in the Royal Academy she married William Carpenter, who also became connected with the visual arts when, in 1845, he became Keeper of Prints and Drawings at the British Museum. In addition, three of their children, Percy and William (twins), as well as Henrietta, became painters themselves (Peters 1991, 5-8).

Of course, this inclination toward painting and the visual arts also thrived on Collins's father's side of the family. Collins's grandfather worked in his own shop as a dealer and restorer of pictures, where his son, Francis, later joined him. Perhaps most well-known to us, however, is his other son and Collins's father, William Collins, who attended the Royal Academy and found great success as a landscape painter, eventually gaining the title of Associate and then later Academician of the Royal Academy (ibid., 10-5). Like his father, Charles Collins, Wilkie's brother, pursued painting as a career. Many of his works were exhibited at the Royal Academy, and he was associated with (though not included in) the original Pre-Raphaelite Brotherhood. In fact, John Everett Millais and William Holman Hunt were frequent visitors to the parlor of Harriet (Wilkie's mother), Charles, and Wilkie Collins, further expanding this network of influence. Wilkie, too, tried his hand at painting, his work "The Smuggler's Retreat" having been accepted for the 1849 Royal Academy Exhibition (ibid., 84-5, 91). Though Collins continued to paint only as a hobby, devoting more and more of his time and skill to writing, the influence of these friends and family members, as well as his own interest in painting account, at least in part, for the degree to which his creative perspective and style are shaped by visual art and the important position illustration would hold in the pages of his text.

The influence of visual art and its method on Collins's writing is evident in his Preface to the 1850 three-volume edition of *Antonina, or the Fall of Rome*, in which he presents his rationale for the book's divisions by likening them to the compositional elements of painting:

> By this plan, it was thought that the different passages in the story might be most forcibly contrasted one with another, that each scene, while it preserved its separate interest to the mind of the reader, might most clearly appear to be combining to form one complete whole; that, in the painter's phrase, the "effects" might thus be best "massed", and the "lights and shadows" most harmoniously "balanced and discriminated". (Collins 1850, xi-xii)

His conception of his work in terms of painting suggests the extent to which these two artistic forms were intertwined for Collins. We see this again in his Preface to the 1862 three-volume edition of *No Name*, in which he justifies his style as one in keeping with "the laws of Art". He also claims to have successfully created Magdalen as "a pathetic character even in its perversity" due to "a resolute adherence, throughout, to the truth as it is in Nature" (Collins 1862, vii-viii). This reinforces his reliance on art while suggesting at least a modicum of sympathy with certain tenets of Ruskin and the Pre-Raphaelites.[1] All of this indicates his predisposition towards the visual, which, for Collins, was inextricably linked to his writing, in either pictorial or dramatic form.

In addition to his personal aesthetic leanings, Collins, like his peers, had to respond to the demands and tastes of his readers. This audience often desired the visual realisation of their text, especially in a time when culture relied on what Kate Flint terms "the very practice of looking" and "the visible" (Flint 2000, 2) and Patricia Anderson identifies as its "increasingly pictorial character" (Anderson 1991, 2). To fully appreciate this, we must place Collins in the context of the Victorian market.

Much of the Victorian period, and especially in the 1860s (considered the pinnacle of Collins's career), saw a surge in illustration in both periodicals and popular novels. The success of illustrated fiction during the Victorian period has been largely attributed to the creative and editorial savvy of Charles Dickens. Dickens's scrupulous management of the illustration and marketing of his work greatly influenced the evolution of these cooperative media in the work of his peers, including Collins. However, as is hinted by Holly Furneaux's essay in this collection, Collins is often cast in the shadow of Dickens in terms of his marketing savvy and appreciation for audience appeal. Collins himself had a keen sense of the Victorian audience and how to market himself. He shrewdly set aside his novel *Antonina* to honor his father with *Memoirs of the Life of William Collins Esq., R. A.* (1848) in order to gain the interest of the reading public via the life of a well-known painter (Peters 1991, 76). Collins's awareness of his audience and the power of a mass readership is evident in his essay "The Unknown Public", published in *Household Words* in 1858 (reprinted in a collection of Collins's essays entitled *My Miscellanies* in 1863). In this piece we see a rather indignant and even haughty Collins referring to an "Unknown Public" that "is, in a literary sense, hardly beginning, as yet, to learn to read" (Collins 1863, 189). We sense his attention to, and anxiety about, this mass of potential readers. In fact, it was this anxiety that, according to Graham Law, may have compromised the quality of his later fiction (Law 2003, 329-32). Clearly, the preferences of his audience impacted Collins and his writing, including its illustration and publication. Though Collins learned a great deal from Dickens, his strategic career decisions show him to be an astute writer and businessman, sensitive to the tastes of his intended audience.

Collins's Texts and their Illustrations

Tracing the exact stages in production for the illustrations of certain of Collins's works is at best a challenge, but we can see the occasional brief reference to an illustrator in Collins's published letters. In a letter dated 23 October 1851 addressed to Richard Bentley, we get a glimpse of Collins's interest in illustration as he presents his idea for a short Christmas story to be titled "The Mask of Shakespeare"—later changed to "Mr. Wray's Cash-Box"—and his vision for its illustration:

> My idea is that a Frontispiece Vignette and Tail Piece would be quite enough–*well* done–ordinary mediocre work won't do–work by the famous men is only to be had at a high price; and, as far as my knowledge of the great names goes, not even *then* to be had in time. I should propose that the three illustrations should be done by three young gentlemen who have lately been making an immense stir in the world of Art, and earned the distinction of being attacked by *The Times* (any notice *there* is a distinction)–and defended in a special pamphlet by Ruskin–the redoubtable *Pre-Raphael-Brotherhood*!!
>
> One of these "Brothers" happens to be *my* brother as well–the other two Millais and Hunt are intimate friends. For *my* sake as well as their own they would work their best–and do something striking, no matter on how small a scale–I could be

constantly at their elbows, and get them to be [erased word] ready as soon as I should. Should you be willing to try them?–and give them *some* re[mun]eration– the amt of which I could easily settle between you and them. (Baker and Clarke 1999, vol. 1, 73, italics in original)

Collins shows not only an interest in who illustrates his work but how it is accomplished. Such concerns indicate more than just an interest in securing work for his friends and his brother but also his acknowledgment of the power of an illustrator to shape the experience of the reader. We see his desire to protect his authorial autonomy by placing the visual realisation of his work in familiar, trustworthy, and even sympathetic hands.

As indications of the interests of the Victorian market, illustrations and illustrated texts are important in re-constructing the social and historical heritage of publishing. However, they are also critically important in the microcosm of the book, for although they are often overlooked in contemporary criticism, they have in fact the power to subvert the text. As Stephen C. Behrendt points out, illustrations "facilitate the act of seeing, but they also significantly limit it: the illustrator makes visual choices *for* us" (Behrendt 1988, 29-30, italics in original). Möller describes illustration as "imagination on a long rein", "decorative as an embellishment to the book, interpretive as a commentary, frequently a source of inspiration and sometimes corrective" (Möller 1988, 8). Examining the function of these in cooperation with the text through what Möller terms a "synchronic" approach, in which one "assess[es] the compatibility of text and picture in individual instances" allows us to more fully appreciate the experience of Collins's work by both the Victorian and the modern reader-viewer (ibid.). With this much influence, attempting to interpret these illustrations in the context of the book is imperative.

"Mr.Wray's Cash-Box", published in one volume by Richard Bentley in 1851, appeared with only one illustration, a frontispiece, and the first book illustration, by Millais (see fig. 4). The relationship of this image to the central dynamic and narrative trajectory of the text reflects both the story's content and the nature of writer-illustrator cooperation when the writer has not completed the story and must convey its subject in a mere sentence or two to an illustrator facing a looming deadline. As a frontispiece, this image safely preserves the story's "mystery" and does not reveal the contents of Reuben Wray's cash-box. As an amalgamation of visual keys to the text, the illustration identifies Annie Wray as the nurturing heroine, perhaps even hinting at her ultimate role as savior to her aged grandfather. However, the image also suggests that the story will focus on the relationship between Annie and the gentleman portrayed with her. This dynamic may mistakenly prepare the reader for either a love story with a seemingly older gentleman or lead to the incorrect assessment of this suspended moment as one between Annie and her grandfather.

Fig. 4. John Everett Millais, frontispiece to "Mr. Wray's Cashbox" (1851).

Though an element of the romantic certainly appears in the text as Annie and Martin Blunt, "*alias* Julius Caesar" (Collins 1852, 89, italics in original), reveal their secret engagement, the relationship between grandfather and granddaughter ultimately becomes the center of our attention. Yet closer scrutiny of the image, with the help of the text's details, suggests that the image still serves as an important means of conveying the story's content and drawing our eyes to the role of Annie. The actual details of Blunt's appearance in this drawing, with his lanky, awkward frame and scraggly, balding head reflect Collins's textual description of him:

> His features […] large and ill-proportioned, his face […] pitted with the small-pox, and what hair he has on his head–not much […] growing in all sorts of contrary directions at once […]. Honesty and kindliness look out so brightly from his eyes, as to dazzle your observation of his clumsy nose, and lumpy mouth and chin, until you hardly know whether they are ugly or not. Some men, in a certain sense, are ugly with the lineaments of the Apollo Belvidere; and others handsome, with features that might sit for a caricature. Our new acquaintance was of the latter order. (ibid., 88-9)

Additionally, though Annie looks up to knot Blunt's tie, we feel her gaze indirectly aimed beyond the two-dimensional page, inviting us to connect with her and her perspective throughout the story. At the same time, her simple gesture toward Blunt and his posture, resulting in his bent body being only inches away from leaning on her diminutive yet firmly upright frame, indicate the role she will play in caring for him and saving their unconventional family. Collins's desire that Millais illustrate "Mr. Wray's Cash-Box", as well as later works, indicates his belief in their creative compatibility and his contentment with Millais's ability to visually interpret his work, even with access to only a nominal description of its content.

The rather complex relationship between this frontispiece and the story it illustrates complicates our understanding of the collaboration between writer and illustrator, giving us insight into a process that was not always a smooth one, the illustrator often lacking seemingly necessary narrative information and having to illustrate text for which an ending, and even subsequent action, had not been written. Though the story's illustrator certainly suffered from the inconvenience and disadvantages of this limited knowledge, the final mixed-media product could be what ultimately suffered the most, for the power of the image "to subvert text" might result in an inconsistent final product and a confusing experience for the reader. However, when the image's tone and use of line and symbol are sufficiently in keeping with the mood and content of the narrative, an illustrator in tune with the author can create an effective final product and a compelling union of image and text, as evident in "Mr. Wray's Cash-Box" and Collins's and Millais's future collaborations.

A later work by Collins, *No Name* (1862), also appeared with a frontispiece by Millais in a one-volume book edition published in 1864 by Sampson Low (see fig. 5).[2] Though very much in keeping with Collins's description of the scene, Millais's drawing increases the suspense of this episode in its minor deviations from the text. Looking at the image we see Millais's illustration of Magdalen's potential suicide. In this scene, Magdalen believes she has this last chance to extricate herself from the devious plot to marry her sickly, selfish cousin under an assumed name and so reclaim the inheritance that should have been hers and her sister's had they not been illegitimate. She contemplates suicide as the only way she can stop the plans that have already been set in motion, knowing she will not be able to look back once she proceeds down either course:

> She resolved to end the struggle, by setting her life or death on the hazard of a chance. On what chance?
>   The sea showed it to her. Dimly distinguishable through the mist, she saw a little fleet of coasting vessels slowly drifting towards the house, all following the same direction with the favouring set of the tide. In half an hour—perhaps in less—the fleet would have passed her window. The hands of her watch pointed to four o'clock. She seated herself close at the side of the window, with her back towards the quarter from which the vessels were drifting down on her—with the poison placed on the window-sill, and the watch on her lap. For one half-hour to come, she determined to wait there, and count the vessels as they went by. If, in that time, an even number passed her—the sign given, should be a sign to live. If the uneven number prevailed—the end should be Death. (Collins 1862, 499)

The selection of the scene for illustration can possibly be attributed to its suspense; it heightens the anxiety of the text by freezing this gripping moment in the life of Magdalen. Interestingly, rather than simply waiting and watching, perhaps "rest[ing] her head against the window" as Collins describes her (ibid., 499), Magdalen appears in the process of reaching for the poison. The voluptuous but static folds of the satiny dress that envelops her contrast powerfully with this activity of her hand and leaning upper body, captured mid-movement. This results in an image that conveys a physically and emotionally suspended moment, heightening the audience's experience of the text. Though Millais takes small liberties with this image in order to achieve a bold, immediate impact, Collins's satisfaction with his work is evident in his future attempts to secure Millais's services.

Fig. 5. John Everett Millais, frontispiece to *No Name* (1864).

However, Millais was not the only illustrator of Collins's work, as is evident in his novel *Armadale*, which appeared serially in the *Cornhill Magazine* from November 1864 until June 1866 and retained the same illustrations in its two-volume edition in 1866. In a letter to his mother, Harriet Collins, dated 9 September 1864, Collins reveals his desire that Millais illustrate *Armadale*. However, unable to secure the artist's services, he is content with the work, at least what he has seen thus far, of an alternative illustrator, George Housman Thomas: "Millais can't do the illustrations–but a very good design for the first number has been done by Mr Thomas" (Baker and Clarke 1999, vol. 1, 250). One of Thomas's first illustrations for *Armadale*, though not a frontispiece, serves much the same function as that for "Mr. Wray's Cash-Box" as, like Millais's illustration, Thomas's image suggests the narrative trajectory and character dynamics that will shape the story. This may suggest either Thomas's adoption of Millais's methods or the existence of a formula for illustration to which they both subscribed. In his illustration "The Two Armadales", Thomas draws together information from multiple pages of text in a visual key, focusing our attention and sympathy on the darker of the two Allan Armadales, at this point known only as Ozias Midwinter (see fig. 6). Thomas pulls from the description of Midwinter as "a startling object to contemplate" with a "shaven head, tied up roughly in an old yellow silk handkerchief", "tawny, haggard cheeks", "bright brown eyes, preternaturally large and wild", a "tangled black beard", and "long supple, sinewy fingers, wasted by suffering, till they looked like claws". In his depiction of Midwinter's gaze, which does not meet the eyes of his companion, Thomas also conveys the suspicion that most others feel toward Midwinter because of their belief that "[I]f this man was honest, his eyes showed a singular perversity in looking away and denying it" (Collins 1866, 50). As in Millais's depiction of Annie Wray, Thomas directs Midwinter's gaze beyond the limits of the page, into our world, as we share with Midwinter the knowledge of his true identity. Even the architecture and décor of the room, as well as the figures' posture, visually realise this narrative perspective and our connection with him. The bed and window curtains angle down towards the centrally placed Midwinter, while two overlapping triangles, formed by Armadale's posture toward Midwinter and the base angles of Armadale's lower legs and the cloak at Midwinter's feet, posit Midwinter at the apex of this scene. The chair that frames Midwinter's face and the light from the window that falls upon him also indicate the important part he will play. Likewise, the point where the ceiling and walls come together aligns with Midwinter's figure so that, again, Thomas draws our eyes to him, his secret identity, and his central role in the story. Thomas combines Midwinter's physical description with the slightly earlier narrative of Allan Armadale's being "the first who appeared at his bedside". We see Armadale having "taken a violent fancy to the castaway usher" so that "a bond of union between them was formed on the spot" (ibid., 49-50) in his captivated gaze directed at the face and story of Midwinter. Thomas's illustration can be traced to the descriptive details Collins provides and to the broader scope of the novel as a whole, making this illustration more than mere visual trimming but rather a means of providing insight into the narrative moment as well as the relational dynamic that shapes the entire novel. Though Thomas's illustration seems in keeping with Collins's content and his efforts to make the reader connect with Midwinter, his stylistic depiction of Midwinter, perhaps more doe-eyed than "wild"-eyed, hints at the limits of the visual medium. These limits compel him to use a somewhat exaggerated style in pushing the audience to sympathise with Midwinter, for the illustrator lacks the luxury of page after page of nuanced, descriptive text. Of course, by the same token, it is the illustrator who possesses the power to shape the reader's visualisation, and so interpretation, of the writer's words. This highlights the potentially precarious balance between image and text and what could be either a cooperative or a contentious dynamic.

In another equally significant and intriguing illustration, titled "Miss Gwilt", from *Armadale*, we see the devious Miss Gwilt walking with her pupil, Miss Milroy, through a garden, as Midwinter watches them from the shadow of the Milroys' summer-house doorway (see fig. 7). In the illustration, Thomas has depicted all three of the figures unnaturally compressed in the tight space of the image's frame. In fact, they have been consigned to such a tight space that the figures of Miss Milroy and Midwinter are strangely cut almost in half so that the lines bordering the image actually divide their bodies, making them half in and half outside the scene. The wooden doorframe further compresses Midwinter's body and emphasises the division between his figure and the approaching women. The space that divides them within the scene, filled by the shrubbery that surrounds the doorway, in fact takes up an equal, if not greater, amount of space in the image as the figure of the centrally placed Miss Gwilt who fills the central place in the image's composition. The effect of this distancing emphasises the content and tone of the story, as well as Collins's characterisation of both Midwinter and Miss Gwilt, who each in their own way feel isolated from those around them, and society as a whole, due to their mysterious and less than respectable pasts. Miss Gwilt, in this central position, draws the viewers' interest immediately, reflecting the attention Collins has given her in the text and that she has drawn from both the characters and the readers. The strategic placement of the parasol, which functions as a tool to highlight Miss Gwilt's profile, draws our attention from the top of the open umbrella down the eye-line created by the angle of the parasol's pole and handle, clutched by the lady's hand, further emphasizing Miss Gwilt as it forms an angle that opens upon her face. This same angle extends in the direction of her gaze aimed at the dark image of Midwinter. Despite the fact that Midwinter takes up the least amount of space in the scene, our attention still falls on him as he alone seems to gaze outside the boundaries of the image and into the reader-viewer's world, once again reinforcing his connection to the reader and our awareness of his true identity. Shrouded in darkness, which again echoes the mystery that surrounds him, we, like the strolling ladies, still notice Midwinter, although the details of his body seem to dissolve into the shadow around him. This also serves to highlight his face, the only part of him not absorbed by the darkness, and to distinguish him from the women and his surroundings even more powerfully.

THE TWO ARMADALES.

Fig. 6. John Housman Thomas, "The Two Armadales" (1866).

Fig. 7. John Housman Thomas, "Miss Gwilt" (1866).

The text which this image visually represents and compresses falls in
the chapter titled "The Housemaid's Face", revealing the thematic importance of
the visual in this particular section. The narrative relevant to the aforementioned
illustration includes Midwinter's comparison of a "written portrait" with the
physiognomy of Miss Gwilt as she approaches him (Collins 1866, 276).
Midwinter has received a letter that provides this detailed description from the
Reverend Decimus Brock, who warns him of the possible arrival of a certain
woman in the neighborhood of Thorpe-Ambrose who may be plotting to take
advantage of the wealthy, young Armadale. Brock's letter describes her
appearance and directs Midwinter to compare his description to the recently
arrived Miss Gwilt and so "[t]est her by her features" (ibid., 274). Of course,
Brock does not realise that he has been deceived by this woman and has
mistaken someone else for the real villainess. At this point in Collins's story,
Midwinter "[finds] himself in a summer-house, thickly covered with creepers,
and commanding a full view of the garden from end to end" (ibid., 276), from
which position he scrutinises the figure of Miss Gwilt:

> He was still absorbed over the description, when he heard the smooth rustle of
> the dresses travelling towards him again. Standing in the shadow of the summer-
> house, he waited while she lessened the distance between them. With her written
> portrait vividly impressed on his mind, and with the clear light of the morning to
> help him, his eyes questioned her as she came on [...].
>   Nearer and nearer, fairer and fairer she came, in the glow of the morning
> light—the most startling, the most unanswerable contradiction that eye could
> see, or mind conceive, to the description in the rector's letter.
>   Both governess and pupil were close to the summer-house before they
> looked that way, and noticed Midwinter standing inside. The governess saw him
> first. (ibid., 276-7)

Intriguingly, while this visual experience deceives Midwinter in its incongruity
with his text at hand, the experience of text and image in this moment is a
revealing one for the reader. In the illustration, as in the text, we see that Miss
Milroy "drew back from the summer-house with an expression of merciless
surprise" (ibid., 277). However, unlike the textual description in which Miss
Gwilt "returned Midwinter's look still steadily fixed on her, with equal
steadiness on her side" (ibid., 277-8), the visual representation of their meeting
denies this mutual exchange in favour of further cementing the audience's
connection with Midwinter, who appears not in profile like the others but gazing
forward beyond the confines of the page. Thomas's visual realisation of
Collins's text conveys the narrative content and captures the tension among and
within its characters. Although it functions more correlatively with the text and
less as a means to arouse and stimulate in the way Millais's *No Name*

frontispiece does,[3] it still artfully represents the tone and subject of this important moment in the story.

The role of illustrations then, as both a means of mass appeal and a mode of instant interpretation, emphasises the importance of considering text and image on a work-by-work basis in relation to the publishing history of popular Victorian fiction, particularly in the work of a writer as invested in the visual arts as Wilkie Collins. By interpreting these texts in their original, mixed-media format, we can draw attention to this often overlooked visual element, reclaiming Collins's illustrated fiction while complicating and enriching our understanding of these works and acknowledging the influence and experience of the Victorian reading market. Without the illustrations, we cannot understand these texts as their author intended, for experiencing the original invites us not only to interact with the mixed-media product encountered by the nineteenth-century reader but compels us to acknowledge the richness and complexity of Collins's work. The power and significance, creatively and historically, of this experience calls for the recovery of not only Collins's other illustrated work but that of the many other Victorian writers whose illustrated fiction has been long forgotten. We compromise the creative nuances and thrilling sensation envisioned by their creators and experienced by their first readers when we ignore these illustrations and their organic relation to the text. The work of Wilkie Collins, as these illustrated novels demonstrate, loses its intensity and vitality with the exclusion of these images–something that represents a grave injustice to one of the most popular writers of the nineteenth century and our own literary history.

Notes

[1] For an analysis of other links between Collins and the Pre-Raphaelites, especially regarding his use of certain stylistic and descriptive techniques such as shading, see Andres 1995 and article Dolin and Dougan 2003 on the relationship between Collins's novel *Basil* (1852) and William Holman Hunt's painting *The Awakening Conscience* (1851-3). For a consideration of connections between Collins and Ruskin see Frick 1985. An anonymous defense of the Pre-Raphaelites (often attributed to Collins) also suggests this sympathy with at least some elements of Pre-Raphaelites, though we know, as Catherine Peters points out in her biography *The King of Inventors*, that his preference in art was a style different from that of the Pre-Raphaelites (Peters 1991, 89).

[2] As in *The Woman in White*, the subject of visual art and illustration appear in *No Name* and is evident in the repeated references to objects and methods of portraiture, such as when the narrator introduces Captain Wragge by "taking his portrait, from top to toe". (Collins 1862, 25). The presence of visual art as a narrative trope, in this text and others, may indicate the influence of particular works of art encountered by the author and underscore the significance of both the artifact within the text and the visual images that accompany certain scenes.

[3] The difference in effect between these illustrations lies not only in the stylistic and visionary differences of the artists but, admittedly, in the subject of the moment they illustrated—one a matter of life and death and the other a matter of mystery and mistaken identity. Additionally, these illustrations served different functions, for Thomas's illustrations for *Armadale* were numerous, allowing for images that represented a range of emotional and narrative significance, while Millais's illustration for *No Name* was the only image accompanying the text and served as a frontispiece, requiring it to capture an extremely important and emotionally charged moment that would rouse sufficient suspense to compel reader interest in the novel.

Works Cited

Allingham, Philip V. 2003. Charles Dickens's *A Tale of Two Cities* (1859) illustrated: A Critical Reassessment of Hablot Knight Browne's Accompanying Plates. *Dickens Studies Annual*. 33:113.

Andres, Sophia. 1995. Pre-Raphaelite Paintings and Jungian Images in Wilkie Collins's *The Woman in White.Victorian Newsletter* 88:26-31.

Altick, Richard D. 1998. *The English Common Reader*. Columbus: Ohio State University Press.

Anderson, Patricia. 1991. *The Printed Image and the Transformation of Popular Culture: 1790-1860*. Oxford: Clarendon Press.

Bachman, Maria K. and Don Richard Cox (eds). 2003. *Reality's Dark Light: The Sensational Wilkie Collins*. Knoxville: University of Tennessee Press.

Baker, William. and William M. Clarke, eds. 1999. *The Letters of Wilkie Collins*. 2 vols. London: Macmillan

Behrendt, Stephen C. 1988. The Functions of Illustration–Intentional and Unintentional in *Imagination on a Long Rein: English Literature Illustrated*. Marburg: Jonas Verlag. 29-44.

Collins, Wilkie. 1850. *Antonina; or The Fall of Rome*. London: Richard Bentley.

—. 1851. A Pictorial Tour to St. Geroge Bosherville. *Bentley's Miscellany* 29:493-508.

—. 1852. *Mr. Wray's Cash-Box; or The Mask and the Mystery: A Christmas Sketch*. Guernsey: Alan Sutton, 1996.

—. 1860. *The Woman in White*. New York: Modern Library, 2002.

—. 1862. *No Name*. Oxford: Oxford University Press, 1998.

—. 1863. The Unknown Public, in *My Miscellanies*. London: Sampson Low.

—. 1866. *Armadale*. London: Penguin, 1995.

Dolin, Tim. and Lucy Dougan. 2003. Fatal Newness: *Basil*, Art, and the Origins of Sensation Fiction, in Bachman and Cox 2003, 1-33.

Flint, Kate. 2000. *The Victorians and the Visual Imagination*. Cambridge: Cambridge University Press.

Frick, Patricia. 1985. Wilkie Collins and John Ruskin. *Victorians Institute Journal* 13:11-22.

Hughes, Linda K. and Michael Lund. 1991. *The Victorian Serial.* Charlottesville: University Press of Virginia.

Law, Graham. 2003. Yesterday's Sensations: Modes of Publication and Narrative Form in Collins's Late Novels, in Bachman and Cox 2003, 329-360.

Möller, Joachim. 1988. *Imagination on a Long Rein: English Literature Illustrated.* Marburg: Jonas Verlag.

Peters, Catherine. 1991. *The King of Inventors: A Life of Wilkie Collins.* London: Secker and Warburg.

Peters, Julie Stone. 2000. *Theatre of the Book 1480-1880: Print, Text, and Performance in Europe.* Oxford: Oxford University Press.

THE FACE OF THE ADVERSARY IN THE NOVELS
OF WILKIE COLLINS

AOIFE LEAHY

Joseph Noel Paton's *The Adversary* (see fig. 8) is not a famous Pre-Raphaelite painting,[1] yet it addresses key themes that arise in John Ruskin's defences of the Pre-Raphaelites. Subtitled "Where Their Worm Dieth Not, And the Fire is Not Quenched", a biblical reference to the eternal torments of hell, the painting represents Satan brooding in the fiery pit. Although Satan is frowning intently, he is a strikingly beautiful figure, apart from a slight scar or disfigurement on his right cheek. His pose is a familiar one and recalls the position of Apollo in Raphael's *Apollo and Marysas* (see fig. 9)[1] from the Stanza della Segnatura in the Vatican, although the figure is rotated so that Satan/Apollo is facing the viewer rather than Marysas, whom Apollo has condemned to death by flaying. The implication is that the viewer is taking the place of the unfortunate satyr and will be tortured in hell at Satan/Apollo's command. In this essay, I will point out why Paton's painting can provide us with a face–or, perhaps, the type of face–for the more attractive male villains in the novels of Wilkie Collins.

Paton may have had a good reason for representing Satan as a Raphaelesque Apollo. John Ruskin argues in his 1853 lecture "Pre-Raphaelitism" that Raphaelesque art (art in the style of Raphael) holds a fatal seduction, taking the viewer away from godly art. The fatal turning point in Raphael's career comes with his project in the Stanza della Segnatura, when he paints Christ as the ruler of Theology in the *Disputa* (see fig. 10) and Apollo as the ruler of Poetry in *Parnassus* (see fig. 11):

[H]e was sent for to Rome, to decorate the Vatican for Pope Julius II [...]. On one wall of that chamber [the Stanza della Segnatura] he placed a picture of the World or Kingdom of Theology, presided over by Christ. And on the side wall of that same chamber he placed the World or Kingdom of Poetry, presided over by Apollo. And from that spot, and from that hour, the intellect and the art of Italy date their degradation. (Ruskin 1853, 162)

The art of the Vatican, according to Ruskin, should recognise Christ and not Apollo as the supreme ruler of the arts: Apollo is allowed to displace Christ in a way that should be unacceptable to the Christian viewer. The effect is felt up to the present day, as it is all too common to see pictures of the Greek gods in Victorian homes rather than images of Christ or the Virgin Mary. The degradation that enters into Raphael's work is proved by his substitution of idealised beauty for a truth to nature as God created it. Artists who follow his style in the present day are similarly degraded, seeking "beauty rather than veracity" (ibid.,163). Conversely, the Pre-Raphaelites are moral reformers in art because they paint from nature, "the thing itself" (ibid., 169), and resist the deceitful idealisation found in Raphael's paintings.

    The Adversary cleverly reinterprets *Apollo and Marysas*, since the Apollo/Satan figure has changed only a little. Apollo's crown of laurels has become a circle of horns, while the mound of earth he sits upon has become the back of a serpent. Paton has unobtrusively added a spear, a weapon commonly found in representations of Satan,[3] in the place of Apollo's lyre. Apollo/Satan's bent knee and beautiful long hair remain the same, however, as does his maliciously cruel intent. Paton's representation of the Raphaelesque figure thus invites the viewer to recall Ruskin's arguments in order to understand the painting. Paton was not a member of the Pre-Raphaelite Brotherhood, but he exhibited with the P. R. B. in the 1850s. His style was considered Pre-Raphaelite at the time[4] and Paton was analysed with the Brotherhood in Ruskin's Royal Academy Notes of the 1850s. Although Ruskin is critical of some aspects of Paton's work, including the "prevailing gloom" (Ruskin 1858, 278) of his subjects, he also praises him for "exquisitely articulated" (ibid., 279) details in his paintings. By Ruskin's standards, Paton was capable of a Pre-Raphaelite truth to nature. Paton's use of Raphael's Apollo pose must suggest either a deliberate rejection of Ruskin or, as is more likely, the depiction of the enemy of the movement. Satan's Raphaelesque beauty–particularly the beauty of Apollo–makes him more evil, not less, and he is *The Adversary* both of mankind in general and of Pre-Raphaelite artists in particular. In this case, the gloom of the subject matter is appropriate and perfectly in line with Ruskin's own theories.

    The biblical context of the painting is emphasised by the subtitle, taken from Mark 9:48. The description of hell follows the horrible instructions in the Gospel of Mark on how to avoid damnation:

> If thy hand offend thee, cut it off. If thy eye offend thee, pluck it out. It is better
> for thee to enter the kingdom of God with one eye, than having two eyes to be
> cast into hell-fire: Where their worm dieth not, and the fire is not quenched.

Fig. 8. Illustration of Joseph Noel Paton, *The Adversary* (1879).

Fig. 9. Engraving of Raphael, *Apollo and Marysas* or *The Victory of Apollo*.

Fig. 10. Engraving of Raphael, *Disputa*.

Fig. 11. Engraving of Raphael, *Parnassus*.

Fig. 12. Engraving of Raphael, *The Portrait of Bindo Altoviti.*

A possible reading of this quote in a Pre-Raphaelite context would be that bodily perfection is not linked to redemption, a challenge to the association of idealised beauty with spiritual well-being in High Renaissance art. Suggestively, Ruskin uses the same quote[5] in a series of didactic letters in 1867 (published as *Time and Tide*) to argue that Satan, the serpent of hell, is as real as the adder or asp on earth:

The puff-adder or horned asp is not more real. Unbelievable—those—unless you had seen them; no fable could have coined out of any human brain so dreadful, within its own material sphere, as that blue-lipped serpent—working its way sidelong in the sand. As real, but with sting of eternal death—this worm that dies not, and fire that is not quenched, within our souls or around them. (Ruskin 1867, 160)

Paton's choice of the Apollo from *Apollo and Marysas* rather than *Parnassus* is a clever one, since the *Parnassus* figure is not an obviously threatening one. Ruskin refers to Satan in *Time and Tide* as "The Lord of Lies and the Lord of Pain" (ibid., 161) and both aspects are found in the deceptively beautiful Apollo who is intent on flaying his victim alive. Like *Parnassus*, *Apollo and Marysas* is found in the Stanza della Segnatura, and is thus part of the doomed project that Ruskin rather melodramatically condemns as the source of the schism between godly medieval art and ungodly modern art. The original *Apollo and Marysas* also shows Apollo at a moment of victory, having defeated Marysas in a competition,[6] so Paton's reinterpretation of the scene may be a comment on Ruskin's argument that Apollo gains an inappropriate and blasphemous victory over Christ in the Vatican.[7]

Like Paton, Wilkie Collins shows a clear awareness of Ruskin's attack on the Stanza della Segnatura, and both the artist and the novelist seem to have independently picked up on the same key points, in identifying deceit and evil in ideal beauty. Ruskin defended the work of Charles Allston Collins in the 1850s alongside the official members of the P. R. B., so the anti-Raphael argument was likely to be of interest to his brother from the start.[8] Ruskin claims in "Pre-Raphaelitism" that the attempts of modern artists to emulate Raphael have brought about "the doom of the arts of Europe" (Ruskin 1853, 163). Collins picks up on the copying of Raphael as a harmful practice[9] and exploits it in his fiction, often in a context of horror. The ghastly room in *The Haunted Hotel* (1879), the scene of a grisly murder and subsequent ghostly apparitions, is painted with copies of "the exquisitely graceful designs of Raphael in the Vatican" (Collins 1879, 193), recalling Ruskin's condemnation of Raphael's work in the Stanza della Segnatura. Disaster occurs in *The Moonstone* (1868) on the very day that Franklin finishes painting the "griffins, cupids and so on" on Rachel's bedroom door (Collins 1868, 66) which are copied from arabesques by Raphael, the artist who "had a sweetheart at the baker's" (ibid., 56). Gabriel Betteredge disapproves of the work and warns the reader that "Satan finds some mischief still for idle hands to do" (ibid.), thus suggesting that there is something Satanic or wicked about the act of copying Raphael's art. In *The Black Robe* (1881) a novel that deals with supernatural premonitions of disaster, the fact that Stella and Roymayne begin their relationship in a gallery dominated by "beautiful copies of Raphael's *Cupid and Psyche* designs" (Collins 1881, 65) signals their fate as ill-starred lovers. To copy and display a Raphael is a dangerous thing in the fictional world that Collins creates, since the practice always brings bad luck.

Characters themselves, however, can also embody figures from Raphael's paintings. Many readers will notice that Wilkie Collins's young male villains tend to be dazzlingly good-looking. It is tempting, perhaps, to dismiss such criminals as the effeminate contrast to manly heroes, but this does not account for their spellbinding power over others and their extraordinary capacity to make their deceptions believable. In fact, characters like the thieving Godfrey Ablewhite in *The Moonstone* (1868) are ideally beautiful, in that they embody the standardised proportions found in ancient Greek sculpture while also possessing the pleasing colouring found in Raphael's paintings. From a Pre-Raphaelite point of view, ideal beauty is a lying substitute for nature. Like Satan, Godfrey is a great deceiver: his very face misleads the viewer by looking innocent. His physical description conforms to that of the powerful Apollo, or to a figure in a typical Raphael portrait such as *The Portrait of Bindo Altoviti* (see fig. 12). Gabriel tells us he "stood over six feet high; he had a beautiful red and white colour; a smooth round face, shaved as bare as your hand; and a head of lovely long flaxen hair, falling negligently over the poll of his neck" (Collins 1868, 60). Ironically, at times of particular wickedness and deceit, he also resembles figures in Raphael's religious paintings; when lying to Miss Clack, he compares himself to "a little angel put[ting] a finger in its mouth" (ibid., 281) like one of the putti at the bottom of *The Sistine Madonna*. The evangelical Clack, who is obsessed with defeating Satan and "the blinded children of the devil" (Collins 1868, 230), is nevertheless blinded by Godfrey's beauty and serves as his devoted follower. Like Paton's *Adversary*, Godfrey is godlike in his Raphaelesque beauty and Satanic in his Raphaelesque capacity for deceit. Looking at Paton's depiction of Satan should give us a good idea of how Collins visualised his villainous character.

Not all of Collins's male villains resemble Raphael's young men, yet even the exceptions can be enlightening. Mannion in *Basil* (1852) is bald and lacks the pleasing colouring of a Raphael painting, but he possesses other qualities of ideal beauty, since he resembles a Grecian statue, with his "extraordinary regularity of features" (Collins 1852, 110), features that are "smooth and massive as marble" (ibid.). This perfection is unsettling rather than pleasing in the novel, since Basil cannot read Mannion's emotions from his mask-like face. Mannion is particularly noteworthy since Collins created the character before most of Ruskin's Pre-Raphaelite arguments had appeared. This implies that Collins was already biased against the ideally beautiful and took advantage of Ruskin's arguments to focus on attacking Raphael in his subsequent work.

Fig. 13. Illustration of Raphael, *St Cecilia with Saints Paul, John the Evangelist, Augustine and Mary Magdalene.*

The obese Fosco in *The Woman in White* (1860) is not a youth with beautiful flowing hair, but in one extremely humorous moment in the text, he is compared to "a fat St Cecilia masquerading in male attire" (Collins 1860, 250). The fact that Fosco is singing with "graceful twistings and turnings of his head" (ibid.) suggests that he may resemble Raphael's plump St Cecilia, and that Collins is parodying the famous *St Cecilia with Saints Paul, John the Evangelist, Augustine and Mary Magdalene* (see fig. 13). While many representations of Cecilia were also painted in the nineteenth century, most can be considered Raphaelesque in that they pay homage to Raphael's original.

More often, however, the temptation inherent in Raphael's art is encapsulated in the irresistible attractiveness of the male villains. Mr Thorpe in *Hide and Seek* (1854) loses his looks in later life, but as a youth his fatal beauty leads to Mary Grice's seduction and tragic death:

> He was quite a young man,–I should say not more than four or five and twenty– very quiet mannered, and delicate–or rather effeminate looking, as I thought–for he wore his hair quite long over the shoulders, in the foreign way, and had a clear, soft complexion, almost like a woman's. (Collins 1854, 268)

Similarly, in *Poor Miss Finch* (1872), Nugent Dubourg uses his overwhelming beauty to steal his brother's fiancé. Blind for many years, Lucilla cannot believe that the blue-skinned Oscar is her lover once her sight is restored, allowing Nugent to impersonate her husband-to-be. Nugent exploits the trustworthiness implied by his appearance to deceive others, and those close to him eventually realise their faith in him is misplaced:

> [Oscar] had not shed a tear since the fatal day when he had discovered that his brother had played him false–that brother who had been the god of his idolatry, the sacred object of his gratitude and his love! (Collins 1872, 405)

Nugent's punishment when his deception is exposed is to be cast out of favour and to suffer like Satan: "There he stood, in the hell of his own making–and devoured his torture in silence" (ibid., 419). At this moment, Paton's *Adversary* would be a wonderful illustration to the text.[10] In contrast, his once-identical twin brother Oscar is a strong and virtuous character by the end of the novel, after his face is "painted" (ibid., 162) dark blue by his medical treatment, which he undertakes voluntarily so that he can look forward to a full life with Lucilla. It is as if sacrificing his ideal beauty can eliminate the negative influences on Oscar's personality.

The tragic Miserrimus Dexter in *The Law and the Lady* (1875) is not a true villain, since the ideal aspects of his beauty are fragmented: he has no legs. Yet he is "an unusually handsome man [...]. A painter would have revelled in him as a model for St John" (Collins 1875, 214). Dexter is most likely to be the image of Raphael's young John the Evangelist, Christ's most beloved disciple, since that figure is standing at the back of the group of figures in *St Cecilia with Saints* (see fig. 13) and has no visible legs. Although St John is a Christian saint, he looks quite similar to Apollo and to Raphael's portraits of young men. Interestingly, the beautiful young men Collins creates are often idolised by other characters in an almost devotional manner, as if the worship intended for religious figures had been misdirected towards the subject of a secular portrait. Ariel certainly worships Dexter as if he were a saint or a god rather than a man. In one sense, Dexter is a complete Raphaelesque character since Raphael's John the Evangelist also has missing or out of view limbs. In another sense, his handicap is a denial of the reassuring affirmation of bodily conformity that is imparted by ideal beauty and falsely linked to moral worth. He does damage by lying, like Godfrey Ablewhite or Nugent Dubourg, but he ultimately repents and reveals the truth about Sara Macallan's death.

The loveliness of male characters in Collins's novels seems less easy to define than female attractiveness, and it is the allurements of villainesses that gain the most critical attention. Dexter is compared to St John in *The Law and the Lady* (1875), but it is striking that while Collins's novels are filled with women that are likened to Raphael's Madonnas by name, the author is more reluctant to overtly identify men as particular Raphael subjects. Perhaps this is because of confusion caused by Raphael's art itself, however. The beautiful young men in Raphael's secular portraits look identical to his depictions of comely saints like John the Evangelist and gods like Apollo. Not naming a subject also leaves open the possibility that Collins is depicting the artist Raphael himself, and indeed, Raphael includes a self-portrait in *The School of Athens*, which is also in the notorious Stanza della Segnatura. Victorians frequently confused Raphael's identity with that of the male figures in his paintings; the figure in *The School of Athens* is not dazzlingly attractive, but theories that identified Raphael as the youth in *The Portrait of Bindo Altoviti* (see fig. 12) were very popular.[11] Ruskin points out in "Pre-Raphaelitism" (1853) that Raphael was a brilliant young man when he fell from grace by denying Christ his rightful place in Christian art. By implication, if Raphael's Apollo is Satanic, then so is Raphael himself, as he shares his subject's beauty and guilt.[12] Tellingly, Nugent Dubourg and Dexter are artists, as is "The Cur" in *The Guilty River* (1886), as if being a certain kind of artist may lead to crime.[13]

In *The Guilty River* (1886), the artist who refers to himself as "The Cur" possesses a beauty that enables him to hatch murderous plans while looking perfectly innocent. Roylake, the narrator, is hypnotised by The Cur when he first sees him:

> If I could be sure that the light of the moon had not deceived me, the most
> beautiful face that I had ever seen was looking down on us–and it was the face of

a man! By the uncertain light I could discern the perfection of form in the features, and the expression of power which made it impossible to mistake the stranger for a woman, although his hair grew long and he was without either moustache or beard. (Collins 1886, 254)

Roylake struggles to believe that The Cur could be capable of wickedness, because as the more knowing Cristel points out, "those beautiful eyes of his sometimes tell tales" (ibid., 281) and persuade the viewer into seeing virtue that is not present. Roylake is deceived into interpreting idealised beauty as proof of innocence, but this is a false and dangerous impression. Setting out to find "something devilish" (ibid., 277) in The Cur's face, Roylake can only identify the murderer's "personal advantages" (ibid.). He does not understand that he could interpret this type of beauty as proof of Satanic evil and is saved from a horrible death by poisoning only through Cristel's intervention. It is only when The Cur is weakened by an operation to restore his hearing (and is on the point of death) that he repents.

The less perfect that Collins's characters are in their physical appearance and well being, the more likely they to be redeemed. One rather unsuccessful aspect of *The Adversary* is that Paton places a scar on Satan's right cheek, something common in representations of the fallen angel, but inappropriate in this case. The blemish dilutes the message of Ruskin's Pre-Raphaelite argument, which is based on the idea that the seductive beauty of the Raphaelesque is in itself evil. The perfect proportions found in Greek sculpture and Raphael's paintings cannot be found in nature in an absolute form. Real people have small peculiarities that deviate from the standardised norm found in idealised art, attesting to the individuality of the living model. That is why characters like Oscar Dubourg often become better people after a disfigurement of some kind, since Collins links morality to personal growth and individuality throughout his fiction. Apollo's perfection is sinister if the viewer takes his lack of real human features to mean the lack of a soul;[14] a scar makes *The Adversary*'s Satan seem more human. The excellent illustration of Paton's painting from *The Magazine of Art* (1879, 265) that I have included in this essay (see fig. 8) makes the Apollo parallel a little clearer than the original work itself, since the disfigurement of Satan is represented as a less obvious shadow on the face. Perhaps, however, Paton does wish us to feel some measure of sympathy for Satan. It could be argued that, whatever Satan's intention towards the viewer, he has himself taken the place of Marysas since he is being tortured by his exile.

The Adversary is cited in Noel Paton's biography simply as "a study for a large picture" (Noel-Paton and Campbell 1990, 101) exhibited at the Royal Scottish Academy in 1879, with a note that it may be compared to other religious paintings by the same artist (ibid., 77-8). Little has ever been written about the painting in its own right, but fortunately its recent auction in 2003 has prevented its disappearance from the attention of the art world. Paton is best remembered today for his book illustrations and his paintings of mischievous fairies,[15] but his fascinating depiction of Satan is more than worthy of attention as a Victorian interpretation of Raphael's Apollo. It would also make a perfect illustration to accompany the novels of Wilkie Collins. Ironically, Collins's official P. R. B. illustrators[16] were ill equipped to draw his wicked characters, since artists who have rejected ideal beauty will not be inclined to represent Raphaelesque figures. Paton's decision to represent Satan in the Raphaelesque style in the 1870s was at a distance from the influence of the original Brotherhood,[17] yet the painting makes perfect sense in relation to Ruskin's critique of Raphael, Apollo, and the Stanza della Segnatura. *The Adversary* helps us to see the fiend that is lurking at the heart of many a Collins villain, despite the diabolical charm of such characters as Godfrey Ablewhite, through a Ruskinian suspicion of ideal beauty.

Notes

[1] However, *The Adversary* sold in Sotheby's, New York, in December 2003 for a price considerably above its reserve. It had previously been a part of a private collection that included many Pre-Raphaelites paintings. See *The Collecting Eye of Seymour Stein.* New York: Sotheby's, 11 December 2003. 112.
[2] I will not address latter-day scholarship that suggests *Apollo and Marysas* is by the hand of an artist other than Raphael, since Paton would have identified it as a work by Raphael.
[3] For a fascinating look at many depictions of Satan, see Woof, et al. 2004. William Blake is a particularly interesting comparison, since Paton admired his work.
[4] See Treuherz 1993, 94.
[5] See also Gibbs and Gibbs 1901, 208.
[6] For an argument that the flaying of Marysas is secondary in importance to Apollo receiving his crown of laurels, see Joost-Gaugier 2002, 47.
[7] For the view that Marysas's sufferings prefigure the crucifixion and are thus quite suitably displayed in the Vatican, see Treip 1985, 21.
[8] Collins also wrote a Pre-Raphaelite review himself, in which he mischievously suggests that most viewers are not clever enough to appreciate Pre-Raphaelite art. (Collins 1851, 617-27.)
[9] Dante Gabriel Rossetti also depicts the copying of Raphael's art as being destructive in "Hand and Soul", as the narrator clashes with a group of students blindly intent on sketching from a Raphael portrait, thus interrupting his study of a superior medieval portrait of a soul. (Rossetti 1850, 23-33).
[10] The original *Cassell's Magazine* (1871-1872) illustrations by Edward Hughes, a second generation Pre-Raphaelite artist, show Oscar and Nugent with chiselled features that could well be considered Raphaelesque. Yet Lucilla is inexplicably represented as a

blonde, although she is clearly identified as the image of the famous brunette *The Sistine Madonna* in the novel.

[11] For insights into Victorian speculations about the portrait, see Cuzin 1985, 236.

[12] I have discussed Ruskin's construction of Raphael as an unwitting Lucifer figure in an overview of his 1850s Pre-Raphaelite criticism. (Leahy 2000, 125-31.)

[13] Different kinds of male artists in the work of Collins are discussed in Denisoff 2003.

[14] In Rossetti's "Hand and Soul", Chiaro's painting of a soul is in sharp contrast to the meaningless Raphael portrait, which is, by implication, entirely soulless.

[15] See Wood 2000, 86-97. As Wood points out, fairies could be sinister or even evil in mid-Victorian art. Fairy art is not as far removed from a depiction of Satan as it might seem.

[16] For a discussion of Millais's illustrations, in particular, see Nadel 1995 and Clare Douglass's contribution to this collection.

[17] Edward Hughes's interesting depiction of Oscar and Nugent in the *Cassell's Magazine* "Poor Miss Finch" serialisation of 1871-2 was, similarly, at a relatively late date.

Works Cited

Bachman, Maria K. and Don Richard Cox. 2003. *Reality's Dark Light: The Sensational Wilkie Collins*. Knoxville: University of Tennessee Press.

Collins, Wilkie. 1852. *Basil*. Oxford: Oxford University Press, 2000.

—. 1851. The Exhibition at the Royal Academy. *Bentley's Miscellany* 174: 617-27.

—. 1881. *The Black Robe*. Stroud: Sutton Publishing, 1999.

—. 1886. *The Guilty River*. Oxford: Oxford University Press, 1999.

—. 1879. *The Haunted Hotel*. Oxford University Press, 1999.

—. 1854. *Hide and Seek*. Oxford: Oxford University Press, 1999.

—. 1875. *The Law and the Lady*. Oxford: Oxford University Press, 1999.

—. 1872. *Poor Miss Finch*. Oxford: Oxford University Press, 2000.

—. 1871. Poor Miss Finch. *Cassell's Magazine* 4: interspersed through volume.

—. 1868. *The Moonstone*. Oxford: Oxford University Press, 1998.

—. 1860 *The Woman in White*. London: Penguin, 1985.

Cuzin, Jean-Pierre. 1985. *Raphael: His Life and Works*. Trans. by S. Brown. London: Alpine Fine Arts.

Denisoff, Dennis. 2003. Framed and Hung: Collins and the Economic Beauty of the Manly Artist, in Bachman and Cox 2003, 34-58.

Gibbs, Mary. and Ellen Gibbs. 1901. *The Bible References of John Ruskin*. London: George Allen.

Joost-Gaugier, Christiane L. 2002. *Raphael's Stanza della Segnatura: Meaning and Invention*. Cambridge: Cambridge University Press.

Leahy, Aoife. 2000. Ruskin and the Pre-Raphaelites in the 1850s. *PaGes 1999* 6:125-31.

Müntz, Eugène. 1882. *Raphael: His Life, Works, and Times*. London: Chapman and Hall.

Nadel, Ira B. 1995. Wilkie Collins and his Illustrators, in Smith and Terry 1995, 149-64.

Noel-Paton, M. H. and J. P. Campbell. 1990. *Noel Paton: 1821-1901*. Edinburgh: Ramsay Head Press.

Rossetti, Dante Gabriel. 1850. Hand and Soul. *The Germ: Thoughts Towards Nature in Poetry, Literature and Art* 1:23-33.

Rhys, E. (ed.). n.d. *Ruskin's Pre-Raphaelitism and Other Essays and Lectures on Art*. London: J. M. Dent.

Ruskin, John. 1858. Academy Notes, 1858, in Rhys n.d. 271-308.

—. 1853. Pre-Raphaelitism, in Rhys n.d.151-74.

—. 1867. *Time and Tide*. New York: United States Book Co., n. d.

Smith, Nelson, C. and R. C. Terry. 1995. *Wilkie Collins to the Forefront: Some Reassessments*. New York: A.M.A. Press.

Treip, Mindele Anne. 1985. *Descend from Heav'n Urania: Milton's* Paradise Lost *and Raphael's Cycle in the Stanza della Segnatura*. E.L.S. Monograph 35.

Treuherz, Julian. 1993. *Victorian Painting*. London: Thames and Hudson.

Wood, Christopher. 2000. *Fairies in Victorian Art*. Woodbridge: Antique Collectors' Club.

Woof, Robert., Howard Hanley, and Susan Hebron. 2004. *Paradise Lost: The Poem and its Illustrators*. Grasmere: Wordsworth Trust.

PART III:
COLLINS AND MEDICINE

MENTAL STATES: POLITICAL
AND PSYCHOLOGICAL CONFLICT IN *ANTONINA*

ANDREW MANGHAM

Political commotions, by arousing to greater activity all the intellectual faculties, by rendering more intense, the depressing and vindictive passions, formenting the spirit of ambition and revenge, overturning public and private fortunes, and changing the circumstances of all men, produce a vast amount of insanity. (Esquirol 1838, 44)

So wrote Jean Étienne Esquirol in his 1838 work *Mental Maladies: A Treatise on Insanity*. Writing in the wake of the French Revolution, Esquirol makes frequent reference to the Reign of Terror as both a cause and symptom of madness. "The influence of our political misfortunes has been so great", he continues,

that I could give the history of our revolution from the taking of the Bastile [*sic.*] to the last appearance of Bonaparte, from that of certain insane persons, whose insanity connects itself with the events which have signalised this long period of our history. (ibid.)

In many ways, *Mental Maladies* delivers exactly what Esquirol promises here: a unique account of the French Revolution based on the individual stories of people who went insane after the political crisis. The book features, for instance, the history of "M. ***, forty years of age", who,

after the storms of the revolution had passed away, returns to France and obtains an honorable subsistence. Two years subsequently, he suffers from loss of memory, and his friends perceive a change in his character. At length, while dining with one of them, he carries off certain pieces of silver plate. (ibid., 26)

This case study is just one of the many examples featured in *Mental Maladies* whereby the revolution is believed to have caused someone to behave strangely. It is evidence, according to Esquirol, of how political crises have a direct link with the onset of madness. Such events seemed to be the "exciting cause of insanity" (ibid.) because they allowed the free run of passions that had been previously curtailed by the monarchic rule, and destabilised a number of key cultural structures that provided the French population with feelings of stability. What emerges from Esquirol's account of the French Revolution is a profound sense of loss: loss of property, loss of purpose, and loss of reason: "The laws which confiscated the property of the condemned, under the Roman Emperors, multiplied suicides. It was the same in France, during the reign of terror" (ibid.).

In England, meanwhile, psychologist James Cowles Prichard corroborated Esquirol's opinion. In a book dedicated to the latter, entitled *A Treatise on Insanity* (1835), Prichard wrote: "At the destruction of the old monarchy many persons became mad through fright and loss of their property" (Prichard 1835, 140). He even speculated that "children born during that era of sorrow and terror must have felt in their mother's wombs the baneful influence" (ibid., 244). According to Esquirol and Prichard, therefore, both of whom were dominant figures in the development of Victorian psychiatry, political unrest had a baneful influence on the minds of the public. In their seminal textbooks, the link between insurrection and insanity is seen as irrefutable.

Yet, Esquirol's book also appears to be in favour of establishing a democracy, despite its concerns over the excesses of revolution. Esquirol argues that greater democracy brings greater insanity and this is actually a positive sign. A country, he writes, that "groan[s] under a despotism, [...] stifles the intellect, and represses the passions" while "a republican or representative government, in giving more play to all the passions, ought, other things being equal, to be more favourable to the production of insanity" (Esquirol 1838, 43). His reference to the old France as groaning under the weight of despotism is hardly a nostalgic ovation of the country's fallen monarchy. Instead, Esquirol appears to suggest that the increase of insanity in France is symptomatic of its transformation into a freer and more independent state. Indeed, throughout *Mental Maladies*, Esquirol claims that madness is a signifier of any given nation's advancement. He writes, for instance: "Without doubt, civilisation occasions diseases, and augments the number of sick, because, by multiplying the means of enjoyment, it causes some to live too well, and too fast" (ibid., 42). For Esquirol, therefore, insanity (like gout) is a natural result of living too well. This is not to suggest, however, that he was unconcerned about the dangers involved in political uprising. Although, as noted above, he seemed in favour of establishing a republic, he was also agitated by the types of behaviour occasioned by revolution. As an illustration of the "critical terminations of insanity" he outlines the story of Téroenne de Méricour—a woman who later seems to have inspired Dickens's representation of Madame Defarge. De Méricour is described by Esquirol as "a celebrated courtesan, [...] of medium height, [with] chestnut colored hair, large blue eyes, a changeful physiognomy, and a sprightly, free, and even elegant carriage" (ibid., 218). Her role in the Revolution is then outlined in literary style:

We immediately see her appear, a red bonnet upon her head, a sword by her side, and a pike in her hand, commanding an army of women. She took an active part in the events of September, 1792. Although it may not be proved that she participated in the massacres, it is said, nevertheless, that she entered the court of the abbey, and with her sword cut off the head of an unfortunate man, who they were conducting to the tribunal of his prison. We are assured that it was a former lover. When the Directory was established, and popular associations ceased, Téroenne lost her reason. (ibid., 219)

We next see De Méricour languishing in an insane asylum:

She articulates phrases, interspersed with the words, *fortune, liberty, committee, revolution, rascal, warrant, decree,* etc. She applies many of them to the moderates. She is angry and transported with passion, when opposed; especially when they desire to prevent her from taking water. She once bit a companion with so much fury, as to take out a piece of flesh. The disposition of this woman had therefore outlived her understanding. (ibid., italics in original)

In a book that frequently warns its readers against the dangers of immoderation, it is no surprise that the hysterical excesses of revolution are viewed as the direct causes of this woman's insanity. In the case of De Méricour, the links between insurgent behaviour and her madness are drawn with unmistakable clarity. Notice how De Méricour's actions during the Revolution are matched by her actions in the lunatic asylum. Her vindictive beheading of an "unfortunate man" is mirrored by her savage violence later. Similarly, the words she repeats in her cell ("fortune", "liberty", "revolution") no doubt echo those uttered during her role in the Reign of Terror. De Méricour appears to pay the price for her unwomanly and immoderate actions.

This blurring of the boundaries between revolutionary and mad behaviour is something that recurs, time and time again, in philosophical, medical, and literary writings following the French Revolution. In his much-quoted *Reflections on the Revolutions in France* (1790), for example, Edmund Burke portrayed the mutinous mobs as irrational and uncontrollable. Years later, writers such as Charlotte Brontë, in *Shirley* (1849), Elizabeth Gaskell, in *Mary Barton* (1848) and *North and South* (1855), and Charles Dickens in *A Tale of Two Cities* (1859), all returned to the notion that, once stirred into political action, a vast crowd of insurgents is a crazy and uncontrollable phenomenon. As is discussed below, moreover, these ideas frequently sat alongside suggestions that such action, although excessive, was not without cause or justification.

Whereas, for Esquirol, the connections between revolution and madness were direct and unmistakable, the links in mid-century writings were much more subtle and metaphorical. Indeed, the perceived connections between insurrection and insanity actually became integral to the very language used by mid-nineteenth-century writers. Belief in the *causal* links between revolution and insanity continued throughout the century. (As late as 1894, for example, Henry Maudsley argued that "political revolution [...] will be followed by a deep exhaustion that may end in disease" (Maudsley 1894, 221).) Yet psychiatrists also began to use images of the fallen, besieged, or restless political state as a metaphor for insanity. More specifically, psychologists depicted the conflict between sane and insane feelings as a struggle to maintain sovereignty over a threatened "state". In 1862, for example, an article in the *Cornhill Magazine* observed that

> a sort of constitutional monarchy exists within us; no power in this small state is absolute, or can escape the checks and limitations which the other powers impose. Doubtless the brain is King; but Lords and Commons have their seats below, and guard their privilege with jealous zeal. (Hinton 1862, 166)

When insanity becomes a factor, psychiatrists argued, this hierarchical order broke down; the King was dethroned and madness reigned supreme. In 1853, the *British Medical Journal* noted that, in insanity, unhealthy thoughts have "*dethroned* the judgment" (Anon. 1853, 619, italics added).

Unsurprisingly, in an era engaged in a great deal of imperial activity, one also finds frequent references to the insane mind as a savage territory and the psychiatrist as a fearless colonist. In a review of Forbes Winslow's *Obscure Diseases of the Brain* (1860), for example, the *British Medical Journal* wrote of Victorian lunatic asylums:

> The springing into existence of these splendid mansions is perhaps the most remarkable feature, in a medical point of view, of the present century. [...] These buildings are, so to speak, the triumphal arches marking the victory of medical science over the instinctive brutality of ignorance. (Anon. 1860, 500)

Here the psychologist is aligned with the bold colonial explorer. Although this writer seems to be working with a different set of images to those employed by Esquirol and his colleagues, he has a similar view of the human mind as caught between two opposing forms of power, one savage and immoderate, the other controlled and civilised.

The fall of Rome, in particular, was a frequent source of reference for nineteenth-century psychologists. This is due in part, no doubt, to the success of Edward Gibbon's *The Decline and Fall of the Roman Empire* (1776-88). Comprising six volumes and written over twelve years, Gibbon's *magnum opus* exerted a profound influence over Victorian views of ancient Rome.[1] As late as 1909, for example, one reads Oliphant Smeaton waxing lyrical about the book's enduring importance:

> No other work has stood the test of time so unflinchingly and so successfully as
> the great history of Edward Gibbon. Other books have had a greater run of
> success, but none has retained the confidence of the critical public so long
> without experiencing some alteration in the blaze of meridian popularity which
> has constantly attended it. (Smeaton 1909, 9)

Gibbon's book, like the psychological texts of the nineteenth century,
frequently aligned images of political disturbance with notions of pathology. He
writes of the Roman Empire, for instance, that "long peace, and the uniform
government of the Romans, introduced a slow and secret poison into the vitals
of the empire" (Gibbon 1776-88, vol. 1, 56). When he describes the empire as
losing some of its colonies, he gruesomely refers to its provinces as
"dismembered" (ibid., 271). *Decline and Fall* also provided the Victorians with
a vocabulary through which to articulate the notion that sanity and insanity were
waging war within every individual. Writing about the state of Rome around
300 A. D., Gibbon writes:

> A perpetual stream of strangers and provincials flowed into the capacious bosom
> of Rome. Whatever was strange or odious, whoever was guilty or suspected,
> might hope, in the obscurity of that immense capital, to elude the vigilance of the
> law. In such a various conflux of nations, every teacher, either of truth or of
> falsehood, every founder, whether of a virtuous or a criminal association, might
> easily multiply his disciples or accomplices. (ibid., 490)

Again, it is possible to see a number of biological images here. Rome has a
"capacious bosom" and, Gibbon implies, that "bosom" is polluted; the passage
could even be seen as anticipating the eugenic ideologies of the early twentieth-
century by suggesting that "a various conflux of nations", a non-uniform state of
population, allows for the formation of unhealthy and "criminal" subgroups; this
is especially possible when the "vigilance of the law" has been relaxed.

For the Victorians, the fall of Rome became an influential image
because it helped them to communicate a paranoid belief that the *mental* state
was in perpetual jeopardy of being overthrown or overrun by pathological
elements. The sane mind was seen as permanently on the verge of becoming
insane. In the preface to *Obscure Diseases of the Brain* Winslow wrote:

> It is wise to be on our guard against the approach of disease, to observe its first
> warnings, and thus, by the use of appropriate remedies, prevent the enemy from
> obtaining a permanent lodgment in one of the vital tissues. (Winslow 1860, xi)

The onset of insanity, he added, is often an "insidious attack":

> The fatal, obscure, and insidious disease has crept quietly and stealthily on its
> victim, giving no sign of its advent, no indication of its advance, no notice of its

presence, until it has surprised the sentinels, boldly seized upon the outposts, scaled the ramparts, and by what may not inaptly be termed a pathological *coup de main*, taken possession of the citadel. (ibid., 7)

Once the citadel has been stormed, he suggests, and the mind laid waste, the effects are devastating–especially for the psychiatrist whose vocation it is to explore the ruins:

> Like the historian and antiquarian wandering with a sad heart over ground made classical and memorable in the story of great men, and in the annals of heroic deeds, surveying with painful interest the ruins of ancient temples, viewing with vivid emotion the sad wreck of proud imperial cities, consecrated by the genius of men renowned in the world's history as statesmen, scholars, artists, philosophers, and poets, so it is the duty of the mental physician to wander through the ruins of still greater temples than any raised in ancient days to the honour of imaginary DEITIES. It is his distressing province to witness great and good intellects, proud and elevated understandings leveled to the earth, and there crumbling, like dust in the balance, under the crushing influence of disease. (ibid., 568, capitals in original)

In a book dense with references to Shakespeare, Winslow appears to owe a lot to the playwright's metonymical links between disordered political and mental states. Winslow also seems to be indebted to Gibbon's work. The latter repeatedly refers to the "curious traveler" or historian whose vocation it is to pick his way through ancient ruins:

> All the other quarters of [Rome], and all the provinces of the empire, were embellished by the same liberal spirit of magnificence, and were filled with ampitheatres, theatres, temples, porticos, triumphal arches, baths, and aqueducts, all variously conducive to the health, the devotion, and the pleasures of the meanest citizen. (Gibbon 1776-88, vol. 1, 47-8)

Like Winslow, Gibbon communicates a sense of loss and nostalgia when wading through the ruinous remains of such grandeur. Yet he retains a sense of optimistic admiration for the fact that the ruins (though they *are* ruins) are still standing: "Among the innumerable monuments of architecture constructed by the Romans, how many have escaped the notice of history, how few have resisted the ravages of time and barbarism!" (ibid., 43). Winslow's metaphorical employment of the same imagery is an example of how medicine drew on historical and literary narratives (especially those outlining the fall–or revolution–of a state) to suggest that insanity is a constant and devastating threat.

Psychiatrists did not suggest, however, that, because insanity is such an evasive condition, all attempts to identify and avoid it were fundamentally redundant. On the contrary, *because* insanity is such an "obscure disease", the individual and his (or her) psychiatrist needed to watch for its beginnings with added vigilance and paranoia. This, reasons Winslow, is why he wrote *Obscure Diseases*. He aimed to excite "a deeper interest" in the causes and treatment of insanity (Winslow 1860, xi). "Mischievous maladies", he hopes, will be "detected in the insipient stage and placed under arrest" (ibid., xii). This statement makes the parallels between politics and psychology particularly clear. As with political uprisings, the rumblings of insanity need to be watched and stamped out in the early stages of development. Of course, Winslow was not intending to make any overt political comment here. Instead, he uses revolutionary metaphors to communicate his view that the intellect, like the sovereignty of any given political state, is something that needs to be watched, controlled, and maintained.

In nineteenth-century psychological texts, then, the fallen empire became a metaphor for the state of an insane mind. In earlier textbooks like Esquirol's, there is a suggestion that revolution is a devastating phenomenon for both the mental and national state. Insurrection seems to destabilise the foundations upon which identities are built and gives full reign to unhealthy passions. Yet there is also the suggestion that these are the signs of a *healthier* political state. By mid century, such associations had become integral to the language used to describe mental disorder. From the writings of Forbes Winslow, in particular, one notices the opinion that everyone is in constant danger of having his or her senses overthrown. The Barbarians, he suggests, have taken permanent camp outside the gates and only a staunch and skilful vigilance will keep them out.

Fictional Representations

What is interesting about the medical writings is that they never offer any explanations for why people become revolutionary. I have already explained, for example, how both Esquirol and Dickens retell the story of Téronne de Méricour. As in *Mental Maladies,* Dickens's portrait of this woman (as Madame Defarge) presents a ruthless, bloodthirsty terrorist who will stop at nothing to overturn the aristocracy. Yet, unlike Esquirol, Dickens also presents the aristocratic behaviour that has instigated such resentment. *A Tale of Two Cities* opens with a small child being run over and killed by an unfeeling aristocrat in his carriage. The scene ends with Defarge looking on, menacingly, and seems to leave no doubt that it is events such as this that spurs her lust for noble blood. In *Mental Maladies,* by contrast, De Méricour's actions are vilified and presented as fittingly rewarded with the loss of reason.

Such differences between literary and medical descriptions of the links between insanity and political revolution are also evident in Wilkie Collins's first published novel *Antonina, or the Fall of Rome* (1850). Collins began writing this book in 1846 but had to delay its completion in order to write a biography of his father (Gasson 1998, 8). The story was eventually published by Richard Bentley in 1850. It has had a lack of critical attention in recent years, primarily because it has many characteristics that differentiate it from the sensational style Collins is seen to spearhead. According to Andrew Gasson, *Antonina* is "absurd", with "many passages read[ing] like a cross between a guide-book to ancient Rome […] and a description of his father's paintings" (ibid.). Lyn Pykett has more recently viewed the novel as a "historical romance"–a genre, she suggests, that had "begun to go out of fashion" by the time Collins started *Antonina* (Pykett 2005, 84). Only Tamar Heller has dedicated any sustained attention to the novel in *Dead Secrets: Wilkie Collins and the Female Gothic* (1992). Heller views it as a text that evidences Collins's struggles between the "radical" "Female Gothic" style and a more conservative attempt to write as a "serious" man of letters (see Heller 1992, 48-57). Heller usefully views *Antonina* in the context of the political instabilities of the 1840s. In 1848, the Chartist movement put forth its third and final petition to Westminster. Following the European Revolutions that same year, which had sought, like the French unprising, to overthrow a number of dynastic governments, the Chartist petition of 1848 was perceived by many to be a highly precarious event. The Queen was dispatched to the Isle of Wight for her own safety and the London streets were lined with soldiers and policemen. It was in this precarious political climate that *Antonina* was written and finally published.

Collins's highly detailed outline of the fall of Rome would have held, therefore, specific meanings for its mid-Victorian readers. Indeed, Collins recognised as much when he wrote to Bentley: "I have thought it probable that such work might not inappropriately be offered for your inspection, while recent occurrences continue to direct public attention particularly on Roman affairs" (quoted in ibid., 49). Here Collins is referring to the European Revolutions. We know from his letters that he also consulted Gibbon's *Decline and Fall* when writing *Antonina*. He borrowed Bentley's edition at the time and owned a twelve-volume edition when he died (Baker et al. 2005, 41; Baker 2002, 111).

What is particularly interesting about Collins's representation of Rome's ancient collapse, in *Antonina,* is how he chooses to parallel those events with the mental breakdowns of two key characters. In the novel, the fall of Rome is both elemental to and reflected in the insanity of Goisvintha, a vengeful Barbarian woman, and Ulpius, a deranged Pagan priest.[2] As with medical writers like Esquirol and Winslow, Wilkie Collins uses the perceived connections between insanity and insurrection as a useful and powerful means of commenting on contemporaneous political events. In *Antonina,* the images of insanity becomes a complex vehicle for expressing the author's ambivalent attitude towards the political instabilities of the 1840s.

Writing from a feminist angle, Heller concludes that, in *Antonina*, "Collins is simultaneously attracted to the rebellion associated with the feminine and repulsed by it" (Heller 1992, 40). To illustrate this, Heller views Antonina, the book's angelic heroine, and Goisvintha, its force of retaliation, as two sides to the same rebellious energy. Yet, as we shall see, Antonina is meant to be a portrait of female submission and weakness. Heller does not capture the complexities of Goisvintha's character who is, in herself, a figure of both attraction and repulsion. Nor does her gender-preoccupied argument allow her to take account of the novel's most significant representation of subversion: Ulpius.

The Fall of Rome

Antonina begins with the Gothic siege of Rome in 408 A. D. Outlined in detail by Gibbon, the domestic and imperial superiority of the Roman empire is shaken one morning by the arrival of the Barbarians.[3] Collins writes:

> A vague, fearful, mysterious desolation seemed to have suddenly overwhelmed the whole range of dwellings beyond the walls. No sound rose from the gardens, no population idled in the streets. The ramparts on the other hand were crowded at every visible point with people of all ranks, and the distant squares and amphitheatres of the city itself, swarmed like ant-hills to the eye with the crowds that struggled within them. Confused cries and strange wild noises rose at all points from these masses of human beings. The whole of Rome seemed the prey of a vast and universal revolt. (Collins 1850, 116)

Numerian, a Roman landholder and Antonina's father, remarks:

> Behold those suburbs! They are left desolate! Hear those cries–they are from Roman lips! While your household's puny troubles have run their course, this city of apostates has been doomed! In the world's annals this morning will never be forgotten! THE GOTHS ARE AT THE GATES OF ROME! (ibid., 116-7, capitals in original)

As with Esquirol's descriptions of revolution, Collins foregrounds here the amount of confusion, devastation, and loss of security resulting from the Gothic invasion. Indeed, he also seems to agree with the medical idea that such crises lead to mental instability:

> Of all the results of the frightful severity of privation suffered by the besieged, none were more common than those mental aberrations which produce visions of danger, enemies, and death, so palpable as to make the persons beholding them, implore assistance against the hideous creation of their own delirium. (ibid., 326)

In agreement with Esquirol and Prichard, Collins suggests that the paranoid and panic-stricken feelings of the "besieged" lead to "mental aberrations" and "delirium". Like the medical writers, he seems to agree that the effects of political instabilities are highly unsettling for those experiencing them.[4]

Goisvintha

Goisvintha seems to typify the kind of threat posed by the Gothic invasion. Infuriated by the Roman slaughter of her husband and children in Aquileia, she becomes a destructive and unstoppable force:

> "Vengeance!" gasped Goisvintha [...]. "We will have vengeance for the massacre of Aquileia! When blood is streaming in the palaces of Rome remember my murdered children, and hasten not to sheathe thy sword!" (Collins 1850, 15)

Finding a passage in the wall surrounding Rome, she becomes the first Goth to enter the city. Intending to slaughter the first Roman she comes across, she chances on Antonina and henceforth sees the latter's death as the only means of appeasing her vengeance:

> Hour after hour [...] had she brooded over the projects of vengeance and blood. Neither the sickness nor the death which she had beheld around her, had possessed an influence powerful enough over the sudden ferocity which now alone animated her nature, to lure it to mercy or awe it to repentance. Invigorated by delay, and enlarged by disappointment, the evil passion that consumed her had strengthened its power, and aroused the most latent of its energies [...]. She detested the girl [...] for her nation; she now hated her for herself. (ibid., 165-6)

Clearly, Collins aims to represent Goisvintha's vengeance as obsessive and irrational. Observe how she "broods" unhealthily over the possibility of killing Antonina and her passions "consume" and fix her attention on this one deadly intention.

Notwithstanding, Antonina manages to escape Goisvintha and hides in a suburban farmhouse. She is discovered by Hermanric, Goisvinth's brother-in-law and fellow Goth. Despite their star-crossed positions, Hermanric and Antonina fall in love and enjoy several innocent "love meetings" in the farmhouse. One evening, however, they are interrupted by Goisvintha:

> Regardless of the darkness and the storm, she had prowled about the house, had raised the latch, had waited for a loud peal of thunder ere she passed the door, and had stolen shadow-like into the darkest corner of the room, with a patience and a determination that nothing could disturb. (ibid., 233)

We see here a crystallisation of the larger, political events. As with the Gothic invasion of Rome, Goisvintha surreptitiously scales the farmhouse's defences and penetrates its unsuspecting parameters. The way in which she creeps upon Hermanric and Antonina also appears to anticipate Winslow's description of insanity as a silent and "obscure" threat. The effects of Goisvintha's invasion, for Hermanric, are fatal. Waiting in the shadows until an opportune moment, Goisvintha savagely wounds his hands:

> Rage, vengeance, ferocity, lowered over them as she crept stealthily forward to the very side of the Goth; and when the next gleam of fire played upon him– drew the knife fiercely across the back of his hands. The cut was true, strong, and rapid–it divided the tendons from first to last–he was crippled for life. […] The cries of his hapless companion, as the whole scene of vengeance, treachery, and mutilation, flashed in one terrible instant, before her eyes, seemed not even to reach his ears. Once he looked down upon his helpless hands, when the sword rolled heavily from them to the floor. Then his gaze directed itself immovably upon Goisvintha, as she stood at a little distance from him, with her blood-stained knife, silent as himself. (ibid., 234)

The fire imagery in this scene underscores how insane, dangerous, and volcanic Goisvintha's passions are. Her vengeance, driven by an uncontrollable fury, is fulfilled with the mutilation of her kinsman. Observe also how Hermanric is effectively emasculated by her violence. A Gothic warrior, he is rendered impotent by her aggressive crippling of his hands–a fact that is highlighted by the way he suggestively drops his sword. Goisvintha says: "I penetrated the paths to your hiding place; I entered it as softly as I once departed from the dwelling where my children were slain! In my vengeance I have treated *you* as treacherously as you would have treated *me*!" (ibid., 236, italics in original). Shortly afterwards, Hermanric is attacked by a troop of rival Huns. Unable to defend himself, he is killed. The Huns, however, do prevent Goisvintha from killing Antonina by carrying the former off with them.

Goisvintha thus becomes the novel's representation of insanity and Gothic invasion. The Goths storm the empire, "surprise the sentiments, seize upon the outposts, scale the ramparts, and […] take possession of the citadel" (Winslow 1860, 7). This is what Goisvintha does with the farmhouse. Insane herself, she also represents madness as she creeps upon Hermanric, crippling and emasculating him. Such political and psychological invasions, the novel seems to suggest, require strong opposition.

Ulpius

Although there are unmistakable similarities between Ulpius and Goisvintha, the former presents an entirely different (and more worrying) kind of threat than the latter. Unlike Goisvintha, who is a foreign, invasive energy, Ulpius is a revolutionary force generated from *within* Rome's defences. Ulpius is a servant of Numerian's and, according to his employer, a recent convert to Christianity. Numerian observes:

> I found him, like me, worn down by the calamities of his early life, and abandoned, as I have once been, to the delusions of the pagan gods. […] I proved to him that the worship he still professed was banished for its iniquities from the land; that the religion that had succeeded it had become defiled by man, and that there remained but one faith for him to choose, if he would be saved—the faith of the early Church. He heard me and was converted. From that moment he has served me patiently and helped me willingly. (ibid., 57)

As with Sim Tappertit and the Maypole's Hugh in *Barnaby Rudge* (1841), however, Ulpius is a servant who harbours revolutionary feelings towards his master and the ruling class. "Greater difficulties" than reinstating Paganism, Ulpius says, "had been overcome by other men. Solitary individuals had, ere this, originated revolutions" (ibid., 95). It is exactly this, a revolution, that Ulpius seeks and believes his purpose is best suited if he manipulates the unsuspecting Antonina:

> Once installed under Numerian's roof, the treacherous Pagan saw in the Christian's daughter an instrument admirably adapted, in his unscrupulous hands, for forwarding his wild project of obtaining the ear of a Roman of power and station who was disaffected to the established worship. […] The ruthless priest patiently awaited the opportunity of commencing his mechanisations. (ibid., 96)

Like the dangers of Goisvintha, Ulpius's threat is primarily directed towards the vulnerable Antonina and the domestic environment she inhabits. Whereas the former invades the suburban farmhouse from outside, however, the latter's dangers are generated from within the home.

One key similarity between Goisvintha and Ulpius, however, is that both characters go mad. The priest believes that the Gothic invasion offers him an ideal opportunity to reinstate Paganism as Rome's primary faith. He therefore seeks an interview with their leader in order to convert them to his cause. He crawls through a hole in the city walls intending to visit the Barbarian camp. While inside the wall he notices how

> an immense rift soared above him, stretching its tortuous ramifications, at different points, into every part of the wall that was immediately visible. The whole structure seemed, at this place, to have received a sudden and tremendous wrench. But for the support of the sounder fortifications at each side of it, it could not have sustained itself after the shock. (ibid., 173-4)

Clearly, the "immense rift" in the city's defences could symbolise Roman vulnerability to Gothic invasion; yet, it also seems to represent how the empire was already weak. The defences, it appears, were crumbling long before the Goths arrived. This gives some clue as to how Ulpius operates within the text. He symbolises how the seeds of revolution, or insanity, were already sewn within Rome's, or the individual's, defences. While inside the wall, part of the structure falls and crushes his shoulder. The shock sends him mad:

> Gradually, the anguish of his body awakened a wilder and stronger distemper in his mind, and then the two agonies, physical and mental, rioted over him together in fierce rivalry, divesting him of all thoughts but such as were by their own agency aroused. [... He] became the victim of a sudden and terrible delusion. [...] There were infantine faces, wreathed about with grave-worms that hung round them like locks of filthy hair; aged faces, dabbled with gore and slashed with wounds; youthful faces, seamed with livid channels, along which ran unceasing tears; lonely faces, distorted into fixed expressions of raging pain, wild malignity, and despairing gloom. (ibid., 177-8)

More significant still, Ulpius's hallucinations feature his own Pagan gods: "Disgorged misshapen figures of priests and idols of the old time, [...] came forth in every hideous deformity of aspect" (ibid., 178). Ulpius's insanity is a unique and important mid-Victorian representation of insanity that anticipates the delirium of the central character in Collins's 1852 novel *Basil*. It is significant how, in the earlier novel, Ulpius goes mad actually *inside* Rome's defences. It underscores how his threat is generated from inside the empire's parameters. There is also a significant similarity between Ulpius and De Méricour, as described by Esquirol. After going mad, De Méricour repeats the words and ideas that had driven her to political insurgency: "fortune", "liberty", and "revolution". Once *he* has gone insane, Ulpius's Pagan obsessions become terrifying delusions. As with Esquirol's example, Collins seems to suggest that there is a direct link between revolutionary thoughts and hallucinatory ideas.

Like the mid-century psychologist, Collins also seems to find revolutionary and military metaphors useful in describing the insanity of the Pagan. "The frame of Ulpius", he writes,

> was still there; but the soul of ferocious patience and unconquerable daring that had lighted it grandly in its ruin, was gone. Over the long anguish of that woful [*sic.*] life, the veil of self-oblivion had closed for ever! [...] Throughout the night

he had wondered about the lonely suburbs, striving in secret and horrible suffering for the mastery of his mind. There, did the overthrow of all his hopes from the Goths expand rapidly into the overthrow of the whole intellect that had created his aspirations. (ibid., 242-3)

The synonyms "ruin", "mastery", and "overthrow" here echo the medical writers' use of similar ideas to describe the onset of lunacy. Collins not only appears to agree that there is a link between the excesses of revolution and insanity, but, by also conflating political and psychological ideas in this way, he seems to confirm that the individual consciousness–like the political state–needs to be watched and guarded. Although Goisvintha and Ulpius represent two different forms of threat (one internal, the other external), the way in which their actions are represented as insane seems to imply that potentially revolutionary action, like the Chartist movement of the 1840s, is itself a mad threat that needs to be overcome. Moreover, and, perhaps more worrying still for the Victorians, there is the implicit suggestion that revolutionary and/or insane behaviour is a possibility in everyone.

Motives

In *Antonina,* Collins goes further than his medical counterparts by presenting mitigating explanations for why Goisvintha and Ulpius become insane and revolutionary. In the opening chapter, for example, Goisvintha describes how the Romans slaughtered her husband and children. Rome had agreed a truce with the Barbarians but demanded to hold the Gothic wives and children as a surety against deceit. Once they hold these innocents (including Goisvintha and her family), they murder them. Although Goisvintha escapes, her children do not. She narrates:

One evening, as I sat on the terrace before the house, [...] a helmet-crest suddenly fell at my feet, and a voice cried to me from the garden beneath–"Priulf thy husband has been slain in a quarrel by the soldiers of Rome! Already the legions with whom he served are on their way to the town; for a massacre of the hostages is ordained. [...] Already, as I rushed towards my children's beds, the fiends of Rome had mounted the stairs, and waved in bloody triumph their reeking swords! I gained the steps; and as I looked up, they flung down at me the body of my youngest child [...]! it was the most beautiful and the most beloved! (ibid., 11-2)

This passage clearly owes much to the gothic texts of the eighteenth century. The helmet-crest falling from the sky, for instance, echoes the opening of Horace Walpole's *The Castle of Otranto* (1764). However, the most gothic element in Collins's narrative is not the Goths, as one would expect, but the "fiends of Rome" waving their reeking swords over the Barbarian innocents. Similarly, revolution is instigated by Roman actions. Goisvintha's husband and children are massacred, not by foreign assailants, but by men with whom they had agreed peace. Barbarity, betrayal, and horror, therefore, are provided by the Romans at the beginning of the novel. It is these events that inspire Goisvintha's insane lust for Roman blood.

A similar explanation for Ulpius's madness is provided by Collins. The Roman conversion from Paganism to Christianity was not, he shows, as peaceful as Numerian would have his listeners believe:

> The Archbishop of Alexandria issued his decree that the Temple of Serapis should be destroyed. [...] As soon as the Archbishop gave the signal for the assault, a band of monks–their harsh discordant voices screaming fragments of psalms, their tattered garments waving in the air, their cadaverous faces gleaming with ferocious joy–led the way, placed the first ladders against the walls, and began the attack. From all sides the Temple was assailed by the infuriated besiegers. [...] Statues were broken, gold was carried off, doors were splintered into fragments. (ibid., 83-4, 86)

These images of plunder clearly anticipate those employed in Collins's later book *The Moonstone* (1868) where the siege of Seringapatam results in the savage murder of three Hindu priests and the theft of a priceless diamond. As with the later episode, the above extract portrays one greedy culture barbarically pillaging the riches of another under the guise of "cultivating" or "enlightening" it. Observe how the monks, like the Romans during the massacre of the Gothic captives, appear savage and animalistic with their fragments of screamed psalms and torn cassocks. Although Gibbon believed Paganism to be a belief in demon idols, he also demonstrated, in *Decline and Fall,* that Christianity was not, initially, a peaceful religion (Gibbon 1776-88, vol. 1). Collins, more ostensibly, portrays a Christian culture that is unwilling to live peacefully alongside other faiths and uses its teachings as a license to kill and steal. As with Goisvintha, it is these inhumanities that fuel the insane obsessions of Ulpius. Collins both provides complex and mitigating reasons for why the Pagan priest resorts to revolutionary behaviour.

This is not to suggest, however, that Collins justifies the actions of Goisvintha and Ulpius. On the contrary, the author's feelings towards their insurgent behaviour seems to remain highly ambivalent as both go on to commit atrocious crimes against Antonina. This is why, it seems, the image of the fallen state is fittingly paralleled by the minds of two insane characters. As the portraits of Goisvintha and Ulpius show, the madman or madwoman is a figure that can be both pitied and feared.[5] If one understands *Antonina* as offering comment on the volatile politics of the early Victorian period, then one could also conclude that Collins viewed those events with equal measures of empathy and concern.

* * *

In the medical literature, I argued, links between insanity and insurrection were drawn to allow psychiatrists the suggestion that the immoderations of revolution were a cause for concern. At mid century, psychologists drew these connections to imply that both the individual and the state needed to be controlled and watched if the onslaught of insanity, invasion, and revolution was to be avoided and/or moderated. In Wilkie Collins's *Antonina*, images of madness retain this high level of political meaning. Yet, through the proffered motives for Goisvintha's and Ulpius's irrational behaviour, it is possible to glean how, in the hands of the popular novelist, the connections between madness and revolution offer means through which the author can explore his culture's ambivalent (and sometimes sympathetic) feelings towards the tempestuous politics of the time.

Notes

[1] In *Barbarism and Religion* (1999) J. G. A. Pocock observes how Gibbon's text emerged from, and helped to shape, the eighteenth-century Enlightenment period. According to Pocock, *Decline and Fall* allowed Gibbon to explore key developments in the period's cultural and political history. As I argue below, *Antonina* allowed Collins to do the same.

[2] Collins was not alone in his representation of the links between insanity and political instability. The 1840s saw a stream of texts portraying images of state insurrection alongside characterisations of madness. In *Jane Eyre* (1847), for example, Jane's and Bertha's passions are paralleled with poignant references to the ill-used millions of the Industrial Revolution. In Gaskell's *Mary Barton* (1848), the Chartist Movement is represented alongside John Barton's increasing abstraction and Mary's own hysterical symptoms. In Dickens's *Barnaby Rudge* (1841), moreover, the eponymous character's idiocy is set in the era of the Gordon Riots of 1780.

[3] Gibbon's outline of the Gothic invasion is contained in chapters 30-1. His is a much more measuredly-written account than Collins's.

[4] Gibbon also wrote about these general feelings of paranoia: "Fear has been the original parent of superstition, and every new calamity urges trembling mortals to deprecate the wrath of their invisible enemies. [...] Such was the public consternation, when the barbarians were hourly expected at the gates of Rome" (Gibbon, vol. 1, 289).

[5] Here I am drawing on the arguments of Helen Small. In her excellent *Love's Madness* she argues that the image of the love-mad woman "provide[d] a controllable narrative framework for thinking about revolutionary politics in a highly unstable political climate. She expresses both a fascination with rebellion and a more sober recognition of its cost" (Small 1996, 112).

Works Cited

Anon. 1860. Review of Winslow, 1860. *British Medical Journal* I:500-1.

Anon. 1853. Mental Disease. *British Medical Journal* II:619.

Baker, William. 2002. *Wilkie Collins's Library: A Reconstruction*. Westport, CT and London: Greenwood Press.

Baker, William., Andrew Gasson., Graham Law. and Paul Lewis (eds). 2005. *The Public Face of Wilkie Collins: The Collected Letters*. 4 vols. London: Pickering and Chatto.

Collins, Wilkie. 1850. *Antonina, or the Fall of Rome*. London: Chatto and Windus, 1896.

Esquirol, Jean Étienne Dominique. 1838. *Des Maladies Mentales, Considérées sous les Rapports Médical, Hygiénique et Médico-légal*. Trans. by E. K. Hunt as *Mental Maladies: A Treatise on Insanity*. Philadelphia: Lea and Blanchard, 1845.

Gasson, Andrew. 1998. *Wilkie Collins: An Illustrated Guide*. Oxford: Oxford University Press.

Gibbon, Edward. 1776-88. *The Decline and Fall of the Roman Empire*. 6 vols. London: J. M. Dent and Sons, 1909.

Heller, Tamar. 1992. *Dead Secrets: Wilkie Collins and the Female Gothic*. New Haven: Yale University Press.

Hinton, James. 1862. What are the Nerves?. *Cornhill Magazine* 5:153-66.

Maudsley, Henry. 1894. *Pathology of Mind*. New York: D. Appleton and Company.

Pocock, J. G. A. 1999. *Barbarism and Religion*. 2 vols. Cambridge, Cambridge University Press.

Prichard, James Cowles. 1835. *A Treatise on Insanity and Other Disorders Affecting the Mind*. Philadelphia: Haswell, Barrington, and Haswell, 1837.

Pykett, Lyn. 2005. *Authors in Context: Wilkie Collins*. Oxford: Oxford University Press.

Small, Helen. 1996. *Love's Madness: Medicine, The Novel, and Female Insanity, 1800-1865*. Oxford: Oxford University Press.

Smeaton, Oliphant. Introduction to Gibbon 1776-88, vii-xxii.

Winslow, Forbes. 1860. *On the Obscure Diseases of the Brain and Disorders of the Mind*. London: John Churchill and Sons, 1868.

READING FACES: PHYSIOGNOMY AND THE DEPICTION OF THE HEROINE IN THE FICTION OF WILKIE COLLINS

JESSICA COX

Physiognomy–the pseudo-science based on the belief that a person's character could be judged by their physical appearance–was popular throughout the nineteenth century, and physiognomical theory was employed by numerous Victorian writers as a means of indicating a character's personality. This essay will examine the character and role of Wilkie Collins's heroines in relation to their physical appearance, examining the different ways in which Collins engaged with physiognomy. Physiognomical descriptions are used for both indicating and concealing character–to suggest to the reader the character of, and, at times, confound expectations of the heroine. I will examine the extent to which Collins's descriptions of his heroines relate to the work of physiognomists such as John Caspar Lavater, and question to what degree Collins employs physiognomical knowledge as a literary device for both indicating and concealing character in his fiction. Finally, I will consider whether Collins's fiction ultimately endorses or questions the "science" of physiognomy.

Physiognomy, and indeed the use of physiognomical detail in literature, dates back much further than the nineteenth century. Aristotle wrote extensively on the subject in his *Historia Animalium* (350 BC) and evidence of physiognomical beliefs can be found in the Bible and in the works of numerous pre-nineteenth century writers including Shakespeare and Milton.[1] The popularity of physiognomy in the nineteenth century, however, can be traced to the publication of John Caspar Lavater's *Essays on Physiognomy* (1772). The text became hugely popular, and sparked a renewed interest in physiognomy and its sister "science", phrenology. The first English editions appeared in the 1780s and, by 1810, at least twenty English editions had been published (Graham 1961, 562)–evidence of the astonishing popularity of the work, which also led to countless articles in periodicals and the publication of numerous other books on the subject. The idea that a person's character could be read in her/his countenance gripped the public's imagination and the reading public became so familiar with the theories of Lavater and other physiognomists that Victorian novelists were able to draw on the principles of physiognomy in their descriptions of central characters.

In his seminal work on physiognomy, Lavater outlined the basic principles of the subject. He defined it as "the science or knowledge of the correspondence between the external and internal man, the visible superficies and the invisible contents" (Lavater 1789, vol. 1, 19), and indicated the meaning behind key facial features: "the forehead, to the eyebrows [is] the mirror, or image, of the understanding; the nose and cheeks the image of the moral and sensitive life; and the mouth and chin the image of the animal life" (ibid., 16-7). He expanded on this with the analysis of numerous countenances and profiles which are reproduced in his work. In the third and final volume of *Essays on Physiognomy*, he discussed his interpretations of facial features at greater length, allowing for some generalisations to be made regarding the meaning found in the eyes, eyebrows, nose, mouth, teeth, and chin. However, Lavater's warning to his readers "to expect only fragments on physiognomy [...] and not a perfect system" (ibid., 18) is indicative of the fact that the author's reliance on specific examples makes generalisations somewhat problematic, as R. D. Stocker, in his short book on physiognomy, *The Human Face* (1900), observed:

> Lavater's writings are [...] of little practical value. [...] His methods of delineating character were largely intuitive, his "Essays on Physiognomy" being almost entirely composed of brief sketches of the dispositions of the countenances which illustrate the work. He [...] laid down very few rules for those who have followed in his steps. (Stocker 1900, vii-viii)

In this respect, later physiognomists, who drew on Lavater's work, such as Stocker, offer a more simplified and logical guide to reading the countenance, which was undoubtedly of greater benefit to the general reader's understanding of the subject.

As well as being limiting in terms of establishing a set of guidelines by which to read countenances, Lavater's work is also problematic in terms of his attitude towards women and this has obvious implications for the application of Lavater's theories to the representations of Victorian heroines. The third volume of Lavater's work includes chapters entitled "Women" and "Male and Female", in which he discusses physiognomy in relation to gender. He opens this discussion by acknowledging that he is "little acquainted with the female part of the human race" (Lavater 1789, vol. 3, 198) which immediately poses problems for applying his theories to descriptions of female fictional characters. This is further underlined by his admission that "I frequently shudder while I think how excessively, how contrary to my intention, the study of physiognomy may be abused, when applied to women" (ibid., 199). However, he goes on to acknowledge that the study of women's faces may be of some benefit, arguing that knowledge of the science of physiognomy may serve to "preserve him who can see from the dangerous charms of their shameless bosoms" (ibid., 202). Lavater's misogynistic attitude is further emphasised by his discussion of women's natures, in which he states that when women rule "with passion and threats [...] they are no longer women, but abortions" (ibid., 207) and suggests that women have an innate "incapacity for deep inquiry and firm decision" (ibid.). He further proposes that "their love, strong and rooted as it is, is very changeable; their hatred almost incurable, and only to be effaced by continued and artful flattery" (ibid.). His assertion that "a woman with a beard is not so disgusting as a woman who acts the free thinker" (ibid., 208) highlights the problem of applying Lavater's ideas to Collins's heroines: in *The Woman in White* (1860), Marian Halcombe, whose character is undoubtedly endorsed by the narrative voice, is both moustached and a free thinker. Thus, Lavater's discussion of women in *Essays on Physiognomy* suggests that he intended his theories to be applied primarily to the reading of men's, not women's, faces.

While Lavater's attitude to women poses inevitable problems in terms of applying his theories to the appearance of female characters in the Victorian novel, however, it is significant that nineteenth-century readers applied physiognomical theory to the countenances of both sexes. Furthermore, Lavater's assertion that women are "the counterpart of man, taken out of man, to be subject to man; to comfort him like angels, and to lighten his cares" (ibid., 205) reflects an attitude common throughout the nineteenth century. His view of women coincides with Victorian society's vision of the idealised feminine—something reflected in the work of numerous nineteenth-century writers, including Collins. In spite of the apparent problems raised by Lavater's misogynistic attitude, his theories of physiognomy nevertheless undoubtedly influenced literary depictions of the Victorian heroine.

In her article, "Physiognomy and the Conventions of Heroine Description" (1980), Jeanne Fahnestock argues that the detailed descriptions of heroines found in fiction dating from approximately the mid-nineteenth century onwards can be explained by the increasing interest in physiognomy. "Physiognomical description", she writes, "was a way of suggesting without proclaiming, of imputing intelligence, caprice, and even sexuality to heroines without indecorous explicitness" (Fahnestock 1980, 326). Fahnestock also notes that a consequence of the Victorian novelists' use of physiognomy was the emergence of "irregularly featured heroines who deviate from the standard of beauty" (ibid., 330), the significance of this being that "the heroine of irregular features is capable of irregular conduct" (ibid., 331). Thus the emergence of the heroine who deviated from the nineteenth-century standard of beauty coincided with the emergence of the heroine whose behaviour also deviated from the norm–something clearly apparent in the female protagonists of the sensation novels of the 1860s, including those of Wilkie Collins. The sensation novelists were not the first nineteenth-century writers to employ physiognomy as a literary trope, however. Victorian writers including the Brontës, Charles Dickens, George Eliot and later Thomas Hardy, all drew on the principles of physiognomy when creating characters.[2] Indeed, by the time the sensation novel appeared in the 1860s, use of physiognomical detail had become something of a literary trope, and this allowed popular writers like Collins to manipulate readers' expectations by offering descriptions of characters which did not necessarily tally with their subsequent behaviour.

Collins's heroines can generally be classified into one of a number of categories of character types: the idealised/conventional feminine (for example, *Hide and Seek*'s Madonna and *The Woman in White*'s Laura Fairlie); the assertive, independent heroine (*The Woman in White*'s Marian Halcombe and *No Name*'s Magdalen Vanstone, amongst others); the penitent sinner (*Man and Wife*'s Anne Silvester and *The New Magdalen*'s Mercy Merrick); the victim (such as *The Woman in White*'s Anne Catherick and *The Fallen Leaves*'s Simple Sally) and the deviant anti-heroine (*Armadale*'s Lydia Gwilt and *The Haunted Hotel*'s Countess Narona). Although these categories are fluid, and there is some blurring of their boundaries, they are nevertheless useful for identifying the key traits of Collins's central female characters. Furthermore, there is often a clear correspondence between these character types and their appearance. The archetypal feminine is idealised in both nature and appearance, according to Victorian convention, while the more assertive and subversive female characters are often marked by masculine and contradictory features. In the case of almost all his central female characters, Collins offers detailed descriptions of their appearance as a means of introducing readers to their personalities.

Collins's detailed descriptions of his central female characters clearly point to an interest in physiognomy. He frequently comments not only on the more obvious aspects of his heroine's appearance, such as hair colour and eye colour, but also on features such as complexion, eyebrows, and the shape and size of the nose, forehead, and chin. Further evidence of Collins's interest in the subject can be found in direct references to physiognomy in a number of his novels. In his description of Madame Fontaine in *Jezebel's Daughter* (1880), for example, he notes that "sensuality shows itself most plainly in the excessive development of the lower part of the face" (Collins 1880, 37), while in *I Say No* (1884), he states, "Francine (as her straight chin proclaimed to all students of physiognomy) was an obstinate girl" (Collins 1884, 8). In *The Evil Genius* (1886), Collins actually alludes to Lavater's *Essays on Physiognomy* in relation to his description of one of the minor characters: "The personal appearance of

Miss Wigger might have suggested a modest distrust of his own abilities to Lavater, when that self-sufficient man wrote his famous work on Physiognomy" (Collins 1886, 78). This confirms that Collins was familiar with the work of Lavater and with the principles of physiognomy, and leaves little doubt that he deliberately engaged with these principles in describing many of his characters.

In spite of the fact that sensation fiction has frequently been identified as subversive, Collins's novels are in fact littered with depictions of the conventional Victorian feminine ideal. While these characters do not necessarily conform to Grecian ideals of beauty, their physiognomical features nevertheless suggest their "proper" womanly natures: passive, unassertive, and dependent. A comparison of some of Collins's idealised women highlights their shared physical attributes. In particular, the idealised feminine in Collins's fiction is generally marked by her pale complexion, blue eyes, and light brown hair. Madonna in *Hide and Seek* (1854) has "incomparable blue eyes" (Collins 1854, 49), while *The Woman in White*'s Laura Fairlie has eyes "of that soft, limpid, turquoise blue, so often sung by the poets, so seldom seen in real life" (Collins 1860, 40). Laura Fairlie's hair is "of so faint and pale a brown–not flaxen, and yet almost as light" (ibid., 39)–identical to that of another of Collins's conventional heroines: Carmina, in *Heart and Science* (1883), whose hair is "of so light a brown that it just escaped being flaxen" (Collins 1883, 53). The eponymous hero's sister, Clara, in *Basil* (1852), and Catherine Linley in *The Evil Genius* are also both marked by their conventionally feminine natures, blue eyes, and pale complexion. Thus Collins's idealised women appear to be typical literary representations of femininity: the blue eyed, light haired, fair skinned heroine represents a standard Victorian literary portrait, gracing the pages of numerous nineteenth-century novels. Nevertheless, these representations engage significantly with physiognomical ideas. Lavater, whose work was so influential on the descriptions of nineteenth-century fictional characters, stated that "blue eyes are, generally, [...] significant of weakness, effeminacy, and yielding" (Lavater 1789, vol. 3, 171)–and this is clearly borne out in the case of Collins's blue eyed, weak, passive heroines. Similarly, physiognomists believed brown hair to be "indicative of a tender disposition" (Stocker 1900, 28), again linking the physical appearance and idealised natures of Collins's more conventional heroines. Pale skin, according to physiognomy, is a sign of a lymphatic temperament (ibid., 2)–the bearers of which are supposedly "dreamy [and] capricious" (ibid., 3). In a number of his novels, Collins provides further physiognomical descriptions of his conventional heroines, and it is clearly significant that both Clara (*Basil*) and Laura Fairlie (*The Woman in White*) are marked by noticeably small chins. Basil, the eponymous narrator, informs the reader that "the lower part of [Clara's] face is rather too small for the upper" (Collins 1852, 19), while "the lower part of [Laura Fairlie's] face is too delicately refined away towards the chin to be in full and fair proportion with the upper part" (Collins 1860, 40). Physiognomy again links a weak chin to a passive disposition: Lavater proposes that the retreating chin signifies an absence of strength (Lavater 1789, vol. 3, 197), while Stocker suggests that "a small chin denotes its possessor to be absent in will power" (Stocker 1900, 26)– both of which are key features of Collins's conventional heroines. As Fahnestock observes, "in the description of Laura Fairlie, Collins gently foreshadows the fate of his heroine, who becomes quite childlike and silly" (Fahnestock 1980, 341).

It is clear from the descriptions of Collins's overtly feminine female characters, therefore, that he deliberately draws on physiognomical theory, and the same is patently true of his more assertive heroines, who often stand in direct contrast to their passive, weak counterparts–in both disposition and appearance. Rosamond Treverton, the assertive, illegitimate heroine in *The Dead Secret* (1857), who takes on the role of moral and physical guide to her blind husband, in a reversal of the traditional marital roles, has thick, dark brown hair, large brown eyes, and a "dusky" complexion (Collins 1857, 69). Similarly, *The Woman in White*'s Marian Halcombe, who provides a direct contrast to her passive half-sister, Laura Fairlie, has an "almost swarthy" complexion, "resolute brown eyes, and thick, coal-black hair" (Collins 1860, 24-5), while Valeria Macallan in *The Law and the Lady* (1875) has black hair and eyes "of so dark a blue that they are generally mistaken for black" (Collins 1875, 14). Again, Collins is drawing on physiognomical ideas that were widely known in the nineteenth century: black hair is suggestive of "intensity of feeling" (Stocker 1900, 28), and black eyes of "a firm mind, not wavering, fearful, but courageous, true and honourable" (Lavater 1789, vol. 3, 179).

It is interesting to note that Valeria's eyes are dark blue, rather than black, and that she does not share the same dark complexion as Rosamond and Marian. Indeed, contrary to this, "her complexion is pale: except in moments of violent agitation there is no colour to be seen in her face" (Collins 1875, 14). This differentiates her from Collins's other assertive heroines, and in fact links her with the more conventional, passive heroine such as *Basil*'s Clara, whose pale complexion also has a "tendency to flush" (Collins 1852, 19). This presents us with further indisputable evidence that Collins draws on the science of physiognomy in his fiction, for Valeria, in spite of undertaking the role of amateur detective, ultimately conforms to Victorian expectations by returning to her husband, and fulfilling the role of dutiful wife and mother. Thus, while her black hair and aquiline nose are indicative of her brief escape from the confines of the domestic sphere, the latter signifying, according to physiognomy, "a penetrating, quick cast of brain" (Stocker 1900, 16) and indicating that the bearer is "capable of command, can rule, act, overcome, destroy" (Lavater 1789, vol. 3, 187), her pale complexion and blue, rather than black, eyes suggest her ultimate conformation to Victorian gender codes.

Collins's assertive heroines share further physical attributes which again link their appearance with their dispositions. Both Rosamond and Marian are notable for their hair that "grow[s] unusually low down on the forehead" (Collins 1860, 25; 1857, 68). This, according to the principles of physiognomy, suggests "a sensuous, artistic, and, probably, combative and ardent temperament" (Stocker 1900, 28). While Marian's "large, firm, masculine mouth and jaw" indicate strength of character, (Lavater 1789, Vol. 3, 197) Valeria's face, "too narrow and too long at the lower part, too broad and too low in the higher regions of the eyes and head" (Collins 1875, 14), again suggests the contradictions in her character.

The dark features of Collins's resolute heroines are also shared by a number of his criminal anti-heroines, suggesting the behaviour of both violates the strict Victorian gender and moral codes. Like Rosamond, Marian and Valeria, Margaret Sherwin (*Basil*), the Countess Narona (*The Haunted Hotel* (1879)) and Madame Fontaine (*Jezebel's Daughter*) are distinguished by their dark hair and eyes. Margaret Sherwin, morally and sexually deviant and an entirely unsympathetic character (unlike a number of Collins's later fallen women), has "hair, eyes and complexion [...] darker than usual in English women" (Collins 1852, 30), signifying that she does not conform to Victorian notions of "proper" femininity. Her lips are described as full–possibly "*too* full" (ibid., italics in original), indicating "sensuality and indolence" (Lavater 1789, vol. 3, 192), and thus provide a visual signifier of her sexual deviancy. The criminal characters of the Countess Narona and Madame Fontaine also have predictably dark features, although, significantly, they are marked by their pallor: the Countess Narona's complexion is described as "corpse-like" (Collins 1879, 4), indicating that she is morally dead, while Madame Fontaine's lack of colour (Collins 1880, 37) suggests similar moral deficiencies. Just as the pale complexions of Collins's passive heroines represent mental or physical weakness, those of Collins's deviant criminal women indicate moral weakness. Collins's detailed plotting is thus mirrored by his close attention to his characters' appearances and clear engagement with the theories of physiognomy.

While Collins's representations of the pale, blue-eyed, passive heroine and the dark, masculine, assertive (anti-)heroine are of interest in terms of establishing the extent to which Victorian writers, and Collins in particular, were influenced by Lavater's theories, they nevertheless appear to represent relatively conventional and common use of physiognomical ideas in Victorian fiction. Of greater interest in terms of Collins's engagement with physiognomy are his less conventional descriptions of central female characters, which, as

Lucy Hartley observes, "frustrate the expectations of the observer" (Hartley 2001, 131). Of particular significance are Collins's depictions of fallen women, whom he frequently idealises, contrary to Victorian notions of morality and femininity. Sally in *The Fallen Leaves* (1879), for example, is similar in appearance to Collins's conventional heroines, with light brown hair (Collins 1879, 282) and "eyes, of the purest and loveliest blue" (ibid., 273), thus her appearance links her with the Victorian ideal of femininity. Indeed, the narrative actually describes her as "the true ideal", commenting that "Raphael himself might have painted [her]" (ibid.), a comparison which is also made with reference to *Hide and Seek*'s Madonna and Lucilla in *Poor Miss Finch* (1872)– both conventional, and, it seems, sexually pure, heroines. Sally, however, is working as a prostitute when she is introduced to the reader, thus her portrayal as the feminine ideal is problematic to Victorian notions of morality, although she is indicative of Collins's tendency to depict the fallen woman as a victim. The pale complexion, light brown hair and "finely-proportioned face" (Collins 1873, 6) of Mercy Merrick in *The New Magdalen* (1873), a reformed prostitute, also indicate tenderness and innocence rather than sexual depravity, although her "large melancholy grey eyes" (ibid., 44) suggest both deceit (Lavater 1789, vol. 3, 179) and a "susceptibility to the influence of the opposite sex" (Stocker 1900, 51), thus preparing the reader for Mercy's impersonation of Grace Roseberry, and the positive influence Julian Gray, her future husband, will have upon her. Anne Silvester in *Man and Wife* (1870)–another of Collins's fallen women–appears beautiful in spite of the faults of "a nervous contraction at one corner of her mouth" and a "nervous uncertainty in the eye on the same side" (Collins 1870, 59): the lack of symmetry implying the imperfections in her character. Like Mercy Merrick, she has grey eyes, indicating her susceptibility to the charms of the villainous Geoffrey Delamayn. Thus while Collins idealises, to some degree, the figure of the fallen woman, in the cases of Mercy and Anne Silvester, at least, he provides some visual markers of their immorality.

The contradictions in the appearance and dispositions of Collins's fallen women are particularly evident in the figure of Magdalen Vanstone in *No Name* (1862)–aptly, as her character is a contradictory mix of the unconventional (she repeatedly subverts Victorian expectations of femininity) and the traditional (like so many of Collins's heroines, she concludes the narrative as a soon-to-be, happily married woman). In the course of the novel, Magdalen, after losing her inheritance as a consequence of her illegitimacy, impersonates her governess, marries a man she despises, and repeatedly disguises herself in various attempts to recover her wealth. Although the narrative clearly sympathises with Magdalen's plight, contemporary reviewers were less favourable, describing her as a "perverse heroine" (Page 1974, 131) and condemning the fact that after all her transgression, "she emerges, at the cheap cost of a fever, as pure, as high-minded, and as spotless as the most dazzling white of heroines" (ibid., 143). Critics of the novel were in no doubt that Magdalen's behaviour was somewhat incongruous with her appearance. Indeed one reviewer openly criticised the fact that Magdalen "employ[s] her beauty [...] to grasp back a fortune" (ibid., 132), stating that "[t]here must be coarseness, as well as meanness, in one capable of such actions and expedients as these" (ibid.). However, Magdalen's appearance is not entirely at odds with her behaviour. While her light brown hair, low forehead, the "true delicacy of form" of her lips, the "lovely roundness" of her cheeks and "creamy fairness" of her complexion (Collins 1862, 8) all recall the figure of the idealised feminine, suggesting "a loveable and good natured disposition" (Stocker 1900, 28) and "a sensitive and tender nature" (ibid., 5), other features are indicative of her transgression. Her grey eyes, like those of Mercy Merrick and Anne Silvester, warn the reader acquainted with physiognomy of the deceitful aspect of her character, and hint at possible sexual deviancy. Her capacity for deceit is further emphasised in the opening of the narrative by her love of acting. Her eyebrows, which are "a shade darker than her hair" (Collins 1862, 8) suggest firmness (Lavater 1789, vol. 3, 183) and "force of character" (Stocker 1900, 46), while her mouth, "too large and firm", and chin, "too square and massive for her sex and age" (Collins 1862, 8), recall Collins's description of Marian Halcombe and are "appropriate for the daring heroine" (Fahnestock 1980, 341), intimating her determined and resolute disposition.

In his portrayal of Magdalen Vanstone, Collins offers one of his most detailed descriptions of physical characteristics, and appears to deliberately depict a confused physiognomy, suggestive of contradictory traits, in order to undermine any assumptions the reader may draw about her character from her appearance—which recalls both the ideal feminine and the subversive other. However, given Collins's obvious sympathy for his protagonist, it could be argued that her features are actually intended to indicate her goodness as well as her deviancy—although contemporary critics generally failed to acknowledge any positive aspects in Magdalen's character. It is therefore debatable to what extent Collins uses physiognomy to deliberately confuse readers, and to what degree he intended Magdalen's features to denote what he perceived as genuine contradictions in her character.

However, there can be little doubt that Collins, on occasion, deliberately draws on widely held physiognomical beliefs to undermine and confuse readers' expectations. This, of course, is one of the key elements of sensation fiction, a genre famous for transforming the figure of the blonde angel of Victorian sentiment. One of the earliest and best known examples of this is Mary Elizabeth Braddon's Lady Audley, whose blonde hair and blue eyes suggest she is the epitome of angelic femininity, but who, contrary to readers' expectations, is in fact the epitome of moral deviancy whose crimes include bigamy and murder. The sensation genre's manipulation of the reader's physiognomical assumptions signifies a departure from a more conventional use of physical appearance in fiction. Although Collins appears to use physiognomical descriptions as a conventional literary trope, in several of his novels, his manipulation of physiognomy, through confusing or ambiguous descriptions, ultimately serves to confound expectations about his characters: it becomes unclear whether he expects the reader to infer a character's disposition from his description, or whether their physical appearance is intended to undermine expectation. Thus, Collins plays with widely-held assumptions about physiognomy through his portrayals of central female characters.

In *Armadale* (1866), Collins clearly subverts established notions about physiognomy through his depiction of the depraved Lydia Gwilt–a bigamist, murderess, and fraudster who eventually commits suicide. The narrative's description of the deviant anti-heroine deliberately emphasises her beauty:

> [Her] forehead was low, upright, and broad towards the temples; her eyebrows, at once strongly and delicately marked, were a shade darker than her hair; her eyes, large, bright, and well-opened, were of that purely blue colour, without a tinge in it of grey or green. [...] The line of [her] nose bent neither outward nor inward: it was the straight delicately-moulded nose (with the short upper lip beneath) of the ancient statues and busts. [... Her] lips were full, rich, and sensual. Her complexion was [...] so delicately bright in its rosier tints, so warmly and softly white in its gentler gradations of colour on the forehead and the neck. Her chin, round and dimpled, was pure of the slightest blemish in every part of it, and perfectly in line with her forehead to the end. (Collins 1866, 277)

Critics were outraged by Lydia Gwilt–denouncing her as a "horrible creature" (Page 1974, 148), a "monstrosity" (Page 1974, 156), and "one of the most hardened female villains whose devices and desires have ever blackened fiction" (Page 1974, 147). Their outrage was in no way tempered by Gwilt's physical appearance, and the reviewers' response to her character is of particular interest, as it is indicative of the expectation that a character's moral deficiencies should be reflected in her physical appearance. One reviewer observed:

> She is described as a beautiful, accomplished, plausible lady, approaching middle age, who, after having passed her life in kennels and gambling-houses and casinos and jails, shows no trace in her demeanour of such associations. [...] The criminal dock, the prison, the companionship with a procuress, must tell even on an educated woman who had sunk to such infamy. (ibid., 148)

Another critic, reviewing *Armadale* in the *Spectator*, was outraged by Collins's anti-heroine, complaining that the novel "gives us for its heroine a woman fouler than the refuse of the streets, who has lived to the ripe age of thirty-five, and through the horrors of forgery, murder, theft, bigamy, gaol, and attempted suicide, without any trace being left on her beauty" (Page 1974, 150). However, although there is much in Lydia Gwilt's appearance that, according to physiognomy, contradicts her criminal disposition and deviant behaviour, Collins includes one significant feature in his description of her character which provides a clear warning of her depravity: "[Her] hair, superbly luxuriant in its growth, was of the one unpardonably remarkable shade of colour which the prejudice of the Northern nations never entirely forgives–it was *red*!" (Collins 1866, 277, italics in original). According to the principles of physiognomy, red hair is indicative of vanity and a hot temper (Stocker 1900, 28), and, according to popularly held notions in the nineteenth century, indicated wickedness. Lydia Gwilt's appearance, therefore, is far from that of Braddon's Lady Audley: her red hair provides readers with a clear warning about her character, in spite of her beauty. Collins's decision to include such an obvious visual indication of his character's depravity is interesting, suggesting, perhaps, his own belief that disposition must, in some way, be reflected in physical appearance.

The fervent conviction, held by critics and possibly to some extent Collins himself, that depravity must show itself on the countenance, is somewhat ironic. Lydia Gwilt is partially based on Madeline Smith, who was tried for the murder of her lover in 1857. The popular press leapt to the defence of Smith: "the sympathy for Madeleine was overwhelming", writes Mary Hartman, "newspapers, pamphlets, legal reviews, and even religious publications […] stoutly maintained her innocence" (Hartman 1985, 54). It is particularly interesting that in its report of the trial, the *Spectator* noted Madeline's "most attractive appearance" (in ibid., 82). A verdict of "not proven" was eventually returned and "the decision was greeted with loud cheers in the courtroom" (ibid., 54), although evidence suggests that she was indeed guilty.[3] In spite of such evidence against her, public opinion seemed to adhere to the belief that "young women, respectable ones at least, were by definition not responsible" (ibid., 56) and that appearances were telling.

Towards the end of the century, however, faith in Lavater's theories began to dwindle, and in *The Legacy of Cain* (1889), Collins's penultimate novel, the validity of physiognomy is called into question, paralleling this general decline in the popularity of physiognomical theory. *The Legacy of Cain* tells the story of Eunice and Helena Gracedieu, the former the adopted daughter of a church minister, whose biological mother was convicted of killing her husband, and the latter the natural daughter of the minister and his wife. Fearing repercussions if the daughter of the murderess is identified, the minister keeps the girls' ages secret in order to prevent the identification of the adopted child. The novel thus deals with the subjects of inherited behaviour and human nature, and it is unsurprising, therefore, that it offers some commentary on physiognomy. The most overt statement against physiognomy is found in the opening of the narrative, which relates the story of the final hours of the life of the murderess prior to her death on the scaffold. As in *Hide and Seek*, *Poor Miss Finch* and *The Fallen Leaves*, *The Legacy of Cain* presents a Madonna-esque figure–but she is far from the idealised feminine found in Collins's earlier novels, for it is the murderess herself (with whom the narrative has very little sympathy) who is compared to images of the Madonna:

> Visitors to the picture-galleries of Italy, growing weary of Holy Families in endless succession, observe that the idea of the Madonna, among the rank and file of Italian Painters, is limited to one changeless and familiar type. I can hardly hope to be believed when I say that the personal appearance of the murderess recalled that type. She presented the delicate light hair, the quiet eyes, the finely-shaped lower features and the correctly oval form of face, repeated in hundreds on hundreds of the conventional works of Art to which I have ventured to allude. (Collins 1889, 7)

While this in itself directly contradicts Lavater's theories, the narrator–a prison governor–is even more explicit in his scepticism of the validity of physiognomy, stating that "daily observation of all classes of criminals has considerably diminished my faith in physiognomy as a safe guide to the discovery of character" (ibid.). However, this questioning of the "science" of physiognomy appears to be contradicted by his description of Miss Chance, the mistress of the murdered man. He observes that, "believers in physiognomy might perhaps have seen the betrayal of an obstinate nature in the lengthy firmness of her chin" (ibid., 15). This statement is undermined, however, by the reappearance of Miss Chance (now Mrs Tenbruggen) a number of years later, by which time the "firmness of her chin" has been replaced by a "double chin" (ibid., 232). Upon his re-acquaintance with her, the prison governor fails to identify her because of her drastically altered features, which, he notes, he "had never seen at any former time" (ibid.). While her physical features have changed over time, however, her malevolent disposition does not appear to have altered. Through the changed appearance of Miss Chance, therefore, Collins appears to further dispute the validity of physiognomy by suggesting that it cannot account for changes in appearance caused by the passing of time.

Collins further undermines Lavater's theories in *The Legacy of Cain* through his description of the two female protagonists. Eunice, in spite of being the daughter of a murderess, is the novel's conventional "good" heroine, while Helena, daughter of a church minister, in the course of the novel, betrays her sister by stealing her lover and attempts to poison him when he rejects her. She is subsequently imprisoned for two years before emigrating to America where she establishes a religious cult for women. Thus, as Amanda Mordavsky Caleb will show in the following essay, the novel aims to complicate the idea of inherited evil, and in its description of Eunice and Helena, also contradicts physiognomical ideas. Eunice has brown eyes, a pale complexion and dark brown hair (ibid., 48), while Helena has a "beautiful nose and mouth" (ibid., 152) and a "delicately shaped" face (ibid.). Neither description provides significant clues to their true nature or identity. Indeed, the fact that "not the faintest trace, in feature or expression, of Eunice's mother was to be seen in Eunice herself" (ibid., 195) is clearly contrary to Lavater's assertions that "family physiognomy is [...] undeniable" (Lavater 1789, vol. 3, 128) and that "the daughter partake[s] of the character of the mother" (ibid., 129).

While it is necessary to the plot of *The Legacy of Cain* to confuse the reader through the appearance of the central female characters, the novel nevertheless serves to undermine physiognomical ideas. Further evidence to suggest that Collins came to doubt Lavater's "science" is found in his final novel, *Blind Love* (1890), in which the central female character is described in such confused terms as to render any interpretation of her character from her appearance impossible:

> Miss Henley's chief claim to admiration lay in a remarkable mobility of expression, which reflected every change of feeling peculiar to the nature of a sweet and sensitive woman. For this reason, probably, no descriptions of her will agree with each other. No existing likenesses will represent her. The one portrait that was painted of Iris is only recognisable by partial friends of the artist. In and out of London, photographic likenesses were taken of her. They have the honour of resembling the portraits of Shakespeare in this respect–compared with one another, it is not possible to discover that they present the same person. As for the evidence offered by the loving memory of her friends, it is sure to be contradictory in the last degree. She had a charming face, a commonplace face, an intelligent face–a poor complexion, a delicate complexion, no complexion at all–eyes that were expressive of a hot temper, of a bright intellect, of a firm character, of an affectionate disposition, of a truthful nature, of hysterical sensibility, of inveterate obstinacy. (Collins 1890, 8)

The description is revealing because it indicates that Collins continued to confuse readers with ambiguous descriptions of his heroines, or perhaps even suggests that, at the end of his literary career, he was anxious to dissuade readers from employing the skills of the physiognomist in an attempt to read character.

Collins's work clearly reflects the value of physiognomy as a literary tool. Like so many Victorian writers, Collins clearly engages with Lavater's theories in his fiction, employing physiognomical ideas as a means of both creating and confusing the reader's impressions of characters. In many ways,

Collins's engagement with physiognomy in his fiction reflects changing attitudes towards the subject. On occasion, he employs physiognomical knowledge as a conventional literary trope, reflecting the commonly held belief in Lavater's theories in the mid-nineteenth century. His attempts to deliberately confuse readers through ambiguous physiognomical descriptions reflects the sensation genre's adoption of physiognomy as a means of undermining readers' expectations, while his apparent questioning of the validity of the subject in his later novels is representative of society's declining interest and faith in the pseudo-science. Although the theories of physiognomy have now been entirely discredited, physiognomical ideas remain an important key for reading character in nineteenth-century fiction.

Notes

[1] See Liggett 1974, 185.
[2] For discussions of these, see Shuttleworth 1996, 57-70, Tytler 1994, Jack 1970, Hollington 1992, Tytler 1999, and Tytler 1998.
[3] For further details see Hartman 1985, 51-84.

Works Cited

Collins, Wilkie. 1868. *Armadale*. London: Penguin Books, 1995.
—. 1852. *Basil*. Oxford: Oxford University Press, 2000.
—. 1890. *Blind Love*. New York: Dover Publications, 1986.
—. 1883. *Heart and Science*. Ontario: Broadview Press, 1996.
—. 1854. *Hide and Seek*. Oxford: Oxford University Press, 1999.
—. 1884. *I Say No*. Gloucestershire: Sutton Publishing, 1998.
—. 1880. *Jezebel's Daughter*. Gloucestershire: Sutton Publishing, 1995.
—. 1870. *Man and Wife*. Oxford: Oxford University Press, 1998.
—. 1862. *No Name*. London: Penguin Books, 1994.
—. 1857. *The Dead Secret*. Oxford: Oxford University Press, 1999.
—. 1886. *The Evil Genius*. Hertfordshire: Broadview Press, 1994.
—. 1879. *The Fallen Leaves*. New York: P. F. Collier and Son, n. d.
—. 1879. *The Haunted Hotel*. New York: Dover Publications, 1982.
—. 1875. *The Law and the Lady*. London: Penguin Books, 1998.
—. 1889. *The Legacy of Cain*. Gloucestershire: Sutton Publishing, 1995.
—. 1873. *The New Magdalen*. Gloucestershire: Sutton Publishing, 1993.
—. 1860. *The Woman in White*. London: Penguin Books, 1994.
Fahnestock, Jeanne. 1980. The Heroine of Irregular Features: Conventions of Heroine Description. *Victorian Studies* 24:325-50.

Graham, John. 1961. Lavater's Physiognomy in England. *Journal of the History of Ideas* 22:561-72.

Hartley, Lucy. 2001. *Physiognomy and the Meaning of Expression in Nineteenth-Century Culture*. Cambridge: Cambridge University Press.

Hartman, Mary S. 1985. *Victorian Murderesses*. London: Robson Books.

Hollington, Michael. 1992. Physiognomy in *Hard Times*. *Dickens Quarterly* 9:58-66.

Jack, Ian. 1970. Physiognomy, Phrenology and Characterisation in the Novels of Charlotte Brontë. *Brontë Society Transactions* 15:377-91.

Lavater, John. Caspar. 1789. *Essays on Physiognomy*, trans. by Thomas Holcroft. 3 vols. London: G. G. J. and J. Robinson.

Liggett, John. 1974. *The Human Face*. London: Constable and Company.

Page, Norman (ed.). 1974. *Wilkie Collins: The Critical Heritage*. London: Routledge and Kegan Paul.

Shuttleworth, Sally. 1996. *Charlotte Brontë and Victorian Psychology*. Cambridge: Cambridge University Press.

Stocker, R. D. 1900. *The Human Face*. London: H. J. Glaisher.

Tytler, Graeme. 1999. "The Lines and Lights of the Human Countenance": Physiognomy in George Eliot's Fiction. *George Eliot–George Henry Lewes Studies* 36:29-58.

—. 1998. "Know How to Decipher a Countenance": Physiognomy in Thomas Hardy's Fiction. *Thomas Hardy Yearbook* 27:43-60.

—. 1994. Physiognomy in *Wuthering Heights*. *Brontë Society Transactions* 21:137-48.

QUESTIONING MORAL INHERITANCE IN *THE LEGACY OF CAIN*

AMANDA MORDAVSKY CALEB

The laws governing inheritance are quite unknown; no one can say why a peculiarity in different individuals of the same species, or individuals of different species, is sometimes inherited and sometimes not so; why the child often reverts in certain characters to its grandfather or grandmother or other more remote ancestor. (Darwin 1859, 13)

There is nothing accidental, nothing supernatural, in the impulse to do right or in the impulse to do wrong; both come by inheritance or by education. (Maudsley 1874, 28)

Despite his popularity with *The Woman in White* (1860) and *The Moonstone* (1868), Wilkie Collins faced criticism and disapproval for his last completed novel, *The Legacy of Cain* (1889). In his review in the *Spectator*, J. A. Noble suggested that no work by Collins can be a complete failure; however, *The Legacy of Cain* "is not one of its author's conspicuous successes" (Noble 1889, 120). Even in the twentieth century, critics have maintained disapproving opinions of the novel; Kenneth Robinson considered it to be one of Collins's worst texts, indicating that it "might almost be mistaken for a parody of the Collins sensation novel" (Robinson 1951, 317). In addition to these negative criticisms there is an overall shortage of critical works on this novel; only Jenny Bourne Taylor, in *The Secret Theatre of Home* (Taylor 1988, 237-9), and Piya Pal-Lapinski, in "Chemical Solutions: Exoticism, Toxicology, and the Female Poisoner in *Armadale* and *The Legacy of Cain* (Pal-Lapinski 2003, 119-22), have dedicated any significant time to *The Legacy of Cain*, yet this is limited to three to four pages in each text. For a writer who was exceptionally popular in his own lifetime and has retained a high level of popularity with modern audiences, the reception and evaluation of this penultimate novel seems curious. Beyond the perhaps unnecessary complexities of the text, I argue here that the general dismissal of this novel is due to Collins's approach to the issues of heredity, madness, and criminality, which differ from his earlier treatments of these issues in works such as *The Woman in White* and *Armadale* (1866). In *The Legacy of Cain*, while Collins presents evidence for inherited madness and criminality, as well as fatalism, he does not completely agree with current, popular theories, instead suggesting that individuals have the ability to defy their parental inheritance through individual moral strength.

The publication of *The Legacy of Cain* in 1889 could not have emerged at a more appropriate time given its discussions of heredity and descent. Although Darwin's *Origin of Species* (1859) had been published thirty years earlier, the implications of theories on heredity were manifest in the popular works of social scientists like Francis Galton, Edwin Ray Lankester, and Cesare Lombroso later in the century. Even Darwin reworked his earlier theories for his treatise on *The Variations of Animals and Plants Under Domestication* (1875). In this work, Darwin argued that domestic animals never lose their natural instincts and abilities. Instead, such impulses become latent through domestication; if returned to the wild, domestic animals could naturally and instinctively recall their ancestral abilities (Darwin 1875, vol. 2, 21, 60). Darwin implied that all animals retained the capability of regressing into a primitive state. At the close of the century, many believed that such ideas could also be applied to humans.

While Darwin avoided the term "hereditary degeneration", the scientific community, aware of the impending *fin de siècle*, referred to his ideas to formulate the notion that humanity had not been evolving over the years but rather degenerating into a morally inferior state. Lankester asserted that despite the illusion that society was evolution in the spirit of "Darwinism", it was actually degenerating (Lankester 1880, 59-60). In 1869, Galton argued that morality and intelligence is inherited rather than cultivated, indicating that current "eminent" men are so distinguished because of their "eminent" ancestors (Galton 1869, 1-4). In 1883, Galton applied these theories to form an early concept of eugenics, a theory which suggests that the selective breeding of humans would improve the species as a whole. He claimed that, in criminals, moral deficiency was inherited. For the benefit of society, therefore, a consideration should be made into "the practicability of supplanting inefficient human stock by better strains and whether it might not be our duty to do so by such efforts as may be reasonable" (Galton 1883, vol. 2, 61-2). Such ideas on moral degeneracy were not considered limited to criminal impulses but were also applied to insanity, most famously by Henry Maudsley. He outlined similarities between the criminal and the insane, suggesting that they shared an inherited moral degeneracy. Although Maudsley implied that human will could influence decisions to a degree, he saw morality as essentially limited by a person's ancestry (Maudsley 1874, 29).

Although such theories have sizeable variations, their unifying factor is a use of heredity as a means of explaining mental illness, criminality, and other deviations from established norms (Taylor 1988, 212). Such scientific postulations represent a significant part of scientific thinking at the time *The*

Legacy of Cain was published. To amend these theories, Collins seems to have accepted and rejected various aspects of them, using the novel as a powerful forum for investigating heredity and creating an alternative idea of moral inheritance.

The Legacy of Cain's examination of inheritance, specifically the "nature-versus-nurture" debate, is evident from the onset of the text. The reader is presented with the Prisoner, a woman arrested for murdering her husband and, as the evidence proves, this act was "deliberate and merciless premeditation, [so] that the only defence attempted by her counsel was madness" (Collins 1889, 2). Sentenced to death, the one concern of this woman is the fate of her daughter, which becomes a topic of debate for three men associated with the prison: the Doctor, the Minister (Mr Gracedieu), and the Governor. Using their knowledge of the Prisoner and their "specialist training", the doctor and Mr Gracedieu consider the fate of the Prisoner's daughter. The Doctor indicates that he has been studying hereditary transmission for twenty years and has come to believe that "vices and diseases descend [...] more frequently to children than virtue and health" (ibid., 19-20). The Doctor, echoing Maudsley, represents the scientific argument on the nature of inheritance.[1] He informs the Governor of his fears that the child will take after her mother, a woman in whom "the virtue is not conspicuous, and the vice is one enormous fact" (ibid., 20). The Doctor's apprehensions evoke ideas also expressed by Andrew Wynter in *The Borderlands of Insanity and other Allied Papers* (1875). He indicated that

> the tendency of the mother to transmit her mental disease is, however, in all cases stronger than the father's; some physicians have, indeed, insisted that it is twice as strong. (Wynter 1875, 281)

Despite the fact that the child in *The Legacy of Cain* cannot be fully exonerated of fault, having a violent temper and unmentionable habits, there is a bias placed against the mother. As a woman with no apparent virtue, it is assumed that she will pass her depravity on to her daughter (Collins 1889, 2).

In opposition to the Doctor's medical viewpoint, Mr Gracedieu trusts in religion and his own righteousness as a means of cultivating the child's good qualities and repelling her immoral ones. He explains to the Governor:

> Trusting as I do, in the mercy of God, I look hopefully to a future time when all that is brightest and best in the nature of my adopted child will be developed under my fostering care. If evil tendencies show themselves, my reliance will be confidently placed on pious example, on religious instruction, and, above all, on intercession by prayer. (ibid., 28)

Mr Gracedieu, like the meaning of his name, believes in the grace of God in preventing the child from assuming her mother's wicked traits. He also hints at the scientific debate between theories of nature versus nurture, unwittingly arguing that an organism can be altered by its environment. This contrast between The Doctor and Mr Gracedieu's views on heredity not only reflect the scientific debates of the period but also address the debate between science and religion. While the Doctor does not completely deny that religion has an influence on people, he does not concede that this can alter the impact of heredity. When the Governor asks him his opinion on the influence of religion, he does not deny its power; however, he does not alter his original prediction either (ibid., 21). Such reluctance mirrors the contemporary debate between science and religion: the contest between two philosophies that equally believe in their respective authority (Turner 1978, 357).

With arguments on both sides of the scientific and religious debate, it is, quite appropriately, the governmental position of the Governor that acts as the intermediary not only in this opening prologue but also in the climax and conclusion of the novel. Despite his narrative position as an arbitrator, the Governor does not maintain his neutrality at any point in the narrative. Between this scientific and religious debate, he supports science:

> On his [Mr Gracedieu's] own showing (as it appeared to me), there would be two forces in a state of conflict in the child's nature as she grew up–inherited evil against inculcated good. Try as I might, I failed to feel the Minister's comforting conviction as to which of the two would win. (Collins 1889, 29)

With the Governor's apprehension that heredity might prevail over a respectable environment, the first part of the novel outlines the themes of the remainder of the novel. In order to explore this theme of heredity with the Prisoner's daughter, a control must be introduced for comparison, and Collins does this through the birth of Mr Gracedieu's biological daughter. With one daughter's iniquitous heritage and another's seemingly pious one, Collins sets the stage for a philosophical debate about the validity of inheritance theories.

In typical Collins fashion, the narration of the text, including this opening section, is achieved through first-person shift, a technique he used "to achieve the effect and create the illusion of evidence presented by a witness at a trial" (Ashley 1952, 68). The particular effect of this, in the second section, is to conceal the identities of Mr Gracedieu's daughters. Thus, the reader is introduced to Eunice and Helena entirely through their personal diary entries. Neither of them knows who is older, nor that one is adopted. Mr Gracedieu does not reveal his information until the climax of the novel, leaving the reader to not only guess which girl is the adopted one but also to objectively examine the influences of both heredity and environment.

Collins does provide clues for the reader in determining the identity of the girls; however, this information sometimes proves unreliable, as neither natural mother was completely virtuous. While the murderous nature of the Prisoner is exposed to all the characters from section one, Mrs Gracedieu's character is only revealed to the Governor and the reader. In visiting the Governor to persuade him to help in placing the adopted daughter in an orphanage, Mrs Gracedieu exposes her unchristian values in her hatred for the adopted daughter. The Governor describes her as a "wicked woman", using similar terminology as used to describe the Prisoner (Collins 1889, 35). While Eunice and Helena are sisters through their common parentage, whether adopted or not, their mothers are also sisters in their wicked natures, demonstrating a level of interconnectivity between the characters through amorality. Because of these similarities between the mothers, it becomes more difficult to distinguish who is the daughter of a murderess.

Without any provocation, the girls' temperaments remain hidden, with only occasional allusions to their inherited flaws. Thus, Helena provides a description of Eunice thus: "Eunice in a state of excitement is Eunice exhibiting an unnatural spectacle" (ibid., 42). Moreover, Helena alludes to her own need to keep her true feelings hidden, writing that when she teaches girls in scripture class, "I may long to box the ears of the whole class, but it is my duty to keep a smiling face and to be a model of patience" (ibid., 45). These slight suggestions do not reveal a particular inherited madness or immorality but rather a universal suppression of desires by women.[2]

However, this "universal suppression" relates to the development of madness in women, as perceived by Maudsley. He argues that a woman's aspiration in life is to marry and, when this does not occur, madness can ensue: "In this disappointment of their life-aim, and the long train of consequences, physical and moral, which it unconsciously draws after it, there is, I believe, a fertile source of insanity among women" (Maudsley 1867, 298). Moreover, Maudsley claims this desire for marriage is hereditary, having been passed on through generations of women in their desire to fulfil their natural inclinations (Maudsley 1867, 298). Thus *The Legacy of Cain* initiates a perceived psychological danger to the girls that is also linked to heredity. The girls have supposedly inherited a need to marry and will therefore consider any man as a potential husband; as such, a rivalry is inevitable. This rivalry emerges in the form of a rich, handsome suitor called Philip Dunboyne, who is, unknown to anyone but Mr Gracedieu, the Prisoner's nephew. While visiting the Staveleys in London, Eunice is introduced to Philip and a romance soon evolves. The result of this brings Philip to Mr Gracedieu's house to seek permission to marry Eunice, which Mr Gracedieu refuses. When Mr Gracedieu's cousin Miss Jillgall first informs Eunice that her father does not intend to let her marry Philip, her reaction demonstrates the excesses of her temper: "I felt aggrieved and angry and puzzled, all in one. Miss Jillgall stood looking at me, with her hands still on the place where her bosom was supposed to be. She made my temper hotter than ever" (Collins 1889, 96).

While Eunice initially demonstrates an ill temper, Helena provides a more calculated, criminal aspect in her thoughts about Philip. After meeting him, Helena determines that she is in love with him and must steal him from her sister. She explains in her diary:

> My fatal passion for Philip promises to be the utter destruction of everything that is good in me. Well! What is good in me may not be worth keeping. There is a fate in these things. If I am destined to rob Eunice of the one dear object of her love and hope–how can I resist? (ibid., 114)

Her desire for Philip turns her against her sister in order to gain Philip's affections. She readily admits that she is willing to reject any virtue to achieve her final aim. Interestingly, she also evokes the idea of fatalism, accepting that she is destined to steal Philip from Eunice, thus strengthening the idea that there is a hereditary bond with her mother (whether she is the Prisoner or Mrs Gracedieu–both of whom, as we have seen, were reprehensible women). Helena achieves her objective, and in doing so, reveals the identity of the two girls through their reactions.

When Eunice learns of her sister's treachery, her response demonstrates her temper and inclinations towards insanity. She writes in her diary: "I am trying to find out some harmless means of employing myself, which will keep evil remembrances from me. If I don't succeed, my fear tells me what will happen. I shall be in danger of going mad" (ibid., 136). The need to distract herself from her maddening thoughts is an active means to suppress her maternal inheritance though she does not recognise it as such. Despite her conscientious endeavours at suppressing her mad desires, Helena's verbal provocation rekindles this threatening side of Eunice. When Helena asks Eunice if she regrets not killing her when the opportunity presented itself, Eunice answers "yes". Eunice then attempts to comprehend the motivation behind this answer:

> My own reply frightened me. I tried to find out why I had said Yes. I don't remember being conscious of meaning anything. It was as if somebody else had said Yes–not I. Perhaps I was provoked and the word escaped me before I could stop it. Could I have stopped it? I don't know. (ibid., 138-9)

Eunice's notion that she had not consciously answered yes to her sister hints at both insanity and a double consciousness, which Collins explores further when Eunice is placed in a state of somnambulism after taking her father's sleeping powders. The use of somnambulism in Collins's novels, a psychological effect that he repeatedly employed in several of his texts including *The Woman in White*, *No Name* (1862) and *The Moonstone*. It is a state that allows one character to influence the behaviour of another. In psychological terms, according to John Addington Symonds, "the person sees, hears, walks, has, in fact, the ordinary attributes of the waking state, and yet is not awake" (Symonds 1851, 130). Taylor expands this idea and notes that somnambulism was "placed between dreaming and insanity" (Taylor 1988, 56). The mere application of somnambulism implies a sense of lost psychological control, and in the context of *The Legacy of Cain*, this altered state allows the reader to surmise that Eunice is the daughter of the Prisoner. The use of somnambulism to disclose this information is fitting given that the Prisoner's crime is associated with madness, and her communication with her daughter is an indication that that insanity has been passed on.

This scene, in which the Prisoner speaks to her daughter, is a critical one not only through its revelation of Eunice's parentage, but also through her successful rejection of that heritage. Any wicked thoughts Eunice has during this scene are experienced while in a state of somnambulism; the reader recognises this when Eunice remarks on her inability to control her limbs (Collins 1889, 144). In her seemingly frozen state, her thoughts turn to murder: "My memory of the love which had begun so brightly, and had ended so miserably, became a blank. Nothing was left but my own horrid visions of vengeance and death" (ibid., 145). These thoughts, experienced in Eunice's altered state, along with her earlier thoughts about her mother, lead to an almost supernatural reappearance of the Prisoner. The Prisoner accuses Eunice of weakness, uttering, "daughter of mine, whose blood is cool; daughter of mine, who tamely submits" (ibid., 146). These accusations imply that Eunice is maintaining a controlled exterior in order to combat any wicked or insane desires. The voice urges Eunice to Helena's room, providing her with the words to say and the means to kill Helena. The counterbalance to the Prisoner, and the agent that stops Eunice, is a picture of Philip that hangs around Helena's neck. She pleads to the picture: "One last mercy, dear, to comfort me under the loss of you. Let the love that was once my life, be my good angel still. Save me, Philip, even though you forsake me–save me from myself!" (ibid., 149). This plea to love serves as a means to break the Prisoner's biological spell over Eunice. The prayerful nature of Eunice's entreaty recalls her virtuous nature from the evil that heredity almost causes. This conscious request to retain her morality indicates a permanent rejection of her maternal inheritance.

This is further realised when the Governor visits Mr Gracedieu's house. In his observation of her appearance, the Governor notes that there is nothing to remind him of the Prisoner (ibid., 194-5). However, when Eunice questions him about her character, he perceives the potential for moral similarities between mother and daughter. He wonders, "in the absence of physical resemblance between parent and child, is an unfavourable influence exercised on the tendency to moral resemblance?" (ibid., 201). Despite this fear, the Governor trusts not only in the environment in which Eunice was raised, but also in her individual sense of morality. He believes that Eunice must possess

> qualities formed to resist, as well as of qualities doomed to undergo, the infection of evil. […] I resigned myself to recognise the existence of counterbalancing influences for good which had been part of the girl's birthright. (ibid.)

Thus the Governor also recognises Eunice's internal battle between inherited depravity and virtue, emphasising that there is a manifest struggle against inheritance.

While the novel's exploration of heredity seems concentrated on Eunice, however, Helena is equally susceptible to maternal heredity, and initially seems to embody all her mother's ruthless traits. The Governor not only recognises Mrs Gracedieu's physical features in Helena but her character as well: "As hard as her mother, as selfish as her mother, and, judging from those two bad qualities, probably as cruel as her mother. That was how I understood Miss Helena Gracedieu" (ibid., 155). Both outwardly and inwardly, Helena seems to embody the traits of her mother. Like Mrs Gracedieu's control over her husband, Helena demonstrates a similar influence over Philip. Before she has stolen him from Eunice, she admits: "I have only to show myself, in my sister's absence, and Philip is mine body and soul. […] He is one of those men–even in my little experience I have met with them–who are born to be led by women" (ibid., 115). After Philip is hers, she acknowledges her control of him: "While I keep my beauty I cannot be in such danger as that–let me say, of permitting time and absence to weaken my hold on him" (ibid., 260). Thus Helena uses her feminine charms to maintain Philip's interest; such emphasis on her beauty and her name alludes to Helen of Troy, further highlighting her controlling and wilful nature.

While there is a similarity between Helena and her mother in regard to their relationships with men, much of the potential maternal inheritance ends there. Although both women have demonstrated a dislike for Eunice for their own selfish reasons, Mrs Gracedieu was more callous than wicked, whereas Helena is actually a potential murderer. When Helena suspects Philip of courting Eunice again, she is at first furious and then conniving: "I am strong again, calm, wickedly capable of deceiving Mr Philip Dunboyne, as he has deceived me" (ibid., 276). Her deception turns to murder, as she continually pours over a story on poisoning and steals the doctor's prescription papers in order to obtain Tincture of Digitalis (ibid., 299).[3] While this act may suggest Helena's attempt at restoring her feminine agency from a male dominated world, as Pal-Lapinski has suggested (Pal-Lapinksi 2003, 12), it is highly likely that Collins was suggesting a link to criminal behaviour through Helena's calculated measures. The premeditation of the murder, as well as a lack of any hesitation in committing it, corresponds with some of Galton's observations and conclusions about criminals (Galton 1883, 42), indicating Helena has a merciless nature before she actually attempts murder. While Helena does entertain the idea of allowing Philip to atone and thus save his life, her immoral judgement does not allow such a perceived weakness. Her decision, despite its consequences, is final.

The result of Helena's attempt on Philip's life leads to a final confrontation between Eunice and Helena, as well as a conclusive discernment of Collins's argument on heredity. When Eunice returns to her father's house to help nurse Philip and confront Helena's treachery, she momentarily represents her mother in her resolution and abhorrence. Miss Jillgall describes the change when she encounters Eunice:

> No! it was not my sweet girl; it was a horrid transformation of her. I saw a fearful creature, with flittering eyes that threatened some unimaginable vengeance. Her lips were drawn back; they showed her clenched teeth. A burning read flush dyed her face. The hair of her head rose, little by little, slowly. And, most dreadful sight of all, she seemed, in the stillness of the house, to be *listening to something*. (Collins 1889, 296, italics in original)

This description not only addresses Eunice's physical change but also demonstrates the pervasive internal struggle with her maternal inheritance. Eunice is listening to her mother's "voice", and, because she does not harm Helena but rather sends her away coldly, we must assume she has again won this internal struggle.

While Eunice maintains her restraint when she encounters the cause of her initial internal conflict, Helena continues in an immoral fashion in an attempt to condemn Eunice as Philip's poisoner. The reader is no longer to privy to Helena's thoughts through her diary; however, the other characters' reactions serve to illustrate her wicked nature. When the Governor encounters her again, he describes her malevolent appearance: "It was a ghastly face. The eye that I could see turned wickedly on me when I came in–then turned away again. Otherwise, she never moved. I confess I trembled, but I did my best to disguise it" (ibid., 306). This shuddering by the Governor, a man who was exposed, daily to criminals, implies that Helena's nature is at least as foul as any criminals.

In a final act to avoid punishment and soil her sister's name, Helena accuses Eunice of poisoning Philip, threatening to report her to the authorities. Helena's accusation may initially seem like a desperate attempt to avoid incarceration, but the calculated nature of the charge, as well as her persistent protest of innocence, implies either madness or careful scheming. Ironically, the Prisoner's daughter avoids any illegalities and marries the wealthy Philip Dunboyne while the minister's daughter receives a prison sentence. After this punishment, Collins sentences her to become a feminist in the Untied States, asserting "the superiority of woman over man" (ibid., 326). While this initially does not seem much of a punishment, Catherine Peters notes that Collins

> could imagine nothing worse. One of his last letters to Andrew Chatto complained of "a German *Female* Doctor" who wanted to translate *Heart and Science*: "I felt inclined to [...] tell her to 'go to hell'. But even when a woman is a doctor, she is a woman still". (Peters 1991, 423-4, italics in original)[4]

Collins's dislike of women in positions of authority is reflected in Helena's own opinion of Mrs Tenbruggen and female doctors in general: "A female doctor is, under any circumstances, a creature whom I detest. She is, at her very best, a bad imitation of a man" (Collins 1889, 258). Thus, while Helena's position as a feminist may seem like a success, for Collins it represents not only an exile from her home country but also an adoption of a position of which he did not approve.

The girls' outlooks seem appropriate given their actions throughout the course of the novel: Eunice is rewarded with Philip's love and Helena is punished with the acceptance of a career condemned by Collins. The result of Eunice maintaining her virtue, despite her maternal inheritance, and Helena becoming wicked, emphasises Collins's disagreement with the narrow view of inheritance theory.

In a cyclical fashion, the rejection of inheritance theories is projected through the Governor. When the Governor first encounters Eunice as an adult, he wonders whether Eunice has inherited her mother's depravity, which demonstrates Collins's shift in his use of inheritance theories. While Collins has, up to this point, agreed with contemporary theories of heredity, he seems to be disagreeing with them here by simultaneously accepting that inheritance will influence Eunice and implying that, not only her environment, but also her individual morality has shaped her character. While Eunice is tempted by her maternal inheritance, outside factors, such as love, affect her actions and convictions. Collins thereby rejects the fatalist view of heredity and adopts a notion that recognises all the potential factors that influence a person, which he demonstrates through the Governor's thoughts:

> Moral resemblances have been traced between parents and children. While, however, I admit this, I doubt the conclusion which sees, in inheritance of moral qualities, a positive influence exercised on moral destiny. There are inherent emotional forces in humanity to which the inherited influences must submit; they

are essentially influences under control–influences which can be encountered
and forced back. (ibid., 201-2)

Collins not only argues that heredity is a factor in the composition of a person's
morality, but also seems to suggest that environment and an innate sense of
morality exert influences beyond a person's direct lineage. He agrees, again
through the Governor, "we, who inhabit this little planet, may be the doomed
creatures of fatality, from the cradle to the grave" (ibid., 202). However, he also
asserts, "I absolutely refuse to believe that it is a fatality with no higher origin
than can be found in our accidental obligation to our fathers and mothers"
(ibid.).

Collins's rejection of the popular ideas of inheritance and fatalism may have
been influenced by his reading of Sir Benjamin Brodie's *Psychological
Inquiries: Being a Series of Essays Intended to Illustrate the Mutual Relations
of the Physical Organisation and the Mental Faculties* (1855).[5] Brodie
contends:

> The child is led to seek the society of other children by an impulse which he
> cannot resist, and which is independent of any intellectual operation. But having
> done so, his moral qualities, which would otherwise have remained in abeyance,
> are gradually developed, and [...] the power of distinguishing right from wrong,
> justice from injustice, follows, as a matter of necessity, the result of an innate
> principle, and not of anything acquired. (Brodie 1855, 218)

Brodie's argument relies on ideas of an innate sense of morality, which he bases
on the Christian doctrine that man was made in the image of God and must
therefore possess His sense of morality (Brodie 1855, 218-9). While Collins was
an opponent of religious cant, and to some extent organised religion, the
influence of his father's spirituality continued to impact his life.[6] Certainly
Collins had some religious agenda in mind when he wrote this novel, which is
not only evident by the title, but by the Governor's final thoughts on Helena as
well: "When I think of Helena, I ask myself, where is the trace which reveals
that the first murder in the world was the product of inherited crime?" (Collins
1889, 326). Collins questions contemporary heredity theories through religion,
implying that Cain, the son of Adam, does not have any ancestors that were
capable of the same type of crime. While Adam and Eve were tempted by the
serpent, their misdeed is not malicious but rather ignorant. Cain, however,
murders his brother because of his envy, a fault that is repeatedly emphasised in
the Bible.

Cain could not have inherited his murderous potential from his parents, nor
did his parents teach him to envy and murder. Instead, this desire must have
been generated within his own lifetime, which is the purport of Collins's
penultimate text. While people may possess an inherently good nature, as

Brodie suggests, they may also possess many vices. The Governor's reflection on Helena emphasises this argument. He indicates:

> It was weak indeed to compare the mean vices of Mrs Gracedieu with the diabolical depravity of her daughter. Here, the doctrines of hereditary transmission of moral qualities must own that it has overlooked the fertility (for growth of good and for growth of evil equally) which is inherent in human nature. There are virtues that exalt us, and vices that degrade us, whose mysterious origin is, not in our parents, but in ourselves. (ibid., 326)

Thus, Collins partly rejects the theories of hereditary transmission and proposes that individual morality is a result not of inheritance, nor of environment, but of an individual potential to wreak good or evil. In order to achieve this final decision regarding hereditary theories, Collins creates two characters who have the potential for opposing or supporting the notion of moral inheritance. Collins establishes a case study that demonstrates not only the complexities of the "nature-versus-nurture" debate but also the potential dangers involved in accepting inheritance theories.

Notes

[1] Jenny Bourne Taylor makes a similar observation. See Taylor 1988, 238.
[2] For more see Taylor and Shuttleworth 1998 and Gilbert and Gubar 1979.
[3] Collins's knowledge of this type of poisoning could have come from Alfred Swaine Taylor's *Poisons in Relation to Medical Jurisprudence* (1849) or *On Poisons* (1859), both of which Collins held in his library at the time of his death. For more on Collins's library, see Baker 2002.
[4] The quote from the letter to Andrew Chatto is dated 2 May 1889.
[5] This text was one of several found in Collins's library at the time of his death. See Baker 2002, 82.
[6] See Wilkie Collins, letter to Edward Pigott (20 February 1852 and December 1854) in Baker and Clarke 1999, 83-6, 130-1. In two letters to Edward Pigott, Collins argued against the any unification with religion and politics, emphasising the importance of religion. Collins seems to have embraced some of his father's spirituality in his recognition of the importance of religion, despite the other differences Collins and his father had, particularly with regard to Collins's freethinking.

Works Cited

Ashley, Robert. 1952. *Wilkie Collins*. London: Arthur Barker.
Bachman, Maria K. and Don Richard Cox (eds). 2003. *Reality's Dark Light: The Sensational Wilkie Collins*. Knoxville: University of Tennessee Press.
Baker, William. 2002. *Wilkie Collins's Library: A Reconstruction*. Westport, CT and London: Greenwood Press.

Baker, William and William M. Clarke. 1999. *The Letters of Wilkie Collins*. 2 vols. Basingstoke and London: Macmillan.

Brodie, Sir Benjamin. 1855. *Psychological Inquiries: Being a Series of Essays Intended to Illustrate the Mutual Relations of the Physical Organisation and the Mental Faculties*, in Hawkins 1865, vol. 1, 117-384.

Collins, Wilkie. 1889. *The Legacy of Cain*. Gloucestershire: Sutton Publishing, 2001.

Darwin, Charles. 1859. *Origin of Species*. Oxford: Oxford University Press, 1996.

—. 1875. *The Variation of Animals and Plants Under Domestication*. 2 vols. New York: Appleton, 1890.

Galton, Francis. 1869. *Hereditary Genius*. London and New York: Macmillan, 1892.

—. 1883. *Inquiries into Human Faculty and Its Development*. London: J. M. Dent and Sons, 1928.

Gilbert, Sandra M. and Susan Gubar. 1979. *The Madwoman in the Attic: The Woman Writer and the Nineteenth-Century Imagination*. New Haven, CT and London; Yale University Press, 1984.

Hawkins, Charles (ed.). 1865. *The Works of Sir Benjamin Brodie*. 3 vols. London: Longman.

Lankester, Edwin Ray. 1880. *Degeneration: A Chapter in Darwinism*. London: Macmillan.

Maudsley, Henry. 1867. *The Physiology and Pathology of Mind*, in Taylor and Shuttleworth 1998, 297-300.

—. 1874. *Responsibility in Mental Disease*. London: Henry S. King.

Noble, J.A. 1889. Recent Novels. *Spectator* 62:120.

Otis, Laura. 1994. *Organic Memory: History and the Body in the Late Nineteenth and Early Twentieth Centuries*. Lincoln, NE and London; University of Nebraska Press.

Pal-Lapinski, Piya. 2003. Chemical Seductions: Exoticism, Toxicology, and the Female Poisoner in *Armadale* and *The Legacy of Cain*, in Bachman and Cox 2003, 94-130.

Peters, Catherine. 1991. *The King of Inventors: A Life of Wilkie Collins*. London; Secher and Warburg.

Robinson, Kenneth. 1951. *Wilkie Collins: A Biography*. London: The Bodley Head.

Symonds, John Addington. 1851. *Sleep and Dreams*, in Taylor and Shuttleworth 1998, 130-2.

Taylor, Jenny Bourne. 1988. *In the Secret Theatre of Home: Wilkie Collins, Sensation Narrative and Nineteenth-Century Psychology*. London and New York: Routledge.

Taylor, Jenny Bourne and Sally Shuttleworth (eds). 1998. *Embodied Selves: An Anthology of Psychological Texts, 1830-1890*. Oxford: Clarendon Press.

Turner, Frank M. 1978. The Victorian Conflict Between Science and Religion: A Professional Dilemma. *Iris* 69:356-76.

Wynter, Andrew. 1875. *The Borderlands of Insanity and other Allied Papers*, in Taylor and Shuttleworth 1998, 280-1.

HABITUATION AND INCARCERATION: MENTAL PHYSIOLOGY AND ASYLUM ABUSE IN *THE WOMAN IN WHITE* AND *DRACULA*

WILLIAM HUGHES

Modern academic criticism has been quick to perceive a relationship between *The Woman in White* (1860) and *Dracula* (1897), emphasising not merely the similar epistolary and documentary structure shared by the novels, but also the presiding evil of the two Continental Counts, Fosco and Dracula (Hennelly 1982). Less attention, however, has been directed towards the manner in which both novels embody the assumptions and logic of an identifiable medical discourse–a systematic, physiologically orientated psychology that was arguably as influential at the *fin de siècle* as it was at mid century. The two narratives sporadically depict not merely the psychopathology of the deviant individual but also the culture of the asylum practices through which such individuals were variously treated or contained. Culturally, of course, the lunatic asylum was–and indeed remains–a classic locus of unease with regard to abuse and wrongful incarceration, and this potential is retained openly in *The Woman in White* and in a muted incarnation in *Dracula*. As both novels demonstrate, though, there is a further potential for abuse and manipulation vested within the very practices which organise asylum life, and whose therapeutic import has always formed part of the curative justification of such institutions. The substantive villains in *The Woman in White* and *Dracula*, it may indeed be argued, are not the rapacious noblemen outside of the medical profession, but those professionals implicated in its financial profitability and experimental development.

Through *Dracula* criticism in particular, the nineteenth-century medical phenomenon of "unconscious cerebration" has in a sense been rediscovered.[1] Popularly theorised by the British physiologist William Carpenter (1813-85), the process of "unconscious cerebration" is premised upon the notion that the unconscious mind is effectively "habituated" or trained into reproducing regular and repeatable actions through its emulation of the conscious mind. Once habituated, these characteristic actions or modes of thought may function without prompting when the mind is either unconscious or is otherwise occupied: popularly, the term was used to describe essentially accurate conclusions produced unconsciously and without prompting when the mind is engaged or asleep, though Carpenter also considered the phenomenon to be demonstrable in, for example, the ability of pianists to play complex pieces of music while engaged in conversation (Carpenter 1896, 217). The implications are ideational as well as physiological, in that the actions of the mind may be trained like those of the body. Hence, "every state of ideational consciousness which is either *very strong* or is *habitually repeated*, leaves an organic impression on the cerebrum", and

> any sequence of mental action which has been frequently repeated, tends to perpetuate itself; so that we find ourselves automatically prompted to *think, feel,* or *do* what we have been before accustomed to think, feel, or do, under like circumstances, without any consciously-formed purpose, or anticipation of results. (ibid., 344, italics in original)

In the words of Collins's Count Fosco, therefore: "Mind, they say, rules the world. But what rules the mind? The body" (Collins 1860, 617). It is not merely the chemist, the focus of Fosco's rhetorical question here, that may rule the mind but he or she that manipulates and trains the bodily organs and their reactions, who facilitates the regeneration of that which is "very strong" into that which may be "habitually" undertaken without perception on the part of the affected individual. The mind, as it were, is a limb to be trained physiologically, much as a hand is trained to manipulate a musical instrument.

Such practices were central to the management of the mentally ill in British public and private asylums from the mid-nineteenth century. In essence, the "moral treatment", and later "moral management", of asylum inmates aimed "to occupy patients'" thoughts and to lead them away from the distressing or irrational preoccupations that had led to incarceration" (Smith 1999, 208). Errors of cognition or logic, like errors of behaviour, were discouraged through admonishment and correction, just as approved behaviour was stimulated and sustained by repetition and favourable acknowledgement (ibid., 191-2, 211-2). This is the context of the depiction of both lunacy and the therapeutics of moral management in *Dracula* and *The Woman in White*.

Though *The Woman in White* opens with Walter Hartright's encounter with Anne Catherick, a lunatic recently escaped from a private asylum, the reader is given very little insight into her treatment therein. The reader, though, *does* subsequently learn a great deal more with regard to contemporary asylum therapeutics from the experience of the escaped patient's half-sister, Laura, Lady Glyde, who is incarcerated in the asylum in the former's place, and under the former's name, following the death of Catherick and her fraudulent burial as Lady Glyde. Laura, drugged and disorientated, is accepted without question into the asylum in the guise of Catherick, despite the perceptible presence of some "curious personal changes" and a "modification in the form of [her] delusion" (ibid., 428). This ready acceptance is not surprising, for reasons other than the financial considerations of retaining a profitable patient. Medically, Laura, in her current distressed and drugged state, may easily be conflated with her body double. Lunacy, as a concept, is conveniently signified through a general confusion or lack of reason on the part of the patient, rather than by an individual obsession or symptom. The erratic behaviour of Laura–manifested in her insistence that she *is* Laura and not Anne, as well as her disorientation within the unfamiliar geography of the asylum–may thus link her to the "confusion" (ibid., 23) that typifies the demeanour of the "flighty and unsettled" (ibid., 28) patient. Similarly, any statement on Laura's part with regard to her husband's role in her incarceration would serve to confirm the endurance of a central focus of Anne's obsession, the "maniacally intense hatred and fear" (ibid., 104-5) of the spendthrift baronet, Sir Percival Glyde.

Laura, in effect, cannot avoid being identified with her body double in this context. As Hartright, narrating a story which Laura cannot–or dare not–recall herself, confides:

This was the Asylum. Here she first heard herself called by Anne Catherick's name; and here, as a last remarkable circumstance in the story of the conspiracy, her own eyes informed her that she had Anne Catherick's clothes on. The nurse on the first night in the asylum had shown her the marks on each article of her underclothing as it was taken off, and had said, not at all irritably or unkindly, "Look at your own name on your own clothes, and don't worry us all any more about being Lady Glyde. She's dead and buried; and you're alive and hearty. Do look at your clothes now! There it is, in good marking ink; and there you will find it on all your old things, which we have kept in the house–Anne Catherick, as plain as print!" (ibid., 436)

This encounter with those who have known the patient's body, and the invitation to view the self *as* that body, and in the context of items intimate *to* that body, marks the first phase of Laura's participation in the regime of mental management which will temporarily destabilise her identity. Laura's new–or supposedly renewed–identity is reinforced by the consistent use of Anne's name in her presence, both visually and aurally. Her name is not merely written in "good"–that is, durable–"marking ink", but stands out boldly, "as plain as print"–though, as the novel progressively shows, by way of a misleading death certificate (ibid., 413), an inaccurately inscribed tombstone (ibid., 414), and a forged parish register (ibid., 512, 544), "print", or writing of any sort for that matter is, as Philip O'Neill argues, a far from stable medium for evidence (O'Neill 1988, 112). Leaving this aside, the gesture–and its reinforcement through the presence of witnesses who are intimates of the former patient–

represent an appeal to the past, and to the continuity implied by the current reunion with that past: "all your old things" are here, and so are you.

The stress on underclothing as well as outer garments is equally important. Clothing is an item of peculiar intimacy for the genteel, as well as for those aspiring to gentility. Though Dickens's Nancy may wear Bill Sikes's disreputable clothing without comment or perturbation, it is unthinkable that Lady Glyde should wear outer garments "not composed of very delicate or very expensive materials" (Collins 1860, 21), let alone the intimate apparel of another woman. As Laura Glyde woke up in these garments, which have that woman's name clearly marked upon them, so it is logical to suggest that she put them on.[2] The breach of etiquette, therefore, in itself testifies that she cannot be who she claims she is–Laura, Lady Glyde, a lady in demeanour as well as by title, would not, indeed could not, contemplate such things.[3] *If* she would not dress herself, then would she allow herself to be dressed in such garments, made doubly alien by their ink-authenticated intimacy and their inferior quality? Only such desperate personal circumstances as beset, for example, Dickens's Lady Dedlock, could justify such an act of social cross-dressing–though Laura's desperation here might again serve to confirm her mental instability rather than the truth of her assertions, if it were to be acknowledged at all by the asylum authorities.[4] A completeness, a logical series of relations and consequences, has been set up, and is backed here by witnesses and written testimony. Finally, the Absolute evidential standard of Death is appropriated, much indeed as it is in the enduring "Narrative of the Tombstone" (Collins 1860, 437, 418): if "She's dead and buried" and "you're alive and hearty" (ibid., 436), then your insistence on this identity can only be a delusion.

The implications are clear, therefore. If a lunatic may be, in Carpenterian terms, habituated or educated out of a false train of thought through a regime which continually replaces or reproves the illogical processes and false evidences which support the delusion, then a sane person may, by exercise of the same technique, be tutored or habituated into the semblance of lunacy. It is not a total identity with Anne that is aspired to here: rather, the mere appearance of confusion, the insistence upon an impossible identity and a fixated grievance, are in themselves enough to convey the superficial appearance of an unsettled mind. Laura's re-education will here transform her into a figure which might conveniently be read as a lunatic, irrespective of whether she eventually comes to identify with Anne Catherick. As Hartright tellingly concludes, "she had been under restraint; her identity with Anne Catherick systematically asserted, and her sanity, from first to last, practically denied. Faculties less delicately balanced, constitutions less tenderly organised, must have suffered under such an ordeal as this. No man could have gone through it, and come out of it unchanged" (ibid., 436–7).

This change, though, is not absolute, if the Carpenterian model of the mind is adhered to. Hence, on Laura's escape from the asylum, she is exposed to a programme of re-education managed by her half-sister, Marian, and her declared lover, Hartright. Effectively, the structured home environment functions in the place of the asylum regime, in order to counteract the mental distortion brought about by institutionalisation. Under this regime, all references to and memories of the asylum are discouraged, while a gradual programme of reintroduction to the activities of her past life, most importantly the water-colour painting which links her both to her former home and to Hartright as her former painting-tutor, is undertaken.[5] The results of this regime of mental management, which embraces both a stimulated recollection of the generalities of a past life as well as the observation of a stable present conducted by two trustworthy mentors, become evident later in the novel:

> More pliable under change than her sister, Laura showed more plainly the
> progress made by the healing influences of her new life. The worn and wasted
> look which had prematurely aged her face, was fast leaving it; and the expression
> which had been the first of its charms in past days, was the first of its beauties
> that now returned. (ibid., 570)

Though "she sometimes looked and spoke like the Laura of old times", the evidentially important memory of the events immediately prior to her awakening in the asylum is, according to Hartright, "lost beyond all hope of recovery" (ibid., 570, 574). The "slightest reference" (ibid., 570) to this period, indeed, aggravates a relapse so severe that "her words became confused; her memory wandered and lost itself as helplessly as ever" (ibid., 570). All roads, despite the corrective work of Marian and Walter, seemingly lead back to confusion or mental evasion, and thus, potentially point also to a false identity and an all too real asylum. As soon as the patient is subjected to the pressure of asserting her own identity, she risks again the loss of personal integrity within the self and in addition all pretence of creditability in the eyes of others.[6] Despite the corrective efforts of Marian and Walter, therefore, a sense of finality, or of cure, is evaded, even when Laura becomes chatelaine of Limmeridge. It is only the impossibility of the return of those key figures–Glyde, Fosco, and Anne Catherick–to Laura's world that prevents her (one assumes) ever again displaying the stigmata of the confused mind she once possessed. Her "sane" condition is, in a sense, maintained only by the absence of the signifiers of persecution and the stabilising presences of Walter, lover, teacher, and husband, and Marian, sister, friend, and "the good angel of our lives" (ibid., 643).

No such beneficent support, however, is extended to the unfortunate R. M. Renfield, Laura Fairlie's incarcerated counterpart in Bram Stoker's *Dracula*.

The psychology and therapeutics of *Dracula* and *The Woman in White*, it may be argued, are strikingly similar, though no evidence exists–despite Mark Hennelly's assertion to the contrary–that Stoker was specifically influenced by this or any other fiction when planning his own epistolary work.[7] Stoker's literary (and by way of the literary, medical) influences might well have included *The Woman in White*, though the author might have as easily encountered both the medical theory and a selection of case studies not merely through the popular press but through conversation with his own brothers, three of whom were qualified medical practitioners.[8]

Like Collins's Count Fosco, who is "Attached (in Honorary Capacities) to [...] Societies Medical [...] throughout Europe" (ibid., 613–4), Stoker's fictional British clinician, the alienist Dr John Seward, enjoys the benefit of professional recognition and fellowship. Unlike Fosco, however, Seward expresses an *explicit* commitment to Carpenterian medicine, the latter testified through his frequent (and, indeed, often openly acknowledged) recourse to the process of "unconscious cerebration" in explanations both of his own mental reasoning and in comprehending the neuroses of his patients.[9] Bearing this in mind, it is unsurprising that Carpenterian practices of habituation and re-education are central to the management of lunacy within Seward's private asylum. The comparative experiences of Laura Fairlie and R. M. Renfield, Seward's patient in *Dracula*, are remarkably similar. In contrast to those depicted in *The Woman in White*, however, the asylum staff within *Dracula* are engaged in a malicious and experimental manipulation of their patient, a breach of medical trust that is comparable to that committed upon a human subject by Collins's vivisectionist Nathan Benjulia in *Heart and Science* (Collins 1883, 280).[10]

Renfield has been committed to the asylum by his "alarmed" friends as a consequence of the persistence of his "strange belief" (Stoker 1897, 273) that life might be absorbed, cumulatively and mathematically, by the ingestion of living creatures–the spiders, flies, and birds which supplement the conventional diet granted him by the asylum. Conventionally, this delusion–which is a idiosyncratic adaptation of an otherwise unexceptional principle of economics–ought to be treated by diverting the patient's attention away from the focus of the neurosis, and by proving that the creatures which Renfield aims to ingest carry little or no intrinsic nutritional or energetic value, irrespective of what they themselves have consumed during their lifetime. A regimen of vegetarianism, or a protracted exposure to the energetic value of meats derived, as is conventional in the West, from herbivores, ought to be a first stage in curing the patient's fixation upon carnivorous species, however humble they may be. Renfield, though, is not habituated away from the focus of his delusion but rather, though a perverse adaptation of Carpenter's methods, driven persistently towards the contemplation of his "strange beliefs". Variously styled as Seward's "pet lunatic" (ibid., 272–3), and as "a study of much interest" (ibid., 93), Renfield becomes little more than an animal to be provoked and observed within the alienist's theatre of bloodless human vivisection.

After selecting Renfield from a range of patients, Seward recalls:

> I questioned him more fully than I had ever done, with a view to making myself master of the facts of his hallucination. In my manner of doing it there was, I now see, something of cruelty. I seemed to wish to keep him to the point of his madness–a thing which I avoid with the patients as I would the mouth of hell. (ibid., 93)

Seward's customary practice, as his statement, above, suggests, is to persistently marginalise or evade the "point" of focus of the patient's "hallucination" rather than to dwell upon its presence. This is, of course, an orthodox application of Carpenterian therapeutics. For the sane mind, such an evasion is a matter of personal management:

> For there can be no doubt that while the tendency to *brood upon* a particular class of ideas and on the feelings connected with them, gives them, if this tendency be habitually yielded to, an increasing dominance,–so that they at last take full possession of the mind, overmaster the Will, and consequently direct the conduct,–there is a stage in which the Will *has* a great power of preserving the right balance, by steadily resisting the "brooding" tendency, calling-off the attention from the contemplation of ideas which *ought not* to be entertained, and directing it into some entirely different channel. (Carpenter 1896, 671, italics in original)[11]

Renfield's "brooding", indeed, affects his entire epistemological viewpoint, destabilising not merely personal identity–the level at which Laura Fairlie, in the person of Anne Catherick, is supposedly deluded–but the entire value system that governs an anthropocentric culture. This is a culture based as much on intimations of spiritual immortality as it is upon the species' ability to both perceive and communicate a sense of difference from all other life forms. It is hardly surprising, therefore, that Seward subsequently taunts Renfield with the implication that living beings may have souls, and thus more than a merely nutritional value (Stoker 1897, 308–12).

The nutritional nature of that value, of course, is the sole factor important to Renfield, though Seward's interests lie as much in the explication of *how* the lunatic has reached his conclusion as to *what* he actually concludes. "How well the man reasoned" (ibid., 104), Seward admits of Renfield, who has effectively demonstrated through the calculations in his notebook the systematic workings of the individual logic behind his delusion. The alienist's immediate admission, though, that "lunatics always do [reason successfully] within their own scope" (ibid., 104) suggests that Seward has not facilitated the comparative interaction of his own conceptual and logical "scope"–his "sane" world view, in other words–with that of the lunatic. Indeed, Seward's intention at this earliest stage of observation is not to correct Renfield's delusion but to "test him with his present craving and see how it will work out" (ibid., 103). Such an approach can only aggravate Renfield's condition–a condition which has almost certainly been caused by his "brooding" on such questions of value prior to his incarceration.[12] As Carpenter observes: "It is [...] in the persistence and exaggeration of some emotional tendency, leading to an erroneous interpretation of everything that may be in any way related to it, that Insanity very frequently commences" (Carpenter 1896, 671). The implications of Seward's practice are clear, and the risk that the alienist is taking is underscored all the more by his own diagnosis that the patient is "an *undeveloped* homicidal maniac" (Stoker 1897, 103, italics added).

Seward's diagnostics are at times self-reflective, however, and in the alienist's private phonograph journals the reader may view the practitioner's record of his own obsessive behaviour, set down in much the same way as Renfield's tabulation of his diet. As in Renfield's consumption of food, so Seward's hunger for scientific data appears sane according to its own logic. There is a perceptible uneasiness, though, in his own assessment of his brilliance as an experimentalist. Speaking of Renfield, whose obsession he has for a while inhibited, he speculates:

> What would have been his later steps? It would almost be worth while to complete the experiment. It might be done if there were only a sufficient cause. Men sneered at vivisection, and yet look at its results today! Why not advance science in its most difficult and vital aspect–the knowledge of the brain? Had I even the secret of one such mind–did I hold the key to the fancy of even one lunatic–I might advance my own branch of science to a pitch compared with which Burdon-Sanderson's physiology or Ferrier's brain knowledge would be as nothing. If only there were a sufficient cause! I must not think too much of this, or I may be tempted; a good cause might turn the scale with me, for may not I too be of an exceptional brain, congenitally? (ibid., 104)

Seward's desire for a "cause" or justification for his continued aggravation of Renfield's potentially homicidal psychopathology must be read in the context of the alienist's earlier assessment of his patient. Renfield is

> a possibly dangerous man, probably dangerous if unselfish. In selfish men caution is as secure an armour for their foes as for themselves. What I think of on this point is, when self is the fixed point the centripetal force is balanced with the centrifugal: when duty, a cause, etc., is the fixed point, the latter force is paramount, and only accident or a series of accidents can balance it. (ibid., 93–4)

Seward, too, treads a finely balanced line between altruism and egotism, between the personal and the professional. Given that the alienist enters into his own "cruel" research for the sole purpose of distracting himself following the refusal of his marriage proposal by Lucy Westenra–"my rebuff of yesterday" (ibid., 93), as he styles it–his ambition is at least initially inhibited by the position of the "self" as the fixed point. Should Seward's ambition, reinforced by his success in interpreting Renfield's monomania, overcome this, then the alienist, too, may not so much "be tempted" as fall without realising it into an obsession which parallels that of his patient. Irrespective of this, the patient, as it were, may be sacrificed to Seward's "duty" as a physician, and the impersonal "cause" represented by an enhanced public health.

Only high-minded excuses such as those based upon duty or the greater good can make vivisection, as Seward himself implies above, if not acceptable then at least justifiable. The names of John Burdon-Sanderson and David Ferrier, British experimental physicians evoked as the current guardians of the boundaries of medical science by Seward, are significant in this context. Both were associated in the popular mind with the practice of vivisection, the latter being prosecuted–and acquitted–under the Cruelty to Animals Act in 1881.[13] Both, as it were, compromised their humanity through a programme of open-ended experimentation which separated the human from the animal, manipulating and mutilating one for the alleged benefit of the other. It is the self, seemingly, that is dehumanised, desensitised, as it in turn separates human selfhood from the lower species which, ironically, when dissected yield information relevant to the human condition. Though not actively a vivisectionist, Seward is implicitly condemned by the congruence which his research bears to that of those who inflict pain on animals. Seward's drive, though, to recognise his experimental subject's humanity further condemns him as a physician in breach of his Hippocratic Oath, one who encourages pain and suffering without any intention of effecting a cure. It is small wonder that Seward feels uneasy about his work or, indeed, about his implicit extension of the justification of vivisection to his own work on the human subject.

It is only when a more "human" and personal "duty"–the abstract defence of womanhood which is enjoined upon a gentleman, and the specific defence of two women of his acquaintance, Lucy Westenra and Mina Harker–eclipses the experimental "cause" that Seward becomes associated with the therapeutic and curative aspects of medicine. This is Seward's own fixed point, as it were. The physician's sense of unease, and the frequency with which he agitates his patient, markedly decrease as his interests are directed elsewhere, first to Lucy then to Mina. Notably, Renfield's battered, though still living, body is discarded with almost indecent haste as soon as the physician and his circle have extracted from it the last fatal confession which ties the lunatic to the predatory vampire (ibid., 321). He dies alone (ibid., 325), and Seward is happy to conclude his case, and Renfield's life, with a fraudulent "certificate of death by misadventure in falling from bed" (ibid., 330) which exonerates the physician from all complicity in the undue development of the lunatic's fatal obsession. A cause which is external yet close to the self, as it were, saves Seward from becoming too much like his patient, and dissipates the "brooding" upon a problem in psychopathology occasioned by his failure in love. Fortified by such a cause, he need not brood, either, on his professional misconduct. Whatever the case, though, such equivocal feelings of unease are not displayed by the staff of the asylum in which Laura Fairlie is incarcerated in *The Woman in White*. They, unlike Seward, do not knowingly abuse the patients entrusted into their care.

The uneasy interface between curative therapy and manipulative abuse thus links *The Woman in White* and *Dracula*, two novels published some forty years apart. It would be reductive to suggest that a direct lineage of literary inspiration connects the latter to the former, though it might justifiably be argued that the two are mobilised through the presence of a medical discourse as accessible to Stoker as it had been to Collins. Significantly, though, the implications of how this discourse is applied by the responsible staff within the two asylums ethically and morally divides the two novels as effectively as similarity of therapeutics unites them. Conventionally, in *The Woman in White*, the asylum is associated with the wrongful incarceration of the innocent and the apparently sane, "the most horrible of false imprisonments" (Collins 1860, 28), as Hartright phrases it after his initial encounter with Anne Catherick. There is no suggestion in *Dracula*, in contrast, other than by way of two momentary periods of unwonted lucidity, that Renfield is in any way inappropriately detained within Seward's establishment. Yet the two mental institutions do occupy moral and ethical spaces diametrically opposed to each other and, indeed, under close scrutiny, might be said to exchange places with regard to their status as locations under which acts of abuse may be knowingly perpetrated by practitioners upon patients. In *The Woman in White*, the asylum is effectively neutral, its negative function in the lives of both Anne and Laura originated not by its own management but as a consequence of the machinations of those outside of the medical profession. It is Glyde's money and influence that first ensures Anne's committal, and the same factors, allied to Fosco's ingenuity and chemical skill, that ensures that Laura takes her place. In the case of Laura, there is no suggestion of cruelty, and no implication that the staff are knowingly attempting to impose a false identity upon their patient. They are merely acting as if the patient is who the legal and medical authorities say she is. At most, the culpability of the asylum-keeper is vested in his inability to see beyond the most obvious symptom displayed by the newcomer, her disordered state of mind. In *Dracula*, though, the abuse is knowingly and deliberately undertaken by the presiding physician, who not merely sees the state of mind but fosters it in the face of all risks and with a total disregard for the humanity of his subject. There is no mistake and, indeed, no excuse either. Seward–vain, egocentric, arrogant, and ambitious–is villainous in a way his counterpart in *The Woman in White* may never be.

Notes

[1] See, for example, Glover 1996, 76–8, Hughes 2000, 142–7, Greenway 1986. Byron's excellent annotated edition of *Dracula* incorporates an extract from William Carpenter's seminal chapter on the phenomenon of "unconscious cerebration", as published in the 1874 edition of his *Principles of Mental Physiology*: see Stoker 1897, 458–61.

[2] It is later revealed, in the confession of Count Fosco, that Laura's "own clothes were taken away from her at night, and Anne Catherick's were put on her in the morning, with the strictest regard to propriety, by the matronly hands of the good Rubelle" (Collins 1860, 626).

[3] As if to recall this episode of social cross-dressing, Count Fosco, himself the perfect European nobleman, dresses as "a French artisan" in order–unsuccessfully–to evade his former Italian associates (Collins 1860, 640).

[4] See Dickens 1853, 260-1, 363-4.

[5] The encouragement of these accomplishments again recall those imposed upon the patient by conventional asylum practice, in that they are appropriate to her gender and social class. No doubt, had Laura remained in the asylum, she would have found herself engaged in the practical needlework of the lower classes rather than the decorative arts of the gentry. See Taylor 1988, 38. Intriguingly, Laura's later attempts to sell her artwork through Walter's agency, however deluded, rather compromise her gentility.

[6] On the fragility of identities produced under Moral Management, see Taylor 1988, 31.

[7] See Hennelly 1982, 15. The two authors did, however, share a common acquaintance in the Manx novelist Hall Caine (1853–1931), the dedicatee of *Dracula*. See Gasson 1998, 25, 67.

[8] Stoker's eldest brother, William Thornley Stoker, was President of the Royal College of Surgeons in Ireland, George Stoker served as a surgeon in the Turkish Army prior to his return to practice in the United Kingdom, and Richard Stoker was engaged in the Indian Medical Service. See Belford 1996, 25. While resident in Dublin, Stoker shared houses not merely with William, Richard, and George but also with the playwright John Todhunter, who had practised medicine in the Irish capital between 1870–4. See Haining and Tremayne 1997, 88, 91.

[9] See, for example, Seward's growing conviction that Renfield's eccentric diet is governed by a form of systematic logic, a logic which Seward understands incompletely at first but gradually comprehends as his mind digests the problem while he is occupied with his other patients and, indeed, his own personal disappointments. See Stoker 1897, 102.

[10] Nathan Benjulia is constructed as an experimental physician who, in part at least, reaches conclusions with regard to his experiments through "unconscious cerebration" (Collins 1883, 271), a detail which links him to Seward.

[11] Carpenter's approach, of course, is hardly novel. Similar strategies had been applied with some success by Pinel and his followers in France, following the cultural change of the French Revolution. The British culture of moral management, heavily influenced by the work of the York retreat, was broadly in agreement with this. Writing in 1813, however, Samuel Tuke notes that attempts "to refute their [the lunatics'] notions, generally irritates them, and rivets the false perception more strongly on their mind". See Tuke 1813, 240.

[12] Indeed, Seward specifically records how Renfield "sits in the corner *brooding*, with a dull, sullen, woe-begone look in his face", following one of his occasional outbursts of violence. See Stoker 1897, 151, italics added.

[13] The issue of vivisection, as Valerie Pedlar observes, links the writings of Collins and Stoker. Where Stoker's condemnation of Seward's avowedly self-serving experimentation is implicit, Collins produces "an unashamed piece of polemic cast in fictional form" in the portrayal of the vivisectionist, Nathan Benjulia, in *Heart and Science* (1883). Pedlar's article makes valid comparison between *Dracula* and *Heart and Science*, particularly in the abuse of the human subject when alive, dead or–in Stoker's case–un-dead. See Pedlar 2003, 172, 173-4. For further information on Ferrier and Burdon-Sanderson see Jann 1989, 277 and n.12.

Works Cited

Belford, Barbara. 1996. *Bram Stoker: A Biography of the Author of Dracula*. London: Weidenfeld and Nicolson.

Carpenter, William B. 1896. *Principles of Mental Physiology, With their Applications to the Training and Discipline of the Mind and the Study of its morbid Conditions*. London: Kegan Paul, Trench, Trübner and Company.

Collins, Wilkie. 1860. *The Woman in White*. Oxford: Oxford University Press, 1996.

—. 1883. *Heart and Science: A Story of the Present Time*. Peterborough: Broadview, 1996.

Dickens, Charles. 1853. *Bleak House*. London: Penguin Books, 2003.

Gasson, Andrew. 1998. *Wilkie Collins: An Illustrated Guide*. Oxford: Oxford University Press.

Glover, David. 1996. *Vampires, Mummies and Liberals: Bram Stoker and the Politics of Popular Fiction*. Durham: Duke University Press.

Greenway, John L. 1986. Seward's Folly: *Dracula* as a Critique of "Normal Science". *Stanford Literature Review*, 3:213-30.

Haining, Peter. and Peter Tremayne. 1997. *The Un-Dead: The Legend of Bram Stoker and Dracula*. London: Constable.

Hennelly, Mark M. 1982. Twice-Told Tales of Two Counts: *The Woman in White* and *Dracula*. *Wilkie Collins Society Journal* 2:15-31.

Hughes, William. 2000. *Beyond Dracula: Bram Stoker's Fiction and its Cultural Context*. Basingstoke: Macmillan.

Ingram, Allan (ed.). 1998. *Patterns of Madness in the Eighteenth Century: A Reader*. Liverpool: Liverpool University Press.

Jann, R. 1989. Saved by Science? The Mixed Metaphors of Stoker's *Dracula*. *Texas Studies in Literature and Language* 31:273-87

O'Neill, Philip. 1988. *Wilkie Collins: Women, Property and Propriety*. Basingstoke: Macmillan.

Pedlar, Valerie. 2003. Experimentation or Exploitation? The Investigations of David Ferrier, Dr Benjulia, and Dr Seward. *Interdisciplinary Science Reviews* 28:169-74.

Smith, Leonard D. 1999. *"Cure, Comfort and Safe Custody": Public Lunatic Asylums in early Nineteenth-Century England*. London: Leicester University Press.

Stoker, Bram. 1897. *Dracula*. Peterborough: Broadview, 2000.

Taylor, Jenny Bourne. 1988. *In The Secret Theatre of Home: Wilkie Collins, Sensation Narrative and Nineteenth-Century Psychology*. London: Routledge.

Tuke, Samuel. 1813. Moral Treatment. Section II. Of the Means of Assisting the Patient to Control Himself, in Ingram 1998, 235-45.

HEART AND SCIENCE AND VIVISECTION'S THREAT TO WOMEN

GRETA DEPLEDGE

It is, indeed, obvious that to found diagnosis exclusively on objective symptoms, is to treat human beings as if they were dumb animals, and to degrade medicine to the level of veterinary surgery. (Anon. 1871, 690)

The purpose of this essay is to provide a re-examination of Wilkie Collins's much-underrated 1883 novel *Heart and Science*. *Heart and Science* is a work of fiction that has many of the traits we associate with a classic Collins novel: there is mystery and intrigue; a defenceless heroine, Carmina; an absent hero, Ovid; and a mysterious and dangerous stranger, Dr Benjulia. *Heart and Science* is a page-turner with battles over inheritance, allegations of illegitimacy, and the constant threat of danger for the central heroine. It has, therefore, all the feverish qualities we have come to expect from a Collins novel yet it has not always received positive reviews.[1] The novel's preoccupation with the vivisection debate has been the reason for much of the negative criticism it has received. However, I would suggest the configuration of the perceived threat to women by the vivisecting doctor as portrayed in *Heart and Science* is intrinsic to its dramatic momentum. Collins accurately pinpoints fears and concerns that were at the very heart of the nineteenth-century vivisection debate: the extension of vivisection from animals to humans; the allegedly dehumanizing effect vivisection would have on its practitioners; and the professed futility of vivisection given the physiological differences between animals and humans. All of these fears are dramatised through the interactions of Dr Benjulia and several of the female characters.[2] This essay will discuss how Collins has configured a very accurate depiction of the concerns that were voiced about the vulnerability of women to medical malpractice and how women were seen as the potential victims of the experimental vivisectionist.

In *Heart and Science* Collins depicts a classic nineteenth-century figure–the hysteric–in his central heroine Carmina. Through his use of this long-established figure we see the dangers Victorian women faced at the hands of career-advancing experimental physicians. It is well proven that women were at the mercy of medical practitioners in the nineteenth century, a time of rapid advance in the specialisation of diseases for women and their treatment. The pathologisation of women's behaviour and bodies accelerated rapidly throughout the century and improved asepsis techniques made it a time when women were "under the knife" more than ever (Dally 1991, 146-84).[3] The hysteric was, arguably, one of the most pathologised and at-risk groups of the period. The experimental procedures of clitoridectomy and oophorectomy, as possible "cures" for hysteria, sensationally illustrate how vulnerable women were to the vogue of "cutting to cure".

Therefore, because new surgical cures for female maladies were, by definition, experimental, there is little wonder that women began to identify with the "dumb animals" pinned to the vivisector's table. Women were repeatedly branded as one of the groups most vulnerable to vivisection: "It's worst feature is that it falls with peculiar severity on the helpless, the long-suffering, the innocent, on the dumb animals, on women and on little children" (Shiell 1903, 3). Furthermore, there was a very real fear that experimentation on animals would lead to experimentation on humans throughout the nineteenth century. In the Second Royal Commission on Vivisection in 1906, the Secretary of the Personal Rights Commission gave evidence that "these experiments are not confined to animals [...] they have always been performed on human beings" (Westacott 1949, 496). Furthermore, T. Spencer Wells, who was an active supporter of the need to experiment on animals (as necessary for the advancement of surgery), wrote, in 1879, of the advances that had been made possible due to experiments on animals. He referred to some of his lectures "which may show what is thought (by men capable of judging) of the value of improvements learned by experiments on a few animals, which could not have been learned so well in many years instead of a few weeks, even by experimenting on women" (Wells 1882, 6).

Clearly, the progression from animal to human experimentation had already happened in the form of experimental gynaecological surgery. This is clear in the following quotation concerning ovariotomy: "One can hardly understand the so-called reasoning which insists that this [advancement of a particular aspect of the ovariotomy operation] should not be demonstrated once and for all in a few narcotised animals, but that we should grope our way to the realisation of the truth through he sufferings and by the dissection of a series of women" (ibid., 39-40). Indeed it is the operation of oophorectomy that provides the most valuable example of the link between vivisection and women and, while there is no direct reference to surgical procedures in Collins's novel, Benjulia, as an established specialist in nervous diseases, would have been familiar with the experimental treatments women were subjected to. An awareness of the surgical threat that became a reality to Carmina's real-life sisters enables the reader of *Heart and Science* to appreciate the extent of the danger that surrounds her as the novel progresses.

The movement from animal to human vivisection seems to have been epitomised by oophorectomy, and medical journals from the period clearly illustrate how many "experts" could not separate the human from the animal when discussing this procedure. In the *British Gynaecological Journal* of 1890 we read the following: "To unsex a woman is surely to maim or affect injuriously the integrity of her nervous system. Observations of the effect of castration and spaying animals might throw some light upon this question. Appeal may be made to the experience of veterinary surgery to help" (Barnes 1890, 400). The article goes on to state that "gynaecology is largely surgical [...]. Surgery of the brain and spinal cord, and of the abdominal and pelvic cavities, is at once experimental and therapeutical. It is vivisection of the noblest kind" (ibid., 392).

It is fears surrounding the association of human medicine and vivisection that Collins exploits in *Heart and Science*. Benjulia's interaction with the hysterical Carmina, Zo, and his cook become the medium through which Collins subtly explores aspects of the vivisection movement.[4] Collins portrays Benjulia as a cold, calculating character who seems to epitomise all that women feared in the medical profession. He appears desensitised, and delights in observing and provoking the women in the novel. He observes, tests, and experiments with Zo, Carmina and his cook and appeases his scientific desires with their responses. Furthermore, he illustrates just how resourceful this vulnerable group—women—could be.

Benjulia's youngest "victim" is Zo, half-sister of Ovid. Collins's introduction of Zo instantly characterises her as vulnerable; she is a child in a somewhat dysfunctional family and is apparently defenceless. She also displays a lack of obvious intelligence that adds to her vulnerability (although she is remarkably perceptive). Zo personifies the categories that were seen to justify experimentation on humans—female, child, and idiot: "Mr Gallilee turned to his youngest daughter—aged ten, and one of the unsuccessful products of the age we live in. This was a curiously slow, quaint, self-contained child; the image of her father, with an occasional reflection of his smile; incurably stupid" (Collins 1883, 64).

Benjulia treats Zo just like one of the dumb animals that he conducts experiments on:

> When men in general thoroughly enjoy the pleasure of talking nonsense to children, they can no more help smiling than they can help breathing. The doctor was an extraordinary exception to this rule; his grim face never relaxed—not even when Zo reminded him that one of his favourite recreations was tickling her. She obeyed, however, with the curious appearance of reluctant submission showing

itself once more. He put two of his soft big finger-tips on her spine, just below the back of her neck, and pressed on the place. Zo started and wriggled under his touch. He observed her with as serious an interest as if he had been conducting a medical experiment. "That's how you make our dog kick with his leg", said Zo, recalling her experience of the doctor in the society of the dog.

"How do you do it?"

"I touch the Cervical Plexus", Dr Benjulia answered as gravely as ever.

This attempt at mystifying the child failed completely. Zo considered the unknown tongue in which he had answered her as being equivalent to lessons. She declined to notice the Cervical Plexus, and returned to the little terrier at home. "Do you think the dog likes it?" she asked.

"Never mind the dog. Do *you* like it?" (ibid., 96)

Benjulia's experiments extend to taking even greater liberties with other females in the novel. The tormenting of his cook can be read as a great comic scene. However, Collins makes explicit the fact that Benjulia is "experimenting" on her, and our knowledge of the bloody experiments he conducts in his laboratory raises the tension. Benjulia is angry with his cook for sending his supper in late; the reason for her tardiness is that she had become distracted, reading a romantic novel. The romance on the pages of the novel, named as Samuel Richardson's *Pamela* (1740), has clearly affected the cook, when summoned to Benjulia's study she ponders: "Why had she not thought of going upstairs first, just to see whether she looked her best in the glass? Would he begin by making a confession? or would he begin by kissing her?" (ibid., 213). Benjulia torments this woman. He is astute enough to be aware of the foolish, romantic notions that have filled her head. She, however, little suspects what is going through his mind: "If she had seen the doctor at his secret work in the laboratory, the change in him might have put her on her guard. He was now looking (experimentally) at the inferior creature seated before him in the chair, as he looked (experimentally) at the other inferior creatures stretched under him on the table" (ibid., 215).

Benjulia dismisses his cook for her poor housekeeping and impudent manner. (In her excitement at the fancied proposal she had dared to fling her arms around his neck.) When Benjulia laughs at the game he has played on cook "the cook's fury in its fiercest heat became frozen by terror. There was something superhuman in the doctor's diabolical joy" (ibid., 216). Benjulia is thereafter informed by his housemaid that the cook has taken refuge in tears:

> Benjulia turned away again with the air of a disappointed man. A violent moral shock sometimes has a serious effect on the brain–especially when it is the brain of an excitable woman. Always a physiologist, even in those rare moments when he was amusing himself, it had just struck Benjulia that the cook–after her outbreak of fury–might be a case worth studying. But she had got relief in crying; her brain was safe; she had ceased to interest him. (ibid., 217)

While there is great comedy to be had in the cook's romantic notions about Benjulia, and his exploitation of them, the sinister undertone is undeniable. Carol Lansbury reads this scene as an example of Benjulia's sadism. He is, she suggests, "a man who can derive pleasure only from inflicting pain upon others" (Lansbury 1985, 138-9). While I do not dispute Lansbury's reading, I would suggest the scene offers a lot more than this. Collins is wittily satirizing the experimental scientist who is keen to use every available opportunity to study, observe, and learn. He is also underscoring the vulnerability of the victim. Cook is not terribly bright. As a female domestic, she is also beholden to Benjulia. The distinction in class between him and his cook heightens her vulnerability and highlights the class-based fear that was predominant in the concerns over human vivisection. The rich had the luxury of selecting their medical attendants from the poor, needy, and vulnerable. In *Death, Dissection and the Destitute* Ruth Richardson writes: "Medical authorities were loth publicly to admit that patients treated in charitable institutions were generally regarded as experimental material" (Richardson 2001, 47). Cook is representative of the nineteenth-century working class whose limited income would have led her to receive medical aid at charitable institutions with all the alleged risks that this would have involved. She has neither the wit nor wherewithal to prevent Benjulia's experiments on her. Her position as cook and servant expose her to every whim and caprice of her wage payer; the cook, arguably, represents the many women who trusted male authority figures (like doctors) and had little awareness of what was truly happening to them when they sought medical advice.

While Benjulia's experiments with Zo and cook appear vaguely threatening it is the central "heroine" Carmina who is most at risk. Through her illness Collins is able to provide the reader with a carefully woven depiction of the nineteenth-century medical man who specialises in nervous diseases. Slowly the narrative builds to reveal the vulnerability of the female patient and the ruthless, career-minded orientation of the physician who desires kudos, recognition, and honour. To such a man patients are necessary, yet dispensable. Of all the females in this novel Carmina is subjected to Benjulia's most dangerous experiment. She has characteristics which clearly define her as a hysteric. While Carmina's hysteria is not the main theme of the novel, however, it is a plot device that links her to the vivisection debate as a potential site for experimentation.

Carmina's hysteria and nervous sensibility are apparent from very early in the novel. She is rendered "helpless and speechless" (Collins 1883, 57) when she witnesses a stray dog meet with an accident in the street. Shortly after this she faints on encountering her aunt, who is to be her guardian, for the first time: "Perhaps, it was the heat of the room. Perhaps she had not perfectly recovered the nervous shock of seeing the dog killed. Carmina's head sank on good Teresa's shoulder. She had fainted" (ibid., 60). Carmina's aunt, Mrs Gallilee, ponders over the nervous state of her young charge:

> Why, if she must faint when the hot room had not overpowered anyone else, had she failed to recover in the usual way? There she lay on the sofa, alternately flushing and turning pale when she was spoken to; ill at ease in the most comfortable house in London; timid and confused under the care of her best friends. Making all allowance for a sensitive temperament, could a long journey from Italy, and a childish fright at seeing a dog run over, account for such a state of things as this? (ibid., 67)

Relations between Carmina and her aunt are strained from the beginning. Mrs Gallilee sees Carmina merely as a source of income.[5] Carmina is wary of her aunt and a sense of suspicion and distrust pervades the house. Carmina's sensitivity predisposes her to hysteria: "All symptoms of hysteria have their prototype in those vital actions by which grief, terror, disappointment, and other painful emotions and affectations are manifested under ordinary circumstances, and which become signs of hysteria as soon as they attain a certain degree of intensity" (Anon. 1866, 245). Clearly Carmina's sense of insecurity leaves her exposed to heightened emotional reactions, undermining her precariously balanced sense of equilibrium. Carmina becomes friends with Miss Minerva, the family governess. Mrs Gallilee however, resents this friendship and continually seeks to challenge it. Her mechanisations push Carmina to breaking point:

> Somehow, I got out of the room. On the landing, a dreadful fit of trembling shook me from head to foot. I sank down on the stairs. At first, I thought I was going to faint. No; I shook and shivered, but I kept my senses […]. I tried to rise. It was not to be done. My head turned giddy. She must have seen that I was quite prostrate–and yet she took no notice of the state I was in. Cruel, cruel creature! (Collins 1883, 166-5)

Collins accurately depicts a girl on the verge of hysterical collapse. The reader knows that the intervention of Dr Benjulia is, without doubt, only a short time away: "Brains and nerves are Benjulia's diseases. Without quite discontinuing his medical practice, he limits himself to serious cases–when other doctors are puzzled, you know, and want him to help them" (ibid., 97). The depiction Collins gives of a clearly vulnerable and relatively defenceless girl, at the mercy of the ministrations of such a sinister figure as Dr Benjulia, is a brilliant representation of some of the worst fears that were expressed by the anti-vivisectionists.

Dr Benjulia's interest in vivisection is implicit from the very beginning of the novel; that he may "experiment" on Carmina raises tension in the text.

Benjulia's investigations on the "hysterical girl" are never what he would call complete. In the following quotation his need for on-going experiments are discussed with Ovid when they meet at the Zoological Gardens. Benjulia tells Ovid:

> "One of the monkeys has got brain disease; and they fancy I might like to see the beast before they kill him. Have you been thinking lately of that patient we lost?"
> Not at the moment remembering the patient, Ovid made no immediate reply. The doctor seemed to distrust his silence.
> "You don't mean to say you have forgotten the case?" he resumed. "We called it hysteria, not knowing what else it was. I don't forgive the girl for slipping though our fingers; I hate to be beaten by Death, in that way" (ibid., 99-100).

There is a sense of work to be done. Furthermore, this tale foreshadows Carmina's future, when her hysteria becomes more acute we wonder if she will "beat" Dr Benjulia as this previous patient did. Shortly after the above exchange Benjulia leaves the zoo with the heavily-drugged monkey, described as being in a "state of stupor" (ibid., 109).

We know what the fate of this monkey will be—what remains of his life will be spent on the vivisection table in Benjulia's lab. The image of the stupefied, drugged monkey is extremely evocative, invoking the plight of the female patient drugged and at the mercy of the surgeon who aims to cure her malady by whatever means necessary, perhaps clitoridectomy, perhaps oophorectomy.

The monkey dies in Benjulia's laboratory and the primate's death juxtaposes Benjulia's quest for professional glory with the traces of humanity that remain in his ruthless soul:

> My last experiments on a monkey horrified me. His cries of suffering, his gestures of entreaty, were like the cries and gestures of a child. I would have given the world to put him out of his misery. But I went on. In the glorious cause I went on. My hands turned cold—my heart ached—I thought of a child I sometimes play with—I suffered—I resisted—I went on. All for Knowledge! all for Knowledge! (ibid., 191)

Within this harrowing quotation Collins uses a topical allusion to theories of evolution, closely connecting the monkey with the child. Clearly, this direct reference to man's simian ancestry conveys the vulnerability of the human to experimental vivisection.

As the novel progresses Mrs Gallilee's machinations drive Carmina closer to hysterical collapse, while Benjulia continues to watch her disintegrate. He calls one day when Mrs Gallilee is out and so Carmina receives him. Benjulia's "vivisection" of Carmina accelerates from this point. Carmina's hospitality renders her "an object of medical inquiry, pursued in secret [...]. Under certain conditions of nervous excitement, Carmina might furnish an interesting case" (ibid., 243). Benjulia also passes time "vivisecting" Zo:

> "You haven't tickled me yet", she said. "Show Carmina how you do it".
> He gravely operated on the back of Zo's neck; and his patient acknowledged the process with a wriggle and a scream. (ibid., 243)

Carol Lansbury, in her reading of this scene, argues that Benjulia's tickling of Zo, and her fascination with his stick, which she had ordered Benjulia to bring with him, can be given a graphic sexual reading: "Tickling, in the language of pornography, is a synonym for flogging or sexual intercourse, and we have met the stick before in all its manifestations of whip and male organ" (Lansbury 1985, 140). Justifying her interpretation thus, "Collins enjoyed a reputation for depravity that both offended and gratified his friends, and it was rumored that he secretly wrote pornography" (ibid., 134). Lansbury's extensive study of pornographic writing from the nineteenth century enables her to justify a sexual interpretation of tickling and walking sticks. However, Collins was writing this novel for a general readership so I would question an interpretation of thinly veiled sexual interplay between a middle-aged man and a small child. These scenes are designed to raise the tension in the novel, as we fear the depravity of the vivisector, wondering if his experiments could become more invasive, bloodier. Collins's use of language–note the words "operated" and "patient"–indicate that a clinical interpretation of this scene is called for. Earlier in the novel a visit by Ovid to Benjulia's study makes explicit the usual, sanguinary occupation of the scientist:

> His eyes wandered a little aside, towards the corner formed by the pillar of the chimney-piece and the wall of the room. The big bamboo-stick rested there. A handle was attached to it, made of light-coloured horn, and on that handle there were some stains. Ovid looked at them with a surgeon's practised eye. They were dry stains of blood. (Had he washed his hands on the last occasion when he used his stick? And had he forgotten that he handle wanted washing too?) (Collins 1883, 133)

These are the hands that tickle Zo and observe her "wriggling and screaming" reaction. However Benjulia's interest in Zo is puzzling:

> Zo impatiently reminded him of her presence–she laid her hand on his knee.
> It was only the hand of a child–an idle, quaint, perverse child–but it touched, ignorantly touched, the one tender place in his nature, unprofaned by the infernal cruelties which made his life acceptable to him; the one tender place, hidden so deep from the man himself, that even his far-reaching intellect groped in vain to find it out. There, nevertheless, was the feeling that drew him to Zo,

> contending successfully with his medical interest in a case of nervous derangement. That unintelligible sympathy with a child looked dimly out of his eyes, spoke faintly in his voice, when he replied to her. (ibid., 246)

So there is a complexity to Benjulia's character which is seemingly at odds with the threatening, inhuman aspects of his portrayal. The scenes with Zo prevent Benjulia from appearing completely loathsome. Collins does seem intent on presenting Benjulia as a man not completely devoid of humanity. Dougald MacEachen, in his essay on this novel, argues that Benjulia is "merely a melodramatic monster, a kind of scientific bogeyman, the vivisector burned in effigy" (MacEachen 1966, 25). I would suggest that Benjulia is much more than "merely" a monster. When Zo and Carmina have a discussion about love, Benjulia contemplates their conversation: "For the first time, a doubt about himself forced its way into his mind. Might he have looked higher than his torture-table and his knife? Had he gained from his life all that his life might have given to him?" (Collins 1883, 247). These finely drawn moments prevent Benjulia from becoming a monster of gothic proportions.[6] It was argued that a doctor, who was also a vivisector, would become brutalised: "Participation in such practices must harden and coarsen all in any way engaged in or consenting to them, must dehumanise both actors and spectators and disqualify them for the sympathetic discharge of the duties of their beneficent profession" (Shiell 1903, 7). Collins achieves a complexity with Benjulia which shows how the vivisector is challenged, morally and humanely, by his young patient.

However, Carmina's nervous temperament makes her irresistible to Benjulia. As yet his experimentation is non-invasive, his voice and his eyes do all the work:

> Thanks to Zo, Carmina's sense of nervous oppression burst its way into relief. She laughed loudly and wildly–she was on the verge of hysterics, when Benjulia's eyes, silently questioning her again, controlled her at the critical moment. Her laughter died away. But the exciting influence still possessed her. (Collins 1883, 244)

Uncontrolled laughter was viewed at this time as symptomatic of hysteria. In the *British Medical Journal* a case history of a woman deemed suitable for oophorectomy after a diagnosis of nymphomania is provided. The diagnosis was made in light of the patient frequently breaking into "wild hysterical laughter" (Anon. 1881, 921). The critical phase of Carmina's mental illness is reached when Mrs Gallilee challenges her with an accusation of illegitimacy:

> A ghastly stare, through half-closed eyes, showed death in life, blankly returning her look. The shock had struck Carmina with a stony calm. She had not started, she had not swooned. Rigid, immovable, there she sat; voiceless and tearless;

insensible even to touch; her arms hanging down; her clenched hands resting on either side of her. (Collins 1883, 250)

Benjulia diagnoses catalepsy.[7] However, he tells Mr Gallilee to "send for your own medical man. The girl is his patient, and he is the person on whom the responsibility rests" (ibid., 253). The sinister reason for this professional reserve is soon revealed:

> He was not yielding obedience to the rules of professional etiquette, in confiding the patient to her regular medical attendant, but following the selfish suggestions of his own critical judgment.
>
> His experience, brief as it had been, had satisfied him that stupid Mr Null's course of action could be trusted to let the instructive progress of the malady proceed. Mr Null would treat the symptoms in perfect good faith–without a suspicion of the nervous hysteria which, in such a constitution as Carmina's, threatened to establish itself, in course of time, as the hidden cause. These motives–not only excused, but even ennobled, by their scientific connection with the interests of Medical Research–he might have avowed, under more favourable circumstances. While his grand discovery was still barely within reach, Doctor Benjulia stood committed to a system of diplomatic reserve. (ibid., 254-5)

Benjulia's actions epitomise the fears many antivivisectionists had that practitioners of medicine withheld treatment that would cure patients, allowing cases to become more interesting for research. A pamphlet published by the International Society for the Protection of Animals from Vivisection in 1894 stated the following:

> The poor, when ill, or when the victims of injury or accident, have no choice but to resort to the hospital for cure or relief. When inmates of the hospital they have no choice either, but to submit to the treatment there prescribed. Nor have they the means of ascertaining whether that treatment is adopted for their benefit, or merely for the advancement, at their expense, of scientific discovery. (Thornhill 1894, 8)

While Carmina is neither poor, nor in a charity hospital, she is without protection at this time and is therefore vulnerable. Collins integrates the very real fears of the public into his novel.

With the debates around genital surgery raging in the latter half of the nineteenth century, conjecture about where Benjulia is planning to go next in terms of treatment for Carmina is, I feel, apposite. We do not know if Benjulia is a proponent of such surgery so could clitoridectomy or oophorectomy be options he is considering? We are given no indication of these brutal measures being utilised by Collins in this novel.[8] It is only our knowledge of Benjulia as a vivisector that gives a sense of foreboding. However, the absence of clitoridectomy or oophorectomy from this text does not detract from their cultural relevance. We know that Collins deliberately shied away from overtly gruesome material that would disconcert his readers:

> Having given my reasons for writing the book, let me conclude by telling you what I have kept out of the book.
>
> It encourages me to think that we have many sympathies in common; and among them, that most of us have taken to our hearts domestic pets. Writing under this conviction, I have not forgotten my responsibility towards you, and towards my Art, in pleading the cause of the harmless and affectionate beings of God's creation. From first to last, you are purposely left in ignorance of the hideous secrets of Vivisection. The outside of the laboratory is a necessary object in my landscape–but I never once open the door and invite you to look in. I trace, in one of my characters, the result of the habitual practice of cruelty (no matter under what pretence) in fatally deteriorating the nature of man–and I leave the picture to speak for itself. (Collins 1883, 38)

Collins is acknowledging the likelihood of nervous sensibilities amongst his readers and so he refrains from depicting bloody surgical techniques on animals or humans. However, Carmina's nervous debilitation makes her a prime candidate for the procedures that nineteenth-century women frequently faced. Her fate, while less bloody, remains precarious. Mr Null's treatment, ineffectual because of his inexperience and incompetence, brings no improvement. Benjulia is recalled to the case:

> Time (as he had anticipated) had brought development with it, and had enabled him to arrive at a conclusion. The shock that had struck Carmina had produced complicated hysterical disturbance, which was now beginning to simulate paralysis. Benjulia's profound and practised observation detected a trifling inequality in the size of the pupils of the eyes, and a slightly unequal action on either side of the face–delicately presented in the eyelids, the nostrils, and the lips. Here was no common affection of the brain, which even Mr Null could understand! Here, at last, was Benjulia's reward for sacrificing the previous hours which might otherwise have been employed in the laboratory! From that day, Carmina was destined to receive unknown honour: she was to take her place, along with the other animals, in his note-book of experiments. (ibid., 280)

Benjulia has now got the case that, if treated successfully, will bring all the kudos he desires: "I am working for my own satisfaction–for my own pride–for my own unutterable pleasure in beating other men–for the fame that will keep my name living hundreds of years hence" (ibid., 190). Such greedy ambition was an allegation successful doctors often faced. Career success seemed to go hand-in-had with innovation: "Since human surgery established any claim to be numbered amongst the sciences, its brightest ornaments and greatest practitioners have been amongst the boldest, and most indefatigable, experimenters on living animals" (Gamgee 1882, 1). Ultimately Benjulia is prepared to risk Carmina's life. However, the ending of the novel becomes classic Collins, when Ovid, the wandering hero, returns in time to save the heroine with a treatment plan that has been developed without vivisection.[9] Despite Ovid's success, Benjulia's belief in his approach remains steadfast. In a confrontation with Ovid he defends his treatment:

> "You were called into consultation by Mr Null", Ovid continued; "and you approved of his ignorant treatment–you, who knew better".
> "I should think I did!" Benjulia rejoined.
> "You deliberately encouraged an incompetent man; you let that poor girl go on from bad to worse–for some vile end of your own".
> Benjulia good naturedly corrected him. "No, no, For an excellent end–for knowledge". (Collins 1883, 306–7)

Benjulia's triumph is short-lived. Ovid's cure is the result of a manuscript from a fellow doctor, lingering on his deathbed, whom Ovid had met while on his travels. This, fortuitously, provides the elusive cure for brain disease while also being a vigorous condemnation of vivisection. Benjulia is denied the glory he so strongly desires and he takes his own life.[10] Before setting fire to himself, and his laboratory, Benjulia releases his vivisection subjects from their torment. Those unable to survive he destroys, the others he sets free. The freeing of the animals, and Benjulia's suicide, provides the reader with a final symbolic condemnation of vivisection and clearly represents the beliefs of so many of its opponents that, ultimately, it was a futile practice.

In conclusion, *Heart and Science* incorporates the arguments and concerns that surrounded the vulnerability of women within the vivisection debate. The configuration of the female characters provides a challenging literary representation of the complexities that surrounded medicine for women in the nineteenth century and their place as potential sites of experimentation. Moreover, Collins has achieved this within a novel that is full of intrigue, has sinister characters, and superb comic moments.

Notes

[1] Contemporary reviews were mixed. An unsigned review in the *Academy* thought the book had no "polemical value" but was "readable and enthralling from its first page to its last" (Page 1974, 213). Another review in the *Athenaeum* thought the novel "good enough to make one almost fail to notice that it was written against vivisection. Unfortunately the story has a weak ending" (ibid., 215). Another response published in the *British Quarterly Review* in 1883 praises Collins for the preparation he has done to research and understand the technicalities of the subject matter (Farmer 1996, 338). *Heart and Science* has received negative criticism from critics in more recent assessments. William H. Marshall considers it Collins's "most unfortunate work [...]

based upon sentiment and inclination rather than upon understanding" (Marshall 1970, 104). In his biography of Wilkie Collins Kenneth Robinson refers to *Heart and Science* as "yet another failure" (Robinson 1951, 302). Sue Lonoff believes that the novel was "far below his earlier standard" sinking in to a "deserved obscurity" (Lonoff 1982, 78). However, a more recent appraisal by Catherine Peters considers *Heart and Science* "to be one of the best and liveliest of his later novels" (Peters 1991, 399). Graham Law refers to the novel as "the gradual retreat into sentimental Christianity" (Law 2003, 352).

[2] The anti-vivisection stance of this novel has been well documented and it is not the intention of this chapter to discuss either the pros or cons of the vivisection debate or the nineteenth-century response to this controversial topic. For further reading on the history of the vivisection debate in the nineteenth century and a history of the anti-vivisection movement see Rupke 1987, French 1975, Rudacille 2001. Both French and Rupke also have chapters which focus specifically on the role of women in the anti-vivisection movement.

[3] For an excellent history of surgery developed through experimental procedures on women see chapters nine and ten of Dally 1991. She provides a detailed study of the clitoridectomy and oophorectomy debates, the two procedures most controversially used to "cure" hysteria.

[4] Arguably chapters thirty-one and thirty-two, where Collins depicts Benjulia and his brother debating the pros and cons of vivisection, do appear rather heavy-handed.

[5] Carmina's parents are dead and Mrs Gallilee has been entrusted with the job of Carmina's guardian. Mrs Gallilee will be given an allowance to defray the expenses of this obligation. More importantly, should Carmina die unmarried, while still Mrs Gallilee's ward, Carmina's inheritance will pass to her aunt.

[6] In his introduction to the Broadview edition of the novel, Steve Farmer refers to a letter Collins wrote to Frances Power Cobbe discussing Benjulia and the contradictions he wished to portray (Farmer 1996, 10). The letter, quoted in full in the appendix, reads: "I shall be careful to present him to the reader as a man not infinitely wicked and cruel, and to show the efforts made by his better instincts to resist the inevitable hardening of the heart [...]. I [will try and] succeed in making him, in some degree, an object of compassion" (ibid., 370). This letter was originally published in Cobbe 1904, 558-9.

[7] Chris Wiesenthal comments on the accuracy of Carmina's "catalepsy" in her study of this novel: "the description of clinical hysteria offered by the text", she writes, "accurately reflects fundamental principles of contemporary psychiatric thought" (Wiesenthal 1995, 259). Isaac Baker Brown, who specialised in treating hysteria and whose career became notorious due to his championing the operation of clitoridectomy, saw catalepsy as one of the more dangerous stages in the progression of hysteria that could ultimately result in death (Brown 1866, 7). Brown gave the following signs and symptoms as indicative of catalepsy: "muscular contraction" where "perception and volition are lost" (ibid., 49). Clearly Collins's description of Carmina would fit with these acknowledged symptoms.

[8] However, representations of these procedures did make their way in to fiction of the time. Consider the slaying of Lucy in *Dracula* (1897), the disfiguration of Lady Sannox in Arthur Conan Doyle's short story "The Case of Lady Sannox" (1894), and Zola's 1899 novel *Fruitfulness*.

162   *Heart and Science* and Vivisection's Threat to Women

[9] The allegedly less-than-bright Zo had the wit to send Ovid a poorly spelt letter alerting him to Carmina's illness. The somewhat contrived appearance of Ovid just in time to save Carmina's life is a little obvious but does enable Collins to "punish" Benjulia.
[10] Both Jenny Bourne Taylor and Valerie Pedlar look in more detail at the relationship Collins sets up between Ovid and Benjulia as, respectively, good-versus-bad physicians (see Taylor 1988, 231 and Pedlar 2003, 170).

Works Cited

Anon. 1866. *British Medical Journal.* Vol. 1. 245.
Anon. 1871. *British Medical Journal.* Vol. 2. 690.
Anon. 1881. *British Medical Journal.* Vol. 2. 921.
Bachman, Maria. and Don Richard Cox (eds). 2003. *Reality's Dark Light: The Sensational Wilkie Collins.* Knoxville: University of Tennessee Press.
Barnes, R. 1890. On the Correlations of the Sexual Functions and Mental Disorders of Women. *British Gynaecology Journal* 6:390-413.
Bending, Lucy. 2000. *The Representation of Bodily Pain in Late Nineteenth-Century English Culture.* Oxford: Oxford University Press.
Brown, Isaac Baker. 1866. *On the Curability of Certain Forms of Insanity, Epilepsy, Catalepsy and Hysteria in Females.* London: Robert Hardwicke.
Cobbe, Frances Power. 1904. *The Life of Frances Power Cobbe as Told by Herself.* London: Swan Sonnenschein.
Collins, Wilkie. 1883. *Heart and Science: A Story of the Present Time.* London: Chatto and Windus.
Dally, Ann. 1991. *Women Under the Knife.* London: Random Century.
Farmer, Steven (ed.). 1996. Introduction and contextual material in Collins 1883.
French, Richard D. 1975. *Antivivisection and Medical Science in Victorian Society.* Princeton NJ and London: Princeton University Press.
Gamgee, Sampson. 1882. *The Influence of Vivisection on Human Surgery.* London: J. and A. Churchill.
Lansbury, Carol. 1985. *The Old Brown Dog: Women, Workers, and Vivisection in Edwardian England.* Wisconsin and London: The University of Wisconsin Press.
Law, Graham. 2003. Yesterday's Sensation: Modes of Publication and Narrative Form in Collins's Late Work, in Bachman and Cox 2003. 329-60.
Lonoff, Sue. 1982. *Wilkie Collins and his Victorian Readers.* New York: A. M. S. Press.
MacEachen, Dougald B. 1966. Wilkie Collins's *Heart and Science* and the Vivisection Controversy. *Victorian Newsletter* 29:22-5.
Marshall, William H. 1970. *Wilkie Collins.* New York: Twayne Publishing.

Page, Norman (ed.). 1974. *Wilkie Collins: The Critical Heritage.* London and Boston: Routledge and Kegan Paul.

Pedlar, Valerie. 2003. Experimentation or Exploitation?: The Investigations of David Ferrier, Dr Benjulia, and Dr Seward. *Interdisciplinary Science Reviews* 28:169-74.

Peters, Catherine. 1991. *The King of Inventors: A Life of Wilkie Collins.* London: Secker and Warburg.

Richardson, Ruth. 2001. *Death, Dissection and the Destitute.* London: Phoenix Press.

Robinson, Kenneth. 1951. *Wilkie Collins: A Biography.* London: The Bodley Head.

Rudacille, Deborah. 2001. *The Scalpel and the Butterfly: The War between Animal Research and Animal Protection.* New York: Farrar, Straus, and Giroux.

Rupke, Nicholas A. (ed.). 1987. *Vivisection in Historical Perspective.* Kent: Croom Helm.

Shiell, Anthony George. 1903. *Dogs and their Dissectors: Addresses on Vivisection.* Brighton: W. J. Smith.

Smith, Nelson. and R. C. Terry (eds). 1995. *Wilkie Collins to the Forefront: Some Reassessments.* New York: A. M. S. Press.

Taylor, Jenny Bourne. 1988. *In the Secret Theatre of Home: Wilkie Collins, Sensation, Narrative and Nineteenth-Century Psychology.* London and New York.

Thornhill, Mark. 1894. *Experiments on Hospital Patients.* London: Victoria Street and the International Society for the Protection of Animals from Vivisection.

Wells, T. Spencer. 1882. *Correspondence with T. Spencer Wells, F.R.C.S. on Ovariotomy.* London: Pickering.

—. 1885. *The Revival of Ovariotomy and its Influence on Modern Surgery.* London: J. and A. Churchill

Westacott, E. 1949. *A Century of Vivisection and Anti-Vivisection.* Essex, Rockford: C. W. Daniel.

Wiesenthal, Chris S. 1995. From Charcot to Plato: The History of Hysteria in *Heart and Science,* in Smith and Terry 1995, 257-68.

PART IV:
COLLINS AND THE LAW

THE SCOTCH VERDICT AND IRREGULAR MARRIAGES: HOW SCOTTISH LAW DISRUPTS THE NORMATIVE IN *THE LAW AND THE LADY* AND *MAN AND WIFE*

ANNE LONGMUIR

Wilkie Collins's interest in the heterogeneous and the hybrid has become the subject of much critical discourse. As Tamar Heller writes, recent Collins criticism has given "sustained attention [...] to various kinds of hybridity–of race, gender, ideology, class, and even aesthetic value" (Heller 2003, 363). Collins peppers his fiction with androgynous characters, such as the moustachioed Marian Halcombe of *The Woman in White* (1860), and racially mixed characters, like the "piebald" Ezra Jennings of *The Moonstone* (1868). However, critics have not given Collins's interest in the heterogeneous nature of the British state the attention it deserves. This lack of attention is regrettable as Collins's understanding of national identity shares many similarities with his understanding of individual subjectivity. Like many of his characters, Collins's Britain exhibits a split personality as it attempts to repress drives considered uncivilised by Victorian society. Of key importance is Scotland, a country popularly held to suffer from a kind of cultural schizophrenia, its identity divided between the sophisticated and civilised Lowlands and the barbaric and wild Highlands. Collins depicts this hybrid, heterogeneous country as a place that represses its uncivilised and irrational drives less successfully than England. This essay examines how intrusions from Scotland disrupt and disturb the English social sphere in Collins's novels, *Man and Wife* (1870) and *The Law and the Lady* (1875). These intrusions are in the form of legal judgements, as Collins reveals that uncertainty and irrationality infect even that most civilised of discourses, the law, north of the border. This essay demonstrates that Collins's vision of Britain serves not to build and support the notion of a unified British nation, but to undermine it–just as his vision of individual subjectivity subverts the pre-Freudian Victorian ideal of the whole and essential self.

Like Sir Walter Scott, Collins depicts a largely imaginary Scotland. With the exception of references to Edinburgh, Glasgow, and Perthshire, the place names of Collins's Scotland are inventions: Gleninch, Dingdovie, Caldershaws, Kirkandrews. And like Scott, Collins subscribes to the commonly held perception of Scotland as a country divided between the metropolitan and sophisticated Lowlands and the rugged and barbaric Highlands. But while Scott's fiction assumes internal British conflict to be in the past, Collins's novels present the assimilation of the Highlands into present-day Scotland and Britain as less assured. Indeed, Collins sets much of *Man and Wife* directly on the border between the Highlands and Lowlands, emphasizing Scotland's schizophrenia: "The situation of Windygates had been skilfully chosen in that part of the country, where the fertile lowlands first begin to merge into the mountain-region beyond" (Collins 1870, 53). The danger represented by the Highlands in Collins's Britain is not violent rebellion or revolution. Rather, the danger represented by Scotland and the Highlands, in particular, is the eruption of the uncivilised and the irrational into the British public sphere. Just as Collins's characters strive–often unsuccessfully–to repress the "'darkness' native to the English self" (Carens 2003, 240), so Great Britain must attempt to suppress its own internal "savagery".

Jenny Bourne Taylor explores the Victorian ideology of the self in her book, *In the Secret Theatre of Home* (1988). She argues that the "dominant model" of the self was one "of containment and control", which promoted "moral management" as a method by which "a stable, sane identity could be built up by proper training and self-regulation" (Taylor 1988, 31). Pointing to Matthew Arnold's fear of "Barbarians" in *Culture and Anarchy* (1869), she contends that the Victorians believed they could only achieve their ideal of the rational, whole self if they repressed the savage, the irrational and the uncivilised. In part, this fear of the primitive was a result of Empire building, as John Herdman writes:

> The concept of moral evil became associated with the primitive, the savage and the untamed in the human spirit, which contact with the native cultures of newly explored or colonised lands was forcing upon the collective attention, and still more upon the collective unconscious of Enlightenment man. (Herdman 1990, 11) [1]

However, Victorian Britain's obsession with this notion of a civilised, rational self also indicates an implicit fear of the savagery that threatens individual subjectivity at home.

Few nineteenth-century writers play upon this fear of the irrational and savage quite as extensively as Collins. His fiction is dominated by characters whose subjectivities are under threat. He repeatedly employs psychological doubles, from the strange symbiotic relationship of Basil and Mannion in *Basil* (1852), to doppelgangers like Laura Glyde and Anne Catherick in *The Woman in White*. But Collins also extends this fear to national identity in *The Law and the Lady* and *Man and Wife*. Not only does Collins depict Scotland as divided from England, but he also connects the internal divisions of Scotland with the internal divisions of the Victorian self. Like James Hogg's *Confessions of Justified Sinner* (1824), Collins's fiction manifests the sense that Scotland is "a cultural amalgam" (Crawford 2000, 252) at the level of individual, as well as national, identity.

Collins's characters consist of two kinds of Scots, the assimilated metropolitan "North Briton" and the unashamedly unassimilated "rough" Scot. The sophisticated lawyers and gentry of the Lowlands, such as Eustace Macallan of *The Law and the Lady* and Sir Patrick Lundie of *Man and Wife*, scarcely seem Scottish, while Blanche, Sir Patrick's niece, even goes so far as to deny her Scottish roots, during an argument with her friend, Janet:

> "Am I to hear my native country run down, and not to say a word in defence of it?"
>
> "Oh! you Scotch people make such a fuss about your native country!"
>
> "*We* Scotch people? you are of Scotch extraction yourself–and you ought to be ashamed to talk that way. I wish you good morning!" (Collins 1870, 333, italics in original)

Here Blanche attacks Janet for her attachment to a Scottish, rather than British, identity. Janet's unabashed Scottishness is, of course, an uncomfortable reminder of Blanche's own hybrid position in English society. The Anglicised manners and speech of these characters, indicates that they are products of the "internal colonisation" (Crawford 1998, 8) that took place in eighteenth-century Scotland, "in which Scots schooled other Scots to conform to an Anglocentric norm in order to advance in Britain and the British empire" (ibid.). But learning to "pass" as British or English in Collins's world means more than economic success: it also signals a form of "moral management", that is, the individual repression of uncivilised desires and drives.

Alongside these Anglicised Scots, Collins depicts the unassimilated Scot. Anne Silvester encounters such Scots when she flees to Craig Fernie Inn. While Windygates is on that imaginary border between the Highlands and the Lowlands, Craig Fernie Inn, with "mountain on one side and moor on the other" (Collins 1870, 119) is very definitely part of the "Scotch wilderness" (ibid.). The inn and its people are explicitly described as "uncivilised", a "barbarous house, and [...] barbarous people" (ibid., 123). Furthermore, as Emily Brontë renders Joseph's language in dialect in *Wuthering Heights* (1847), so Collins renders the speech of Mistress Inchbare and her waiter, Bishopriggs: "'It just comes to this, mistress', she [Mistress Inchbare] answered. 'I'm no' free to tak' your money, if I'm no' free to let ye the last rooms left in the hoose'" (ibid., 120). While Scots such as Eustace Macallan and Sir Patrick Lundie "pass" as

English by eradicating all traces of Scots dialect and accent, neither Mistress Inchbare, nor her waiter, Bishopriggs, exhibit such internal colonisation, which in Collins's world is also a form of "moral management" of the self. That Bishopriggs should also disclose a degree of dishonesty is therefore unsurprising. Like Mistress Inchbare's temper and meanness, Bishoprigg's dishonesty is a sign that he has not fully conquered the "savage" within himself.

Collins offers us a similarly divided picture of the Scottish character in *The Law and the Lady*. Valeria identifies "'The Sabbath' in Scotland" as a cause of the Scots' apparent split personality. Crucially, she couches this divide in terms of the civilised and the uncivilised. The Scots are for the most part a rational, modern people, Valeria tells us: "There are no people more cheerful, more companionable, more hospitable, more liberal in their ideas, to be found on the face of the *civilised* globe than the very people who submit to the Scotch Sunday" (Collins 1875, 255-6, italics added). However, the Sabbath points to an instance of Scotland's latent irrationality and barbarism, because it is, in Valeria's words, a "senseless and savage austerity" (ibid., 255). Eustace's Scottish seat, Gleninch, similarly reveals "the dark other" that haunts Scottish identity. Despite its location near Edinburgh, the house seems tainted by the wildness of the Highlands:

> The country round was pretty and well cultivated, and nothing more. The park was, to an English eye, wild and badly kept. The house had been built within the last seventy or eighty years. Outside, it was as bare of all ornament as a factory, and as gloomily heavy in effect as a prison. Inside, the deadly dreariness, the close oppressive solitude, of a deserted dwelling wearied the eye and weighed on the mind, from the roof to the basement. (ibid., 268)

Furthermore, its "otherness" is most apparent to the English visitor, signaling a difference in the sensibilities of the Scots and English with regard to the "uncivilised". The garden is mainly "a wilderness of weeds" (ibid., 270), while the dust-heap is more visible than it would be in England:

> "In tidy England, I suppose you would have all that carted away, out of sight", said the lawyer. "We don't mind in Scotland, as long as the dust-heap is far enough away not to be smelt at the house". (ibid.)

Scotland, it seems, is less concerned than England is to suppress the unwanted and unacceptable traces of civilised society.

Crucially, the decay encountered at Gleninch, and initially at Windygates, is the result of legal action. Gleninch was "shut up at the time of the trial" (ibid., 268) of Eustace Macallan for the poisoning of his first wife, and has been left to fall into disrepair. Similarly, when we first encounter Windygates, the summer retreat of Lady Lundie and her stepdaughter Blanche, "the mansion" is "closed"

(Collins 1870, 54) and "the garden" is "a wilderness of weeds" (ibid., 53). Like Dickens's Bleak House, "an interminable lawsuit [has] coiled itself closer and closer" around Windygates "sequestering it from human habitation, and even from human approach" (ibid.). That the law should promote the growth of the wild and the uncivilised at both Gleninch and Windygates is significant, indicating that Scots law is figured in *Man and Wife* and *The Law and the Lady* as a disruptive element. While the law is traditionally regarded as a civilising force, Collins depicts Scots law–just like Scotland–as having irrational elements that subvert the English social sphere. Furthermore, the vagaries of Scots law also threaten the subjectivity of two English women, Anne Silvester and Valeria Macallan, as Collins reinforces the connection between national and individual identity in each novel.

Like his close friend Charles Dickens, Wilkie Collins was deeply interested in legal matters. Just as Dickens repeatedly employs court cases and wills as plot devices in novels such as *Bleak House* (1853) and *Our Mutual Friend* (1865), so the law is central to many of Collins's novels, from the issue of illegitimacy in *No Name* (1862) to marriage settlements and wills in *The Woman in White*. The apparent affinity between law and literature, as witnessed in the fiction of Collins and Dickens, is not entirely surprising. Both the law and literature, after all, function as narratives by which we represent the world to ourselves. But while the proliferation of literature creates multiple, rival realities, legal discourse is commonly held to restrict and limit meaning, employing its narrative "to maintain a normative order" (Clayton 1993, 14). The law, we assume, is a rational discourse, that undertakes the "moral management" of the nation, containing and controlling the uncivilised. But for Victorian Britain, striving to create a unified sense national identity from disparate kingdoms, the different legal system in "North Britain" raised problems. Not only did the very existence of another legal system inject relativism into the "truths" of English law, but the peculiarities of Scots law, seized on by Collins, introduce epistemological uncertainty and irrationality into the British social sphere—just as the wild Highlands admit the latent savagery at the heart of Britain and its inhabitants.

Collins interrogates the peculiarities of Scots law in *The Law and the Lady* and *Man and Wife*. He depicts Scots law as doing precisely what the law should not do, that is, introduce ambiguity and the proliferation of meaning. In *Man and Wife*, Collins examines the impact of the "Scotch marriage". These irregular, but perfectly legal marriages, could occur in three ways in Scotland: by the mutual consent of the couple, by a public declaration followed by consummation, or by cohabitation and repute. In the first instance, no witnesses were required nor, significantly, was any authority figure, such as a clergyman or judge. Indeed, these marriages were often not recorded by any official body, and hence were entirely unknown to the state. The result in practice—and in *Man and Wife*, of course—is confusion and uncertainty, as it becomes difficult to ascertain whether a marriage has taken place. In *The Law and the Lady*, Collins approaches another aspect of Scots law, which undoes the fixed binaries of English law, namely the verdict of "not proven". This so-called "Scotch verdict" is unique to Scots law, and supplements the traditional verdicts of "guilty" and "not guilty". Commonly understood as meaning, "we know you did it, but we cannot prove it", "not proven" was, perhaps most famously, the verdict in the Madeline Smith trial, which numerous critics have cited in connection with *The Law and the Lady*.[2] This verdict, which is still controversial in Scotland,[3] introduces epistemological uncertainty into the courtroom. Rather than attempting to fix meaning, as other legal discourses aim to do, Scots law admits the possibility of "undecidability".

In both novels, the peculiarities of Scots law disrupt the identity of the novel's principal female character. Unless she can legitimate her marriage to Geoffrey Delamayn, Anne Silvester faces losing her social identity, as Lady Lundie's refusal to refer to Anne's sex or name indicates: "I won't have the name mentioned. I won't have the sex mentioned. Say, 'The Person', if you please. 'The Person'" (Collins 1870, 306). Similarly, Eustace's decision to marry Valeria under an assumed name forces her to question the validity of her marriage and her identity. The shadow of suspicion that hangs over Eustace severely compromises Valeria's social self as his legal appendage. Anne Silvester's attempt to prove the legitimacy of her marriage to Geoffrey Delamayn and Valeria's decision to challenge the "Scotch verdict" are therefore means of restoring both the normative English social sphere and their own identities.

Man and Wife was published in 1870, the same year that the Married Women's Property Act became law. Like *No Name*, *Man and Wife* has an overt social agenda. *No Name* challenges the status of illegitimate children under English law, while *Man and Wife* confronts marriage law in the Victorian period. Through the story of Hester Durthbridge, Collins reveals the iniquitous state of marriage, whereby "There is no limit, in England, to what a bad husband may do–as long as he sticks to his wife" (ibid., 590). Through the story of Anne Silvester, he exposes the impact of Scottish marriage laws, which judge that:

> Consent makes marriage. No form or ceremony, civil or religious; no notice before, or publication after; no cohabitation, no writing, no witnesses even, are essential to the constitution of this, the most important contract which two persons can enter into. (ibid., 231)

However, while the Married Women's Property Act went some way to alleviating the problems of women like Hester Durthbridge, irregular marriage was not abolished in Scotland until 1939. And it is this second aspect of marriage that disrupts the English social sphere and subverts the subjectivity of Collins's characters in this novel. Significantly, Collins employs the same civilised/uncivilised axis in his discussion of Scottish marriage laws as he uses it to depict Scotland in general. Scottish marriage laws are deemed to be of a "scandalous uncertainty [...] entirely without parallel in any other *civilized* country in Europe" (ibid., 522, italics added). They permit sexual relations without the sanction of the state or church, and legitimise the "bestial" drives of men like Geoffrey Delamayn.

Delamayn epitomises Victorian fears of the rise of the savage. He is the most prominent exponent of physical exercise and muscular development in *Man and Wife*, which Collins firmly associates with the primitive drives that threaten the psychic wholeness of the civilised individual and nation. As Sir Patrick Lundie puts it, "there is far too much glorification in England, just now, of the mere physical qualities which an Englishman shares with the savage and the brute" (ibid., 68). Collins repeatedly describes Delamayn in terms that emphasise his "uncivilised" nature; he is a "savage" (ibid., 177, 359), a "wild beast" (ibid., 495), an "animal" (ibid., 194). Collins also signals the lack of "moral management" in his sexuality; it is no coincidence that Geoffrey "ruins" Anne Silvester. Furthermore, even her attraction to him stems from his animal physicality:

> She had seen him, the central object of the interest of a nation; the idol of the popular worship and the popular applause. *His* were the arms whose muscle was celebrated in the newspapers. *He* was first among the heroes hailed by ten thousand roaring throats as the pride and flower of England. A woman, in an atmosphere of red-hot enthusiasm, witnesses the apotheosis of Physical Strength. Is it reasonable–is it just–to expect her to ask herself, in cold blood, What (morally, and intellectually) is all this worth?–and that, when the man who is the object of the apotheosis, notices her, is presented to her, finds her to his taste, and singles her out from the rest? No. While humanity is humanity, the woman is not utterly without excuse. (ibid., 77, italics in original)

While English law will not sanction the uncontrolled sexual relationship of Geoffrey Delamayn and Anne Silvester, the uncertain and confused marriage laws of Scotland legitimate their earlier uncontained desire. Here Collins depicts Scotland once more permitting the savage and uncivilised to disrupt English society, as Anne's Scotch marriage to Geoffrey Delamayn derails the socially approved match of Geoffrey and the wealthy widow, Mrs Glenarm.

But not only does the confusion engendered by Scotland's "uncivilised" marriage laws upset a "society wedding", these laws also undermine the individual subjectivities of three of Collins's characters. Anne Silvester is in a "hybrid" role from the novel's opening. As a governess she finds herself, like Charlotte Brontë's Jane Eyre, in an awkward position somewhere between the serving and the served classes. Lady Lundie refers to her directly as "half-bred" (ibid., 90), while Mrs Glenarm asks of her: "Dressed like a servant, and looking like a lady. What *does* it mean?" (ibid., 429, italics in original). Her sexual relationship with Geoffrey Delamayn threatens her identity further, because she is pregnant and unmarried. Her only hope of retaining her social identity is to marry Geoffrey–a course he is unwilling to take for fear of losing his allowance and inheritance. Anne's solution is a secret Scotch marriage, which would legitimate their sexual relationship. But such are the uncertainties and confusion of Scots law that Anne succeeds not in restoring her own self, but only in further destabilizing her identity and that of two others.

Instead of successfully marrying Geoffrey Delamayn, Anne discovers that he hopes to use Scots marriage laws against her. After Anne and Arnold Brinkworth spend the night together at a local inn, masquerading as man and wife, Geoffrey accuses them of being legally married. His accusation leaves Anne uncertain whether she is an unmarried "ruined" woman, whether her husband is Arnold Brinkworth, or whether she is married to Geoffrey Delamayn. Arnold does not know whether his legal wife is Anne or Blanche, while Blanche must discover whether she is Arnold's wife or whether she too has been "ruined" by inadvertently living with a man outside of marriage. Blanche also finds herself outside of patriarchal control for the first time in her life, further destabilising her identity. As her uncle, Sir Patrick Lundie, tells her would-be husband, Arnold Brinkworth:

> My difficulty is, that I can't assert my authority, as guardian, if I assume my niece (as I do) to be a married woman. Your difficulty is, that you can't assert your authority as her husband, until it is distinctly proved that you and Miss Silvester are *not* man and wife. (ibid., 464-5, italics in original)

Anne attempts to resolve the issue by visiting two lawyers in Glasgow. Each, however, gives her a different opinion. To the first she is indubitably "a married woman" (ibid., 321), to the second there is "no marriage" only "evidence in favour of perhaps establishing a marriage" (ibid., 322). Like Sir Patrick Lundie, the lawyers acknowledge "the confusion and uncertainty in the marriage-law of Scotland" (ibid., 322). Crucially, Anne attempts to prevent Arnold's possibly bigamous marriage to Blanche until their status has been resolved. But like marriage law in Scotland, her letter to Arthur is marked by "confusion and uncertainty": "It was blotted, it was illegible in more places than one. With pains and care they made out the address at the beginning, and here and there, some fragments of the lines that followed" (ibid., 326). Anne's undecided legal status seems to have resulted in the collapse of her language.

In Scotland, the language of marriage is, it seems, truly performative. So much so, that Collins warns us few people have "any inadequate idea [...] of the infamous absence of all needful warning, of all decent precaution and restraint, which makes the marriage law of Scotland a trap to catch unmarried men and women" (ibid., 132). Here Scots law not only threatens identity, but also conceptions of language that privilege the intention of the speaker or writer, because in Scotland it is possible to get married *without really meaning to do it*. This "confusion and uncertainty" is eventually resolved in *Man and Wife* by the intervention of English law–and, significantly, not through a spoken promise, but a written one. Geoffrey's note to Anne at the inn, signed "Your loving husband" (ibid., 482), is deemed proof of their prior marriage:

> Loose and reckless as the Scotch law is, there happens, however, to be one case in which the action of it has been confirmed and settled by the English courts. A written promise of marriage exchanged between a man and woman, in Scotland, marries that man and woman by Scotch law. An English Court of Justice (sitting in judgement on the case I have just mentioned to Mr Moy) has pronounced that law to be good—and the decision has since been confirmed by the supreme authority of the House of Lords. (ibid., 523)

However, while English law seems to bring resolution here, some residue of the uncivilised confusion introduced by Scots law remains. Anne's marriage to Geoffrey is, after all, not based on love, but their previous carnal relationship. As Collins comments sarcastically, their marriage is "done, in the name of Morality. Done, in the interests of Virtue. Done, in an age of progress, and under the most perfect government on the face of the earth" (ibid., 527). In other words, Scots law forces English society to incorporate an element of "bestial savagery".

The Law and the Lady hinges on a verdict unique to Scots law, the verdict of "not proven". Like Scottish marriage laws, the Scotch Verdict offers a direct challenge to the black and white orthodoxies of English law, by admitting into its "normative universe" the existence of grey areas. As such, it is deeply threatening to the English establishment. Again the threat posed by Scotland is rendered along the barbaric/cultured axis. As Major Fitz-David states, this verdict "is not permitted by the laws of any other *civilised* country on the face of the earth" (Collins 1875, 95, italics added). The impact of the verdict on Eustace and Valeria is significant, as it does not just introduce uncertainty over Eustace's guilt, it also undermines and problematises the identity of each. The shame resulting from the verdict persuades Eustace to change his name from Macallan to Woodville. He marries Valeria under his assumed name. On discovering this deception Valeria finds her own identity and social self fundamentally disturbed. Firstly, there is the question of whether she is legally married at all. As her landlady puts it, "you are neither maid, wife, nor widow. You are worse than nothing, madam" (ibid., 40). To have lived with a man outside of marriage, even unwittingly, would, of course, destroy Valeria's social identity in nineteenth-century Britain, rendering her "nothing". Secondly, there is the question of what Valeria's name now is, whether it be her maiden name, Brinton, or Eustace's assumed name, Woodville, or his real name, Macallan.

Crucially, the disturbance in the identities of Eustace and Valeria, introduced by the Scotch verdict, also manifests itself as a disturbance in their gender. Eustace is a singularly weak and submissive character, who cries on his wedding day. He is described at his trial as showing "far less self-possession than the last prisoner tried in that Court for murder—a woman, who had been convicted on overwhelming evidence" (ibid., 121). By contrast, his second wife Valeria possesses many masculine qualities, as her first name hints. Though lacking "the dark down on her upper lip" that "was almost a moustache" adorning Marian Halcombe's face in *The Woman in White* (Collins 1860, 58), Valeria nevertheless has some masculine features. Her eyebrows are "too dark, and too strongly marked" (Collins 1875, 14); she describes herself in masculine terms, deriding herself for her "weakness and my want of spirit" (ibid., 36), while her decision to move out of the private sphere of the home to investigate the poisoning of her husband's first wife compromises her femininity by Victorian standards. As her uncle comments sarcastically, the account of Eustace's trial makes "nice reading for a young woman" (ibid., 112).

In solving the mystery of the first Mrs Macallan's death, there seems to be some reordering of the gender identities of Eustace and Valeria. She returns to her "proper" domestic sphere: "The quiet, monotonous round of my new life was far from wearying me. I, too, wanted repose–I had no interests, no pleasures, out of my husband's room" (ibid., 346). Yet Valeria is still haunted by "secret longings, in those dangerous moments when I was left to myself" (ibid., 347). These "secret longings" remind us that while Collins's characters can manage their uncivilised drives, they cannot eradicate them from the self or the nation. Fittingly, *The Law and the Lady* does not therefore see the entire restitution of the English normative order. Instead the epistemological uncertainty engendered by Scots law prevails, with the mystery solved, not through rational enquiry, but through the ramblings of a "madman", Miserrimus Dexter.

In Miserrimus Dexter, Collins creates another hybrid creature–a man whose hybridity manifests itself not just in his character and language, but also in his physical appearance. Dexter was born without legs–and perhaps also genitals. He is at once half-man, half machine, half masculine, half feminine, even half human, half animal. He is a classic instance of a Collins's character whose "moral management" of the self repeatedly fails, as the description of his performance at Eustace's trial reveals:

> But as he went on, the mad side of him showed itself. He mixed up sense and nonsense in the strangest confusion: he was called to order over and over again; he was even threatened with fine and imprisonment for contempt of Court. In short, he was just like himself–a mixture of the strangest and the most opposite qualities; at one time, perfectly clear and reasonable, as you said just now; at another, breaking out into rhapsodies of the most outrageous kind, like a man in a state of delirium. A more entirely unfit person to advise anybody, I tell you again, never lived. (ibid., 187)

However, it is only when Dexter succumbs entirely to madness that Valeria solves the mystery of *The Law and the Lady*. In other words, Valeria discovers that she can only restore her identity by giving free reign to the irrational and the uncivilised. Having come to this realisation, Valeria discovers the solution to the first Mrs Macallan's poisoning in that symbol of Scottish "wildness", the dustheap at Gleninch. Her decision to allow the Scottish verdict of "not proven" to stand at the close of the novel, indicates her final rejection of the doctrine of self-control and containment.

Critics often note the disruptive impact of distant colonies on the English social sphere in Victorian literature. This essay, however, demonstrates that just as a stolen Hindu diamond can throw a household into disarray in *The Moonstone* (1868), so an intervention from much closer to home–Scotland–can unsettle the English social sphere. But while Edward Said interprets the interventions of empire in nineteenth-century literature as a means of consolidating British identity (Said 1993, 88), the intrusion of Scotland and Scots law in particular does something quite different in the fiction of Wilkie Collins. Rather than support a homogeneous ideal of "Britishness", intervention from the outsider/insider culture of Scotland points to the heterogeneity at the heart of Britain. Thus, while the Moonstone is eventually returned to India, Collins never quite eradicates the uncertainty and confusion introduced by Scots law into national and individual identity in *The Law and the Lady* and *Man and Wife*.

Notes

[1] For more on this relationship between empires and selfhood see Andrew Mangham's contribution, "Mental States", to this collection.

[2] Karin Jacobson, Jenny Bourne Taylor, and Dougald MacEachen all cite Wilkie Collins's fascination with Smith 1857 trial in Edinburgh for poisoning her lover, Emile L'Angelier.

[3] Labour M. S. P., Michael McMahon, is currently working on a private members bill, which proposes the scrapping the not proven verdict (MacDonnell 2004).

Works Cited

Brontë, Emily. 1847. *Wuthering Heights*. London: Penguin, 1965.
Carens, Timothy L. 2003. Outlandish English Subjects in *The Moonstone*. *Tennessee Studies in Literature* 41:239-65.
Clayton, Jay. 1993. *The Pleasures of Babel: Contemporary American Literature and Theory*. New York: Oxford University Press.
Collins, Wilkie. 1852. *Basil*. Oxford: Oxford University Press, 1990.
—. 1870. *Man and Wife*. Oxford: Oxford University Press, 1995.
—. 1862. *No Name*. London: Penguin, 1994.
—. 1875. *The Law and the Lady*. London: Penguin, 1998.
—. 1868. *The Moonstone*. London: Penguin, 1986.
—. 1860. *The Woman in White*. London: Penguin, 1974.
Crawford, Robert. 2003. *Devolving English Literature*. Edinburgh: Edinburgh University Press.
—. 1998. *The Scottish Invention of English Literature*. Cambridge: Cambridge University Press.
Dickens, Charles. 1853 *Bleak House.* London: Penguin, 1971.
—. 1865. *Our Mutual Friend*. London: Penguin, 1971.
Heller, Tamar. 2003. Masterpiece Theatre and Ezra Jennings's Hair: Some Reflections on where we've been and where we're going in Collins Studies. *Tennessee Studies in Literature* 41:361-70.
Hogg, James. 1824. *Confessions of a Justified Sinner*. London: Everyman, 1994.
Herdman, John. 1990. *The Double in Nineteenth-Century Fiction*. Houndsmill: MacMillan.
Jacobson, Karin. 2003. Plain Faces, Weird Cases Domesticating the Law in Collins's *The Law and the Lady* and the Trial of Madeleine Smith. *Tennessee Studies in Literature* 41:283-312.
MacDonnell, Hugh. 2004. Not proven verdict under threat. *The Scotsman*. <http://news.scotsman.com/topics.cfm?tid=441&id=1341582004> accessed 31 July 2006.
Maceachen, Douglas B. 1950. Wilkie Collins and British Law. *Nineteenth Century Fiction* 5:121-39.
Said, Edward W. 1993. *Culture and Imperialism*. London: Vintage.
Taylor, Jenny Bourne. 1988. *In the Secret Theatre of Home: Wilkie Collins, Sensation Narrative and Nineteenth-Century Psychology*. London, Routledge.

COLLINS ON INTERNATIONAL COPYRIGHT: FROM "A NATIONAL WRONG" (1870) TO "CONSIDERATIONS" (1880)

GRAHAM LAW

The Anglo-American copyright controversy has been for the last thirty years the Schleswig-Holstein Question of literature. It has appeared equally insoluble, and has been almost as tedious. (Leader in the *Times*, 24 May 1879, 11)

Towards the end of his famous first North American tour, the youthful Charles Dickens had written as follows:

I have always felt, and do always feel, so keenly, the outrage which the existing Piracy inflicts upon writers [...] that I cannot, though I try ever so hard, discuss the question as one of expediency, or reason it as one of National profit and loss. [...] I had always said, and always intended to say, that the question was one of Plain Right and Wrong, and was not to be considered, honestly, in any other Light. (Tillotson et al. 1965-2002, vol. 3, 221-2)

This, we should note, was before Britain itself had signed its first reciprocal copyright agreement, with Prussia in 1846. Compare a similar comment written over forty years later, shortly before the opening in 1885 of the Berne Convention, which led to the creation the International Copyright Union.[1] More than a decade after his only trip across the Atlantic, the aging Wilkie Collins wrote thus, again to a sympathetic American literary acquaintance:

At sixty years old, I have not yet learnt to control the rage that possesses me under a strong sense of injustice–or, in plain English, under a sense of the robberies committed on me [...] by the pirates. (Baker and Clarke 1999, vol. 2, 469-71)

This pair of quotations suggests correctly that, concerning his opinions on intellectual property, as in so many other respects, Collins took the lead from his literary mentor Dickens. Nevertheless, the consistency of sentiment and tone across such a wide historical gap is surprising.

In the course of their respective literary careers both Dickens and Collins were irritated from time to time by the inadequacies or intricacies of the regulations protecting English authors on the European Continent and in the British Colonies, but remained perpetually incensed by their non-existence in the United States. Both tended, however, to direct their anger less intensely and less frequently at the "self-interested" legislative bodies that neglected to enact an international copyright code than at those "dishonest" parties who exploited the absence of such a code. Both thus employed provocative terms like "piracy" with great frequency, but rarely distinguished between practices that were in breach of a specific copyright law and those which infringed some general notion of natural justice.[2] Though both authors could and sometimes did claim a measure of professional legal knowledge and experience–Dickens had worked as a junior clerk to a solicitor while Collins was formally qualified to practice as a barrister–neither is much inclined to offer a theoretical basis for such a notion. It is nevertheless clear that the foundation of the position shared by Dickens and Collins was a belief in the absolute, inalienable and perpetual moral right of authors to control their own literary productions.[3] Such a position, it must be noted, was by no means compatible with the principle underlying British and American copyright law throughout their lifetimes. That is, that publication conferred on the author a proprietary right limited in duration that could be freely assigned to another, and that was in practice typically leased or sold outright to a publishing house. At the same time, the growth of liberal-democratic ideals during the nineteenth century ensured that copyright protection would often be seen, like duty on paper, as both a restriction of free trade and a "tax on knowledge", so that there were many calls for its curtailment or abolition. Without taking account of the tensions between the interests of authors as individuals, publishers as a class, and the people as reading public, with the varying concepts of right that they gave rise to, it is impossible to understand why the Anglo-American copyright conflict remained so intractable.

The specific purpose of this paper is to provide such a context for a reading of Collins's only substantial publications on the issue of international copyright. These are: "A National Wrong", an unsigned contribution to *Chambers Journal* in early 1870, written in collaboration with James Payn; and "Considerations on the Copyright Question", an article published in mid-1880 in the *International Review*, a New York monthly which also circulated in London. Collins's role as co-author of the earlier article has only recently been recognised, so that this represents the first opportunity to give a comparative assessment of the two pieces.[4] These prove again to be rather similar in terms not only of their basic stance on the copyright issue, but also of their rhetorical strategy and prevailing tone. Nevertheless, I will argue that the specific public and private contexts in which they were written, and the distinct debates to which they contribute, give the two pieces a rather different significance. I will thus discuss in turn the "moments" of "A National Wrong" and "Considerations", separated by an *intermezzo* spanning the decade in between, and followed by a *coda* on the passage of the Chace Act, which gave the United States a code of international copyright for the first time.

I. The Moment of "A National Wrong"

In the autumn of 1869 Collins's novel *Man and Wife* was just beginning its serial run in *Cassell's Magazine*. The London publishers were approached by Belinfante Brothers of the Hague, who wished to use the electrotype plates of the illustrations to accompany a Dutch translation of the novel in their own house magazine. Though Holland had signed a reciprocal copyright treaty with France as early as 1855, there was still no mutual agreement between the Dutch and British governments, so that Belinfante Brothers were under no legal obligation to request permission from or offer remuneration to the writer himself. Annoyed particularly by the fact that they were prepared to pay for the illustrations but not for the novel, Collins promptly decided to treat the occasion as a chance to draw public attention to "the dishonesty of the publishers in Holland" (Baker and Clarke 1999, vol. 2, 157-8). He thus engaged in a provocative exchange of letters with the Dutch house, which he intended from the outset to publish in the press. Messrs Cassell themselves were happy to oblige, and the correspondence duly occupied two inside columns of their new halfpenny evening paper the *Echo*. Collins's argument was simply that a "sense of honour" should oblige any respectable publisher to acknowledge the moral right of the author even in the absence of legal protection. It concluded resoundingly:

> I persist, in the interest of public morality, in asserting my right to regard as my own property the produce of my own brains and my own labour, any accidental neglect in formally protecting the same in any country notwithstanding. I declare any publisher who takes my book from me with a view to selling it, in any form, for his own benefit–without my permission, and without giving me a share in his profits–to be guilty of theft, and to be morally, if not legally, an outlaw and a pest among honest men. ("International Copyright", *Echo*, 24 November 1869, 3)

This probably represents the clearest and most succinct summary of the author's general position. More characteristically in the Belinfante correspondence, though, Collins adopts a sardonic tone, taking advantage both of the less than perfect command of English of his correspondents and of the fact that they had addressed him initially as "Madame Wilkie Collins". In support of his position he thus compares the Dutch publishers to pickpockets, contrasting their base commercial values with the chivalric ideals of Baron von Tauchnitz of Leipzig, long the publisher of the "Collection of British Authors". According to Collins, in issuing English editions of his own novels for a continental audience, the Baron "is not obliged by law to pay me a farthing for doing so, but he invariably does pay me" (ibid.). Here Collins was in fact mistaken. As Simon Nowell-Smith has demonstrated (Nowell-Smith 1968, 41-63), in the case of Prussia from 1846, and thereafter regarding an increasing number of areas of Europe as new reciprocal treaties were gradually concluded with Britain, the Baron *was* obliged by international law to negotiate the right to market the novels of his British Authors. Indeed, Collins only had to glance at one of his own novels in the Tauchnitz series, where the legend "Copyright Edition" appeared prominently on the title-page, to see that his claim was false.

Nevertheless, the Dutch publishers eventually accepted Collins's argument. They agreed thereafter to recognise the moral right of all English authors and were thus welcomed as Collins's authorised publishers in Holland, a role which they continued to perform into the 1880s. In the meantime, though, the correspondence in the *Echo* had come to the attention of Collins's friend and fellow novelist, James Payn, editor since 1858 of *Chambers' Journal*. The outcome was that the two agreed to collaborate on an article concerning "The Belinfante Affair" for that paper, with Collins sketching the outline and Payn filling in the details. When it emerged that Belinfante Brothers had capitulated, the two writers clearly decided to shift the target in the English author's battle for overseas rights from the little kingdom across the Channel to the large republic on the other side of the Atlantic.[5] When "A National Wrong" duly appeared in February 1870, it thus incorporated the *Echo* correspondence in large part, but added an original framing commentary. The exchange between Collins and the Belinfante Brothers itself was figured consistently as a triumphant encounter between a gallant English merchant ship ("the *Man and Wife* of London, master and owner, Wilkie Collins") and a rogue Dutch vessel hoisting "the Black Flag" (Collins and Payne 1870, 108). But the article begins with, and in its conclusions returns to, the copyright conflict with the United States. There the piratical American publisher is compared sarcastically to a woman who is prepared to steal the home-made clothes off the back of her cousin's child, or even to kidnap the child itself. At the same time, the "spry American senator" is depicted as hypocritically cloaking self-interest in the rhetoric of Free Trade, "with his tongue in one cheek and his quid in the other" (ibid., 107). Though there is a passing blow concerning the deleterious effects of this situation on the standing of the American author and the standards of American literature, the main thrust of the argument remains a defense of a sense of natural justice that upholds the moral right of the author.

"A National Wrong", however, can be seen to reflect deeper concerns and should not simply be read as an opportunistic response to the Belinfante business, allowing the author once more to ride a favourite hobby horse. The turn of the 1870s represented a crucial period not only in the course of Anglo-American diplomatic relations (I shall come back to this) but also in the professional literary career of Wilkie Collins.

The loss of his mentor Dickens in June 1870 merely confirmed a sense of crisis that had been building for some time. The 1860s had opened triumphantly for Collins with the resounding success of *The Woman in White*, which had allowed the author to negotiate favourable publishing deals for the issue of his fiction alike as serials, triple-deckers, and single-volume reprints. These secured him a substantial income into the second half of the decade, but by then it was clear his literary stock was in decline. Dickens's weekly miscellanies, which had provided a regular venue for Collins's serials since *The Dead Secret* in 1857, were themselves losing ground; Collins had failed to establish a stable relationship with a publishing house for his new triple-deckers, so that *The Moonstone* (1868), for example, fell into the grimy hands of William Tinsley; and, most significantly, the uniform edition of his reprinted novels, though now bearing the prestigious imprint of Smith, Elder, was selling poorly. The underlying causes were probably more complex, but Collins himself blamed the conservatism of the British book trade, which geared the production of new fiction to the fastidious demands of Mudie's circulating library. This prevented his brand of sensationalism from reaching immediately the broad popular audience to which it most appealed. He responded in a variety of ways. One was to try to explore new popular serial outlets like the weekly numbers trade or cheap papers such as *Cassell's Magazine*; another was to pour a good deal of literary energy into the drama, where he hoped to bypass the publishers and librarians and address the people directly. In both areas, however, the results were often frustrating.[6]

In such a situation it was especially irritating to be reminded that his fiction was in fact already reaching an appreciative mass audience–but in North America where the rewards to the author remained both limited and uncertain. From the beginning, Collins had in fact been able to arrange the sale of early copies of his new fiction to the established New York house of Harper and Brothers, thus allowing them to gain an advantage of a few weeks over any unauthorised rivals. The sums involved were initially paltry–as little as £15 for his first novel *Antonina, or the Fall of Rome* in 1850–but following the success of *The Woman in White* rose to the more substantial sum of £500. Indeed, by offering *Man and Wife* simultaneously to their major rivals Putnam's and Appleton's, Collins had persuaded Harper's to pay a record £750–still, of course, only around a third of what the smaller British market gave him for equivalent rights. What Collins does not seem to have understood was that the most generous *ex gratia* payments came from the established East Coast firm most firmly opposed to international copyright legislation. At the time of Dickens's first visit to America, the Harpers were still seen as "the redoutable champions of literary piracy" (Barnes 1974, 80), and even after the Civil War continued overtly or covertly to undermine attempts to enact copyright legislation (Putnam 1915, 367-70). When Collins sent the Belinfante correspondence to Cassell's in London, he also forwarded copies to his authorised publishers in New York with a similar request that it be published to further the cause of international copyright. When Collins wrote to S. S. Conant, editor of *Harper's Weekly*, to repeat his request that the correspondence appear despite the capitulation of the Dutch house, he argued:

> It appears to *me*, to be *something* to have obtained a recognition of the principle of international copyright, in a country which has hitherto set that principle at defiance. All legal protection to property springs, in the first instance, from authoritative recognition of moral right. (1 January 1870, Baker and Clarke 1999, vol. 2, 335-7, italics in original)

Conant's response has unfortunately not survived, but it is likely to have been an exercise in tact. What is certain is that the letters were not published in any of Harper's periodicals, so that the Belinfante Affair received no publicity in New York.

What is also certain is that, in public terms, the moment of "A National Wrong" was an inopportune one to accuse the United States so stridently of piracy. The key issue of the period in Anglo-American relations was the diplomatic dispute arising from the Civil War and known as the "*Alabama* Claims". The *Alabama* was the best known of a number of warships secretly ordered by Confederate agents and built surreptitiously in British shipyards, which were to cause enormous damage to the Northern merchant fleet and thus help to prolong the Southern rebellion. On the grounds that, in permitting the construction of vessels like the *Alabama*, Britain had failed to follow its own neutrality laws, the US demanded substantial compensation–over two billion dollars or the ceding of the Canadian colonies were among the more extravagant claims. The long-running dispute was only settled after a Joint High Commission met in the United States. This led to the signing of the Treaty of Washington in May 1871, by which the British Government apologised and agreed to pay compensation–in the event, under sixteen million dollars–as decided by a committee of arbitration (Cook 1975, 167-86, 233-40).

While the *Alabama* Claims remained unresolved, British authors were generally more circumspect in asserting their own grievances and in pressing for relief. (The measured open letter from Arthur Helps to Charles Eliot Norton, published in *Macmillan's Magazine* in June 1869, is a good example.) After the *Alabama* dispute was settled, many British commentators were quick to suggest that the mechanism of arbitration might also appropriately be used in an attempt to settle a conflict of even longer standing. In particular, the autumn of 1871 saw a lengthy debate on international copyright in the correspondence columns of the *Times*, sparked off by a letter from "A Traveller":

> Now that the time has come for settling once for all whatever grievances may have existed between England and America, it would be a serious mistake to overlook one grievance which for many years past has caused a feeling of irritation and estrangement between the two countries. ("American Pirates", *Times*, 27 September 1871, 9)

As a leader pointed out (24 October, 9), the key exchange was between the New York publisher William Appleton and his London counterpart Frederic Daldy. Appleton's letter set out the case, grounded in the rights of the people to cheap literature, that no reciprocal copyright agreement would be acceptable if the result were to allow the British publishing trade to impose its own restrictive practices in America. In his own memorable words: "every arrangement that England has hitherto offered is but a kind of legal saddle for the English publisher to ride his author into the American book market" (20 October, 10). Though Daldy pointed out that the kind of domestic manufacturing clause which Appleton advocated would also serve the interests of the established houses in New York and Boston (24 October, 6), there is no doubt that the American publisher had stoutly defended a position of which many British authors were not fully aware.[7] Although there were a number of telling interventions from British scholarly writers, the novelists acquitted themselves rather poorly in *The Times* debate, often using the opportunity to air personal grievances as trivial as they were obscure. In particular, Caroline Norton muddied the waters with a wild attack on all and sundry (25 October, 6), provoking angry responses from, among others, Ellen Wood (28 October, 6), Harrison Ainsworth (31 October, 6), and Mary Braddon (2 November, 10).

Though he was a subscriber to *The Times*, Wilkie Collins did not participate in the debate. Indeed, we must note that, at the time of the Belinfante Affair itself, Collins had failed to react to public criticism of his own position. When the Belinfante correspondence was published in the *Echo*, the editors themselves had commented in an editorial:

> We are afraid the remedy does not consist in an appeal, with Mr Wilkie Collins, to an innate "sense of justice" or "the dignity of man". A general agreement between all civilised nations on the terms of a treaty of international copyright is the only effective protection that can be devised for the rights of authors. ("Mr Wilkie Collins on his Rights", *Echo*, 24 November 1869, 1)

J. H. Kruyt of Rotterdam was even more forthright in his criticisms of the English author's stance (2 December, 3). These were principally two. Firstly, that that it was unjust to suggest that Holland was solely or even principally responsible for the absence of protection for British authors there. Secondly, Kruyt argued that Collins's own appeal to a code of honour was an anachronism under the modern system of commerce, under which the chivalrous publisher would undoubtedly lose out in competition with the unscrupulous. Both of these statements were roundly ignored by the author. What nobody pointed out, however, was that, according to his own declared ideals, in arranging the publication of the letters of the Dutch publishers without their agreement, Collins had infringed their indefeasible moral rights as authors. It is difficult to escape the conclusion that, regardless of its stated aims, "A National Wrong" itself shares something of the buccaneer spirit.

II. In the Interim

During the course of the 1870s Collins gradually established more stable arrangements with British publishers of his work in both volume and serial form. After briefly resuming business relations with his original publishers, Bentley, in late 1874 he came to a long-term agreement with the up-and-coming firm of Chatto and Windus. Thereafter they not only published all of his new novels in circulating-library format but also took over the rights to all of his available earlier fiction and established a range of uniform editions, including cheap railway yellowbacks. This was rather too late to see anything like the level of backlist sales achieved by his sensational rival Ellen Wood, who had stuck by Bentley from the beginning, but it nevertheless offered Collins a greater degree of economic security. During the 1870s Collins explored a wide range of new serial venues during the decade, including prestigious metropolitan pictorial papers like the *Graphic* and the *Illustrated London News*. Towards the end of the decade he followed the lead of Mary Braddon and signed his first contract with Tillotson and Son, the Lancashire syndication agency which supplied fiction mainly to provincial journals. Though there were to be many annoyances and frustrations, the newspaper market was thereafter to provide the principle outlet for his short and serial fiction up to the end of his career. This allowed his novels to reach a far wider social readership, while offering significantly more substantial rewards than those from middle-class literary monthlies like *Belgravia* from Chatto and Windus or Bentley's *Temple Bar*.

Over the same period, though, his long-term publishing partnership with Harper's across the Atlantic began to unravel. This was especially upsetting to Collins as he had assiduously cultivated the human side of the relationship during his reading tour of North America of 1873-4, taking as his model Dickens's second visit to the United States during 1867-8. At that rather delicate period in Anglo-American relations, and with resentment at his outspokenness on his earlier visit still in the air, Dickens had taken considerable care both to court those American publishers who had paid him for advance sheets and not to speak in public on the copyright question. Collins did much the same. While in New York he was treated lavishly by his authorised publishers, meeting staff members like S. S. Conant for the first time. The British author got on well with Joseph W. Harper Jr, a fellow sufferer from gout who now headed the firm, and established a lasting personal friendship with William A. Seaver, a senior editor of *Harper's Magazine* (Harper 1912, 522). The most tangible result was the establishment of Harper's "Illustrated Library Edition" of his works, which eventually extended to seventeen titles, each bearing the facsimile inscription: "I gratefully dedicate this collected edition of my works, to The American People" (see Gasson 1998, 74-5). The primary reason for the souring of this apparently idyllic relationship was related to the increasingly fraught question of colonial copyright.

In theory, British copyright law held sway throughout the Empire. This implied that the artificially high prices charged by British metropolitan book publishers for work both new and not so new would apply also at the colonial periphery, where even Mudie's volumes could not penetrate and where local circulating libraries were scarce. In practice, there were several remedies, more or less legal, grounded in the recognition that what English-speaking settlers required–in Australia, say, just as much as in America–was the opportunity to buy cheap publications not to borrow luxury editions. One remedy was the production of compact colonial editions in London; another was through the international syndication of literary material in newspapers or magazines, with or without permission; perhaps the simplest and most effective was, officially or unofficially, to permit the importation of cheap foreign volume editions, whether from America or from Leipzig. With the long open border with the United States, it was obviously in Canada that Imperial copyright legislation came closest to a purely fictional status (Copinger 1893, 609-12; Bowker 1912, 381-5). From around 1850 American editions of British copyright works had been allowed into the Canadian colonies on payment of a duty that was in fact rarely exacted. This was clearly in the interests neither of British authors nor of fledgling Canadian publishing houses. Thus, after the creation of the Dominion in 1867, such houses began to approach English writers with a view to issuing authorised cheap Canadian editions of their work in return for a small payment. Hunter, Rose, and Co. of Toronto was one of these firms, and Wilkie Collins was one of the first authors with whom they established business relations.

Throughout the 1870s from *Man and Wife* onwards, virtually all of Collins's new fiction thus appeared in such editions, and the author encouraged colleagues such as Charles Reade to follow suit. When he gave a reading in Toronto at Christmas 1873, Collins thus enjoyed a cordial dinner with Robert Hunter, George Rose, and their respective families. The problem was that the interests of his authorised publishers in Toronto and New York were diametrically opposed, since there was little to stop both editions crossing the open border and competing head-on on both sides. When he became aware of the problem, at first Collins tried to negotiate a gentlemanly comprise, then to favour the New York house since it paid significantly more, but the final outcome was an abrupt break in business relations with Harpers from early 1878. The precise details remain unclear, but on 1 May Collins had written to George Rose to suggest that there was "certainly a chance of attacking the Harper monopoly this time" (Baker et al., 2005, vol. 3, 193). As a result, at the end of the decade both *The Fallen Leaves* (1879) and *Jezebel's Daughter* (1880) failed to appear in authorised versions in the United States, whether in serial or volume form, while the honorarium on the Illustrated Library Edition precipitately dried up.

III. The Moment of "Considerations"

"Considerations on the Copyright Question" takes the form of a protest letter "Addressed to an American Friend", in the words of the subtitle. It was written for the *International Review*, then an intellectual monthly published in New York by A. S. Barnes and distributed in London by Trübner, who also re-issued the piece in the form of a sixteen-page pamphlet. The small New York house was that to which Collins had first turned when his arrangement with Harper's broke down. Though A. S. Barnes and his editors supported the cause of international copyright, they were clearly uncomfortable with the strong language and belligerent tone of Collins's contribution, and appended a note to that effect. The letter opens:

> You were taking leave of me the other day, Colonel, when I received from the United States a copy of a pirated edition of one of my books. I threw it into the waste-paper basket, with an expression of opinion which a little startled you. As we shook hands at parting, you said, "When you are cool, my friend, I should like to be made acquainted with your sentiments on the copyright question". I am cool now–and here are my sentiments. (Collins 1880, 609)

As with "A National Wrong", the author's sentiments spring from a passionately held belief in the indefeasible moral right of authors to control their own intellectual properly. Again as in "A National Wrong", the argument opens in a personal vein and with an analogy, in this case comparing the American publisher's piracy of the English author's work to an Iroquois chief stealing a hand-made watch from the Colonel's ancestor, an early Dutch visitor to Manhattan Island. This time, however, though they are dismissed rather impatiently and peremptorily as "American delusions" (ibid., 613), Collins does acknowledge, in the body of the article, a number of the objections to an Anglo-American copyright treaty modeled on that with France. Finally the letter tries to compute the extent of the financial losses suffered by Dickens and Collins due to their lack of protection in the American marketplace, concluding abruptly: "Good-by for the present, Colonel. I must go back to my regular work, and make money for American robbers, under the sanction of Congress" (ibid., 618).

In the process of rapidly dispelling the "American delusions", in "Considerations" Collins makes the following claims:

> 1) that there should be no distinction between the protection of English copyrights in Europe and in America, despite the necessity of translation and republication in the former case;
> 2) that the responsibility for the lack of copyright protection for foreign authors lies not with the American people but with the American legislature;
> 3) that books, whether addressed to an elite or a popular audience, are in reality no cheaper in America than they are in Britain; and
> 4) that the leading American publishing houses oppose international copyright out of self-interest whereas their counterparts in London support it from a sense of justice.

Three of these claims were probably defensible, though the first and last were in fact contested in London as well as in New York, while the second might be seen as relying on a rather naïve misunderstanding of the nature of the American Constitution. But the third–and here the crux of the conflict lay–is one of the few instances where Collins can be accused not of honest error but of sophistry. It is not just that the figures he cites are unrepresentative and the calculations subject to special pleading. Throughout his career, in his correspondence Collins rails against the "extravagantly absurd prices charged for works of fiction" in Britain (Baker et al. 2005, vol. 1, 87-8) with its "vicious circulating library system" (ibid., vol. 3, 452-3). But in "Considerations" we find him brushing aside the long wait before new British novels reappear in yellowback format, and even extolling the value of a Mudie subscription–"If this is not cheap reading, what is?" (Collins 1880, 614). To understand the private motives underlying this extraordinary lapse we need to return briefly to his dispute with Harper and Brothers.

A closer reading of "Considerations" suggests the depth of the author's personal resentment towards the New York house. There it is Harper's that stands as the leading example of a major American house that puts its own trade interests before the cause of an honourable settlement. And there it is Harper's old catalogues (dating from just before the break in relations) that provide the damning evidence that American books are not so cheap. Most importantly, Collins leaves plenty of circumstantial evidence to allow the curious reader to identify the American friend to whom the protest is addressed. The reference to Dutch ancestry, the military epithet, and the recent house-call leave little doubt that the friend is Colonel William A. Seaver, the Civil War hero who had recently retired from his editorial post at Harper's and paid a couple of visits to London. Despite the row, Collins and Seaver remained close friends until the latter's death in 1883, shortly before Collins would cautiously resume his literary dealings with the New York firm. The fact that Collins chose to address his "Considerations on the Copyright Question" to the Colonel can thus be seen as a further expression of his sense of betrayal by Harper and Brothers.

As we have seen, Collins's authorised publishers in the United States had long remained opposed to international copyright. But in the late 1870s they had changed their position and come round to supporting the idea of an Anglo-American treaty with a clause guaranteeing domestic manufacture. This was what W. H. Appleton had advocated back in 1871, though the idea itself had been around since at least 1837 (Barnes 1974, 62-3; Bowker 1912, 341-7). The Harper proposal to establish a joint commission with a view to effecting such a compromise was sent privately to the American government in November 1878. It was made public in a pamphlet issued on 17 March 1879 and entitled *Memorandums in regard to International Copyright*, which also contained extracts from Appleton's 1871 letter. This pamphlet was widely discussed in Britain, initially in the correspondence columns of the *Times,* to which the American house itself contributed (30 May 1879, 10). Though most London publishers remained firmly opposed to the proposal,[8] there were by now quite a number of British authors who welcomed the initiative. Collins of course was not one of them, though he must have seen a copy of the pamphlet, since *Memorandums* is used in "Considerations" as evidence of the self-serving views of the leading American houses. This reading had indeed some justification. As an editorial in the *Times* had pointed out (19 April 1879, 11), the background to Harper's change of heart was the increasing competition that the established houses based on the eastern seaboard were facing within the American marketplace. This was not only from Canadian publishers such as Hunter, Rose but also from brash new American houses further west in Chicago. For something like a quarter of a century the major American houses had agreed to abide by rules of trade "courtesy", respecting agreements for advance sheet from English authors and combining to crush opposition from newer concerns. Thus, during Collins's long partnership with Harper's, there had in fact appeared relatively few "pirated" editions of his works–notably from T. B. Peterson in Phildaelphia (Gasson 1998, 122)–competing with the authorised versions. But as the centre of American gravity shifted westwards after the Civil War, and as the American reading public gradually began to acquire a taste for English novels at under 20 cents a volume, it became increasingly difficult to maintain this form of cartel. Soon even upstart New York houses like Munro and Lovell were able to enter the same market unopposed (ibid., 98, 137-8). This was also, of course, the main reason why, from the later 1870s, Harper's began to behave less generously and less accommodatingly to British authors like Collins (Conant 1879, 159).

Before concluding, we should recognise that, when the Harper proposal was made public, the debate on protection in America for English authors had already been reactivated on both sides of the Atlantic by the publication of the Report of the Royal Commission on Copyright. This took place in the summer of 1878, after three years of hearings. The Commission's brief was a very wide one, covering domestic issues of serial publication and dramatic performance, as well as problems of colonial and international copyright. In addition to the consideration of specific grievances and remedies there was general discussion of the juridical principles underlying copyright law, with much argument devoted to the question of whether literary property had been protected in common law since Magna Carta or whether it was a purely statutory creation. Here a yawning gap emerged between witnesses committed to the creation of a perpetual copyright founded in the indefeasible moral rights of the author and those wishing to abolish the concept and replace it with a limited royalty payment in the interests of free trade and social progress. As a result it was difficult to establish a consensus among the commissioners, so that, though the final report recommended against a departure from the existing legal principles, several members would only sign with reservations and one submitted a dissenting opinion. Though the commissioners were unanimous only in condemning the confused and confusing state of existing legislation, there was in the event to be no major overhaul until the Copyright Act of 1911 (Bonham-Carter 1978, 98-100).

Nevertheless, the publication of the report encouraged a vigorous exchange in the periodical press which was still in progress when "Considerations" appeared. Notable here are: the two articles of late 1878 by Froude and Farrar representing the battle between the absolutists and abolitionists; the paired articles by S. S. Conant and Leonard Courtney in the

June 1879 issue of *Macmillan's Magazine*, respectively representing American and English views; and, most famously, Matthew Arnold's valiant attempt to give an overview of the issues at stake, and to steer a middle course, in his *Fortnightly Review* article of March 1880. There Arnold centres his argument on the contrast between the cheap book revolution taking place in France at mid century, thanks to the vision of publishers like Michel Lévy, and the reactionary practices of the British book-trade still clinging to the skirts of Charles Mudie. Though he is well aware of the self-interestedness of the arguments of American publishers like Harper's, as regards the crucial question, in the end Arnold is "at one with Mr Conant":

> The Americans ought not to submit to our absurd system of dear books; I am sure they will not, and, as a lover of civilisation, I should be sorry, though I am an author, if they did. I hope they will give us copyright; but I hope, also, they will stick to Michel Lévy's excellent doctrine: "Cheap books are a necessity, and a necessity which need bring, moreover, no loss to either authors or publishers".
> (Arnold 1880, 334)

It is important to remember that "Considerations" appeared three months *after* this challenging intervention.

* * *

As is well known, the British circulating-library system finally fell apart only in 1895, around six years after the death of Wilkie Collins. There have been many attempts to explain why this happened when it did, including the anecdotal, bibliometric, and neo-Marxist approaches of, respectively, Guinevere Griest, Royal Gettmann, and Norman Feltes. In the light of the international copyright conflicts discussed above, it seems to me that all of these very different interpretations share a tendency to overplay domestic determinants and underestimate external pressures. Rather earlier, in March 1891, Congress had approved the Chace Act, thus conceding copyright to foreign authors whose governments offered reciprocal protection, but on condition that the works in question were republished within the United States within a limited period. Though this clause disappointed many idealists on both sides of the Atlantic and prevented the United States from joining the International Copyright Union, in practice it represented a significant step forward for British authors at least. It seems possible that, if popular writers like Dickens and Collins had listened more sympathetically to the case being made across the Atlantic, and with a view to compromise, a similar step might have been taken a generation or so earlier. This might in turn have helped to advance the collapse in Britain of what Arnold called "our highly eccentric, artificial, and unsatisfactory system of book-trade" (ibid., 334). While Wilkie Collins's two articles represent a lively and engaging point of access to "the Schleswig-Holstein Question of literature", revealing much about the personal passions and anxieties it aroused, it would be unwise to take them as the last word on the subject.

Notes

[1] Generally on the creation of international copyright law during the nineteenth century, see Bowker 1912, Copinger 1893, and Nowell-Smith 1968.

[2] Though the topic is beyond the scope of the present article, we should note that both Dickens and Collins were also vociferous against the infringement of other literary "rights" unprotected by statute, notably the unauthorised theatrical adaptation of works of fiction.

[3] The most systematic defence of this position is found in the lengthy treatise of 1879 by the American jurist Eaton S. Drone.

[4] The attribution is found in the recent annotated edition of *A National Wrong* from the Wilkie Collins Society (July 2004), edited by Andrew Gasson, Paul Lewis, and Graham Law.

[5] See the letters to Payn of 26 and 30 November 1869, and 14 January 1870, Baker et al. 2005, vol. 2, 162-3, 165, 168.

[6] For a fuller version of this argument, see the Introduction to Baker et al., 2005, vol. 1, xxx-xxxix.

[7] In response a petition to the British Foreign Secretary in support of the Appleton proposals was signed in 1871 by fifty British authors, including Collins's journalist friends George Sala and Edmund Yates, as well as names like Carlyle, Ruskin, Mill, Spencer, and Darwin (Didier 1880, 137; Bowker 1912, 350-1).

[8] Edward Marston, a partner in the firm of Sampson Low, was both a representative voice and a regularly contributor to the debate; see Marston 1904, 306-14.

Works Cited

(Material from daily newspapers is cited fully in the body of the essay but omitted here.)

1879. *Memorandums in regard to International Copyright between the United States and Great Britain*. New York: Harper and Brothers.

Arnold, Matthew. 1880. Copyright. *Fortnightly Review* 27:319-34.

Baker, William and William M. Clarke (eds). 1999. *The Letters of Wilkie Collins*. 2 vols. Basingstoke: Macmillan Press.

Baker, William, Andrew Gasson., Graham Law and Paul Lewis (eds). 2005. *The Public Face of Wilkie Collins: The Collected Letters*. 4 vols. London: Pickering and Chatto, 2005.

Barnes, James J. 1974. *Authors, Publishers and Politicians: The Quest for an Anglo-American Copyright Agreement, 1815-54*. London: Routledge and Kegan Paul.

Bonham-Carter, Victor. 1978. *Authors by Profession: Vol. 1 From the Introduction of Printing until the Copyright Act of 1911*. London: Society of Authors.

Bowker, R. R. 1912. *Copyright: Its History and its Law*. Boston: Houghton Mifflin.

Collins, Wilkie. 1880. Considerations on the Copyright Question. *International Review* 8:609-18.

Collins, Wilkie and James Payn. 1870. A National Wrong. *Chamber's Edinburgh Journal* 17:107-10.

Conant, S. S. 1879. International Copyright: I. An American View. *Macmillan's Magazine* 40:151-61.

Cook, Adrian. 1975. *The Alabama Claims: American Politics and Anglo-American Relations, 1865-1872*. Ithaca: Cornell University Press.

Copinger, W. A. 1893. *The Law of Copyright in Works of Literature and* Art. London: Stevens and Haynes.

Courtney, Leonard H. 1879. International Copyright: II. An Englishman's View of the Foregoing. *Macmillan's Magazine* 40:161-6.

Didier, Eugene L. 1880. Congress and International Copyright. *Scribner's Magazine* 10:132-8.

Drone, Eaton S. 1879. *A Treatise on the Law of Property in Intellectual Productions in Great Britain and the United States*. Boston: Little Brown.

Farrer, T. H. 1878. The Principle of Copyright. *Fortnightly Review* 24:836-51.

Feltes, N. N. 1986. *Modes of Production of Victorian Novels*. Chicago: University of Chicago Press.

Froude, J. A. 1878. The Copyright Commission. *Edinburgh Review* 148:295-343.

Gasson, Andrew. 1998. *Wilkie Collins: An Illustrated Guide*. Oxford: Oxford University Press.

Gettmann, Royal A. 1960. *A Victorian Publisher: A Study of the Bentley Papers*. Cambridge: Cambridge University Press.

Griest, Guinevere L. 1970. *Mudie's Circulating Library and the Victorian Novel*. Bloomington, IN: Indiana University Press.

Harper, J. Henry. 1912. *The House of Harper: A Century of Publishing in Franklin Square*. New York: Harper.

Helps, Arthur. 1869. International Copyright between Great Britain and America: A Letter to Charles Eliot Norton. *Macmillan's Magazine* 20:89-95.

Marston, Edward. 1904. *After Work: Fragments from the Workshop of an Old Publisher*. London. Heinemann.

Nowell-Smith, Simon. 1968. *International Copyright Law and the Publisher in the Reign of Queen Victoria*. Oxford: Clarendon Press.

Putnam, George Haven. 1915. *Memories of a Publisher, 1865-1915*. New York: Putnam.

Tillotson, Kathleen., Graham Storey., et al. (eds). 1965-2002. *The Letters of Charles Dickens*. 12 vols. Oxford: Clarendon Press.

THE DANGEROUS BROTHER: FAMILY
TRANSGRESSION IN *THE HAUNTED HOTEL*

LYNN PARKER

Although one of Wilkie Collins's most financially successful short novels, *The Haunted Hotel* (1879) has received relatively little critical attention. The sparseness of critical interest in the text is made especially clear when reading Norman Page and Toru Sasaki's interesting introduction to the Oxford World Classics edition of the text (see Page and Sasaki 1999). Since this edition brings together three different short novels by Collins, much of the introduction draws attention to the seeming discomfort that critics of the Victorian novel have had with the novella form.[1] When it turns to discuss *The Haunted Hotel* independently, the introduction is forced to spread a wide net, citing brief mentions of the novella that can be found in critical works that primarily focus on other Collins's works. Part of the critical discomfort with discussing the novella stems from its seeming failure to be conveniently labelled. Lacking both the critical acclaim and length of Collins's more widely discussed novels, *The Haunted Hotel* has also been excluded from the discussion of what some critics term Collins's "social cause" novels, such as *The Fallen Leaves* (1879).[2]

Critics who have addressed the text have tended to focus on Countess Narona, "one of Collins's grand Gothic villainesses", to use Tamar Heller's fine description. The Countess's presence does dominate much of the text, and her apparent insistence upon deliberately acting to ensure her own destruction has fascinated some scholars (Heller 1992, 164). In fact, as Page and Sasaki note, T. S. Eliot considered Narona's obsession with fatality as the single factor which makes "the text better than a mere readable second-rate ghost story" (Eliot 1932, 380).[3] The text's interest in fate can be clearly seen in its representation of two "opposites" who seem to be connected by fate. *The Haunted Hotel*, first published in *Belgravia* magazine in 1879, traces the relationship between a sexually compelling villainess, the Countess, and Agnes Lockwood, the virginal woman whom Narona inadvertently displaces from her fiancé, Lord Montbarry's, affections. Using third person narration, the novella explores the mystery surrounding Montbarry's death in Venice shortly after his marriage to Narona, after which she receives a large life insurance payment. Collins identifies Countess Narona as a beautiful but "unwomanly" villain almost immediately in the text, carefully pointing to the "total want of tenderness" in her eyes, and her unpleasant smile, which was "at once sad and cruel" (Collins 1879, 90, 93). Believing, like Ozais Midwinter with reference to Lydia Gwilt in *Armadale* (1866), that she is doomed to commit some crime and then face just retribution, the Countess initially attempts to fight her "destiny", only to realise that she inevitably enacts it through her struggle. After establishing that a mysterious fate appears to link the two women, the text offers a series of interconnected mysteries, culminating in the discovery of a severed head that is eventually proven to be that of Narona's husband, Lord Montbarry. The murder and destruction of the body is linked to Narona and her ostensible brother, Baron Rivar, although both die before they can give a formal confession, evading, in legal terms at least, retribution.

Drawing upon elements of sensation and detective fiction, the text's exploration of the Countess's complex relationship to fate is indeed compelling. However, as the title *The Haunted Hotel* would suggest, the novella also presents a ghost story that is central to the plot. Of course, the term "haunted" may be a blind here, identifying the ways in which the Countess is herself haunted by her belief in fate. But, in addition to this interesting type of haunting, the text portrays a series of spectral visitations that provide the focus and resolution of the novella's mystery plot. By looking "past" the ghost story as readers such as T. S. Eliot suggest, critics have potentially overlooked the complex way in which Collins employs this spectral narrative to explore dangerous flaws in the nature of sibling bonds, "bonds", moreover, that were considered central to the affectionate Victorian family.

The novella reveals its interest in examining the strength and nature of sibling ties in its third chapter, when Montbarry's younger brother, Henry Westwick, inadvertently overhears several members of his club gossiping about Montbarry's upcoming marriage to Narona. Contrary to what the gentlemen of the club seem to expect, Henry does not defend his brother. Rather, he tells the men to continue talking about Montbarry, since "not one of you can despise him more heartily than I do" (ibid., 101). Henry's public renunciation of his brother appears to be based upon Montbarry's own prior rejection of family ties. As Narona explains earlier in the text, the stigma attached to Montbarry's rejection of Agnes Lockwood as his fiancé is amplified because she is "of his own blood and family" (ibid., 93). The hauntings that occur later in the novella reinforce this interest in the strength of blood ties: although the authenticity of the hauntings is verified by the authority of the third person narrator, the manifestations are only perceived by the murdered man's blood kin. Thus, considering the novella's ghostly elements as central to, rather than an adjunct of, the text reveals the story's interest in exploring the potentially unstable nature of familial bonds. The apparent tendency of Collins's fiction to challenge ideas at the heart of Victorian culture was nicely identified by Heller in her classic study of Collins and the Female Gothic (Heller 1992, 164). Yet, as part of her brief discussion of *The Haunted Hotel*, which is limited to a short, but interesting analysis of Narona as creator of the play-within-the-novel, Heller laments the disappearance of this complex blend of narrative efficacy and subversive focus in Collins's later fiction. I would suggest that this dissident tendency is present in a powerful way in *The Haunted Hotel* as Collins employs the spectral to challenge the stability of sibling ties. By employing the hauntings as a device to investigate the Victorian family, through the shifting dynamics of sibling interactions, Collins manages to construct a subtle exploration of social concerns within the demands and freedom of the spectral novella.

Both historians and literary critics have increasingly turned their attention to the importance of sibling bonds in the Victorian idealisation of the family. In *Family Fortunes* (1987), for example, family historians Leonore Davidoff and Catherine Hall have traced the significance of sibling relationships as social markers for the emerging affectionate family of the nineteenth century, pointing to the many ways in which business and personal life were inevitably determined by sibling relationships. Most recently, Valerie Sanders has suggested that brother-sister relationships serve an important ideological function in Victorian literature, providing Victorians with their most dominant image of familial and social bonds (see Sanders 2002). I would suggest that, as these sibling ties became increasingly imbued with social and narrative responsibility, however, the danger that these relationships might be unsound challenged the stability of the family itself. In its interesting exploration of potentially unstable sibling ties, *The Haunted Hotel* challenges fiction's increasing reliance upon sibling bonds to support both narrative and cultural authority.

The novella offers an intriguing view of sibling ties in its outline of the way in which Montbarry's severed head is discovered. Readers eventually learn that Countess Narona and Baron Rivar hide Montbarry's severed head, the only part of his body that they are not able to destroy with acid, in a chamber of the Venetian palace that Montbarry has rented. The head is hidden in a secret compartment near a fireplace, left over from "the last evil days of the Inquisition" (Collins 1879, 208). The palace is eventually converted into a hotel, and each member of Montbarry's family, who spends time in the room with the fireplace (or the room directly below the hiding place), has some kind of supernatural experience: one brother, Henry, feels restless and depressed and is forced to leave the hotel; Montbarry's sister, Mrs Norbury, who "in olden times had been noted in the family as the one member of it who lived on affectionate terms with Montbarry", dreams that her brother Montbarry is killed over and over in a number of different ways; a second brother, Francis, smells an overpowering "offensive" odour that drives him from the room, and so on. It is of course important that only family members experience such hauntings. When strangers sleep in the room there is no phenomena, and even when the guilty and seemingly guilt-ridden Countess sleeps in the room, she experiences nothing ghostly. In addition to Montbarry's siblings, only Agnes, his former fiancé, experiences a manifestation and indeed hers is the most powerful. While sleeping in the room beneath where the victim's final remains are hidden, Agnes sees a severed head floating above her bed; the head turns to face her and begins to descend upon her. The disturbing sexual resonances of the head's descent are telling, as is the fact that the haunting is predicted, and experienced vicariously, by Countess Narona. Having used a variety of means to sneak into Agnes's room, the countess stealthily sits by Agnes's bed, waiting for and apparently finally experiencing, the haunting that she cannot experience alone.

That Agnes receives a more intense supernatural visitation than the others seems predicated on her status as both blood relative and devoted jilt. The Countess explains that Agnes was "nearer to the heart" of Montbarry than anyone else, and she is also the only family member who does not renounce her family tie to Montbarry when he marries the Countess (ibid., 89). The blood tie is central to the unfolding of these haunting scenes: only family members can see or smell the ghost, and, at the same time, the spectral experience reaffirms kinship connections. Although the siblings renounce him, and several admit that they indeed never liked him when he was alive, the supernatural occurrences seem to assert that Montbarry's blood tie is irrevocable since it reaches across a far wider divide than any separation created by personal dislike or disapproval. Furthermore, while the hauntings ostensibly serve the narrative and spiritual purpose of alerting the family members to Montbarry's death by violence, the hauntings also reinforce affection and family allegiance. Although the siblings admit that they are angry at his past behavior towards Agnes, the hauntings powerfully remind them of their blood tie; as the brother who becomes the new Lord Montbarry attests near the end of the story, "I remembered, with something like remorse, that the same mother bore us" (ibid., 235). Montbarry's spectral, severed head allows him to assert and maintain his literal "head of the family" status, forcing his siblings to acknowledge the family ties that they would like to renounce.

The Haunted Hotel's ghost story thus reaffirms the importance of sibling relationships suggesting that these bonds cannot be severed by behaviour or choice. Neither eradicating the body and severing the head, nor choosing to sever personal ties to one's siblings is enough to cut the power of sibling blood bonds. This seemingly straight-forward narrative affirmation of the priority of family ties is challenged and undermined, however, by an alternative portrait of the instability of sibling ties. While Agnes's dual status as lover and cousin might signal the strength of her attachment on the one hand, the double role also opens up the possibility of confusion.

Agnes's initial refusal to "blame" Lord Montbarry for breaking their engagement and marrying someone else suggests a quality of selflessness and devotion that would certainly be in keeping with Victorian cultural beliefs about the nature of women. From Sarah Stickney Ellis's conduct books, such as *The Women of England* (1843), which ring with the phrase "self-sacrifice" and insist that a woman must "lay aside [...] her very *self*" for the good of her family (ibid., 15, italics in original), to Ruskin's famous call in *Sesame and Lilies* (1865) for women to be "wise, not for self-development, but for self-renunciation" (Ruskin 1862, 78), presenting self-sacrifice as a moral force, much Victorian literature advocated female self-sacrifice for the benefit of her family and even her nation. Certainly the majority of the characters in *The Haunted Hotel* appear to admire Agnes's loyalty, even if they believe that her devotion is misplaced. Regardless of the basis for her devotion, the supernatural world also appears to give authority to Agnes's selfless behavior, potentially validating her devotion by giving her the most intense haunting experience. However, the text challenges the nobility of this portrait by pointing out the possibility that this kind of devotion might be misplaced or exploited. While the novella does not attempt to explain or justify Agnes's choice of Lord Montbarry, it is clear that he does not deserve this special devotion. In addition to describing Montbarry's betrayal of Agnes, the narrator explains that most of his siblings did not like Montbarry and that "even his mother owned that her eldest son was of all her children the child whom she least liked" (Collins 1879, 172). Agnes's preference for Montbarry goes beyond the claim of blood ties, since Montbarry's younger brother Henry "had been the unsuccessful rival of the elder for the hand of Agnes" (ibid., 108). While Agnes does not harbour resentment against Montbarry, he is suitably punished for his sins against her with a failed marriage to the Countess and horrific final days of incarceration in a dungeon-like cellar, poisoning, and dismemberment.

There is an irony, however, in this narrative enactment of revenge against a man for failing to value a woman's devotion, since the text also reveals a different enactment of womanly devotion through the Countess Narona. Like Agnes, the Countess reveals an intense, persistent devotion to a man in her life, her alleged brother, the Baron Rivar. The Countess commits a variety of crimes, including helping to murder her husband, in order to provide Baron Rivar with money to pay his gambling debts and finance his experiments in chemistry. While the consequences of her devotion to the Count are certainly condemned by the novella, the text also reveals the potential problems of female self-sacrifice by revealing how the Countess perceives her nefarious actions to stem from her feminine "duty".

The Countess suggests the intensity of her devotion to her brother in the confessional "play" which she writes in the hopes of earning some money from Montbarry's theatre-producing brother. This play echoes scenes from the Countess's own experiences, identifying characters by title rather by name, including the countess, the baron, the Lord, the courier, and so on. The play describes the "Baron's" attempt to coerce his sister, a Countess, into marrying a Lord for money. After the Baron makes the curious ultimatum that he will marry "the wealthy widow of a Jewish usurer", if the Countess herself will not "marry for money", the play describes the Countess's immediate declaration to sacrifice herself:

> All the noblest sentiments in her nature are exalted to the highest pitch. "Where is the true woman", she exclaims, "who wants time to consummate the sacrifice of herself, when the man to whom she is devoted demands it? [...] She holds out her hand to him, and she says, Sacrifice me on the altar of your glory! Take as stepping-stones on the way to your triumph, my love, my liberty, and my life!" (ibid., 223)

By prefacing the *play's* Countess's offer to sacrifice herself with the authorial descriptor, ("all the noblest sentiments in her nature are exalted to the highest pitch") the *novella's* Countess reveals her own approval and admiration of such sacrifice. The melodramatic excess of the Countess's proclamation not only emphasises the intensity of her attachment to "the man to whom she is devoted", but also points to the sexual nature of that devotion, for which she longs "to consummate the sacrifice of herself". The excessiveness of this portrait of womanly and sisterly self-sacrifice, is, of course, also part of a Victorian culture of sisterly devotion. Nineteenth-century fiction abounds with images of sisterly loyalty to potentially undeserving brothers, such as Lizzie Hexam's adherence to Charley in *Our Mutual Friend* (1864-5) or Maggie Tulliver's to Tom in *The Mill on the Floss* (1859). The social importance of such sisterly behavior is specifically articulated by Sarah Stickney Ellis, who calls upon sisters to be selfless in order to maintain the sibling tie. Referring to a sister's need to cultivate her sibling bond to a brother, Ellis suggests that she should be

> watchful and studious to establish this intimate connexion, and to keep entire the golden cord by which they are thus bound. Affection does not come by relationship alone; and never yet was the affection of man fully and lastingly engaged by woman, without some means being adopted on her part to increase or preserve his happiness. (Ellis 1843, 67)

Ellis's language clearly echoes that used to describe a wife's domestic obligations, and indeed Ellis insists that the brother-sister bond can be a substitute for marriage. In what may seem to twenty-first-century eyes a dangerous observation, Ellis confidently asserts that "[a] young man of kind and social feelings is often glad to find in his sister, a substitute for what he afterwards ensures more permanently in a wife" (ibid., 67). The exact nature of these "substitute" duties is, of course, not clear, but the potential connotations of Ellis's point are disturbingly visceral. Within this context, then, the *play's* Countess's decision to maintain her fraternal tie to her brother at all costs might be seen as an alarming exaggeration of Ellis's "safe" domestic advice.

Like the blurring of cousin and lover in Agnes, and the subtle connotations of Ellis's observations suggest, the Countess's role as sister seems blurred by the intensity of this imagery. Indeed, both the third-person narrative and the enclosed play-within-the-narrative continually suggest that the Countess and Baron's relationship has a sexual component. Early in the third chapter, for example, some gentlemen at gossip in their club outline a list of rumours about the Countess's behaviour and relationships, ranging from claims about her nationality and gambling habits to the assertion "that it is doubtful whether the man who accompanied her in her travels (under the name of Baron Rivar, and in the character of her brother) was her brother at all" (Collins 1879, 99). These rumors about the Baron's "name" and "character", are extended in the text by further hints and conjectures about their relationship. For example, without specifying what the "other things" are, Ferrara, the courier who works for Montbarry and Narona when they are married and living in Venice, hints at the Countess and Baron's sexual relationship when he writes to his wife:

> I have seen other things besides, which–well! which don't increase my respect for my lady and the Baron. The maid says she means to give warning to leave. She is a respectable British female, and doesn't take things quite so easily as I do. [...] If my lord's suspicions are once awakened, the consequences will be terrible. (ibid., 117)

The maid, the "respectable British female" who eventually leaves the Countess out of moral indignation, serves as patriotic contrast to the continental Countess, whose sexual indiscretions have not yet, but will presumably at some time, come under "my lord's suspicions". Indeed, the "evidence" provided by the maid's desertion and the courier's intimations is strong enough to be presumed factual by Agnes's lawyer, who is acting for the courier's wife. As these rumours and the play's authorial intrusions suggest, the Baron may merely be posing as the Countess's "brother" in order to disguise his actual role as her lover. The Baron's hope of establishing either his own, or Narona's, mercenary marriage could explain why their sexual relationship would need to remain illicit.

This straightforward explanation is challenged, however, by the Countess's response to such accusations. Indeed, as author of the "play" enclosed within the text, Narona describes the *play's* Countess as the victim of malicious gossip "which falsely and abominably points to the Baron as her lover instead of her brother" (ibid., 223). The play obliquely asserts that the Lord does eventually accuse his wife of infidelity, at the very least, but that once he articulates his "suspicions", he then appears to repent and second guess his conclusions. The Countess's claim, in the play, that the unspecified accusations are "false" and "abominable", questions her guilt of adultery, while simultaneously suggesting the alternate explanation that the Baron is *both* her lover and brother. The dangerously intimate imagery present in Sarah Stickney Ellis's description of a sister's duties and obligations is made evident here in a powerful suggestion of incest predicated upon sisterly self-sacrifice. The Countess's status as villainess is thus implicitly challenged for a brief moment when she appears to be the possible victim of brotherly exploitation.

The novella's recognition of the potential for familial exploitation suggests that such "exploitation" or misrepresentation might underlie Agnes's status as both "cousin" and "lover". By deliberately complicating any simple correlation between a selfish brother and a self-sacrificing sister, Collins reveals the sexual motivations that potentially underlie the brother-sister bond, even as he reveals how dangerously open to deception, and misappropriation, the affectionate social relationship of brother and sister may be. The constricting sense of brotherly abuse implied in this relationship potentially undercuts the "happy ending" offered to Agnes at the close of the novella. Seemingly unable (or unwilling) to break from this potentially constricting circle of fraternal power, Agnes marries her fiancé's brother, thus redefining her connection to the deceased Montbarry from lover to sister and simultaneously reversing those familial connections to his brother Henry. This marriage reinforces Agnes's blood relationship to the family, doubling, as it were, her connection by replacing the cousin tie with the dual status of spouse/sister.[4]

Agnes's marriage to one brother, after being engaged to another, hints at issues of incest through interfamily remarriage that were strenuously debated, in both legal and moral terms, as part of the discussion surrounding "The Deceased Wife's Sister Bill". The morality and legality of a marriage between a widower and his deceased wife's sister became part of a very public discussion when a new Act, known as "Lord Lyndhurst's Act" and passed in 1835, legalised any such marriage that had taken place before 1835 and *banned* any subsequent ones. As Chase and Levenson explain in "Love After Death: The Deceased Wife's Sister Bill", before 1835 such marriages where considered morally ambigous, being in violation of Archbishop Parker's Table of Kindred and Affinity, but in practice remained legal as long as no one officially challenged the marriage during the couple's lifetime. Although a vigorous attempt, centered around "The Deceased Wife's Sister Bill", was made to reverse Lord Lyndhurst's Act, it was not until 1907 that the law was changed. The Act and the resulting attempts to reverse it brought the issue of domestic sexuality and sibling relationships into public discussion, a discussion whose echoes Chase and Levenson trace through several of Dickens's novels. (Chase and Levenson 2000, 107, 113-4).

Read in this context, Agnes's decision to marry her deceased fiancé's brother seems far more loaded with familial and sexual meaning. Of course, the novella allows Agnes to sidestep these questions of morality since she never married her first lover and only considers a marriage to Montbarry's brother after her first lover jilts her and then dies. However, as Chase and Levenson point out rather briefly, the prohibition against a widow marrying her deceased husband's brother was far stronger than that accorded to a deceased wife's sister and thus Agnes's behavior as psuedo-widow would carry a further stigma, as well (ibid., 114). While such prohibitions may seem more of an intellectual puzzle than an actual concern, one only has to think of the importance that Hamlet places on Gertrude's marriage to her deceased husband's brother in *Hamlet* to understand the resonance. Hamlet's interest in "defining" incest is echoed by *The Haunted Hotel*, as is the interesting device of using loosely-veiled doubles in a "play within a play" (in this case a "play within a novel") to determine guilt.

This emphasis on doubles and the possibility of misinterpreting them is reflected in myriad ways throughout the text, including the two brothers/fiancés, double meanings, the double set of characters created by the play's mirroring of the novella's events, the roles of cousin/brother and lover, and so on. In an echo of *The Woman in White* (1860), for example, the mystery plot itself revolves around doubles and substitutions when Narona and the Baron switch the identity of the dying courier for a relatively healthy Lord Montbarry, allowing the world to think Montbarry has died of natural causes. The stakes of substitution have been raised from the earlier novel, however: whereas the Italian villain, Count Fosco (with the aid of Sir Percival Glyde) imprisons Laura in an asylum, *The Haunted Hotel*'s Italian villain and villainess imprison, and eventually murder, Lord Montbarry. Of course, murder is perhaps "necessary" in this text because the victim is not a woman with limited social claims to a public identity, but a man and a "Lord" who could presumably prove his identity by a host of legal and familial means. Although the severed head, which has been submerged in acid, cannot "prove" the identify of the victim by its features, the gold teeth inside, markers of his wealth and status, are able to assert his identify with equally sure conviction. The substitution of courier for Lord—made possible not by their physical similarity but by the fact that the two men are strangers to the Venetian medical establishment—is perhaps more precarious than the one perpetrated in *The Woman in White*, but the closure offered by the evidence of the golden teeth is known only to Montbarry's brother Henry.

A text infused with doubles closes with the murdered man's brother/double marrying his jilt and refusing to answer her questions about the identity of the severed head. Henry's unwillingness to authenticate the "meaning" of the hauntings for Agnes or his other siblings reflects the narrative's refusal to provide closure. Hence, the text's refusal to name the Baron as lover or brother is part of a series of narrative refusals, including the unwillingness to offer "authenticated" testimony, as in Collins's other texts, to support the story.

Although it employs both a third-person narrator and the type of documents that play a key narrative role in such texts as *The Woman in White*, the text asserts authority selectively. The third-person narrator establishes the authority of the haunting experiences, for example, by providing a careful chronicle of the various siblings' responses to the room. But this same narrator is curiously silent on the question of the Countess and Baron's true relationship, leaving rumor and the "play" as unstable documentary evidence. The novella teases the reader about the veracity of the play, linking details of the hauntings to specific parts of the drama. For instance, the visions that Montbarry's sister sees of her brother being murdered in a variety of different ways is eventually replicated in, and "authenticated" by, the play, when its Countess and Baron characters discuss different ways of killing the Lord. Similarly, the horrible odour that Montbarry's brother smells as part of his haunting is described in the play as the odour of chemicals and human decay that is created by the play's Baron when destroying the corpse.

Hence, the novella "explains" the unexplainable in some ways, but elects to leave the question of incest tantalisingly open. Rejecting the option of easily clearing the confusion between the brother and lover roles by showing how the sibling tie between Nerona and Rivar is false, Collins portrays a darker possibility beneath the brother-lover relationship and presents sibling desire as irresolvable a mystery as the haunting and murder themselves. Indeed, the truth of sibling connection seems to be one that lies beyond conventional, "proper" means of understanding, and can only be put to the test through supernatural intervention. Thus, even as the novella offers the ultimate validation for the primacy of sibling bonds, it simultaneously reveals the inability of those bonds to function successfully in the Victorian social realm. Wilkie Collins suggests that Victorian insistence upon the nobility of sibling bonds and sisterly self-sacrifice serves to mask the more dangerous aspects of the brother-sister relationship. In *The Haunted Hotel,* this is represented as the brother's desire to exploit his sister's sexuality for his own pleasure and personal gain.

Notes

[1] I have chosen to use the term novella to describe *The Haunted Hotel* though I do so in agreement with Page and Sasaki who point out that there is "no satisfactory term in English" for the form (Page and Sasaki 1999, vii).

[2] Critical discussions of the novella are, of course, potentially biased by Swinburne's dismissal of *The Haunted Hotel* as "hideous fiction" (Swinburne 1889, 263).

[3] Page and Sasaki (1999, ix; xvi-xvii) agree with Eliot that the text's primary focus is on fatality, but they see the text as a narrative return to the issues raised in *Armadale.*

[4] The Victorians used the term "sister" to refer either to a blood sibling or to a sibling gained through marriage, a figure who might now be named a "sister-in-law".

Works Cited

Chase, Karen. and Michael Levenson. 2000. Love After Death: The Deceased Wife's Sister's Act, in *The Spectacle of Intimacy*. Princeton: Princeton University Press.

Collins, Wilkie. 1879. *The Haunted Hotel*. Oxford: Oxford World Classics, 1999.

Davidoff, Leonore. and Catherine Hall. 2002. *Family Fortunes: Men and Women of the English Middle Class, 1780-1850*. London: Routledge.

Eliot, T. S. 1932. Wilkie Collins and Charles Dickens, in *Selected Essays, 1917-1932*. New York: Harcourt, Brace, and Co.

Ellis, Sarah Stickney. 1843. *The Woman of England*. New York: J. H. G. Langley.

Heller, Tamar. 1992. *Dead Secrets: Wilkie Collins and the Female Gothic.* New Haven: Yale University Press.

Page, Norman. 1974. *Wilkie Collins: The Critical Heritage*. London: Routledge and Kegan Paul.

Page, Norman and Toru Sasaki. 1999. Introduction to Collins 1879, vii-xxiv.

Ruskin, John. 1862. Of Queens' Gardens, in *Sesame and Lilies*. New Haven: Yale University Press, 2002.

Sanders, Valerie. 2002. *The Brother-Sister Culture in Nineteenth-Century Literature.* New York: Palgrave.

Swinburne, Algernon Charles. 1889. In Defence of Collins's Artistry, in Page 1974, 253-64.

PART V:
COLLINS, THEATRE, AND FILM

"TWIN-SISTERS" AND "THEATRICAL THIEVES": WILKIE COLLINS AND THE DRAMATIC ADAPTATION OF *THE MOONSTONE*

RICHARD PEARSON

"The final plays were largely adaptations of the novels" (Marshall 1970, 12). In this succinct and dismissive comment rests a critical attitude that is largely unchallenged, despite the resurrection of Collins's novels in the last two decades of critical interest. In their approaches to Collins's plays, biographers and critics have repeated the tenor of Marshall's note time and again. Like the general academic attitude towards the Victorian stage, critical opinion is comfortable with the notion that Collins either dashed off his adaptations to secure dramatic copyright against pirated stage versions, or that he produced mistakes, full of "drastic changes" from the original novel (Pykett 2005, 195). The temptation to compare an adaptation to its original, and find it wanting, is always present in the critical writings on the plays. In every study of Collins, the plays have functioned merely as extraneous footnotes on the novels themselves. With the occasional exception,[1] Collins's plays, when discussed, are simply described, and with an air of critical curiosity that seems almost astonished that Collins could have been bothered with such trifles. Collins, on the other hand, suggested that, had he been born in France where the opportunities for a successful career as a dramatist existed, "all the stories I have written [...] would have been told in dramatic form". Summing up his artistry, he added, "if I know anything of my own faculty, it is a dramatic one" (Ashley 1952, 132). Robert Ashley takes issue with this; like many of his fellow critics, he is unable to see the value of Collins's drama (indeed, he spends only two pages of his book discussing the post-1870 plays), agreeing only that his critical assessment "would not be complete without some mention of his dramatic work" (ibid., 125). "Of true dramatic ability Collins possessed little", Ashley suggests; "none of his original dramas achieved any conspicuous success; his stage hits were all adaptations" (ibid., 133).

And yet, quite clearly, Collins and the stage were intimately acquainted and the author paralleled a career as a novelist with that as a dramatist. As he said in the Preface to *Basil* (1852), "the Novel and the Play are twin-sisters in the family of Fiction; that the one is drama narrated, as the other is a drama acted; and that all the strong and deep emotions which the Play-writer is privileged to excite, the Novel-writer is privileged to excite also" (Collins 1852, letter of dedication). And like the "twin-sisters" or doubled-characters of most of his fiction, the interrelation between these like members of the same family was problematic, deeply divided, schizophrenic, antagonistic, passionate, and sensational. Collins wrote at least fourteen plays in his career, many of which had very successful runs in the theatre; he wrote drama across four decades from the 1850s to the 1880s. His last play, *The Evil Genius*, part of an interesting simultaneous production of play and novel, was read only as a "copyright performance" on 30 October 1885 (Gasson 1998, 42). Even at the end of his career, however, Collins clearly had intended *The Evil Genius* for production, writing to A. P. Watt, "It *is* a good play 'though I say it that should't'" (cited Peters 1991, 418), and taking enough care to revise a transcript.[2] Collins's playwrighting career was serious enough that he worked tirelessly on some productions that may never even have made it onto the boards–his letters describe the months of working with Regnier in Paris on a French version of *Armadale*, for example. At the height of his novel-writing career, he revised the 1857 text of *The Frozen Deep* for the 1866 production at the Olympic Theatre, and, after *No Thoroughfare* (which ran for 200 nights at the Adelphi from 26 December 1867), Collins secured lucrative runs of his adaptations in the first half of the 1870s. *The Woman in White* (Olympic, 9 October 1871), ran for nineteen weeks; *Man and Wife* (Prince of Wales, 22 February 1873), twenty-three weeks; *The New Magdalen* (Olympic, 19 May 1873), nineteen weeks (and a provincial tour); *Miss Gwilt* (the second adaptation of *Armadale* which opened in Liverpool, 9 December 1875), ran at the Globe for twelve weeks from 15 April 1876[3]; and finally *The Moonstone* (Olympic, 17 September 1877), ran for nine weeks. Although usually described as a failure, and, in comparison to other runs, *The Moonstone* certainly did not remain on the stage as long, still from the playbill of Saturday, 13 October, the public were informed that "in consequence of numerous enquiries, and for the convenience of families residing at a distance, a Morning Performance of the above successful Drama, by Wilkie Collins, will take place on Saturday 27th October" (bill printed in Gasson 1998, 107). The success of Collins's works on the stage demand more than the cursory glances and negative comparisons they have received thus far; they are the unjustly neglected "twin-sisters" of their novel counterparts, and, as with the "doubles" of Collins's texts, without them, we see only part of the scene.

T. S. Eliot's introduction to the Oxford University Press 1928 edition of *The Moonstone* identifies the significance of the "dramatic" impulse in Collins's works, and the irremovable connection between the writings of Collins and those of Charles Dickens. From 1850, Eliot argues, Collins's writings instilled in Dickens a new sense of the dramatic, encapsulated in the fatalistic atmosphere of his narratives. Summarising his view of the two writers, he argues that:

> The distinction between drama and melodrama is a fine one. In relation to the work of Wilkie Collins it is probably this – that in drama the coincidences, the fatalities, appear to be the visible manifestations of some obscure power beyond human knowledge. The dramatist seems to be sensitive, more than we, to the Dark Forces. When we intellectualise his work, we say that he has a "philosophy". The melodramatist, on the other hand, is the author who appears to be interested in the effects as effects, without knowing or caring what lies behind. Wilkie Collins is the pure melodramatist. Dickens, without belonging to that group of dramatists of fate which includes Sophocles and Shakespeare, is yet separated from Collins by the difference between pure unaccountable genius and pure consummate talent. (Eliot 1928, x)

Dickens has "drama", Eliot suggests, where Collins has only "melodrama". This critical opinion has three significances. Firstly, it establishes the essential inseparability of Dickens and Collins: "[y]ou cannot appreciate Collins without taking Dickens into account; and the work of Dickens after 1850 would not be what it is but for the reciprocal influence of Collins", he writes, almost replicating that fascination with "fatality" that he describes as central to Collins's work (ibid., v). Secondly, he reflects that critical hierarchy which places melodrama below an idealised drama–a shaping of literary tradition that has been responsible for consigning Collins's plays (and, indeed, much of Victorian drama) to the archive, and moreover of estimating the novels above their dramatic adaptations. But, thirdly, he identifies that central dramatic quality of Collins's work that makes the plays so significant and makes the need to challenge this hierarchy so essential. Eliot represents a twentieth-century critical complacency about authorial identity that was not, I would argue, achieved until that same period.

The relationship between fiction, drama, and poetry in the mid-nineteenth century was problematic. Drama was an ancient mode of writing with authorial legitimacy, but was in decline as an art form; the novel was new, young, experimental, but also popular, "low", and commercial. For a young writer, drawn to the stage but perceiving the hazards of making a career in such a mode, successful with the novel but aware of its populist connotations, and, moreover, living in the shadow of a writer who himself occupied the borderland between legitimacy and commercial popularity, Collins must have found his authorial direction confusing. Much as Dickens believed the drama to be in a state of poverty, so Collins, writing for *Household Words* in the late 1850s, thought the same. In his essay on "Douglas Jerrold", he complained that "[i]t is sad, it is almost humiliating, to be obliged to add, in reference to the early history of Jerrold's first dramatic triumph, that his share of the gains which *Black-Eyed Susan* poured into the pockets of managers on both sides of the water was just seventy pounds" (Collins 1858a, 219). The paucity of payment in writing for the stage drove authors in one direction only: "in England, the most eminent literary men", he wrote, "write for the library table alone; and, in England, the theatre is the luxury of the illiterate classes" (Collins 1858b, 266). This analysis of the situation of the modern stage, in an article entitled "Dramatic Grub-Street", describes a complicated system of actor-manager domination, cheap French translations, and ignorant audiences, as accumulating to the detriment of good theatre. However, Collins argues for a more financially successful future for the dramatic author: "At the present low rate of remuneration", he remarks, "a man of ability wastes his powers if he writes for the stage" (ibid., 269). He calls for an enlightened "theatrical speculator" or manager, who would do for the drama what the serial novel has done for the financial success of novelists and publishers. If such emerged, he suggests, "names that are now well known on title-pages only, would then appear on play-bills also; and tens of thousands of readers, who now pass the theatre-door with indifference, would be turned into tens of thousands of play-goers also" (ibid., 270).

   In much of Collins's work, legitimacy validates identity. We see this in the position of characters like Laura Fairlie in *The Woman in White* (1860) and Magdalen Vanstone in *No Name* (1862). As Magdalen writes in the latter novel, with irony following her marriage to the obnoxious Noel Vanstone, "it has made Nobody's Child, Somebody's Wife" (Collins 1862, 590). The illegitimacy of the Drama as a space of activity and as a mode of writing is reflected in both Collins's attitude towards playwriting as a profession, and the stage as a means of livelihood. In *No Name*, the novel most associated with the stage in its portrayal of Magdalen's short career on the boards and in its own theatrical construction in eight "Scenes", Collins portrays a theatrical life as commonly viewed with moral abhorrence, "a suspicious way of life to all respectable people" (ibid., 313). Magdalen is a "mimic", brilliantly adept at playing "character parts and disguises", and successfully working on the stage in a one-woman show, based on Charles Mathews's "At Homes", "an imitation of the great imitator himself" (ibid., 236-7). This association of the theatre with imitation and disguise, as well as illegitimacy, connects with Collins's anxieties about dramatic authorship, and provides a fresh angle from which to approach the plays. Theatrical versions of the novels are at once interventions in an illegitimate arena of dubious respectability, the sister Magdalen in disguise, as it were, to her morally superior sister Norah, and alternative versions of a text that provoke a rereading of the "legitimate" founding text.

In addition, the adaptations stand in unique relationship with the unacknowledged and forbidden illegitimate, pirate dramatic versions of the texts that circulate in a popular "illiterate" theatre (the versions that Collins's own dramatic texts were supposed to prevent, but consistently failed to do so). Collins's adaptations of his own novels, then–whether written for copyright purposes or for genuine performance–are anxiously situated between a popular novel (itself the subject of critical debate: was sensation fiction truly intellectual or mere popular nonsense?) and the spectre of an illegitimate piracy. But in their own way, they could never approach a representation of the novel on stage–always "falling short" of an audience's expectations–nor could they be any more "legitimate" than any other dramatic version of the novel, except in that they were authored by the actual novelist. It is important, when examining Collins's plays, we recognise that, rather than attempting repetition and replication of his novels, the dramatic adaptations of the 1870s, as Janice Norwood demonstrates in the next essay, deliberately distance themselves from the originals. In this way, Collins makes his plays truly "twin-sisters" of his fiction: not replicas, but different and independent; not misreadings, but rereadings or even counter-readings. Yet in their revisiting of the original texts, the whole process of duplication and dramatisation becomes an activity fraught with authorial identity-crisis: a theft, a disguise, an imitation, that puts in doubt the author's ability to establish a stable self, an homogenous whole, as Foucault might have described it. In writing for both the respectable "library-table" and the disreputable "illiterate classes", Collins divides himself as an author in such a way that threatens his survival in both. It was a ground he loved to haunt, as he did as "Mr William Dawson" visiting his Morganatic family and flirting with public respectability in a life between Caroline Graves and Martha Rudd (Pykett 2005, 18-22). But it also fuelled the anxious fractures evident in his literary output and is exposed in the broken identities of central characters in his plays.

Collins began writing the dramatic version of *The Moonstone* as early as the beginning of 1876, when the performances of *Miss Gwilt* were running successfully. The first act was completed by February 1876 (Baker et al. 2005, vol. 3, 115). The play was prepared for performance during the following year, Collins writing to the American actress Fanny Davenport, 28 July 1877, to ask whether she would play the lead part in the New York production. He indicated to her that *The Moonstone* would open at the Olympic in London on 1 or 8 of September, but in the event it was the 17th, an indication that rehearsals had taken longer than anticipated. The casting had also been a problem. On 25 May 1877, Collins wrote to Laura Seymour (who was the play Miss Clack), "the misfortune is that I am still crippled by my rheumatic knees–when I ought to be going to the theatres and looking out for the men that the piece wants" (ibid., 159). Collins was taking a close interest in the vehicles for his drama. Indeed, he remained annoyed with Henry Neville for producing *No Thoroughfare* at the Olympic in a revival in November 1876, without consulting him on the casting– he thought the production weak and initially refused to attend rehearsals (ibid., 139, 143). In July 1877, he wrote to Laura Seymour again, saying he was correcting the second act for her part, and still debating the cast with Neville: "We have decided this difficult question to my entire satisfaction", he wrote, and added optimistically, "if the negotiations succeed, the complete performance will, as I believe, be really remarkable" (ibid., 162). However, the "negotiations" clearly did not succeed; he wrote with scarcely veiled annoyance to Charles Collette on 6 August–just a few weeks before the performance was due to begin–to query why he had still not confirmed that he would play Cuff, and that Neville had been forced to delay the start date in order to accommodate him. The part was finally played by Thomas Swinbourne (ibid., 165-6).

The play opened on the 17 September 1877, and the first week indicated an initial positive reception. Collins was quickly negotiating with colleagues in America for productions over there, assuring Fanny Davenport on the 8 September, and Daly on the 22nd, that "it may be as well to add (on the question of protecting the piece in America) that many of the chief scenes and situations are not in the novel at all, and are now first invented by me", and, for this reason, "no paste-and-scissors version of the novel can compete with my version: for this plain reason that many of the chief scenes and situations are of my own invention, and *are not in the novel at all*" (ibid., 168, 171, underlining in original). That Collins saw the drama as a new text is clearly evident from these remarks. He took things a stage further with Daly on 25 September, proposing that the title of "*The Moonstone*" be altered for the stage version in the States:

> If it is a success there will be plenty of paste-and-scissors Moonstones issued by plenty of theatrical thieves. […] There is no fear of piratical adaptations doing any injury to my piece–because the best scenes and situations are not in the novel at all, and cannot be pirated. *But we cannot protect the title of "The Moonstone"*–and rival "Moonstones" may mislead the public and do serious injury. I am all for a new title–which *can* be protected, and which will therefore always distinguish the genuine version of the story from the counterfeit. (ibid., 177, underlining in original)

Collins suggested several new titles: "The Colonel's Diamond", "The Yellow Diamond", "The Innocent Thief", "Dreaming and Waking", "The Adventures of a Night", "The Dressing Gown", and "False Appearances"–feeling himself that "The Yellow Diamond" was the best and "Dreaming and Waking" his second choice.

Collins left too much to his initial euphoric optimism, and set off for a tour of the Continent before the performance had really established itself. He was in Brussels on 25 September, and passed through Paris, Munich, South Germany, and the Tyrol, before spending several weeks in Italy. When he collected his letters in Paris on 4 December, he was in for something of a shock, and was forced to write to Daly on 10 December cancelling any immediate American production of the play

> with great regret–but I felt at the same time that it was the safest course to take, under the circumstances. If I obtain a great success with another piece in the States, we will then return to the question of producing "The Moonstone" at a time when the opinions of playgoers are specially predisposed in my favour. In the meanwhile, let the work repose on your shelves. I am very glad to hear that you thought well of it. In spite of the indifference of the public reception here, I think it myself one of the best things of the kind that I have written. (ibid., 177)

Collins's final sentence shows how highly he regarded the play, and, with several years of experience in adapting his works, he was disappointed that the public had not taken to it. With matter enough to make it a new text, with over eighteen months in the writing, casting, and rehearsing, the failure signalled practically the end of his playwriting career. A one-night production of *The Evil Genius* and the disaster of *Rank and Riches* were all that remained for the future.

    Certainly, as with the other long novels of the 1860s, adapting *The Moonstone* for the stage was a difficult task. Not only does the novel range widely over the globe, but it also appeared as a series of narratives told by different characters, a method that enabled Collins to maintain the suspense and secret at the heart of the novel–who stole the diamond? The play version dispensed with all of these attributes: it was set in a single room with one point of view (that of the audience), and the secret of the theft of the diamond is revealed at the end of the first act (of three but seemingly extended to four in performance), when the audience sees Franklin Blake take it. The audience watches as Blake, with the slow, measured steps of a sleep-walker, and muttering "it's not safe in the cabinet", takes the diamond, observed by a horror-struck Rachel Verinder. The scene is the end of Rachel's love for him, she having been lately disappointed by Blake's unthinking admission that he owes a poor Parisian restaurant owner two hundred pounds and does not care (Collins 1877, 12) and who now thinks Blake's debts have "utterly degraded him" as Godfrey Ablewhite declares (ibid., 13). Blake takes the diamond, having intended, as the audience knows, to give it to Godfrey to take to his father's bank in London for safe keeping (ibid., 24). In his sleep, disturbed by the rich food and drink he has taken against his doctor's advice, Blake performs what his mind is dwelling on, but recalls nothing of having done so in the morning. The play removes the laudanum as a catalyst here and places more emphasis on Blake's own personality–as Collins does with Lydia Gwilt's character in *Miss*

Gwilt–making him more responsible for the theft itself, more reckless and flawed, and thus more related to the symbol of the diamond.

The play is marked by a shift in emphasis from sensation and suspense to audience expectation and dramatic irony. A review of the play in the *Illustrated London News*, while somewhat supportive, argues this point well and demonstrates that the audience's prior knowledge of the novel made their experience of the play a challenging one:

> All novel readers are well acquainted with the incidents of this clever story [...].
> Mr. Collins has arranged [the adaptation] upon a safe plan. He has successfully
> resisted the temptation to found his plot upon the principle of surprise, and has
> substituted for it that of expectation [...]. By the observance of this principle,
> much pain is spared the spectator of the play, when the perplexed agents in the
> action are placed in situations of moral difficulty. (22 September 1877, 290)

This shift in focus provides the audience with a greater knowledge than the characters in the drama (which indeed they hold from having read the novel): identifying the interest of the scenes in the interaction of characters who distrust each other's motives and honesty, rather than the search for the diamond. However, it also means that the role of the detective, Sergeant Cuff, is problematised. Since Cuff cannot surprise the audience with his sudden revelations, the play must work more like many contemporary detective television programmes work: tracing the detective's unravelling of the guilt of the perpetrator, who is already suspected by the viewer. Thus the final scene of the play is probably the first example of the detective's "trap": Cuff's revelation of Blake's sleepwalking reveals the horror in Ablewhite's face and exposes him as the real thief of the diamond. In the play, Cuff has been watching Ablewhite for some time: he is suspected of embezzlement, and keeps a "private villa in the suburbs" and a "contraband lady with the carriage and the jewels" (Collins 1877, 86). The *dénouement* both exposes and entraps the guilty Ablewhite, and, though he calmly exits as he acknowledges his crime (while calling himself a "victim of circumstances", in naturalistic style), a casual Cuff reassures the household that "the policeman is outside" (ibid., 87).

The play's detective plot is, however, subservient to the domestic story it relates. Unlike the novel, where extraneous incident constructs an elaborate colonial world around the diamond and the main characters, symbolised by the foreboding presence of the Indian jugglers, the play quite deliberately shuts this world out. The play is set entirely in the same place, indeed, in a single domestic space–not quite a room, more a hallway. The theft of the moonstone from and Indian idol is not touched upon in the play; indeed the source of disturbance in the play is class-based, not racial–the house is described as being in a neighbourhood of beer-shops: as Miss Clack finishes her champagne she remarks, "how unspeakably dreadful! Rachel! Do you hear that? A neighbourhood of beer-drinkers all round this beautiful house. And that neighbourhood your property!" (ibid., 17). The class snobbery of the characters hints at their feelings of insecurity in a "beer-drinking" neighbourhood. Miss Clack proposes the establishment of a new charitable society for the neighbourhood: the Branch-Mothers'-Small-Clothes-Conversion-Society, linked to returning items from the pawn-brokers (an ironic parallel to the need for such in the lives of both Blake and Ablewhite). Indeed, the characters' class snobbery is exposed in these references and they appear as ill-thinking "champagne socialists".

As the first act ends, the doors to the house are tightly locked in an elaborate closing-up ceremony for the night, by Betteredge and his assistant, and the French windows in the main hall are "protected by a broad iron-sheathed shutter, which covers two-thirds of it from the floor upwards" (s. d., ibid., 26). Ironically, the diamond is placed in a cabinet where the locks are broken–Rachel confident that her house is not "an hotel": "Are my faithful old servants thieves?" (ibid, 22). When the diamond is finally recovered, rather than return it to India, as in the novel, Rachel invests its value in helping her neighbourhood. Rachel decides to sell the diamond, "and the money shall be a fund for the afflicted and the poor" (ibid., 88). The theft of the diamond is displaced by its conversion into charitable aid.

The most conspicuous transformation in the play is that of the traveller Franklin Blake, who, despite his nervous disorder, is changed into the domestic husband, asleep at the end of the play, waking to be claimed by his wife. The play's narrative enacts Collins's own process of dramatisation (transforming the exotic into the domestic) and reverses the effect of the novel, investing the stolen jewel in the reconstruction of British society, assuaging the guilt of the wealthy in the poor neighbourhood. The active charity workers are exploded by the novel–Ablewhite as fraud and Clack as hypocritical (she drinks champagne with delight), but the wealthy Rachel, hemmed in by her iron doors and social proprieties, can only appropriate the wealth of empire to sort out her neighbourhood. Ablewhite and Blake are not far apart–indeed Ablewhite pawns the diamond at Luker's, the money-lender, whose name he was given by Blake in act one. Rachel and Blake take centre stage, and their story is a love story, with both of them reflecting the qualities of the diamond in turn–to fascinate and to repel. This is made explicit at the end where Rachel refers to Blake as her "jewel". Her link to the moonstone is indicated in Betteredge's comment that "there's a mine of hidden perversity in the best woman that ever lived". The diamond itself is seen as a curse and a gift; brought from "robbery and murder" in India, yet something that has great beauty–"a perfectly unearthly light shines out of the diamond in the dark" (ibid., 21).

The play also revolves around Ablewhite's attempt to gain Rachel's hand in marriage over Blake–Rachel finally agreeing to this when her belief in Blake is destroyed and she feels degraded. Rachel and Blake are closely linked through their own sense of self-degradation in the eyes of the other:

> Suppose you discovered the woman to be utterly unworthy of you–a false, shameless, degraded creature. And suppose your faithful heart still clung, in spite of you, to that first object of your love? Suppose– [...] oh how can I make a *man* understand that a feeling which horrifies me at myself can be a feeling which fascinates me at the same time? Godfrey, it's the breath of my life, and it's the poison that kills me–both in one! [...] Is there a form of hysterics, Godfrey, that bursts into words instead of tears? (ibid., 60)

Rachel's self-understanding is one of deeply rooted anxiety at desires beyond her control. She "horrifies" and "fascinates" herself in a dual response that again mirrors the status of the moonstone in the play. This tension between desire and degradation is never resolved in the production; Blake's final awakening, significant from the hint of Collins's alternative title for the play–"Dreaming and Waking"–might be to a domestic bliss, but it is in the context of a loss of the exotic traveller's life he was leading and that itself creates anxiety that leads to the theft of the diamond. Collins presents us with a narrative of cause and effect. It is also a narrative of the anxiety of identity: Blake's very identity is threatened by his self-same desire to marry Rachel and settle down. This causes the loss of the diamond, since through his nervous tension, Blake's actions become uncontrollable and unknowable. He is divided between unconsciousness and consciousness–sleeping and waking–but his final sleep is disturbed by Rachel. Blake's final line is one of confusion and doubt: "Franklin (*Looking up, bewildered*): Who is it?" "Only your wife", Rachel replies as the curtain falls, but as he has slept through the entire final scene, Franklin has no knowledge of the chain of events that led him to that chair, or of the "happy ending" in store for him (ibid., 88).

As a play, Collins's *The Moonstone* softens the incidents of the novel. Where the play version of *The Woman in White* concludes with a new climax that displays to the audience the actual murder of Count Fosco by the Italian assassins (where the novel just describes the discovery of his body in the morgue), *The Moonstone* describes the exposure of Ablewhite and his apprehension by Cuff, rather than his murder in a boarding-house by the Indians (as in the novel). This alteration signals the central theme of transformation in the play–symbolic of its alteration as a cultural artefact, from novel to play, from private parlour to public stage. The influence of the moonstone, the change in Blake from exotic traveller to domestic husband, in Rachel from independent heiress to domestic wife, and in the literal alteration of Blake's state of mind under physiological and mental stress, all figuratively repeat the fundamental transformation of the narrative under Collins's process of adaptation.

The alternative title of "Dreaming and Waking" provides another metaphor of alteriarity that also mirrors the text's formal shift from sensational romance to realist drawing-room drama. The adaptation of the private, more secretive process of personal reading that is the normative mode of experience for novel-reading into a public exhibition of the narrative as performance is symbolically represented in *The Moonstone*'s static stage set. The simple interior scene of the inner room of the Verinder mansion permits the very public exposure of the family's inner secrets; like a doll's house with its front removed, the set exposes all of the sordid motives and guilty actions of the characters, within this most exclusive and protected of sanctified environments–the private dinner party. The unlockable and unprotected cabinet at the rear of the stage, where the moonstone is placed and from which it is stolen, provides a metaphor for the uneasy revelations of the characters' inner drives. Indeed, Blake's theft of the diamond is prompted by his subconscious anxieties over the diamond's safety, a pre-Freudian understanding of the leakage of inner motivations into the public arena that the intense atmosphere of the closeted party encourages, and that is expected by the intense scrutiny of the audience. No more apt metaphor for this kind of personal exposure and public scrutiny can be suggested perhaps than the gazing into the heart of the diamond to see its exotic flaw–its "mine of hidden perversity".

The final interlocking theme in this nest of symbolic boxes is that which is prefigured by the enclosing of the house itself–with its metal shutters and heavy-duty security locks. These precautions separate the house from the "undesirable" neighbourhood or beer shops that surround it. Like the theatre, which removes its growing middle-class audience from the real struggles of the Victorian class system and industrial society, so the play enacts the desire to conceal, exclude, or shut out the social problems concomitant with capitalist wealth. Rachel's conviction that none of her servants could possibly be thieves, exposes her blind prejudices: her words might be admirable, but they fail to consider that even her middle-class friends might be guilty. It is the man of charity, Godfrey Ablewhite, who actively takes money from the charity he serves, to fulfil his desires (the kept woman in the fashionable villa), and who takes the diamond to feed his addictions. When the diamond is returned, it is to be reinvested in neighbourhood improvements–an acknowledgement of a need for interaction and communication between classes (but also a further deflection of the guilt away from the aristocratic mansion). This benevolent paternalism only serves to return the play's social order to one that centralises concealment and maintains the hidden secret of the source of the diamond's value. This shift of attention and textual alertness to the novel's colonial acknowledgments suggests both a change of heart on Collins's part towards the political substructure of the original story, and also that the adaptation of the text from private to public sphere enacts a reburial or re-hiding of society's colonial props. The proclamation of Queen Victoria as Empress of India on 1 January 1877, as Collins began his adaptation, changed the ideological landscape of British society and made anti-imperial sentiments less appropriate for a theatrical show. It was not a time to look back to the excesses of the 1850s. Perhaps Collins saw the audience as subtly different from that which read his fiction ten years earlier, although it is possible he had anticipated capturing a renewed interest in the Indian subcontinent. In the event, public focus shifted to South Africa (with the annexation of the Transvaal in April), Russia declaring war on Turkey also in April and escalating the Eastern Crisis, and Ireland (with the Parnell becoming leader of the Home Rule party in late August). 1877 was a busy year.

The play's concealment of the novel's connections to Empire is bought at the expense of the emasculation of Franklin Blake, whose transformation is an uninspiring end to his global adventuring, being a silenced and startled awakening into the role of disempowered domestic patriarch. The anxieties he feels on the threshold of this change that lead to the theft–a kind of social suicide or self-destruction subconsciously propelling him into an act that is simultaneously benevolent (protecting Rachel's diamond) and subversive (engaging in burglary)–are placing him in a position that will undermine his reputation and make him the social pariah that, in turn, will see him exiled into that same wandering lifestyle. There is an element of wish-fulfilment that is not seen in the novel. However, Franklin does not awaken into a state of resolution; he sleeps through the entire final act (unconsciously re-enacting his theft and implicating Abelwhite), and takes no part in the exposure of the truth and the unmasking of Ablewhite. His dazed reaction to Rachel's pronouncement of their new relationship only serves to enforce the sense of his disempowerment. Seated in a chair, looked down on by Rachel, he is the embodiment of the impotent armchair husband. This is a far cry from the thoughtless and carefree man who leaves his French creditor's family wanting, but a transformation that leaves unconfronted the roots of his psychological anxiety and loss.

That Collins himself should intertwine the adaptation of novel to play with the concept of theft, as suggested earlier by his reaction to the dramatic pirating of his novels–particularly in America–makes for another level of symbolic linkage of *The Moonstone* to the process of literary adaptation. Moreover, the anxiety felt by Blake at the reduction of his sphere of activity from international explorer to domestic husband, further symbolised by the locking and shuttering of the house and claustrophobic single set, replicates metaphorically the reduction of the novel from wide Imperial cinemascope to narrow naturalistic drawing-room. Collins and critics recognised *The Moonstone* as probably his greatest literary achievement as a novel, and the stage production clearly had the potential to damage his reputation. That he cancelled the American production after the lukewarm reception of the London play is a further indication of another concealment or burial. But the anxiety embodied in Franklin Blake suggests something more needs to be said. Collins's literary identity crossed the boundary between the private and the public in adapting his novels and writing for the stage. Though often denigrated as mere sensation fiction today, Collins pitched his novels to an increasingly high-brow audience wanting acceptable artistic merit; indeed, he had made that switch from Dickens's *All the Year Round* to the majesterial *Cornhill* in the mid-1860s (though *The Moonstone* appeared in Dickens's magazine). But the stage was a space beyond the reputable establishment; although haunted by literary alter egos (like G. H. Lewes's "Slingsby Lawrence"), it remained artistically and morally marginalised. As Blake sullies his diamond with theft, a curse, and a flaw, so Collins risked his literary identity on a dramatic career that could confound his reputation. The jewel in his own literary crown was compromised and sullied by this very association. *The Moonstone* was–though a lacklustre "success"–the penultimate curtain in his stage career before the crippling failure of *Rank and Riches*. Perhaps the diamond had its final revenge.

Notes

[1] *The Frozen Deep* has been the most widely discussed play, especially in connection with Dickens and its influence on his later career and biographical details.

[2] The play was probably refused by the cautious theatre managers after the cat-calls that ruined the production of *Rank and Riches* in 1883. This play was intended as a major venture, including George Alexander and G. W. Anson in the cast, but has received no critical attention, despite a run in the States, "where, strangely enough [... it] enjoyed a considerable success", Kenneth Robinson notes as if this were preposterous (Robinson 1951, 277).

[3] The play included A. W. Pinero (as Darch) and Ada Cavendish–she also opened it in New York, Wallack's Theatre, 5 June 1879 (Gasson 1998, 11); a parody, *The Gwilty Governess and the Downey Doctor*, played in Brighton, July 1876 (ibid., 11).

[4] Although a letter of December 1867 on *No Thoroughfare* comments "the 'Armadale' play is also being finished in Paris. So the [deuce] is in it if the stage doesn't bring in some money now!" However, there is no evidence that it was ever finally produced (Baker and Clarke 1999, vol. 2, 299).

[5] The "long descriptions" referred to here do not really exist: there are little more than five pages in eighty-eight that deal with the subject, and only two or three paragraph-long speeches by Candy on the matter, and no reference to Elliotson's book at all. Indeed, Collins makes one of his slight alterations here: where the novel cites Elliotson's citing of Combe's case of the Irish porter from his *Phrenology* (1819), the play simply cites the original and omits any reference to Elliotson (Collins 1877, 75-6).

Works Cited

Ashley, Robert. 1952. *Wilkie Collins*. London: Arthur Barker.

Baker, William. Andrew Gasson., Graham Law., and Paul Lewis (eds). 2005. *The Public Face of Wilkie Collins: The Collected Letters*. 4 vols. London: Pickering and Chatto.

Baker, William and William M. Clarke (eds). 1999. *The Letters of Wilkie Collins*, 2 vols. Basingstoke: Macmillan.

Clarke, William M. 1988. *The Secret Life of Wilkie Collins*. Stroud: Alan Sutton, 1996.

Collins, Wilkie. 1852. *Basil*. Oxford: Oxford University Press, 2000.

—. 1858a. Douglas Jerrold. *Household Words* 19, 217-22.

—. 1858b. Dramatic Grub-Street. *Household Words* 17, 265-70.

—. 1875. *Miss Gwilt*. London: Privately published.

—. 1868a. *The Moonstone*. London: Oxford University Press, 1928.

—. 1868b. *The Moonstone*. Ontario: Broadview, 1999.

—. 1877. *The Moonstone: A Dramatic Story, in Three Acts*. London: Privately published.

—. 1862. *No Name*. Oxford: Oxford University Press, 1998.

Eliot, T. S. 1928. Introduction to Collins 1868a.

Gasson, Andrew. 1998. *Wilkie Collins: An Illustrated Guide*. Oxford: Oxford University Press.

Hutton, Laurence (ed.). 1892. *Letters of Charles Dickens to Wilkie Collins, 1851-1870*. London: J. R. Osgood.

Lonoff, Sue. 1982. *Wilkie Collins and his Victorian Readers: A Study in the Rhetoric of Authorship*. New York: A. M. S. Press.

Marshall, William Hall. 1970. *Wilkie Collins*. New York: Twayne.

Peters, Catherine. 1991. *The King of Inventors: A Life of Wilkie Collins*. London: Secker and Warburg.

Pykett, Lyn. 2005. *Authors in Context: Wilkie Collins*. Oxford: Oxford University Press.

Robinson, Kenneth. 1951. *Wilkie Collins: A Biography*. London: Bodley Head.

Taylor, Jenny Bourne. 1988. *In the Secret Theatre of Home: Wilkie Collins, Sensation Narrative and Nineteenth-Century Psychology*. London: Routledge.

SENSATION DRAMA? COLLINS'S STAGE ADAPTATION OF *THE WOMAN IN WHITE*

JANICE NORWOOD

Wilkie Collins's *The Woman in White* (1860) has frequently been cited as the first sensation novel. It is tempting to suppose therefore that his stage adaptation, also entitled *The Woman in White*, must have belonged to the theatrical genre known as "sensation drama", which dominated the British and American stage in the 1860s. To test the veracity of this categorisation we need to ascertain whether Collins's play exhibits the key elements of the genre. It is also instructive to see how contemporary critics viewed it and to compare the author's production with other dramatisations of the famous novel.

History of Adaptations

Serialisation of *The Woman in White* finished in August 1860, the same month that the three-volume novel was published. The first stage adaptation, by J. R. Ware, appeared at the beginning of November at the Surrey Theatre, situated on the south side of the Thames in London. It earned a favourable response from both audiences and critics, the latter recognising the difficulties inevitably encountered in adapting a lengthy novel for the stage. The report in the *Era*, for example, praises the adaptation while suggesting that the character of Count Fosco is predictably less subtle in the dramatic version because he has to portray "and speak acts, and ideas only dimly hinted at by the author, and supposed by the reader":

> In this manner the cleverly-drawn part of Fosco in the novel, on the stage, wanting the halo of mystery, becomes a familiar individuality. A fault, which is owing to the stern and uncompromising requirements of the stage, and not to the adapter, who, with a lively knowledge of the difficulties of his task, has executed it in a manner very highly to his credit. (11 November 1860, 11)

However, another reviewer in an unidentified newspaper cutting at the British Library dissented from the general approval of the production. His review is scathing:

We have seen many adaptations, but this is the worst. Had it not been for the blue fire, shooting, &c., the piece would have been a decided failure. We would suggest to the management to call this drama a farce, and the audience will laugh at it and enjoy it accordingly. [...] The irresistibly funny way in which Mr. Holloway [playing Sir Percival Glyde] did a tragic scene also deserves mention. (10 November 1860, Theatre Cuttings, book 63)

Further adaptations followed in January and August 1861 at the Theatre Royal, Norwich and at Sadler's Wells respectively. The manuscripts sent to the Lord Chamberlain's office for licensing reveal that W. Sidney wrote the former, but the name of the other dramatist is not given.[1] In September 1862 an adaptation by the actress Josephine Fiddes played at the Theatre Royal, Cambridge with Walter Hartwright enacted by a young Henry Irving.[2] Sadly there is no script of this version in the Lord Chamberlain's collection of plays so we can only rely on a review in the *Cambridge Chronicle and University Journal* (6 September 1862), which stated: "there was no link between the events which occur, the plot was vague and indistinct, and we must add that to those who had not read the novel it was unintelligible". The critic also judged that the "plump, well-rounded figure" of Miss Fiddes was miscast in the dual roles of the woman in white and Laura Fairlie. Irving, however, "did not make a bad Hartwright".

Adaptations were not confined to the British provinces. In Europe there were dramatisations in Berlin in December 1866 (Gasson 1998, 161-2) and at Rotterdam, The Hague, and Delft in the Netherlands in 1870.[3] There was even a version by the English actor-dramatist George Fawcett Rowe at the Princess's Theatre, Melbourne, Australia in March 1862 (Irvin 1974, 34).

It was not until 9 October 1871 (nearly eleven years after the first adaptation) that Collins's own version opened at the Olympic Theatre in London's Wych Street, near Drury Lane. There are another six twentieth-century stage adaptations in the Lord Chamberlain's collection of plays (see appendix). Each makes various alterations to the plot of the original novel and attempts to suit the drama to contemporary audience tastes. Thus while the typescript of the 1938 version by A. R. Janes, which played at the Shanklin Theatre on the Isle of Wight, states that the action is set in 1870, the language of Walter Hartright clearly derives from 1930s' conversational style. In the Prologue, when he literally bumps into Anne Catherick on a road near Hampstead, he says: "Awfully sorry: but it's confoundedly dark. I say, what's the matter? You look scared to death" (f.1). Soon afterwards he complains: "It's a rum go, you know, accosting me like this. I'm not sure that I like it" (f.2).

Theatrical taste had changed again by the 1970s. Victorian melodrama was regarded as laughable, "low" culture and so dismissed as impossible to stage seriously. This is evident in the irreverent treatment of the novel in Tim Kelly's play *Egad, The Woman in White* (1975). The "Story of the Play" gives a good indication of its style:

> Suffering unabated! Human frailty revealed! Here's an old-fashioned melodrama that has only one purpose in mind–LAUGHTER. Based on the classic by Wilkie Collins, it ranks with *East Lynne* and *The Poor of New York*, except that it's wilder, faster and FUNNIER. (Kelly 1975, 5, capitals in original)

The author advises the cast to "treat the play as if it were a deeply moving and completely serious work of dramatic art. They should never 'break up'. Leave that to the audience" (ibid., 78). Even the *dénouement* in which Sir Percival burns to death, is played for laughs, the stage directions describing it as "a frantic, overdone, embarrassingly bad death scene" (ibid., 75). However, in the same decade academics were beginning to re-evaluate popular art forms such as melodrama,[4] thereby making possible serious treatments of Collins's fiction. Thus in 1988 Melissa Murray's adaptation at the Greenwich Theatre, London rendered the novel faithfully and earnestly.

In addition to the stage productions, there have been at least eight film versions, the most famous of which was made in 1948, directed by Peter Godfrey and starred Sydney Greenstreet as Fosco (Goble 1999, 90). Television adaptations include the 1982 BBC version, another from 1997 starring Tara Fitzgerald (Marian Halcombe), Andrew Lincoln (Hartright) and Simon Callow (Fosco), and one filmed by a Colombian company in Sri Lanka and set in the 1950s. Finally, there was the musical that opened in September 2004 at the Palace Theatre in London with Michael Crawford as Count Fosco.

Sensation Scenes and Victorian Drama

To return to the mid-Victorian stage, the first play to be termed a sensation drama was Dion Boucicault's *The Colleen Bawn* (1860), which premiered at the Adelphi Theatre. It was followed by numerous dramas by Boucicault and others, all of which were distinguished by having a least one scene of physical excitement calculated to electrify the audience's nerves. Such scenes were heavily dependent on the latest backstage technology, which was used to create as realistic an impression as possible. Usually the hero, heroine, or both, exhibited physical courage in the face of some kind of adversity. For example, in the famous scene from *The Colleen Bawn* the eponymous heroine (Eily O'Connor) is pushed from a rock into a lake by her husband's servant but is rescued from drowning by Myles-na-Coppaleen. The water was represented by painted scenery and by sheets of blue gauze cloth stretched across the stage and undulated by twenty boys in the wings (Fawkes 1979, 118). The scene caused excitement because Myles (played in the original by Boucicault himself) dived into the water and Eily sunk down below the surface by disappearing through trap doors in the stage floor. Similar lake scenes with spectacular rescues soon abounded on the London stage.

Considering *The Woman in White*, one incident that has the potential to make a memorable sensation scene is the death of Sir Percival Glyde in the fire in the vestry. Conflagrations were certainly a popular feature of sensation dramas. By 1871, when Collins produced his play, this sort of scene had been staged frequently, most notably in Boucicault's *The Poor of New York* (1857), which played in New York in 1857, then came to Britain in 1864 first as *The Poor of Liverpool* and then as *The Streets of London*. In 1863 two rival stage adaptations of Mary Braddon's *Lady Audley's Secret* (1862) at the St James's and Royal Victoria Theatres also featured an on-stage fire as they dramatised the burning inn set ablaze by Lady Audley in her attempt to kill Robert Audley.

Other potential sensation scenes derived from Collins's novel might feature Marian eavesdropping out on the roof in the rain (perhaps a thrilling rival to the famous scene in Boucicault's *Arrah-na-Pogue* (1864) when Shaun-the-Post climbs the ivy-clad wall of the prison), or a scene inside the lunatic asylum when Marian recognises Laura when she expects to encounter Anne. A lifelike representation of the inmates in an asylum would create the sort of shocked comments provoked by the grim prison scene showing convicts on a treadmill in *It's Never Too Late to Mend* (1865) by Collins's friend and fellow novelist and dramatist Charles Reade (Princess's Theatre; Rahill 1967, 199).

It is notable that virtually all the other nineteenth-century versions (and several of the later adaptations) of the play feature the death of Sir Percival in the vestry fire as a sensation scene. The Ware adaptation at the Surrey also added more exciting incident in the form of a duel at the end between Fosco and Walter. Just as Walter is about to be skewered, a member of the Brotherhood suddenly appears and shoots Fosco dead. Most recently the West End musical version, despite being "freely adapted from the novel", interpreted the play more in the spirit of a sensation drama. It depicted Glyde's death under the wheels of a train, a scene clearly derived from Victorian sensation scenes (such as Augustin Daly's *Under the Gaslight* (1867) and Boucicault's *After Dark* 1868)) and owing more than a passing acknowledgement to James Carker's demise in Charles Dickens's *Dombey and Son* (1846-8). Moreover the production featured two other physically exciting scenes: Marian's rooftop eavesdropping during a violent thunderstorm and the pursuit, capture, and drugging of Anne by Glyde's henchmen. It also dramatised the recognition scene in the asylum complete with archetypal psychotic inmates.

By contrast, in Collins's drama Sir Percival is consigned to death off stage, Walter revealing that he was drowned in a fishing boat while attempting to escape to France (Collins 1871, 65); Marian's eavesdropping is carried out from behind a door (ibid., 50-1); and the lunatic asylum is only shown as an anteroom, so no other inmates appear (ibid., 70). Catherine Peters says Dickens thought the opening of the novel depicting the meeting of Walter with the Woman in White was "one of the two most dramatic scenes in literature" (Peters 1991, 208)[5]–yet Collins chose not to put it in the play. He deliberately avoided the obvious sensation scenes. Undoubtedly he knew that the audience was aware of the plot of the novel. This is evident from the *Times* review of the 1860 Surrey production:

> The audience clearly understand the drift and purpose of Count Fosco before that estimable nobleman has spoken half-a-dozen words, whereas if they had never read Mr. Collins's novel, it is very questionable whether they would have completely appreciated the polished villainy even when the curtain had descended. (8 November 1860, 6)

Therefore there was no point in withholding some of the information: suspense is necessarily already dissipated. So rather than maintain mystery around Anne Catherick's parentage, as happens in the novel, in the play Sir Percival guesses who her father is in the prologue. In the same scene the audience witnesses his removal of the incriminating page from the church register, thereby revealing another of the fiction's mysteries at an early stage. Collins as dramatist surprises his audience by changing details. He toys with audience expectation. He thus creates intellectual titillation rather than stimulating physical excitement and suspense.

We might legitimately ask why Collins produced his own version of *The Woman in White* in 1871, especially since the big wave of sensation dramas took place in the mid-1860s. Indeed sensationalism had become the subject of a number of spoofs including H. J. Byron's burlesque of *The Colleen Bawn* entitled *Miss Eily O'Connor* (1861), which was first staged at Drury Lane. More appositely, in his play *The Woman in Mauve* (1864), which played in Liverpool at the end of 1864 and opened at the Haymarket Theatre in London in March 1865, Watts Phillips made fun of both sensation plays and novels. As the title suggests, Collins's *The Woman in White* was one of his targets.

In staging the play Collins's incentive was not to establish copyright as he and Dickens had done a decade earlier with *A Message from the Sea* (Stephens 1992, 98).[6] Instead, a major motivation was almost certainly money, bearing in mind Collins was funding two households and his second child had been born in May. His letters reveal how pleased he was with the financial success of the drama. For example, he wrote to Charles Reade on 20 October 1871 that the "business" "promises famously". "Receipts of the first week £475–which gives a good profit to those interested at starting. This week's returns, steadily larger every day than last week's" (Baker and Clarke 1999, vol. 2, 348). Nevertheless, it is doubtful that money was the only motivating factor. Collins's own pronouncement on the playbill advertising his production, reveals his intention:

> In the first place, he [Collins] has endeavoured to produce a work which shall appeal to the audience purely on its own merits as a play. In the second place, he has refrained from making the interest of his drama dependent on mechanical contrivance, and has relied in the play, as he relied in the novel, on the succession of incident, on the exhibition of character, and on the collision of human emotion rising naturally from those two sources. (Playbill for Monday 9 October 1871)

He goes on to criticise other versions and says "he has not hesitated, while preserving the original story in substance, materially to alter it in form". The changes that he made were not just driven by the need to condense a long novel into a four-hour performance (as Ware and the other adaptors had also had to do): they are more fundamental. Once the play went on tour in the provinces, Collins agreed to let Wybert Reeve, the actor who originally played Hartright but was then playing Fosco, make further cuts and alterations, particularly to the last act (Reeve 1906, 461).

In general, apart from some criticism of George Vining's interpretation of the role of Count Fosco, which Collins felt compelled to defend,[7] and a difference of opinion over the effectiveness of the *dénouement*,[8] Collins's adaptation received positive reviews. The *Daily Telegraph*, for example, reported:

> A drama of extraordinary power was this wonderful story; but, knowing every line of the book as we all do, we are actually able to be excited–if not more–over the play than over the novel. The book has been turned inside out; and probably a more masterly instance of adaptation for the stage from a story has seldom been seen. (11 October 1871, 2)

Picturing the Production

A number of the journals also featured illustrations of the production alongside reviews of the dramatisation. Comparing these images with similar depictions of action-filled sensation scenes, or even the illustration from the *Illustrated London News* (17 January 1857, fig. 14) of the amateur production of *The Frozen Deep* as put on by Dickens, Collins, and friends at Tavistock House, reveals a striking difference. Instead of a scene of climactic excitement, the artists show one of contemplation. There is no physical derring-do or heightened emotion. In *The Frozen Deep* image the viewer's eye is immediately arrested by the dishevelled and half-starved figure of Richard Wardour, who seems to be crying out to Clara. With her back to the audience, she has sunk to her knees in grief, believing that he has murdered her fiancé. In contrast, the most exciting action from *The Woman in White* depicted by the *Illustrated London News* (18 October 1871, fig. 15) is the opening of a door as Fosco bows to Anne Catherick. The expression on her face is the only indication of the hidden menace of the scene. The *Illustrated Times* (15 October 1871, fig. 16) illustrates a more static moment at the end of act two with a fainting Anne lying on the couch, echoing Laura's position when resting earlier in the same act. Fosco silently reveals her to Glyde, whose body position registers surprise. The image in the *Graphic* (16 October 1871, fig. 17) is even more contemplative. It portrays a shadowy Fosco brooding on the brilliantly-lit figure of Anne, highlighting the play's (and the novel's) symbolic counterpoising of light and dark. The fact that the illustrators chose to depict these particular moments rather than more dramatic, physical climaxes suggests that they were picking up on the different mood created by this play compared to that of many contemporary dramas.

Frederick Walker's original artwork for the poster advertising the play portrays a back view of a shrouded woman passing through a doorway into the star-lit night (1871).[9] The image is undoubtedly beautiful, yet because it focuses on the mystery of the woman in white, it is ironically less appropriate for the stage version. The journal illustrations, which spotlight the central character of Fosco, provide a truer indication of the content of the play (perhaps not surprisingly, since they were drawn from the production itself whereas Walker produced his art before the play opened).

Significantly, the notion of "looking" and the implied questioning of identity raised by the *Illustrated Times* and *Graphic* illustrations are also central to *Poor Miss Finch* (1872), the novel Collins was writing at the time of the dramatisation. In that novel a blind girl easily distinguishes between identical twins (even when unable to register the visual clue that one has blue skin caused as a side effect of medical treatment). In *The Woman in White*, Laura Fairlie and Anne Catherick, although only half-sisters not twins, are strikingly similar in appearance. For the Olympic production the actress Ada Dyas played both parts in a blonde wig. At this period it was not unusual for actors to assume multiple roles within one play following the success of Charles Mathews the elder in Colman's *The Actor of All Work* (1817), performed at the Haymarket (Bratton 2003, 113). The main purpose of such doubling was to display the versatility of the performer's dramatic talents, often to comic effect. In the case of the drama of *The Woman in White* the two roles are not radically different and the point of the doubling is physically to embody the exploration of identity that is one of the main motifs of the novel. Ware's version at the Surrey had similarly entrusted the two parts to one actress, Mrs Page, but at least two other versions of the play did not use doubling. The critics were unanimous in their praise of Ada Dyas's acting. The *Daily News* commented:

> Ordinarily these double performances are eminently unsatisfactory–a fact which generally arises from the impossibility of forgetting for a moment the identity of the performer. This objection, however, is entirely removed in this instance by the skill of the actress, who never seems identical, but only strikingly like her counterpart. This happy result [...] lies in the very movements of the actress, and, above all, in the expression of her features, which in the one character is grave, tender, earnest, while in the other her face is alternately lighted up with the happy smiles of a mind too weak for settled sorrow, or convulsed with terror and the sudden remembrance of the persecution that pursues her. (11 October 1871, 9)

A New Style of Drama

The illustrative evidence confirms that Collins's play was not a traditional sensation drama. In fact it pointed the way forward to the more psychological dramas of the final quarter of the nineteenth century. Its opening night preceded by just one month the Lyceum première of Leopold Lewis's *The Bells* (25 November 1871), the play in which Henry Irving, as the burgomaster Mathias, established himself as the major actor of his age. At the very end of Collins's play, Count Fosco is stabbed by two members of the Brotherhood. The action is virtually performed as a dumb show, no words passing between the three men. This serves to underline the ritualistic aspect of the killing. The assassins leave and, as Fosco lies dead on the floor, there is silence, finally broken by a knock on the door. Fosco's wife is heard offstage saying "Count! May I come in?" (Collins 1871, 88). Thus the villain has met his retribution and the audience's attention at the end is turned to the one person who loved him and will mourn his death. In a traditional melodramatic *dénouement*, the audience is invited to applaud the thoroughly deserved death of the villain and so gain cathartic release, but here the effect is to make the audience's response more equivocal, arousing some sympathy at the villain's assassination, justifiable though they know it to be.

Fig. 14. "Private Theatricals at Tavistock House–Scene from *The Frozen Deep*",
Illustrated London News (1857).

Fig. 15. Scene from *The Woman in White* at the Olympic Theatre, *Illustrated
London News* (1871).

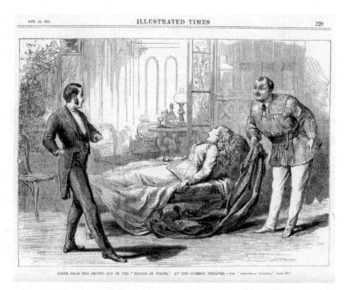

Fig. 16. Scene from the second act of *The Woman in White* at the Olympic
Theatre, *Illustrated Times* (1871).

Fig 17. Scene from *The Woman in White* at the Olympic Theatre, *The Graphic*
(1871).

Compare this with the end of *The Bells* where Mathias is woken from a nightmare in which he has relived the murder he carried out years before and dreams he is sentenced to death by hanging. His wife, daughter, and her fiancé knock on his bedchamber door and discover him close to death, fretting at the imaginary hangman's noose around his neck. He dies. In the text of the Samuel French published edition Mathias's wife places her hand on his chest, pronounces him "Dead!" and his daughter bursts into tears (Lewis 1871, 502). Apparently, Irving often played this slightly differently and delivered the final words himself: "Take the rope from my neck–take–the–rope–neck–" (Mayer 1980, 76, 95). Nevertheless, he always died surrounded by his family so, once again, the audience is aware of the devastation his death will cause to his loved ones.

Both Fosco and Mathias are killed when their pasts catch up with them, but whereas Mathias dies from his internalised guilt, Fosco is despatched by an external agent. Nevertheless Fosco does reveal some complexity of character in seeking to warn Marian before she sees Anne/Laura at the asylum, and this action differentiates him from the one-dimensional stage villain epitomised by Glyde. Fosco is much more complex and both attracts and repels the audience, as he does Marian. (In the West End musical this ambivalence was emphasised by the fact that the audience was encouraged to laugh when Fosco performed a comic song and he was allowed to escape unharmed and unpunished at the end.) Thus Collins's Italian villain is a prototype for what David Mayer has described as the "divided hero-villain" of 1870's melodrama, and which is epitomised by Irving's Mathias (Mayer 2004, 159).

In his entertaining and persuasive article "Fosco Lives!", A. D. Hutter argues that if you take into account the circumstances in which the novel was read as a serial publication, you can deduce that readers were expected to postulate different outcomes (Hutter 2003, 200). He alleges that the novel has been misread, for in fact all the clues in the text suggest that Fosco stages his own death and survives the assassination attempt. Hutter therefore sees the play as an inferior product, which he describes as "frequently horrifying" (ibid., 223), because it removes all ambiguity and therefore does not allow for the possibility of Fosco's resurrection. He contends that the fault is in part due to the Victorian theatre "which had not yet discovered the oblique, the unstated" (ibid., 222), and postulates: "The very complexity of perspective and richness of a character such as Fosco is sacrificed to an overly clear plot" (ibid., 224).

To counter Hutter's criticisms, consider Collins's famous introduction to his earlier novel *Basil* (1852):

Believing that the Novel and the Play are twin-sisters in the family of Fiction; that the one is a drama narrated, as the other is a drama acted; and that all the

strong and deep emotions which the Play-writer is privileged to excite, the
Novel-writer is privileged to excite also. (Collins 1852, letter of dedication)

Significantly he gives the two genres equal billing, the clear implication being
that neither is superior to the other. So instead of judging Collins's drama
against the novel, it is more instructive to view it in its theatrical context, taking
into account the circumstances of its performance. It should thus be recognised
as a valid drama in its own right.

Certainly the production was a great success. It ran for four-and-a-half
months, after which two separate productions toured the provinces. Wybert
Reeve, the actor who played Hartright in the original production, then took over
as Count Fosco, led one tour around the United Kingdom, America, Canada,
and Australia and is said to have played the part of Fosco more than fifteen
hundred times (Pasco 1880, 285). Collins reported in a letter to Charles Ward
(15 October 1871) that extra seats had to be put into the aisles of the Olympic to
accommodate all those who wished to attend performances (Baker, et al. 2005,
vol. 2, 283). At that time the seating capacity of the Olympic was approximately
890 (Howard 1970, 166). In comparison, the Surrey (which staged the first
adaptation) could seat 2,161 and had additional standing room (ibid., 234). This
is relevant because the size of the venue has a direct bearing on the type of
drama produced: the smaller Olympic Theatre being more suited to a more
intimate, less sensational style of production. Contemporary critics
distinguished between the "Olympic drama" and the "Adelphi drama", which
they characterised as cruder and full of melodramatic incident (Sherson 1925,
103).[10] Dramatic fare at the Olympic was regarded as more refined than that of
the Adelphi or the Surrey, which produced a mixed repertoire including opera
and Shakespeare alongside its celebrated nautical melodramas and pantomimes.
Its audience was drawn both from the local vicinity and from respectable West
End visitors (Davis and Emeljanow 2001, 39). As a more upmarket venue than
the Surrey, the Olympic attracted a more fashionable and educated audience and
this too may have influenced Collins's adaptation.

In conclusion, various factors surrounding the play's production in 1871,
including the author's own comments on his writing and the timing and choice
of venue, suggest that Collins did not envisage his dramatic version of *The
Woman in White* as a sensation drama. Studying the play as a text for
performance, comparing it to other adaptations, and noting the absence of
sensation scenes together with the presence of a contemplative mood, as
indicated by the review illustrations, confirm that it does not fit the
classification. So how then should we view the play? In his "Recollections of
Wilkie Collins" Reeve suggested that contemporary critics recognised its
originality: "The drama was a decided success. On its production the
newspapers pronounced it the best drama and the most interesting writer of late

years, and likely to be the forerunner of a new and better school" (Reeve 1906, 458). Perhaps surprisingly, later critics failed to recognise how some elements of Collins's work anticipated the new psychological dramas of the late-nineteenth century. It is therefore ironic that the most recent stage productions of *The Woman in White* have reinvented it as sensation drama.

Notes

[1] British Library, ADD.MS 53000C and ADD.MS 53006D. Neither version was published so these are the only known copies of the dramas.
[2] Collins's play also provided the dramatist Arthur Wing Pinero with his first professional acting role in a production at the Theatre Royal, Edinburgh in June 1874 (Wearing 1972, 140).
[3] I am grateful to Pierre Tissot van Patot for the Dutch information.
[4] See Brooks 1976 and James 1977.
[5] The other scene was the account of the march of the women to Versailles in Carlyle's *The French Revolution* (Peters 1991, 208).
[6] Copyright laws prevented other dramatists adapting an author's work of fiction providing the latter had already registered his or her own adaptation.
[7] He wrote a letter to the *Daily Telegraph* dated 11 October 1871 and published 12 October. Collins also printed the same comments on the Olympic Theatre programmes.
[8] The *Times, Daily News*, and *Morning Post*, for example, made adverse comments, whereas the *Daily Telegraph, Weekly Dispatch,* and *Land and Water* reacted favourably.
[9] Now in the collection of Tate Britain, London.
[10] The Adelphi Theatre had staged the original production of *The Colleen Bawn* and put on Collins's dramas *No Thoroughfare* (1867), *Black and White* (1869), and *Rank and Riches* (1883).

Appendix: Stage Adaptations of *The Woman in White*

1860. *The Woman in White*, Adap. J. R. Ware. Royal Surrey Theatre. ADD.MS 52997B. British Library.

1861. *The Woman in White*. Adap. W. Sidney. No theatre named. ADD.MS 53000C. British Library.

1861. *The Woman in White*. Royal Sadler's Wells Theatre. ADD.MS 53006D. British Library.

1905. *The Woman in White*. Adap. C. W. Somerset. Kennington Theatre. LCP 1905/23. British Library.

1938. *The Woman in White*. Adap. A. R. Janes. Shanklin Theatre. LCP 1938/59. British Library.

1952. *The Woman in White*. Adap. Constance Cox. Theatre Royal, Aldershot. LCP 1952/42. British Library.

Sutherland, Dan. 1955. *Mystery at Blackwater*. Lacy's Acting Edition No. 326. London: Samuel French.
1967. *The Woman in White*. Adap. Constance Cox. Theatre Royal, Northampton. LCP 1967/40. British Library.
Kelly, Tim. 1975. *Egad, The Woman in White*. New York: Samuel French.
1988. *The Woman in White*. Adap. Melissa Murray, Greenwich Theatre. Playscript 3982. British Library.

Works Cited

(Material from daily newspapers is cited in the body of the essay but omitted here.)

Bachman, Maria K. and Don Richard Cox (eds). 2003. *Reality's Dark Light: The Sensational Wilkie Collins*. Knoxville: University of Tennessee Press.
Baker, William., Andrew Gasson., Graham Law., and Paul Lewis. 2005. *The Public Face of Wilkie Collins*. 4 vols. London: Pickering and Chatto.
Baker, William. and William M. Clarke (eds). 1999. *The Letters of Wilkie Collins*. 2 vols. Basingstoke: Macmillan.
Boucicault, Dion. 1860. *The Colleen Bawn*, in Rowell 1972, 173-231.
Bratton, Jacky. 2003. *New Readings in Theatre History*. Cambridge: Cambridge University Press.
Brooks, Peter. 1976. *The Melodramatic Imagination*. New Haven and London: Yale University Press.
Byron, H. J. n.d. *Miss Eily O'Connor*. Lacy's Acting Edition No. 781. London: Thomas Hailes Lacy.
Collins, Wilkie. 1871. *The Woman in White: A Drama, in a Prologue and Four Acts*. London: Published by the Author.
—. 1852. *Basil*. Oxford: Oxford University Press, 2000.
Davis, Jim. and Victor Emeljanow. 2001. *Reflecting the Audience: London Theatregoing, 1840-1880*. Hatfield: University of Hertfordshire Press.
Fawkes, Richard. 1979. *Dion Boucicault*. London: Quartet Books.
Gasson, Andrew. 1998. *Wilkie Collins: An Illustrated Guide*. Oxford: Oxford University Press.
Goble, Alan (ed.). 1999. *The Complete Index to Literary Sources in Film*. London: Bowker-Saur.
Howard, Diana. 1970. *London Theatres and Music Halls 1850-1950*. London: The Library Association.
Hutter, A. D. 2003. Fosco Lives!, in Bachman and Cox 2003, 195-238.
Irvin, Eric. 1976. Nineteenth-Century English Dramatists in Australia. *Theatre Notebook* 30:24-34.

236   Sensation Drama? Collins's Stage Adaptation of *The Woman in White*

James, Louis. 1977. Taking Melodrama Seriously: Theatre, and Nineteenth-Century Studies. *History Workshop* 3:151-8.

Lewis, Leopold. 1871. *The Bells,* in Rowell 1972, 467-502.

Mayer, David (ed.). 1980. *Henry Irving and* The Bells. Manchester: Manchester University Press.

Mayer, David. 2004. Encountering Melodrama, in Powell 2004, 145-63.

Pasco, Charles E. 1880. *The Dramatic List.* London: David Bogue.

Peters, Catherine. 1991. *The King of Inventors: A Life of Wilkie Collins.* London: Minerva.

Phillips, Watts. n.d. *The Woman in Mauve.* Lacy's Acting Edition No.76. London: Thomas Hailes Lacy.

Powell, Kerry (ed.). 2004. *The Cambridge Companion to Victorian and Edwardian Theatre.* Cambridge: Cambridge University Press.

Rahill, Frank. 1967. *The World of Melodrama.* Pennsylvania and London: Pennsylvania State University Press.

Reeve, Wybert. 1906. Recollections of Wilkie Collins. *Chambers's Journal* 9:451-68.

Rowell, George (ed.). 1972. *Nineteenth-Century Plays.* Oxford: Oxford University Press.

Sherson, Errol. 1925. *London's Lost Theatres of the Nineteenth Century.* London: Bodley Head.

Stephens, John Russell. 1992. *The Profession of the Playwright: British Theatre 1800-1900.* Cambridge: Cambridge University Press.

Wearing, J. P. 1972. Pinero's Professional Dramatic Roles, 1874-1884. *Theatre Notebook* 26S:140-4.

DETECTING BURIED SECRETS: RECENT FILM VERSIONS OF *THE WOMAN IN WHITE* AND *THE MOONSTONE*

STEFANI BRUSBERG-KIERMEIER

In his famous essay "Art as Technique", Victor Shklovsky emphasises the important role that non-habitual perception and defamiliarisation play for the function of works of art: "Art exists that one may recover the sensation of life; it exists to make one feel things, to make the stone *stony*. The purpose of art is to impart the sensation of things as they are perceived, and not as they are known" (Shklovsky 1917, 24, italics in original). According to Shklovsky, the appropriate technique of art that serves to recover one's sensations is "to increase the difficulty and length of perception because the process of perception is an aesthetic end in itself and must be prolonged" (ibid.). Due to its very name, sensation fiction can be regarded as following Shklovsky's maxim and help the reader recover the sensation of life by the reception of a work of art. Sensation fiction defamiliarises ordinary reality and, moreover, events are not only presented as logically ordered and purposeful, as in other genres of fictitious writing, but plots in sensation fiction are strange and full of surprises.

Although the famous saying allegedly made by Wilkie Collins–"make 'em laugh, make 'em cry, make 'em wait"–is most probably apocryphal (Peters 1991, xi), it has certainly been ascribed to this sensation fiction writer because of Collins's clever use of serial publication. His topicality can be easily made apparent when one reminds oneself of how closely every television series today still adheres to his techniques of increasing the difficulty and length of perception. Like in Collins's novels, TV series' dramatic dialogues and actions involve the audience intellectually and emotionally and even prolong and heighten their process of perception by the use of "cliff hangers". Also, the topical or even timeless appeal of Collins's plots might be due to the fact that novels like *The Woman in White* and *The Moonstone* are touching love stories of loss and recovery. Sensational occurrences and new acquaintances cause turbulent emotional changes that the characters have to adjust to and consequently shape their self-image. Interestingly enough, Jenny Bourne Taylor explains the effect of the novels' exciting events on the characters' existence with the help of the term "screen": "The self is a screen on which others' perceptions are projected and enacted; a collection of physical signs whose meaning is uncertain; a subjectivity struggling to gain coherence, yet bearing secret and forgotten traces" (Taylor 1988, 63-4). This statement seems especially poignant when it comes to discussing screen adaptations of Collins's work.

But the transfer of Collins's novels onto film is not only a logical consequence with regard to their structure and subject matter. The medial change allows the non-reader to get access to these exciting plots and unusual characters and the reader to perceive and enjoy the novels afresh in a defamiliarised way. When one takes the enormous popularity and financial success of some of Collins's novels into account, it does not come as a surprise that filming of Collins's novels has been attractive for filmmakers from the early days of the moving image. His two most popular novels, *The Woman in White* (1860) and *The Moonstone* (1868), are also the ones that were most frequently put onto the screen. The Internet Movie Database lists two film versions of *The Woman in White* from 1912 and one each from 1917, 1929, 1948, as well as the BBC mini series from 1982. *The Moonstone* was made into a film in 1915 and 1934, and into a TV series in 1959 and 1972. This essay looks more closely at the BBC television versions of *The Woman in White* from 1997 and *The Moonstone* from 1996.

While the serial publication strongly structures Collins's novels, his talent as a dramatist becomes most obvious in the sensational moments in all of his texts irrespective of their genre. The surprising actions of his subversive heroes and heroines fascinate and their secrets puzzle the theatre audience as well as the reader. Collins has the strengths of a theatrical writer and his dramatic plots accelerate or slow down in terms of the speed of the action whenever necessary to enhance their sensational effect. These particulars also make the transfer of his novels into films easier than those by other authors. As I have argued elsewhere, not only does the illusion of reality have to coincide in both media–novel and film–but the emotional and intellectual experience when watching the film should be comparable to the emotional and intellectual experience when reading the novel (Brusberg-Kiermeier 2004, 150). The audio-visual medium has means–though different, just as subtle as literature–through which to create a strong and authentic impression. For a novel or a film to become "important" to an audience, this audience must get involved mentally and emotionally during the reception, constructing "meaning" while reading or watching (Griem and Voigts-Virchow 2002, 159). This process is usually based on the medium's coherent narrative and especially on key moments of great intensity and stimulation.

A contemporary film version of a Wilkie Collins novel will almost necessarily present itself as a heritage movie combined with thriller elements. Films in which the action is located in Britain are prone to fetishise cities or landscapes, gardens, country houses, or other period details. London and Hampstead Heath in *Notting Hill* (1999) and North Yorkshire in *Calendar Girls* (2003) are only two of many contemporary examples. A Victorian setting, like other historical ones, often contributes to the films' visual perfectionism. Over the years something that I would like to call "heritage aesthetics" has been established, an aesthetic approach that film versions of a sensation novel seem likely to adopt. As Imelda Whelehan states, certain features of novelistic expression must be retained in an adaptation, but the idea of which features are essential to a reproduction varies largely (Whelehan 1999, 7). In my view, the question of literary genre comes into play here. For the filming of a Collins novel, the director not only needs to consider appropriate setting, but also needs to retain high levels of realism, and historical verisimilitude, and the degrees of suspense that one comes to expect from a sensation novel. Moreover, the closeness of Collins's novels to the genre of crime fiction will inevitably influence the final product.

Similar to the crime novel, "whodunit", or mystery, the detection of hidden secrets or crimes is essential to the genre of sensation fiction. For instance, in both Wilkie Collins's *The Woman in White* and Mary Elizabeth Braddon's *Lady Audley's Secret* (1862) the reader is confronted with the death of a woman who takes a secret with her into her grave. In her study *Over Her Dead Body* (1992) Elisabeth Bronfen explains the important role that a female corpse can play for the process of detection:

> A corpse spurs on the urge to detect missing facts with death explained by virtue of a reconstruction of the events–the doubled narrative imitating the uncanny position of the dead/remaining woman. Once her death has been explained the corpse can lie peacefully, the end of the narrative double plot equal to the end of her revenant position. (Bronfen 1992, 294)

Collins's novels thus foreshadow the classical crime story, in which a murder brings a whole community into disarray. The detection of the crime by a detective figure serves to gradually establish order again. But sensation novels are more than a plot full of riddles that have to be deciphered. The special uncanny effect of the sensation novel is often brought about by the important role that graves and graveyards play for the mystery plot. In *The Woman in White* and *The Moonstone,* Collins uses a country estate's graveyard and a servant's grave as the sites of hidden secrets.

One of the greatest difficulties for a director who wants to film *The Woman in White* or *The Moonstone* is to decide which narrative perspective s/he is going to choose. In both novels Collins uses a great variety of narrators and narrative devices that all claim authority and truth for themselves. This technique not only makes the novels landmarks of ambivalence (Kendrick 1977-8, 85), but also makes it difficult to transfer them into another medium. The departure from Collins's multiple-voice narration is therefore understandable as a ninety-minute film–even more so than a mini series–cannot represent the novel's complex variety of fragmented texts. In the 1997 version of *The Woman in White*, co-produced by the BBC, Carlton, and WGBH Boston, the film-makers opted for "a feminist revision of the past" (Cartmell and Whelehan 1998, 5) by making Marian Halcombe the main narrator, whose diary only contributes part of the narrative in the book. She is called "Fairlie" in the movie instead of "Halcombe" to clarify the family connection between her, her half-sister Laura, and their uncle Frederick. Marian, played by Tara Fitzgerald, frames the film with her narrative, which is made the more haunting by the excellent photography (Richard Greatrex won a BAFTA TV award for it) and David Ferguson's atmospheric music. While the film's action focuses very much on Marian's determination and energy, the novel's "maternal plot" is cut. In the film, Marian and her other half-sister Anne Catherick go to their father's instead of their mother's grave, and Anne has hidden Sir Percival Glyde's will and her diary therein.

The film oscillates between camera perspectives that represent the viewpoints of Marian and Walter Hartright. Moreover, the changing camera perspectives offer implications concerning the unreliability of a narrator in certain situations. When Walter is to meet his new employer, Mr Fairlie, the servant Margaret Porcher brings him to his room. The camera pretends to give us Walter's perspective by focusing on Margaret's rear part, neck, and face. The view presented has erotic undertones and hints at the theme of sexual harassment that will later play an important role in the film. Adie Allen, who plays Margaret Porcher, delivers an excellent performance as the sensual servant, who is man hunting, and later has an affair with Glyde, thereby holding the story together. The complicated plot of the novel is made more accessible by the centralisation of place; quite a few incidents that happen elsewhere in the book are set at the Fairlie estate in Limmeridge.

Especially interesting with regard to camera perspectives is Marian's illness, her hallucinatory dream, and her recovery. While she suffers from typhus she dreams that Glyde and his helpers murder Laura Fairlie. When Marian wakes up she comments on her dream, "a dream, thank God!", only to be told subsequently that Laura has died. Blurred camera images and hectic shots from unusual perspectives make the viewers unsure what they are to accept as hallucinations and what is actually happening. Thus the viewer adopts Marian's state of mind and is equally transformed into a state of anxiety and shock, especially when s/he finds that Marian stands next to Laura's grave. Here the film's action comes to a halt as the heroine has to decide how to proceed. This two-part structure is reminiscent of Alfred Hitchcock's *Vertigo* (1957), in which the hero also finds himself confronted with the death of his beloved. *Vertigo*, unlike *The Woman in White*, introduces the "other", "similar" woman in the second half and therefore reveals only retrospectively that there were two women from the beginning. Also contrary to *The Woman in White*, in *Vertigo* the wife is really murdered by her husband, while the "other", "similar" woman, who impersonated the wife, finally dies in an accident.

Concerning the mysterious female doppelganger, the film version (like the novel) adopts the viewpoint of the drawing master Walter Hartright. As Bronfen explains, Anne Catherick is buried alive in an asylum to procure her silence, which means that she is socially dead and can only become "alive" again by her escape (Bronfen 1992, 296). While the text makes clear that her white garments allow for a great variety of interpretation–supernatural angelic creature, young lady in her bridal gown, prostitute in her undergarments–the film version gives preference to an association of the white garments with a shroud (see ibid., 297). Moreover, Susan Vidler, who plays Anne Catherick, wears almost-completely white make-up, which makes her look not only disturbed but deathly pale. Since Collins has Anne die young of a heart disease, she represents a combination of mental and physical illness; from the beginning she is the "dead image" and Laura the "living image" of the same woman (ibid., 298). Strangely enough, the film changes her death from a disease to suicide– she throws herself from a tower in desperation–and thus highlights her mental instability and not her unstable physical condition.

However, the drastic scene serves to stress the brutality and villainy of Sir Percival Glyde and his friend, Count Fosco. Due to their conspiracy, Laura takes over Anne's position after her death as an incarcerated living dead, and her fair dress in turn changes its association from bridal gown to shroud. The film cleverly foreshadows the villains' plan of this exchange; first Walter wishes to draw the woman in white and uses Laura as a model. Later again Laura takes Anne's place, this time under her name in an asylum. The motivation for the crimes against the three half-sisters is hidden in Glyde's past. In Collins's novel, Glyde is an illegitimate child as his parents were never married. He forges the church register so that he can inherit his father's estate. In the film, however, his secret is the sexual exploitation of Anne Catherick from her teenager years onwards. The filmmakers' decision to use child and wife abuse as the hidden secret, that has to be discovered by the detective figures, is understandable when one takes the datedness of discourses into account. A contemporary film audience might find it hard to grasp the social implications that illegitimate birth had in Victorian times.

Sir Percival Glyde's friend, Count Fosco, is a mysterious foreigner who is involved in the criminal plot and whose function in the crimes remains unclear for a long time. Fosco has remained one of the leading villains in world literature. In the *Guardian*'s competition for the readers' favourite villain in March 2005, half of the twenty winning entries stem from Victorian novels, and Fosco ranks among Dracula, Heathcliff, Moriarty, and Long John Silver. While in general the screen version of *The Woman in White* can boast excellent casting and performances, Simon Callow's presentation of Count Fosco lacks the sensual attraction that the character is supposed to have in the book, making him a more frightening than fascinating figure. Ian Richardson is more convincing as a physically strong but very affected and dandy-like Mr Fairlie, who leers at a cherub's genitals in a coal drawing. But then Richardson had more time to develop his performance as he had already played the part in the BBC mini series based on the novel in 1982. Alan Badel, who played Count Fosco in this mini series earned good reviews, but then again Badel specialised in playing weird foreigners in Victorian England, having played Svengali in the 1976 TV version of George Du Maurier's famous novel *Trilby* (1894). In the recent film version of *The Woman in White*, Mr Fairlie's exploitation of his servants is immediately made obvious in his greeting of Walter Hartright: "There is in this house none of the horrid barbarity of the local gentry, who would treat artists as their servants. Now would you put this tray of coins back in the cabinet and then go and take down the portfolio". When at the ending of the film Walter announces Laura's recovery and his engagement to her, Richardson has a funny exit as he nearly faints and has to be taken away by two servants.

In this murder mystery, which is characterised by a mistaken identity, Walter joins Marian in her fight against unlawful patriarchal power. The filmmakers even elaborate on the topic of sexual harassment: Glyde sets up a trap for Walter and uses his servant Margaret to falsely accuse him in order to have him removed from the house. Thereby the film cleverly intensifies the tragic love plot between Laura and Walter, introduces the theme of sexual abuse, and points out the difference between an *unmarried* woman being harassed by a stranger and a *married* woman being harassed by her husband. The audience reconstructs the crime alongside Marian and Walter and likewise experiences Marian's and Walter's discovery of Laura in the asylum as the most exciting moment in the film. The scene is especially effective as Anne and Laura are established as not really close look-alikes before. Walter only initially mistakes Laura for the woman in white because the sun blinds him. By choosing actresses with dark hair, the director Tim Fywell stresses the overall similarity of all three half-sisters. The use of Laura's dark long hair to disguise her face and thereby her identity renders the revelation of her true identity the more spectacular and sensational. This scene certainly creates a strong emotional impact, which hardly decreases with repeated viewing. Only when Anne's death is finally acknowledged can Laura fully re-enter the world of the living.

In the neoformalist approach to film criticism the viewer is not passive but active, constructing characters according to their visual and oral presentation. The viewer follows the expressions and actions of the characters and constructs continuity and meaning within the film's narrative. In *The Woman in White* for instance, Laura is introduced "through Walter's eyes", that is, we are blinded by the sun as well and might also mistake her for Anne. The similarity of the two women is alluded to when Laura "represents" Anne in Walter's painting or when Anne is given Laura's clothes, which, it is assumed, will fit her. The highlight of the film is the scene in which Laura has actually become Anne. The secrets that Glyde and Fosco hope to bury forever are thus detected: it turns out that first Anne has to be silenced in some way, because she has been sexually abused by Glyde and threatens to expose him. Secondly, Glyde has only married Laura for her money and is eager to get rid of her in order to inherit it. In the film, Laura's fears are even more unsettling because of her husband's violence and her inability to prove that he wishes to murder her: "I have no evidence against my husband except that he is cruel. What is that? So are half the men in England". Glyde and Fosco, who exchange their identities, exploit this similarity between the two women. The dead Anne is buried under Laura's name, while Laura is brought to a remote asylum under Anne's. The discovery of the dead-alive Laura in the bleak asylum brings about the discovery of the buried secrets and has a strong visual effect that can be better described in terms of excess than lack of meaning, which makes clear that Imelda Whelehan is completely right in arguing that it is not fruitful to regard adaptations of literary texts as necessarily lacking the complexity, substance, or force of the original (Whelehan 1999, 16). Tara Fitzgerald and Justine Waddell rise to the challenge when they depict the shock of one sister at finding the other one alive but mentally disturbed. The photography increases the tension to the extreme by only showing Laura in a close-up after Marian has called out her name.

In her study of neoformalist film analysis, Kristin Thompson differentiates between four types of motivation for the presence of any given device in film: realistic, compositional, transtextual, and artistic (Thompson 1988, 16ff.). While the use of a certain geographical setting might be based on a realistic or compositional motivation, the casting of certain actors is often motivated transtextually, that is, based on the audience's familiarity with an actor's previous work. The viewer who is acquainted with other British heritage films will not be surprised to come across Simon Callow, Tara Fitzgerald, and James Wilby in *The Woman in White* or Patricia Hodge, Peter Vaughan, and Greg Wise in *The Moonstone*. It is fully understandable that the BBC and ITV engage such renowned heritage actors when they wish to produce a "definite" TV film version of a well-known novel. A well-received TV heritage film might even make it into the cinema, like the 1995 BBC version of *Persuasion*. For others, especially younger actors, heritage TV productions prove a great chance to make a name for themselves and gain roles in forthcoming British cinematic projects. *The Woman in White*, for instance, profited from Andrew Lincoln's excellent performance as Walter Hartright. In turn, Lincoln was given the role of Mark, the melancholy admirer of the newly-wed Juliet (played by Keira Knightley) in *Love Actually* (2003).

In British films of the 1990s Tara Fitzgerald became the epitome of the independent, self-assured, and even subversive heritage heroine. Within a few years she made herself a name as an excellent actress, appearing alongside Joseph Fiennes and Samuel West in *The Vacillations of Poppy Carew* (1995), Hugh Grant in *The Englishman Who Went Up a Hill* (1995), and Ewan McGregor in *Brassed Off* (1996). Her most impressive performance is probably her portrayal of the heroine Helen Huntingdon in the 1996 BBC version of Anne Brontë's *The Tenant of Wildfell Hall*. This three-part mini series stars two other outstanding heritage actors, Rupert Graves as Arthur Huntington and Toby Stevens as Gilbert Markham. Like in the novel, Gilbert Markham falls in love with an enigmatic young woman who has moved into his neighbourhood and earns her own living by selling her paintings. Because she is attracted to him, too, she allows him to read her diary, which reveals her hidden secret: she has left her husband and taken with her her young son in order to free him from his father's bad influence. Contrary to the book, in which she finally inherits both her husband's and her aunt's country estates, in the mini series she returns to the dilapidated cottage in North Yorkshire. While most heritage films use locations to create a "Southern, feminine Englishness", the 1992 version of *Wuthering Heights* used the impressive Malham Rocks in North Yorkshire to bring about a "Northern, masculine Englishness" (Brusberg-Kiermeier 2004, 153). In *The Tenant of Wildfell Hall*, this location is used to create a surprising image of a "Northern, feminine Englishness".

Something similar, but more disturbing is achieved by the television version of Collins's *The Moonstone*, which sets the suicide of a female ex-criminal, Rosanna Spearman, who thinks she is involved in the theft of the jewel, in the Shivering Sands, "the most horrible quicksand on the shores of Yorkshire" (Collins 1868, 36). The image of the Shivering Sands provides the frame for the movie, which uses it for the opening and closing credits. The uncanny landscape is then linked to the moonstone. At the beginning of the film we see the hero Franklin Blake in bed with his wife Rachel Verinder, dreaming of the Shivering Sands as well as of the first violent theft of the moonstone from a temple in India. This present-tense start serves to introduce the story of the priceless jewel which the film then unfolds in one big flashback until it ends with exactly the image of the Shivering Sands it started with.

Franklin Blake's function is to bring the moonstone to Rachel on her birthday, to fall in love with her, and to finally marry her. She is delighted by the valuable birthday present and reluctant to accept the difficulties that arise due to the moonstone's worth and history. The film also cleverly introduces the Indian Brahmins who wish to recover it for their temple as "jugglers" on Rachel's birthday. The comments of another party guest, the family doctor Mr Candy, not only indicate the danger in which Rachel is now placed but also that she has no more right to the stone than the first thief John Herncastle, her cousin Franklin Blake, or the second thief, Godfrey Ablewhite. In this the film clearly follows Collins's visionary critique of British colonialisation in India.

Interestingly enough, Rosanna Spearman is much more central to the film's focus than in the book. The lower-class character is slightly handicapped with a twisted back. She is shown witnessing Franklin's singing and piano play and cleaning his room, touching his desk and books. Another servant, Penelope (who is in fact Betteredge's daughter in the book), rightly diagnoses "love-sickness" as the reason for Rosanna's strange behaviour. Rosanna indicates Franklin's involvement in the crime early on in the film, runs off to her friend "Limping Lucy"–another handicapped, lower-class woman, and later hides something in the Shivering Sands. Immediately afterwards she approaches Franklin and steps very close to him. His arrogance and ignorance of her feelings hasten her decision to drown herself in the Shivering Sands. The film adapts the suicide most impressively by showing Rosanna vanish in the mud with the inspector and two other servants watching. The butler Gabriel Betteredge shouts "Rosanna" while the servant Samuel is seized by violent sobs. Rosanna's suicide is certainly one of those key moments of great intensity and stimulation that stay in the audience's memory irrespective of the medium.

Franklin later discovers that Rosanna hid his besmeared nightgown in the Shivering Sands as it indicated that he was the thief. He gradually learns that he took the moonstone under the influence of laudanum and that he unwittingly passed it on to Godfrey Ablewhite who is finally robbed and killed by the Indians. When Franklin reads Rosanna's explanatory letter we hear her voice tell her tale, how she fell in love with Franklin, and tried to shield him from the police. The film beautifully repeats Rosanna's first sight of Franklin, this time in slow-motion, when he comes towards her "like a lover in a dream". This technique prolongs the process and heightens the intensity of perception, establishing Franklin as the romantic hero and thus making Rosanna's infatuation understandable. The film also closely follows Collins's association of the Shivering Sands with mystery, hidden secrets, sexual desire, and female subversion. The film negotiates closure with a short and effective scene of the

featuring the moonstone's restoration and then returns to the opening image of
Franklin and Rachel in bed. But, as in the book, the happy ending of the love
relation between Franklin and Rachel cannot obliterate the disturbing image of
the *unhappy* ending of Rosanna's love for Franklin. The subversiveness of her
desire is again invoked with the film's final image of the Shivering Sands.

Like in the book, the funniest scenes derive from comical behaviour or
remarks made by the butler Gabriel Betteredge or the zealot Drusilla Clack,
played by Kacey Ainsworth. When Drusilla is told about how Godfrey
Ablewhite was attacked in the street, Ainsworth's delivery of her lines–"Lept on
him? And from behind!"–is hilarious. Peter Vaughan plays Betteredge, who is
the main narrator in Collins's novel. This brings about an interesting meta-level
of meaning, as Vaughan has in recent years become the butler actor *par
excellence*, playing butlers in *The Remains of the Day* (1993) and in *An Ideal
Husband* (1999).

The timeless appeal of *The Moonstone* is certainly based on its
structural closeness to the crime novel, with its theft of a priceless jewel, the
curse connected to the gem's initial theft, and its variety of complicated, false
alibis. Moreover, the detection of the crime is repeatedly delayed for various
reasons. This overall pattern, which also characterises the film version, is called
"stairstep construction" (Thompson 1988, 37). While Anthony Sher's mannered
and stagy presentation of Inspector Cuff emphasises the artificiality of the step-
by-step reconstruction of the crime, Greg Wise as Franklin Blake and Keeley
Hawes as Rachel Verinder act sincerely and thereby inject authenticity and
verisimilitude into the complicated plot and its often unlikely twists. However,
the uncanny effect of the movie is mainly based on the topicality of the class
conflict. The presentation of two lower-class women–and moreover two that are
physically handicapped–who are closely linked to upper-class crime and suffer
from this connection has lost nothing of its shocking impact, not even in our
allegedly politically-correct times.

On closer scrutiny it becomes obvious that the beginning of the twenty-
first century sees a renaissance of sensation fiction and of its transfer into other
media. Another example is the film version of Mary Elizabeth Braddon's novel
Lady Audley's Secret (1862) from 2000, which offers an interesting re-reading
of the novel as a French love tragedy. This co-production of ITV, Carlton TV,
and Warner Sisters has obviously taken a statement of the character Robert
Audley–"I feel like the hero of a French novel; I am falling in love with my
aunt" (Braddon 1862, 46)–as a *modus operandi* for the whole movie. Instead of
the novel's blond and childlike Lucy Audley, the film presents a dark, tall, and
womanly heroine, played by Neve McIntosh. Nevertheless, the film stylises
Lady Audley in the sensuous Pre-Raphaelite mode, in which her portrait in the
book is painted (ibid., 56). Steven Mackintosh plays the role of her husband's

nephew, Robert Audley, as that of "the hero of a French novel". The film focuses on Robert's infatuation with his aunt. For instance, he not only gets into her room through a secret passage, he steals one of her hair combs, and secretly watches her while she dresses. As in the novel Robert functions as the detective who reveals that she is a bigamist, has tried to kill her husband, and probably inherited her mother's madness. But while she is incarcerated in an asylum in France till her death in the novel, the film ends with her escape and union with a new victim. Robert sees them at a station and has to accept that he has brought tragedy into his family's lives and lost his love. His final position as a voyeur reminds of French movies like Louis Malle's *Damage* (1992), which concludes with Dr Stephen Fleming (played by Jeremy Irons) moving to Italy after his marriage has come to an end and he has lost his son and his job, because of his infatuation with his daughter-in-law.

But this adaptation of *Lady Audley's Secret* is not the only adaptation to give an impression of the possibilities for topical re-readings of sensation fiction. Another example is a recent musical version of *The Woman in White*. London's Palace Theatre recently showed this musical with the music of Andrew Lloyd-Webber, the lyrics of David Zippel, and the direction of Trevor Nunn. In times of reduced funds for the arts, Lloyd-Webber is not the only one to rely on the magnetism of one of the greatest literary works of all time. What becomes obvious is that the canonisation of a text plays an important role in its adaptation into another medium. In times of enormous cuts in the expenditure for culture and education, filmmakers or composers will rely rather on well-known or at least canonised texts. The film versions of Shakespeare plays–most clearly the films directed by Kenneth Branagh–show this tendency as well as the novels chosen for adaptation as heritage films. One can only hope that filmmakers and others will tackle lesser-known literary texts–like Collins's other fascinating novels–for adaptations in future.

When Jonathan Heawood described how Penguin Classics and Oxford World's Classics rediscovered Wilkie Collins's works, he called it a "vintage scandal" (*Observer*, 2 March 2003, 9). The publishing contest came about because a reading audience brought up on melodramas written by contemporary authors who imitate Victorian genre-fiction were "hungry for the real-thing". Heawood thinks that the current vogue for sensationalism has to do with similarities between modern and Victorian society, as people are increasingly identifying themselves with a society driven by sexual and political double standards. If Heawood is right, the subversiveness of Collins's characters might indeed enhance a political consciousness for social inequality. And even escapist *Harry Potter* readers might finally turn to Collins's fiction after they have seen a film or musical version, because–after all–he still makes us laugh, cry, and wait.

Works Cited

Braddon, Mary Elizabeth. 1862. *Lady Audley's Secret.* Ware: Wordsworth Classics, 1997.

Bronfen, Elisabeth. 1992. *Over Her Dead Body: Death, Femininity, and the Aesthetic.* Manchester: Manchester University Press.

Brontë, Anne. 1848. *The Tenant of Wildfell Hall.* Ware: Wordsworth Classics, 1994.

Brusberg-Kiermeier, Stefani. 2004. Stormy Novel, Thorny Adaptation: Recent Appropriations of *Wuthering Heights,* in Voigts-Virchow 2004, 149-57.

Cartmell, Deborah. and Imelda Whelehan. 1998. Introduction–Sisterhoods: Across the Literature/Media Divide, in Cartmell et al. 1998, 1-15.

Cartmell, Deborah. and Imelda Whelehan (eds). 1999. *Adaptations. From Text to Screen, Screen to Text.* London, and New York: Routledge.

Cartmell, Deborah., I.Q. Hunter., Heide Kaye., and Imelda Whelehan (eds). 1998. *Sisterhoods: Across the Literature/Media Divide.* London: Sterling, VA: Pluto Press.

Collins. Wilkie. 1854. *Hide and Seek.* Oxford: Oxford University Press, 1999.

—. 1868. *The Moonstone.* London: Penguin, 1998.

—. 1860. *The Woman in White.* London: Penguin, 1999.

Giddings, Robert. and Erica Sheen (eds). 2000. *The Classic Novel from Page to Screen.* Manchester: Manchester University Press.

Griem, Julika. and Eckart Voigts-Virchow. 2002. Filmnarratologie: Grundlagen, Tendenzen und Beispielanalysen, in Nünning and Nünning 2002, 155-83.

Heawood, Jonathan. 2003. Vintage Scandal. *The Observer,* 2 March, 9.

Kendrick, Walter M. 1977-8. The Sensationalism of *The Woman in White,* in Pykett 1998, 70-87.

Newton, K. M. (ed.). 1988. *Twentieth-Century Literary Theory: A Reader.* Basingstoke and London: Macmillan.

Nünning, Vera. and Ansgar Nünning (eds). 2002. *Erzähltheorie Transgenerisch, Intermedial, Interdisziplinär,* Trier: W. V. T.

Peters, Catherine. 1999. Introduction to Collins 1854, vii-xxiii.

Pykett, Lyn (ed.). 1998. *New Casebooks: Wilkie Collins.* Houndmills: Macmillan.

Shklovsky, Victor. 1917. Art as Technique, in Newton 1988, 23-5.

Taylor, Jenny Bourne. 1988. *In the Secret Theatre of Home: Wilkie Collins, Sensation Narrative and Nineteenth-Century Psychology.* London: New York: Routledge.

Thompson, Kristin. 1988. *Breaking the Glass Armor: Neoformalist Film Analysis.* Princeton NJ: Princeton University Press.

Voigts-Virchow, Eckart (ed.). 2004. *Janespotting and Beyond: British Heritage Retrovisions Since the Mid-1990s.* Tübingen: Gunter Narr.

Whelehan, Imelda. 1999. Adaptations: The Contemporary Dilemmas, in Cartmell and Whelehan 1998, 3-19.

AFTERWORD

JANICE M. ALLAN

"It is no longer appropriate, or productive, to employ the terms centre and margin when discussing Collins's writing". (Jenny Bourne Taylor)

This comment, offered during the closing discussion of the Wilkie Collins Conference, brought together the various ways in which the papers foregrounded the extent to which Collins's corpus challenged both literary and social boundaries. Looking forwards, as well as backwards, it also serves as an apt point of departure for an Afterword that reads the literary productions of Collins as being characterised by a certain liminality that "can both subsume and transcend a dialectic of margin and center" (Spariosu 1997, 38). Indeed, such a notion of liminality problematises the concept of boundary itself. Consider, for example, the ambiguous position of Ozias Midwinter, standing "between the dead father [...] and the living son" (Collins 1866, 122); the bottle of opium–both remedy and poison–discovered by Miserrimus Dexter "in the space between the outer wood and the lining" of Sarah Macallan's dressing case (Collins 1875, 177); or the missing links supplied by Ezra Jennings in "the intervals between" Dr Candy's delirious wanderings (Collins 1868, 456). If Collins novels are–as was suggested by his contemporary critics–a "puzzle", each of the foregoing examples represents a key piece in their construction.[1] Yet in each case, this key is discovered by a character that embodies the destabilisation associated with the mongrel, that "unnatural" product that calls into question the boundaries between species as well as "the great law of nature" (Gosse 1844, xc). Moreover, explicitly (if precariously) located in the space of the in-between, the understanding provided by such keys becomes provisional, shifting, and unstable.

Such liminal moments proliferate throughout Collins's texts.[2] In this volume alone we find discussions of how his writing lurks–like an uncanny spectre–between fixed generic categories (Beller and Norwood), between text and illustration (Douglass), and the languages of art and literature (Leahy), as well as the novelistic and dramatic (Pearson). We have also seen how it foregrounds a certain slippage between accepted constructions of masculinity and femininity (Furneaux and Cox), between sibling and sexual bonds (Parker) and, in their shared vulnerability to medical experimentation, between women and animals (Depledge). In psychological terms, Collins's novels are seen to explore the fragile borders between mental and political revolution (Mangham) and sanity and insanity more generally (Hughes). Persistently engaging in a range of contemporaneous concerns, it is not surprising to find them blurring the boundaries between heredity and environment (Caleb) and between contemporary constructions of the civilised and the savage (Longmuir). Even the seemingly most discrete explorations of liminality, such as those of Kontou (between the sensational text and the supernatural séance) and Law (between the moral and legal rights of authors) figure forth a more generalised questioning of the relationship between performance and reality and the relationship between natural justice and the contemporary legal system. Despite such topicality, Brusberg-Kiermeier is able to detect an uncanny doubling of nineteenth-century and current concerns, especially in terms of class relations and transgressions. As each of these readings demonstrates, the lure of meaning–like desire itself– draws us on but is destined to remain unfulfilled; endlessly circulating in the liminal space between perceived oppositions and, in the process, disrupting established norms and boundaries. In an age obsessed with classification and taxonomies–an age already rendered anxious by the discoveries of Darwin and the transmutationists–the sensational impact of Collins's novels may, in part, be traced back to such liminal qualities.

Looking forward, I would also suggest that it is precisely this liminality– the ways in which meaning is never simply there to be grasped but, rather, resides in what we might call the space of both interpretation and undecidability–that continues to attract the attention and interest of so many modern readers and critics of various persuasions. Within the proliferation of recent readings of Collins, however, at least one dimension of this liminality remains largely unexplored: the question of language. While many, like William Hughes within this volume, are happy to acknowledge the ways in which a certain notion of textuality problematises the stability of meaning and identity, they are also content to "leave such issues aside" as their interests reside elsewhere. For this reason, I would like to use this Afterword as an opportunity to suggest that this tendency towards liminality–towards slippage and disruption–escapes the confines of plot and infects the politics of representation itself.

To suggest what I mean by this, I would like to turn to *The Woman in White* (1860) and, more specifically, the characters of Anne Catherick and Laura Fairlie. As we all know, Anne enters the text as an "extraordinary apparition" who appears before Walter Hartright in the middle of the night on the deserted road to London (Collins 1860, 47). Thus she is introduced as a quintessential figure of sensation. According to D. A. Miller's reading of this scene, her touch signals the moment when, "released from–and with–the Woman, nervousness touches and enters the Man"; a reading based on the assumption that the novel "makes nervousness a metonymy for reading, its cause or effect" (Miller 1988, 152, 151). In contrast, I would associate this state of nervousness–or anxiety– not with the act of reading but that of writing and, more precisely, with a specifically textual form of the slippage or disruption discussed above.

The effects of such slippage are immediate. As Lyn Pykett suggests, the appearance of Anne produces, in both Walter and the reader, a "sense of disorientation" and "a strange, dreamlike world in which the 'ordinary rules of evidence' are replaced by an associative logic" (Pykett 2005, 177). It is this principle of association that is key to my own reading of this scene. Fatherless and devoid of origin, Anne enters the text as a lack and is condemned to circulate through the text, wandering like a signifier freed from the logos. Analysing his own actions, Walter is forced to ask:

> What had I done? Assisted the victim of the most horrible of false imprisonments to escape; or cast loose on the wide world of London an unfortunate creature, whose actions it was my duty, and every man's duty, mercifully to control. I turned sick at heart when the question occurred to me. (Collins 1860, 55)

As Ann Cvetkovich suggests, "Walter's rather hysterical pronouncement about the consequences of his action suggest that it is being loaded with a significance that cannot be found in the event itself" (Cvetkovich 1992, 32). Yet such an assertion brings us back, once again, to the notion of slippage. For if Anne represents a signifier of absence, she is also a signifier who is inhabited by the trace of another and, more specifically, Laura Fairlie. Recording his early impressions of this character, Walter is continually struck by a sense of "Something wanting–and where it was, and what it was, I could not say" (Collins 1860, 76). The answer to Walter's query is, quite simply, textuality itself: the space of both lack and desire. As an isolated and supposedly stable sign, Laura remains incomplete and illegible. Indeed, it is only when Walter re-inscribes her into a network of referrals–into the space of the in-between–that he is able to recognise that the "Something wanting" is his own "recognition of the ominous likeness between the fugitive from the asylum and [his] pupil at Limmeridge house" (ibid., 86). In this liminal relationship between Anne and Laura, "the presumed interiority of meaning is already worked upon by its own exteriority. It is always already carried outside itself" (Derrida 1972b, 33). Meaning thus resides in neither one nor the other character but, rather, in the space of the supplement that I am calling the space of the in-between. Thus, it is only appropriate that Walter records his experience, "trac[ing] these lines […]

with the shadows of after-events darkening the very paper [he] writes on" (Collins 1860, 50).

This scene is only one of countless examples where Collins foregrounds the instability of meaning, the ghostlike or phantom qualities it assumes as it circulates throughout a chain of signification. Yet the status of this example is exemplary. In her review of *The Woman in White*, an early attempt to define the sensation genre, Margaret Oliphant focuses on the two scenes discussed above; scenes which represent, for her, the exact qualities that render the sensation novel sensational. As she suggests, "the effect is pure sensation, neither more nor less" (Oliphant 1862, 572). Yet in concentrating on these two episodes where the status of a stable meaning is called into question, Oliphant also suggests how textuality–with all its attendant notions of slippage, destabilisation, and liminality–is written into the very heart of Collins's novels.

Consider another significant example from *The Woman in White*. As each of the characters becomes ever more entangled in the mysterious events of the novel, Anne comes to assume, for them, the status of a logos: the origin and guarantee of all meaning. As Walter suggests, "the End is appointed–the End is drawing us on–and Anne Catherick, dead in her grave, points the way to it still!" (Collins 1860, 471). Endlessly elusive, like the textuality she embodies, she is pursued, relentlessly, because it is believed that she holds the key to the text's secret: the illegitimacy of Sir Percival Glyde. In actuality, she knows nothing more than that such a secret exists, a fact that she does not hesitate to communicate to Percival. Yet her mother's description is, for my purposes, telling:

> "Beg my pardon, directly", says [Anne], "or I'll make it the worse for you. I'll let out your Secret. I can ruin you for life if I choose to open my lips". My own words! Repeated exactly from what I had said the day before–repeated, in his presence, as if they had come from herself. He sat speechless, as white as the paper I am writing on, while I pushed her out of the room [...]. I tried to set things right. I told him that she had merely repeated, like a parrot, the words she had heard me say and that she knew no particulars whatever, because I had mentioned none. I explained that she had affected, out of crazy spite against him, to know what she really did *not* know". (ibid., 557, italics in original)

The significance of this communication is illuminated by Derrida's comments on the relationship between repetition (as writing) and truth. As he suggests:

> In the anamnesic movement of truth, what is repeated must present itself as such, as what it is, in repetition. The true is repeated; it is what is repeated in the repetition, what is represented in the representation. It is not the repeater in the repetition, nor the signifier in the signification. (Derrida 1972a, 111)

Yet in the passage above, Anne–the quintessential figure of sensation–"repeat[s] without knowing"; a repetition in which what "is repeated is the repeater, the imitation, the signifier, the representative, in the absence, as it happens, of the thing itself" (ibid., 74, 119). In these terms, she may be read as a figure for the ways in which Collins's writing is characterised by "an incessant sliding of the signified under the signifier": a movement that relegates meaning–as elusive as Anne herself–to the liminal space of textuality (Lacan 1957, 154).

This "incessant sliding of the signified under the signifier" is apparent throughout Collins's corpus. Within *The Law and the Lady* (1875), we can see it at work in Valeria's frenzied movement between a series of clues, located in the house of Major Fitz-David, that gain significance not from any signified but only from their status as signifiers and, more precisely, their relation to other signifiers in the system.[3] It is also evident in *The Woman in White* where Walter's discovery of Sir Percival Glyde's spurious origins at the Church at Welmingham depends, not on the plenitude of the original register, but only on the *difference* between the original and its copy. Speaking more generally, we can see this emphasis on slippage and instability in Collins's treatment of marriage, illegitimacy, and class transgression, his preoccupation with false and multiple names, forgeries, traces, and a suspense that depends, precisely, on a suspension of meaning. But it is, perhaps, most obvious in Rosanna Spearman's revelation of Franklin Blake's guilt within *The Moonstone* (1868). Oblivious of his own culpability, Blake returns from abroad to the scene of the crime in order to resume his investigation of the mystery. His efforts gain new momentum upon the long delayed receipt of a message from Rosanna, a message that transgresses class boundaries and, seemingly, transcends the borders between the living and the dead. Mirroring the play of writing, the "envelope contained a letter: and this, in its turn, contained a slip of paper" (Collins 1868, 354). Failing to explain the meaning of Rosanna's behaviour, this letter only directs him to the memorandum. The play amongst signifiers continues as the memorandum, in turn, directs him to seek another piece of writing by going to the Shivering Sands and, having located a particular spot, "*to pull the chain*" (ibid., italics in original). In offering us the image of Franklin pulling up the tin attached to this chain, Collins is offering us nothing less than a literal representation of a chain of signification. Yet the movement of signification does not end here. Inside the tin, Blake discovers a letter and a nightgown. Spreading the latter out, he "instantly discovered the smear of paint from the door of Rachel's boudoir" (ibid., 358). This textual relay continues as the mark of paint leads Blake to a mark of ink:

> I had discovered the smear on the nightgown. To whom did the nightgown belong? [...] The nightgown itself would reveal the truth; for, in all probability, the nightgown was marked with its owner's name. I took it up from the sand, and

looked for the mark. I found the mark, and read–MY OWN NAME. (ibid., 359, capitals in original).

In the hope that the nightgown is, somehow, "a liar" (ibid., 360), Blake turns to Rosanna's letter. But like all writing, this letter merely repeats the marks that have already identified him as the thief that stole the diamond. And in so doing, it simultaneously confirms and destabilises Blake's identity while also blurring the boundaries between innocence and guilt and, more generally, consciousness and the unconscious. As such, it offers us a clear example of an insistent tendency to privilege the signifier over the signified within a chain of signification, as well as the destabilisation such a process entails.

Even without the benefits of a post-structuralist vocabulary, Collins's contemporary critics did not fail to pick up on this radical re-conception of language. According to one reviewer, "life [for Collins] is a sort of chess-board, in which the pieces have indeed a different value; but this arises *not from anything in the material of which* they are made, but from the *particular moves* to which, by the rules of the game, they are restricted" (Anon. 1872, 479, italics added). Those familiar with contemporary critiques of Collins will recognise the game analogy. It appears with the same regularity as that of the chain–a figure, as I have already suggested, of the endless chain of signification–to which it is related. Collins's novels intrigue us "as a Chinese puzzle might, or a charade, or an ingenious mathematical problem, or a trick of sleight-of-hand with a pack of cards" (Williams 1866, 638). In adopting the analogy of a game, the nineteenth-century critics were particularly astute, for play is the operative principle for this writer. For him, "meaning"–the term signification is obviously more appropriate–is not a process of re-presentation but only the effect of differential articulation. Thus the *Spectator*'s characterisation of Collins's texts as "a discordant mosaic instead of a harmonious picture" (Anon. 1866, 638) is particularly apposite. Like the component pieces of a mosaic, each signifier is, when seen in isolation, devoid of meaning. Only when it is read in relation to others–inscribed into a chain of textual referrals–does signification become possible.

While contemporary critics were willing to acknowledge such textuality and liminality within Collins's novels, it was not received as a welcome development and his novels were routinely criticised for their unnaturalness, illegitimacy, and mechanicalness; all the familiar faults and flaws of writing. Thus, in the course of a review of both realistic and sensational novels–legitimate and illegitimate forms of writing–Margaret Oliphant declares that "we think it right to make as distinct a separation as the printer's skill can indicate between the lower and the higher ground" (Oliphant 1867, 275). This gesture is altogether typical of the critical response to Collins's novels and represents nothing more or less than an attempt "to exclude or to lower (to put outside or below), the body of the written trace" (Derrida 1967, 197). Yet the liminality of Collins's texts, their ability to destabilise boundaries and elude stable categorisation, renders Oliphant's gesture futile. Hence the reviews are also characterised by a strategic deployment of a discourse of disease, contamination, and contagion. Such a discourse implicitly recognises the liminality of Collins's writing and we encounter a series of increasingly anxious acknowledgements that such novels call into question the boundaries between high and low, pure and impure, inside and outside. In geographical terms, the "faults of the French school are creeping into our literature, and threaten to flourish there" (M.-M.- 1860, 210); in terms of class: such novelists may "boast, without fear of contradiction, of having temporarily succeeded in making the literature of the Kitchen the favourite reading of the Drawing room" (Rae 1865, 204); and even in terms of the domestic community itself: "To Mr. Collins belongs the credit of having introduced into fiction those most mysterious of mysteries, the mysteries which are at our own doors" (James 1865, 593). Having begun as an "epidemic", this threat soon transforms into an "endemic. Its virus is spreading in all directions" (Wise 1866, 270).

I would argue, however, that this discourse of *disease* is used to name the much more pervasive and much more elusive sense of *dis-ease* provoked by the liminality of Collins's writing. As Antony Easthope reminds us, "it is not possible for human beings, for speaking subjects, to encounter [...] a gap in signification without immediately trying to close it with fantasy, to recuperate it into some form of coherent meaning" (Easthope 2002, 4). It was precisely such "gap[s] in signification" that were calculated "to make one's audience uncomfortable, without letting them know why" (Page 1974, 151). Furthermore, through its association with writing as a re-inscription that brings to light a buried or hidden textuality–this sense of dis-ease is experienced as uncanny. And here, Anne Williams's suggestion that the uncanny "is like the radioactive energy given off when the atom of signifier and signified is split", is entirely relevant (Williams 1995, 72). If, as it has often been suggested, Collins's novels were experienced as an uncanny return of a destabilising force normally repressed by both the individual and cultural psyche, this force also exists at the level of signification itself.[4]

Within this period, the purity associated with "proper" middle-class femininity was often figured as a blank page and thus, by extension, female sexuality came to be associated with the stain of textuality.[5] If this is the case, then the unruly force and excessive energy of signification within Collins's novels may also shed light on the paradoxical contemporary tendency to construct the sensation genre, not simply as "feminine" but also as "un-feminine", and "anti-feminine".[6] Such a supposition receives some support from

Catherine Gallagher's work on prostitution. As she suggests, the womb of the prostitute–like the body of the sensation novel–is

> too slippery. And yet she is a source of proliferation. What multiples through her, though, is not a substance but a sign: money. Prostitution, then, like usury, is a metaphor for one of the ancient models of linguistic production: the unnatural multiplication of interchangeable signs. (Gallagher 1986, 41)

Like the products of prostitution and usury, Collins's texts–continually criticised for their crass commercialism–produce signifiers whose proliferation and multiplication render them not just "too slippery", but actually illegitimate. For this writer, signs come to embody the qualities of the bastard. And as Jenny Bourne Taylor has suggested, bastardy "is analogous to the 'feminine' position" as analysed by critics such as Cixous and Irigaray, for whom it "'cannot be assigned a fixed spot in the play of difference'" (Taylor 1996, 125). Thus Collins's treatment of language–his tendency towards linguistic undecidability and slippage–is yet another possible reason why this genre was seen to blur the strategic boundaries between the feminine and its "improper" other.

Whether this is the case or not, I would like to suggest that it is possible to read this emphasis on slippage and, more precisely, what amounts to a destabilisation of the sign, through the more general destabilisation of gender that characterised the heyday of sensationalism. Consider, for example, the impact of the Matrimonial Causes Act of 1857, the practice of reporting lurid details of individual divorce cases in the press, and the generally confused state of contemporary marriage laws, a confusion that, at times, seemed to condone bigamy. Such factors produced a widespread anxiety about the stability of marriage. In much the same manner as divorce and bigamy severed and destabilised the bond between man and wife–a bond upheld through the law of coverture–so too does Collins not simply represent such concerns through his narratives, but actually embody them in his language by severing the bond between a single signifier wedded to a single signified. Or again, consider the Contagious Diseases Acts of the 1860s as a response to the uncontrollable circulation of disease from women who, themselves, circulate too freely. In much the same way, Collins's texts–continually likened to a contaminating disease–represent the endless circulation of signifiers with their debilitating effects on meaning.[7] In this sense, Collins's novels function like a performative utterance, putting into action, at the level of representation itself, the destabilisation explored within their narratives. In short, these texts–which continually criticise both the law and the father–foreground a certain destabilisation of the Law of the Father, the Symbolic, and meaning itself.

The effects of such destabilisation bring us back, once again, to the issue of anxiety. Collins's novels were seen to represent both a real and a symbolic threat to the family, the home and, more generally, the boundaries between high and low, the licit and the illicit. Yet, as I have already suggested, such specific threats tend to mask the more general, underlying fear provoked by the pervasive liminality and slippage of which I have been writing. This slippage is decidedly threatening in its ability to destabilise both the subject and the boundaries–be they textual, cultural, or literary–by which it is constituted. Indeed, one might argue that the effects of this slippage may be likened to Kristeva's notion of the abject. As Julian Wolfreys reminds us:

> The abject is an uncanny effect of horror, threatening the logical certainty of either the subject/object or self/not-self binary. Abjection is thus the psychic experience of a slippage across the boundaries of the self, and with that a partial erasure of the borders of the psyche which define the ego. Absolutely essential to all cultures, the abject is, amongst other things, the fluid locus of forbidden desires and ideas whose radical exclusion is the basis of cultural development. (Wolfreys 2002, 3)

Such a reading not only sheds light on the arguably "poetic" nature of Collins's textuality, but also illuminates the horror with which contemporary critics reacted to his novels.

Yet the textuality and liminality that represented such a threat to our Victorian predecessors is now read as a site and source of exciting possibilities. And rather than being disturbed by the shifting and provisional process of signification within Collins's texts, we recognise and welcome the possibilities for reading that it offers. The range and scope of readings that such liminality is able to generate is ably demonstrated by the papers contained within this volume. Looking forward to the future, the proliferation of meaning within Collins's texts will continue to generate a proliferation of readings and, while denying us the possibility of stable meaning–a final signified–promises a multiplication of scholarly interest that will place Collins at the forefront of nineteenth-century studies.

Notes

[1] See, for example, the anonymous review of "*No Name* and *Thalatta*" (Anon. 1863, 84) that describes Collins's novels as "a mere puzzle".

[2] The importance of liminality to Collins's writing has recently been recognised by Lyn Pykett. As she suggests: "Collins was [...] both an insider and an outsider, or, perhaps more accurately, he was neither an insider nor an outsider, but occupied a position somewhere in between–a liminal position. It was a position which gave him a very interesting perspective on Victorian society, and what he described in his Preface to *Armadale* as its clap-trap morality. From his liminal position Collins did not so much

hold up the glass of satire to his contemporaries, as refract or re-present contemporary society through his peculiarly angled lens" (Pykett 2005, 2).

[3] The first significant clue that Valeria discovers is a drawer that "literally contained nothing but the fragments of a broken vase" (Collins 1875, 78). Significantly, she is unable "to estimate the value of the vase, or the antiquity of the vase—or even to know whether it was of British or foreign manufacture" (ibid., 81). Yet, even when devoid of signified meaning, such "fragments" direct Valeria's attention to the "vacant space" on top of the bookshelf (ibid., 81) which, in turn, leads her examine the volumes it contains. Once again, however, we should note that she is drawn, not by their signified content, but only by the differential relationship between them: "Here and there I saw empty spaces from which books had been removed and not replaced" (ibid., 83). It is these gaps between signifiers that eventually leads to the discovery of the trial report from the space "between the bookcase and the wall" (ibid., 93).

[4] According to one contemporary reviewer, Collins's novels "stimulate the very feelings which they should have sought to repress" (Anon. 1866b, 102).

[5] See, for example, Gubar 1982.

[6] For a discussion of such paradoxes, see Pykett 1992, 31-5.

[7] As Marlene Tromp suggests, "The M. P.s felt that sensation literature had been produced by critics of the acts, and was, like venereal disease, uncontrollable and limitlessly contaminating. Not only was it all within the reach of women and children—activists regularly delivered it to 'the drawing rooms and breakfast-tables of the wives and even the maiden sisters of the most respectable families'—but it was conceived of as an 'invasion' and a 'deluge'" (Tromp 2000, 147).

Works Cited

Abel, Elizabeth (ed.). 1982. *Writing and Sexual Difference*. Brighton, Sussex: The Harvester Press.

Anon. 1863. *No Name* and *Thalatta*. *Saturday Review* 15:84-5.

Anon. 1866a. Armadale. *The Spectator* 39:638-40.

Anon.1866b. Recent Novels: their Moral and Religious Teaching. *London Review* 27:100-24.

Anon. 1872. *Wilfrid Cumbermede* and *Poor Miss Finch*. *Rose-Belford's Canadian Monthly and National Review* 1:477-9.

Collins, Wilkie. 1866. *Armadale*. Oxford: Oxford University Press, 1989.

—. 1875. *The Law and the Lady*. Oxford: Oxford University Press, 1992.

—. 1868. *The Moonstone*. London: Penguin Books, 1986.

—. 1860. *The Woman in White*. London: Penguin Books, 1985.

Cvetkovich, Ann. 1992. *Mixed Feelings: Feminism, Mass Culture and Victorian Sensationalism*. New Jersey: Rutgers University Press.

Derrida, Jacques. 1972a. *Dissemination*. Trans. by Barbara Johnson. Chicago: University of Chicago Press, 1993.

—. 1967. Freud and the Scene of Writing, in *Writing and Difference*. Trans. by Alan Bass. London: Routledge, 1993. 196-231.

—. 1972b. *Positions*. Trans. by Alan Bass. Chicago: University of Chicago Press, 1981.

Gubar, Susan. 1982. "The Blank Page" and the Issues of Female Creativity, in Abel 1982, 73-94.

Easthope, Antony. 2002. *Privileging Difference*, ed., Catherine Belsey. Basingstoke: Palgrave.

Fuss, Diana (ed.). 1996. *Human, All Too Human*. London and New York: Routledge.

Gallagher, Catherine. 1986. George Eliot and *Daniel Deronda*: The Prostitute and the Jewish Question, in Yeazell 1986, 39-62.

Gosse, Philip. 1844. *An Introduction to Zoology*, in Ritvo 1996, 37-57.

James, Henry. 1865. Miss Braddon. *Nation* 1:593-4.

Lacan, Jacques. 1957. The Agency of the Letter in the Unconscious or Reason since Freud, in *Ecrits: A Selection*. Trans. by Alan Sheridan. New York: W. W. Norton and Co. 1977. 146-78.

M. M. 1860. Novels of the Day: their Writers and Readers. *Fraser's Magazine* 62:205-17.

Miller, D. A. 1988. *The Novel and the Police*. Berkeley: University of California Press.

Oliphant, Margaret. 1867. Novels. *Blackwood's Edinburgh Magazine* 102:257-80.

—. 1862. Sensation Novels. *Blackwood's Edinburgh Magazine* 91:564-84.

Page, Norman. 1974. *Wilkie Collins: The Critical Heritage*. London: Routledge and Kegan Paul.

Pykett, Lyn. 2005. *Authors in Context: Wilkie Collins*. Oxford: Oxford University Press.

Rae, W. F. 1865. Sensation Novelists: Miss Braddon. *North British Review* 43:180-204.

Ritvo, Harriet. 1996. Barring the Cross: Miscegenation and Purity in Eighteenth- and Nineteenth-Century Britain, in Fuss 1996, 37-57.

Robbins, Ruth. and Julian Wolfreys (eds). 1996. *Social and Cultural Formations in Nineteenth-Century Literature*. Basingstoke and London: Macmillan Press.

Spariosu, Mihai I. 1997. *The Wreath of Wild Olive: Play, Liminality, and the Study of Literature*. New York: State University of New York.

Taylor, Jenny Bourne. 1996. Representing Illegitimacy in Victorian Culture, in Robins and Wolfreys 1996, 119-42.

Tromp, Marlene. 2000. *The Private Rod: Marital Violence, the Law and Sensation in Victorian Britain*. Charlottesville and London: University Press of Virginia.

Williams, Anne. 1995. *Art of Darkness: A Poetics of the Gothic.* Chicago and London: University of Chicago Press.

Williams, D. E. 1872. *Poor Miss Finch*: a Novel. *Athenaeum* 2312:202-3.

Wise, John Richard de Capel. 1866. Belles Lettres. *Westminster Review* 86. n.s. 30: 268-80.

Wolfreys, Julian et al. 2002. *Key Concepts in Literary Theory.* Edinburgh: Edinburgh University Press.

Yeazell, Ruth Bernard (ed.). 1986. *Sex, Politics, and Science in the Nineteenth-Century Novel.* Baltimore and London: Johns Hopkins University Press.

SELECT BIBLIOGRAPHY

1. Wilkie Collins and Sensation Fiction

Allan, Janice M. 1996. Scenes of Writing: Detection and Psychoanalysis in Wilkie Collins's *The Moonstone*. *Imprimatur* I: 186-93

Ashley, Robert. 1952. *Wilkie Collins*. London: Arthur Barker.

Bachman Maria K. and Don Richard Cox. 2003. *Reality's Dark Light: The Sensational Wilkie Collins*. Knoxville: University of Tennessee Press.

Baker, William. 2002. *Wilkie Collins's Library: A Reconstruction*. London: Greenwood Press.

Baker, William. and William M. Clarke, eds. 1999. *The Letters of Wilkie Collins*. 2 vols. Basingstoke: Macmillan.

Baker, William., Andrew Gasson., Graham Law. and Paul Lewis (eds). 2005. *The Public Face of Wilkie Collins: The Collected Letters*. 4 vols. London: Pickering and Chatto.

Carens, Timothy L. 2003. Outlandish English Subjects in The Moonstone. *Tennessee Studies in Literature* 41:239-65.

Clarke, William. 1988. *The Secret Life of Wilkie Collins*. London: Allison and Busby.

Cvetkovich, Ann. 1992. *Mixed Feelings: Feminism, Mass Culture, and Victorian Sensationalism*. New Brunswick: Rutgers University Press.

Eliot, T. S. 1932. Wilkie Collins and Charles Dickens, in *Selected Essays, 1917-1932*. New York: Harcourt, Brace, and Co.

Ellis, S. M. 1951. *Wilkie Collins, Le Fanu and Others*. London: Constable.

Frick, Patricia. 1985. Wilkie Collins and John Ruskin. *Victorians Institute Journal* 13:11-22.

Gasson, Andrew. 1998. *Wilkie Collins: An Illustrated Guide*. Oxford: Oxford University Press.

Grinstein, Alexander. 2003. *Wilkie Collins: Man of Mystery and Imagination*. Madison and Connecticut: International Universities Press.

Harrison, Kimberly. and Richard Fantina (eds). 2006. *Victorian Sensations: Essays on a Scandalous Genre*. Ohio: Ohio State University Press.

Heller, Tamar. 1992. *Dead Secrets: Wilkie Collins and the Female Gothic*. New Haven: Yale University Press.

—. 2003. Masterpiece Theatre and Ezra Jennings's Hair: Some Reflections on Where We've Been and Where We're Going in Collins Studies. *Tennessee Studies in Literature* 41:361-70.

Hennelly, Mark M. 1982. Twice-Told Tales of Two Counts: *The Woman in White* and *Dracula*. *Wilkie Collins Society Journal* 2:15-31.

Hughes, Winifred. 1980. *The Maniac in the Cellar: Sensation Novels of the 1860s*. Princeton: Princeton University Press.

Jacobson, Karin. 2003. Plain Faces, Weird Cases: Domesticating the Law in Collins's *The Law and the Lady* and the Trial of Madeleine Smith. *Tennessee Studies in Literature* 41:283-312.

Lonoff, Sue, 1980. Charles Dickens and Wilkie Collins. *Nineteenth-Century Fiction* 35:150-70.

—. 1982. *Wilkie Collins and his Victorian Readers: A Study in the Rhetoric of Authorship*. New York: A.M.A. Press.

MacEachen, Dougald B. 1966. Wilkie Collins's *Heart and Science* and the Vivisection Controversy. *Victorian Newsletter* 29:22-5.

Maceachen, Douglas B. 1950. Wilkie Collins and British Law. *Nineteenth Century Fiction* 5:121-39.

Mangham, Andrew. 2007. *Violent Women and Sensation Fiction: Crime, Medicine and Victorian Popular Culture*. Basingstoke: Palgrave.

Maunder, Andrew, et al. (eds). 2004. *Varieties of Women's Sensation Fiction, 1855-1890*. London: Pickering and Chatto.

Maunder, Andrew and Grace Moore (eds). 2004. *Victorian Crime, Madness and Sensation*. Hampshire: Ashgate.

Marshall, William H. 1970. *Wilkie Collins*. New York: Twayne Publishing.

Maynard, Jessica. 1998. Black Silk and Red Paisley: The Toxic Woman in Wilkie Collins's Armadale, in *Varieties of Victorianism: The Uses of a Past*, ed. by Gary Day. London: Macmillan. 63-79.

Nayder, Lillian. 1997. *Wilkie Collins*. New York: Twayne.

—. 2002. *Unequal Partners: Charles Dickens, Wilkie Collins and Victorian Authorship*. London: Cornell University Press.

O'Neill, Philip. 1988. *Wilkie Collins: Women, Property and Propriety*. London: Macmillan.

Page, Norman. 1974. *Wilkie Collins: The Critical Heritage*. London: Routledge and Kegan Paul.

Pedlar, Valerie. 2003. Experimentation or Exploitation? The Investigations of David Ferrier, Dr Benjulia, and Dr Seward. *Interdisciplinary Science Reviews* 28:169-74.

Peters, Catherine. 1991. *The King of Inventors: A Life of Wilkie Collins*. London: Secker and Warburg.

Pykett, Lyn. 2005. *Authors in Context: Wilkie Collins*. Oxford: Oxford University Press.

—. 1992. *The Improper Feminine: The Women's Sensation Novel and the New Woman Writing*. London: Routledge.

—. (ed.). 1998. *New Casebooks: Wilkie Collins*. London: Macmillan.

—. 1994. *The Sensation Novel: from* The Woman in White *to* The Moonstone. Plymouth: Northcote House.

Reeve, Wybert. 1906. Recollections of Wilkie Collins. *Chambers's Journal* 9:451-68.

Robinson, Kenneth. 1951. *Wilkie Collins: A Biography*. London: The Bodley Head.

Shuttleworth, Sally. 1993. "Preaching to the Nerves": Psychological Disorder in Sensation Fiction", in *A Question of Identity*, ed. by Miranda Benjamin. NJ: Rutgers University Press. 192-243.

Smith, Nelson, C. and R. C. Terry (eds). 1995. *Wilkie Collins to the Forefront: Some Reassessments*. New York: A.M.A. Press.

Taylor, Jenny Bourne (ed.). 2006. *The Cambridge Companion to Wilkie Collins*. Cambridge: Cambridge University Press.

Taylor, Jenny Bourne. 1988. *In the Secret Theatre of Home: Wilkie Collins, Sensation Narrative and Nineteenth-Century Psychology*. London: Routledge.

Trodd, Anthea. 1999-2000. Collaborating in Open Boats: Dickens, Collins, Franklin and Bligh. *Victorian* Studies 42:201-25

Wiesenthal, Chris S. 1995. From Charcot to Plato: The History of Hysteria in *Heart and Science,* in Smith and Terry 1995, 257-68.

Wynne, Deborah. 2001. *The Sensation Novel and the Victorian Family Magazine*. Basingstoke: Palgrave.

2. Victorian Art and Illustration

Allingham, Philip V. 2003. Charles Dickens's *A Tale of Two Cities* (1859) Illustrated: A Critical Reassessment of Hablot Knight Browne's Accompanying Plates. *Dickens Studies Annual*. 33:113.

Anderson, Patricia. 1991. *The Printed Image and the Transformation of Popular Culture: 1790-1860*. Oxford: Clarendon Press.

Andres, Sophia. 1995. Pre-Raphaelite Paintings and Jungian Images in Wilkie Collins's *The Woman in White*. *Victorian Newsletter* 88:26-31.

Behrendt, Stephen C. 1988. The Functions of Illustration–Intentional and Unintentional in *Imagination on a Long Rein: English Literature Illustrated*. Marburg: Jonas Verlag. 29-44.

Flint, Kate. 2000. *The Victorians and the Visual Imagination*. Cambridge: Cambridge University Press.

Law, Graham. 2003. Yesterday's Sensations: Modes of Publication and Narrative Form in Collins's Late Novels, in Bachman and Cox 2003, 329-60.

Leahy, Aoife. 2000. Ruskin and the Pre-Raphaelites in the 1850s. *PaGes 1999* 6:125-31.

Möller, Joachim. 1988. *Imagination on a Long Rein: English Literature Illustrated*. Marburg: Jonas Verlag.

Nead, Lynda. 2006. *The Haunted Gallery: Painting, Photography and Film c. 1900*. London and New Haven: Yale University Press.

—. 1988. *Myths of Sexuality: Representations of Women in Victorian Britain*. Oxford: Basil Blackwell.

—. 2000. *Victorian Babylon: People, Streets and Images in Nineteenth Century London*. London and New Haven. Yale University Press.

Noel-Paton, M. H. and J. P. Campbell. 1990. *Noel Paton: 1821-1901*. Edinburgh: Ramsay Head Press.

Rhys, E. (ed.). n.d. *Ruskin's Pre-Raphaelitism and Other Essays and Lectures on Art*. London: J. M. Dent.

Treuherz, Julian. 1993. *Victorian Painting*. London: Thames and Hudson.

Wood, Christopher. 2000. *Fairies in Victorian Art*. Woodbridge: Antique Collectors' Club.

3. Victorian Psychology and Medicine

Bending, Lucy. 2000. *The Representation of Bodily Pain in Late Nineteenth-Cenutry English Culture*. Oxford: Oxford University Press.

Burney, Ian. 2006. *Poison, Detection, and the Victorian Imagination*. Manchester: Manchester University Press.

Davis, Michael. *George Eliot and Nineteenth-Century Psychology: Exploring the Unmapped Country*. Hampshire: Ashgate.

Graham, John. 1961. Lavater's Physiognomy in England. *Journal of the History of Ideas* 22:561-72.

Greenslade, William. 1994. *Degeneration, Culture and the Novel 1880-1940*. Cambridge: Cambridge University Press.

Hartley, Lucy. 2001. *Physiognomy and the Meaning of Expression in Nineteenth-Century Culture*. Cambridge: Cambridge University Press.

Hollington, Michael. 1992. Physiognomy. *Hard Times. Dickens Quarterly* 9:58-66.

Ingram, Allan (ed.). 1998. *Patterns of Madness in the Eighteenth Century: A Reader*. Liverpool: Liverpool University Press.

Jack, Ian. 1970. Physiognomy, Phrenology and Characterisation in the Novels of Charlotte Brontë. *Brontë Society Transactions* 15:377-91.

Leavy, Barbara Foss. 1982. Wilkie Collins's Cinderella: The History of Psychology and *The Woman in White. Dickens Studies Annual* 10: 91-141.

Mangham, Andrew. 2003. Hysterical Fictions: Mid-Nineteenth-Century Constructions of Hysteria and the Fiction of Mary Elizabeth Braddon. *Wilkie Collins Society Journal* 6:35-52.

—. 2006. "What Could I Do?": Nineteenth-Century Psychology and the Horrors of Masculinity in *The Woman in White,* in Harrison and Fantina 2006. 115-25.

Micale, Mark S. 1995. *Approaching Hysteria: Disease and Its Interpretations.* Princeton: Princeton University Press.

Moscucci, Ornella. 1990. *The Science of Woman: Gynaecology and Gender in England 1800-1929.* Cambridge: Cambridge University Press.

Oppenheim, Janet. 1991. *"Shattered Nerves": Doctors, Patients, and Depression in Victorian England.* Oxford: Oxford University Press.

Otis, Laura. 1994. *Organic Memory: History and the Body in the Late Nineteenth and Early Twentieth Centuries.* Lincoln, NE and London: University of Nebraska Press.

Pick, Daniel. 1993. *Faces of Degeneration: A European Disorder, c.1848-c.1918.* Cambridge: Cambridge University Press.

Rylance, Rick. 2000. *Victorian Psychology and British Culture 1850-1880.* Oxford: Oxford University Press.

Scull, Andrew (ed.). 1981. *Madhouses, Mad-doctors and Madmen: The Social History of Psychiatry in the Victorian Era.* Philadelphia: University of Pennsylvania Press.

—. 1979. *Museums of Madness: The Social Organization of Insanity in Nineteenth-Century England.* London: Allen Lane/New York: St. Martin's Press.

Showalter, Elaine and English Showalter. 1972. Victorian Women and Menstruation, in *Suffer and be Still: Women in the Victorian Age,* ed. by Martha Vicinus. London: Macmillan. 38-44.

Showalter, Elaine. 1987. *The Female Malady: Women, Madness and English Culture, 1830-1980.* London: Virago.

Shuttleworth, Sally. 1996. *Charlotte Brontë and Victorian Psychology.* Cambridge: Cambridge University Press.

—. 1993. Demonic Mothers: Ideologies of Bourgeois Motherhood in the Mid-Victorian Era, in *Rewriting the Victorians: Theory, History and the Politics of Gender,* ed. by Linda M. Shires. London: Routledge. 31-51.

—. 1993. "Preaching to the Nerves": Psychological Disorder in Sensation Fiction", in *A Question of Identity,* ed. by Miranda Benjamin. NJ: Rutgers University Press. 192-243.

Small, Helen. 1996. *Love's Madness: Medicine, the Novel, and Female Insanity, 1800-1865.* Oxford: Oxford University Press.

Smith, Leonard D. 1999. *"Cure, Comfort and Safe Custody": Public Lunatic Asylums in Early Nineteenth-Century England.* London: Leicester University Press.

Taylor, Jenny Bourne. 1988. *In The Secret Theatre of Home: Wilkie Collins, Sensation Narrative and Nineteenth-Century Psychology.* London: Routledge.

—. 1997. Obscure Recesses: Locating the Victorian Unconscious, in *Writing and Victorianism,* ed. by J. B. Bullen. New York: Longman. 137-79.

Taylor, Jenny Bourne. and Sally Shuttleworth (eds). 1998. *Embodied Selves: An Anthology of Psychological Texts, 1830-1890.* Oxford: Clarendon Press.

Turner, Frank M. 1978. The Victorian Conflict Between Science and Religion: A Professional Dilemma. *Iris* 69:356-76.

Tytler, Graeme. 1998. "Know How to Decipher a Countenance": Physiognomy in Thomas Hardy's Fiction. *Thomas Hardy Yearbook* 27:43-60.

—. 1994. Physiognomy in *Wuthering Heights. Brontë Society Transactions* 21:137-48.

—. 1999. "The Lines and Lights of the Human Countenance": Physiognomy in George Eliot's Fiction. *George Eliot–George Henry Lewes Studies* 36:29-58.

Wood, Jane. 2001. *Passion and Pathology in Victorian Fiction.* Oxford: Oxford University Press.

4. Victorian Law

Ainsley, Jill Newton. 2000. "Some Mysterious Agency": Women, Violent Crime, and the Insanity Acquittal in the Victorian Courtroom. *Canadian Journal of History* 35:37-55.

Barnes, James J. 1974. *Authors, Publishers and Politicians: The Quest for an Anglo-American Copyright Agreement, 1815-54.* London: Routledge and Kegan Paul.

Bonham-Carter, Victor. 1978. *Authors by Profession: Vol. 1 From the Introduction of Printing until the Copyright Act of 1911.* London: Society of Authors.

Bowker, R. R. 1912. *Copyright: Its History and its Law.* Boston: Houghton Mifflin.

Chase, Karen. and Michael Levenson. 2000. Love After Death: The Deceased Wife's Sister's Act, in *The Spectacle of Intimacy.* Princeton: Princeton University Press.

Eigen, Joel Peter. 2003. *Unconscious Crime: Mental Absence and Criminal Responsibility in Victorian London.* Maryland: Johns Hopkins University Press.

—. 1995. *Witnessing Insanity: Madness and Mad-Doctors in the English Court* (New Haven: Yale University Press, 1995.

MacDonnell, Hugh. 2004. Not Proven Verdict under Threat. *The Scotsman.* <http://news.scotsman.com/topics.cfm?tid=441&id=1341582004> accessed 31 July 2006.

Maceachen, Douglas B. 1950. Wilkie Collins and British Law. *Nineteenth Century Fiction* 5:121-39.

Nowell-Smith, Simon. 1968. *International Copyright Law and the Publisher in the Reign of Queen Victoria.* Oxford: Clarendon Press.

Smith, Roger. 1981. *Trial by Medicine: The Insanity Defence in Victorian England.* Edinburgh: Edinburgh University Press.

Zedner, Lucia. 1991. *Women, Crime, and Custody in Victorian England.* Oxford: Oxford University Press.

5. Victorian Theatre and Modern Film Adaptations

Bratton, Jacky. 2003. *New Readings in Theatre History.* Cambridge: Cambridge University Press.

Brooks, Peter. 1976. *The Melodramatic Imagination.* New Haven and London: Yale University Press.

Brusberg-Kiermeier, Stefani. 2004. Stormy Novel, Thorny Adaptation: Recent Appropriations of *Wuthering Heights,* in Voigts-Virchow 2004, 149-57.

Cartmell, Deborah. and Imelda Whelehan, (eds). 1999. *Adaptations. From Text to Screen, Screen to Text.* London, and New York: Routledge.

Cartmell, Deborah., I.Q. Hunter., Heide Kaye., and Imelda Whelehan (eds). 1998. *Sisterhoods: Across the Literature/Media Divide.* London: Sterling, VA: Pluto Press.

Davies, Tracy C. 1991. *Actresses as Working Women, their Social Identity in Victorian Culture.* London and New York: Routledge.

Davis, Jim. and Victor Emeljanow. 2001. *Reflecting the Audience: London Theatregoing, 1840-1880.* Hatfield: University of Hertfordshire Press.

Fawkes, Richard. 1979. *Dion Boucicault.* London: Quartet Books.

Giddings, Robert. and Erica Sheen (eds.). 2000. *The Classic Novel from Page to Screen.* Manchester: Manchester University Press.

Goble, Alan (ed.). 1999. *The Complete Index to Literary Sources in Film.* London: Bowker-Saur.

Howard, Diana. 1970. *London Theatres and Music Halls 1850-1950.* London: The Library Association.

Irvin, Eric. 1976. Nineteenth-Century English Dramatists in Australia. *Theatre Notebook* 30:24-34.

James, Louis. 1977. Taking Melodrama Seriously: Theatre, and Nineteenth-Century Studies. *History Workshop* 3:151-8.

Marshall, Gail. 1998. *Actresses on the Victorian Stage: Feminine Performance and the Galatea Myth*. Cambridge: Cambridge University Press.

Nead, Lynda. 2006. *The Haunted Gallery: Painting, Photography and Film c. 1900*. London and New Haven: Yale University Press.

Peters, Julie Stone. 2000. *Theatre of the Book 1480-1880: Print, Text, and Performance in Europe*. Oxford: Oxford University Press.

Powell, Kerry (ed.). 2004. *The Cambridge Companion to Victorian and Edwardian Theatre*. Cambridge: Cambridge University Press.

—. 1998. *Women and Victorian Theatre*. Cambridge: Cambridge University Press.

Rahill, Frank. 1967. *The World of Melodrama*. Pennsylvania and London: Pennsylvania State University Press.

Rowell, George (ed.). 1972. *Nineteenth-Century Plays*. Oxford: Oxford University Press.

Sherson, Errol. 1925. *London's Lost Theatres of the Nineteenth Century*. London: Bodley Head.

Stephens, John Russell. 1992. *The Profession of the Playwright: British Theatre 1800-1900*. Cambridge: Cambridge University Press.

Voigts-Virchow, Eckart (ed.). 2004. *Janespotting and Beyond: British Heritage Retrovisions Since the Mid-1990s*. Tübingen: Gunter Narr.

Wearing, J. P. 1972. Pinero's Professional Dramatic Roles, 1874-1884. *Theatre Notebook* 26S:140-4.

6. General Nineteenth-Century Criticism

Altick, Richard D. 1998. *The English Common Reader*. Columbus: Ohio State University Press.

Auerbach, Nina. 1982. *Woman and the Demon: The Life of a Victorian Myth*. Cambridge, MA: Harvard University Press.

Barrow, Logie. 1986. *Independent Spirits: Spiritualism and the English Plebeians 1850-1910*. London and New York: Routledge and Kegan Paul.

Beer, Gillian. 1983. *Darwin's Plots: Evolutionary Narrative in Darwin, George Eliot and Nineteenth-Century Fiction*. London: Routledge.

—. 1993. Forging the Missing Link: Interdisciplinary Stories, in *Open Fields: Science in Cultural Encounter*. Oxford: Clarendon Press. 115-45.

Bland, Lucy. and Laura Doan. 1998. *Sexology Uncensored: The Documents of Sexual Science*. Cambridge: Polity Press.

Bronfen, Elisabeth. 1992. *Over Her Dead Body: Death, Femininity, and the Aesthetic*. Manchester: Manchester University Press.

Cantor, Geoffrey, Gowan Dawson, Graeme Gooday, Richard Noakes, Sally
     Shuttleworth, and Jonathan Topham. 2004. *Science in the Nineteenth-
     Century Periodical.* Cambridge: Cambridge University Press.
Cantor, Geoffrey. and Sally Shuttleworth, eds. 2004. *Science Serialised:
     Representations of the Sciences in Nineteenth-Century Periodicals.*
     Cambridge, MA: The Massachusetts Institute of Technology Press.
Chase, Karen. and Michael Levenson. 2000. *The Spectacle of Intimacy: A
     Public Life for the Victorian Family.* Princeton: Princeton University Press.
Crawford, Robert. 1998. *The Scottish Invention of English Literature.*
     Cambridge: Cambridge University Press.
—. 2003. *Devolving English Literature.* Edinburgh: Edinburgh University Press.
Cvetkovich, Ann. 1992. *Mixed Feelings: Feminism, Mass Culture and Victorian
     Sensationalism.* New Jersey: Rutgers University Press.
Dally, Ann. 1991. *Women Under the Knife.* London: Random Century.
Davidoff, Leonore. and Catherine Hall. 2002. *Family Fortunes: Men and
     Women of the English Middle Class, 1780-1850.* London: Routledge.
Fahnestock, Jeanne. 1980. The Heroine of Irregular Features: Conventions of
     Heroine Description. *Victorian Studies* 24:325-50.
Feltes, N. N. 1986. *Modes of Production of Victorian Novels.* Chicago:
     University of Chicago Press.
Flint, Kate. 1993. *The Woman Reader 1837-1914.* Oxford: Oxford University
     Press.
French, Richard D. 1975. *Antivivisection and Medical Science in Victorian
     Society.* Princeton and London: Princeton University Press.
Furneaux, Holly. 2005. 'It is Impossible to be Gentler': The Homoerotics of
     Male Nursing in Dickens's Fiction. *Critical Survey* 17:34-47.
Gallagher, Catherine. 1985. *The Industrial Reformation of English Fiction:
     Social Discourse and Narrative Form, 1832-1867.* Chicago: Chicago
     University Press.
Gettmann, Royal A. 1960. *A Victorian Publisher: A Study of the Bentley
     Papers.* Cambridge: Cambridge University Press.
Gilbert, Pamela K. 1997. *Disease, Desire and the Body in Victorian Women's
     Popular Novels.* Cambridge: Cambridge University Press.
Gilbert, Sandra M. and Susan Gubar. 1979. *The Madwoman in the Attic: The
     Woman Writer and the Nineteenth-Century Imagination.* New Haven, CT
     and London: Yale University Press, 1984.
Griest, Guinevere L. 1970. *Mudie's Circulating Library and the Victorian
     Novel.* Bloomington, IN: Indiana University Press.
Hall, Donald. 1996. *Fixing Patriarchy: Feminism and Mid Victorian Male
     Novelists.* Basingstoke: Macmillan.
Hartman, Mary S. 1985. *Victorian Murderesses.* London: Robson Books.

Herdman, John. 1990. *The Double in Nineteenth-Century Fiction*. Houndsmill: MacMillan.

Hughes, Linda K. and Michael Lund. 1991. *The Victorian Serial*. Charlottesville: University Press of Virginia.

Hughes, William. 2000. *Beyond Dracula: Bram Stoker's Fiction and its Cultural Context*. Basingstoke: Macmillan.

Lansbury, Carol. 1985. *The Old Brown Dog: Women, Workers, and Vivisection in Edwardian England*. Wisconsin and London: The University of Wisconsin Press.

Liggins, Emma. and Daniel Duffy (eds). 2001. *Feminist Readings of Victorian Popular Texts*. Hampshire: Ashgate.

Maunder, Andrew. and Grace Moore (eds). 2004. *Victorian Crime, Madness and Sensation*. Hampshire, Ashgate.

McDonald, Peter. 1997. *British Literary Culture and Publishing Practice 1880-1914*. Cambridge: Cambridge University Press.

Mitchell, Sally. 1977. Sentiment and Suffering: Women's Recreational Reading in the 1860s. *Victorian Studies* 21:29-45.

Oppenheim, Janet. 1985. *The Other World: Spiritualism and Psychical Research in England, 1850-1914*. Cambridge: Cambridge University Press.

Poovey, Mary. 1988. *Uneven Developments: The Ideological Work of Gender in Mid-Victorian England*. Chicago: The University of Chicago Press.

Porter, Katherine H. 1958. *Through a Glass Darkly: Spiritualism in the Browning Circle*. Lawrence: University of Kansas Press.

Punter, David. 1996. *The Literature of Terror*. 2 vols. Essex: Longman.

Pykett, Lyn. 1992. *The Improper Feminine: The Woman's Sensation Novel and the New Woman Writing*. London: Routledge.

Richardson, Ruth. 1988. *Death, Dissection and the Destitute*. London: Phoenix Press, 2001.

Roper, Michael. and John Tosh (eds). 1991. *Manful Assertions: Masculinities in Britain since 1800*. London: Routledge.

Rudacille, Deborah. 2001. *The Scalpel and The Butterfly: The War Between Animal Research and Animal Protection*. New York: Farrar, Straus, and Giroux.

Rupke, Nicholaas A. (ed.). 1987. *Vivisection in Historical Perspective*. Kent: Croom Helm.

Sanders, Valerie. 2002. *The Brother-Sister Culture in Nineteenth-Century Literature*. New York: Palgrave.

Shortt, S. E. D. 1984. Physicians and Psychics: The Anglo-American Medical Response to Spiritualism, 1870-1890. *Journal of the History of Medicine and Allied Sciences* 39:339-55.

Snyder, Katherine. 1999. *Bachelors, Manhood and the Novel 1850-1925*. Cambridge: Cambridge University Press.

Sussman, Herbert. 1995. *Victorian Masculinities: Manhood and Masculine Poetics in Early Victorian Literature and Art*. Cambridge: Cambridge University Press.

Sutherland, John (ed.). 1988. *The Longman Companion to Victorian Fiction*. Essex: Longman Group.

—. 2005. *Victorian Fiction: Writers, Publishers, Readers*. Basingstoke: Palgrave.

Tosh, John. 1991. Domesticity and Manliness in the Victorian Middle Class: The Family of Edward Benson White, in Roper and Tosh 1991, 44-73.

—. 1999. *A Man's Place: Masculinity and the Middle-Class Home in Victorian England*. New Haven and London: Yale University Press.

Turner, Mark. 2000. *Trollope and the Magazines: Gendered Issues in Mid-Victorian Britain*. Basingstoke: Macmillan.

Westacott, E. 1949. *A Century of Vivisection and Anti-Vivisection*. Essex, Rockford: C. W. Daniel.

White, Chris (ed.). 1999. *Nineteenth-Century Writings on Homosexuality: A Sourcebook*. London: Routledge.

Winnifrith, Tom. 1996. *Fallen Women in the Nineteenth Century*. Hampshire: Macmillan.

Winter, Alison. 1998. *Mesmerized: Powers of Mind in Victorian Britain*. Chicago and London: The University of Chicago Press.

Yeazell, Ruth Bernard. 1986. *Sex, Politics and Science in the Nineteenth Century Novel*. Baltimore and London: Johns Hopkins University Press.

LIST OF CONTRIBUTORS

Editor

Andrew Mangham is a lecturer at the University of Reading where he specialises in Victorian literature and culture. His interests are in the intersections between science, literature, and legal documents in nineteenth-century Britain. He has a forthcoming book entitled *Violent Women and Sensation Fiction: Crime, Medicine, and Victorian Popular Culture* (Palgrave). He has also written articles for *Critical Survey*, *Clues*, and the *Wilkie Collins Society Journal*.

Contributors

Janice M. Allan is a Lecturer in English at the University of Salford. In addition to editing *Bleak House: A Sourcebook* (Routledge 2004), she has published various articles on Wilkie Collins and sensation fiction more generally. She is currently guest editing two special issues of *Clues: A Journal of Detection* and is working on a sensation fiction sourcebook for Liverpool University Press.

Anne-Marie Beller completed her PhD at the University of Leicester in 2003 and now teaches in the department of English and Drama at Loughborough University. She has research interests in the Victorian novel, women's writing, and popular genres. Recent work includes essays on sensation fiction, Collins, Mary Elizabeth Braddon, and Charles Reade. Anne-Marie is currently working on a book about Mary Elizabeth Braddon and marginalisation.

Amanda Mordavsky Caleb is finishing her PhD at the University of Sheffield on the decadent scientist in *fin de siècle* popular fiction. She is currently editing a book on science in nineteenth-century Britain which is due out with Cambridge Scholars Publishing in 2007.

Jessica Cox is a research student in the Department of English at the University of Wales, Swansea. Her research interests include gender studies, Victorian sensation literature, and New Woman writing. Her doctoral thesis examines legal and bodily representations of women in the fiction of Wilkie Collins. She has published articles on Wilkie Collins and Mary Elizabeth Braddon in the

Wilkie Collins Society Journal, Philological Quarterly, and the *Journal of Gender Studies*. She is also the editor of the Penguin Classics edition of Charlotte Brontë's *Shirley*.

Greta Depledge has just completed a PhD thesis at Birkbeck College, University of London, on *Female Maladies, Literary Culture and Medicine Practice in the Nineteenth Century*. She is one of the editorial assistants for Birkbeck's new online refereed web journal dedicated to advancing interdisciplinary study in the long nineteenth century: <www.19@bbk.ac.uk>. Her current project is based on the popular nineteenth-century novelist Florence Marryat.

Clare Douglass graduated with a B. A. in English from Wake Forest University and has since earned an M. A. in English at the University of North Carolina, Chapel Hill, where she is presently a PhD candidate and teaching fellow. She has served as Fiction Editor and Managing Editor for *The Carolina Quarterly* and is completing a dissertation on select illustrated, canonical novels by each of four Victorian authors: Collins, Dickens, Gaskell, and Thackeray.

Holly Furneaux is a lecturer in Victorian Studies at the University of Leicester. Having recently completed a PhD thesis examining homoeroticism in the work of Charles Dickens (Birkbeck College, University of London), she is now finishing a book project, *Queer Dickens*, and embarking on a new interdisciplinary book-length exploration of the cultural history of male nursing in the long nineteenth century. She has published articles on the erotics of nursing in Dickens's fiction and on the politics of Dickens adaptation.

William Hughes is Professor of Gothic Studies at Bath Spa University. A graduate of the University of East Anglia, Norwich, he is the author of *Beyond Dracula* (2000), and, with Andrew Smith, is the co-editor of *Bram Stoker: History, Psychoanalysis and the Gothic* (1998), *Fictions of Unease* (2001: edited with Diane Mason and Andrew Smith), and *Empire and the Gothic* (2003). With Richard Dalby he is co-compiler of the definitive *Bram Stoker: A Bibliography* (2004). His current research includes a further edited collection of essays, *Queering the Gothic*, with Andrew Smith, and two volumes on Stoker's *Dracula* for Palgrave. He is the editor of *Gothic Studies*, the refereed journal of the International Gothic Association, published by Manchester University Press.

Stefani Brusberg-Kiermeier has taught English literature and gender studies at the Free University Berlin, the Humboldt University Berlin, Siegen University, and, since April 2004, at Potsdam University. Her PhD thesis on stagings of the body in Shakespeare's history plays (*Körper-Inszenierungen in Shakespeares Historien*) was published in 1999 by Peter Lang, who also published *Shakespeare in the Media: From the Globe Theatre to the World Wide Web* (2004), which she co-edited with Jörg Helbig. She is about to finish a book on Victorian fiction and continues publishing on Shakespeare, the early modern poet Aemilia Lanyer, Victorian literature and culture, as well as contemporary British drama and film.

Tatiana Kontou recently submitted her DPhil thesis on representations of Victorian spiritualism at the University of Sussex, where she is currently working as an associate tutor. Her research interests include sensation fiction, womens' writing, theories of the ghostly, and the relationship between nineteenth-century and contemporary literature and culture.

Graham Law is Professor of Media History at Waseda University, Tokyo. Among other books and articles on nineteenth-century literary and publishing history, he is the author of *Serializing Fiction in the Victorian Press* (2000). He has also produced editions of a number of popular Victorian serial novels, including David Pae's *Lucy, the Factory Girl* (2001), and is co-editor of the *Wilkie Collins Society Journal* and *The Public Face of Wilkie Collins: The Collected Letters* (2005).

Aoife Leahy lectures in the English Studies section of the Department of Languages and Cultural Studies, University of Limerick. Her research interests are interdisciplinary and focus on the links between Victorian literature and art. Her PhD was awarded by University College Dublin in 2003 and her thesis was entitled *The Raphaelesque versus the Pre-Raphaelite in Victorian Fiction: 1850-1900*.

Anne Longmuir is Assistant Professor of English at Kansas State University. Specialising in Victorian literature and contemporary American fiction, she has published articles in *Critique* and *Brontë Studies*, and has articles forthcoming in *The Explicator* and *Modern Fiction Studies*. She is currently working on an article that explores the function of travel in Charlotte Brontë's *Villette*.

Janice Norwood teaches English and drama at the Universities of Leicester (where she completed her PhD in 2006) and Hertfordshire. She has carried out extensive research into the Britannia Theatre, Hoxton and its relationship with popular culture and the local community. She is particularly interested in the interconnections between Victorian theatre and other art forms.

Lynn Parker received her PhD from Brandeis University and is currently an Associate Professor of English at Framingham State College. She has published work on Thomas Hardy and is currently working on a manuscript about the relationship between brother-sister bonds and the marriage plot in the nineteenth-century English novel.

Richard Pearson is Head of Arts, Humanities and Social Sciences at the University of Worcester and lectures in Victorian Literature and Culture. He is the author of *W. M. Thackeray and the Mediated Text* (2000) and is currently project director for an AHRC digitising project to create e-texts of a series of Victorian Plays from Lacy's Acting Edition.

INDEX